Birth of a Nation: Essays on Race, White Identity, and More

Dwayne Wong (Omowale)

ISBN: 9798851693816

Contents

1

THE LEGACY OF AFRICOM

Malcolm X explained that after colonialism in Africa ended, the United States stepped in to fill the role that the European powers had played in Africa. Malcolm explained: "They were trapped on the African continent, they couldn't stay there- they were looked upon as colonial and imperialist. They had to pass the ball to someone whose image was different, and they passed the ball to Uncle Sam. And he picked it up and has been running it for a touchdown ever since."

Malcolm continued to explain that at the time that the ball was passed to the United States, it was passed to John F. Kennedy who adopted a more benevolent approach, which Malcolm described as being philanthropic colonialism or "dollarism." Malcolm noted that the United States couldn't help the Africans in Mississippi, Alabama or Detroit, but the American government was going to send aid to Africa.

The reality is that America's policy in Africa has been no different than the policy of the colonial powers of Europe. Malcolm was well-aware of this. He was very critical of America's role in the Democratic Republic of Congo, where the United States intervened to remove Patrice Lumumba. Malcolm also pointed out that it was American tax dollars which were being used to finance America's imperialistic policy in Congo.

The development of the U.S. Africa Command (also known as AFRICOM) represents the continuation of the colonial policy which Malcolm X spoke about. This was the very point Gilbert Taguem Fah made, stating: "Despite the fact that security and humanitarian aid are often presented as the driving forces behind America's push into Africa, the growing interest in Africa is shaped not only by global strategic concerns but also and most importantly the growing demand for oil coupled with the quest for access to foreign markets."

Fah noted that prior to the AFRICOM, America's policies in Africa were shaped by the lens of the Cold War. During this period

1

the United States was engaged in proxy wars and coups, but Africa was of relatively little concern for the United States. Fah noted that after the end of the Cold War, America became more concerned with Africa.

President George W. Bush announced AFRICOM on February 6, 2007. Following the terrorist attacks in 2001, Bush pursued a very aggressive foreign policy. This "War of Terror" which Bush launched was marked by the invasion of Afghanistan and the invasion of Iraq. Bush also took a more aggressive approach to North Korea. AFRICOM was part of this more aggressive foreign policy by the Bush administration.

The aggressive foreign policy of the Bush administration was justified by the notion that waging an international war on terrorism was necessary for America's national security. Africa became an important strategic location to pursue this policy given that Osama bin Laden had previously lived in Sudan and his terrorist attacks included targeting American embassies in Tanzania and Kenya. American military presence was seen as being necessary to counter Al Qaeda's activities in Africa, especially in Muslim regions in Africa.

The United States was unable to find a country in Africa which was willing to host the headquarters for this new initiative. President Ellen Johnson-Sirleaf of Liberia was willing to host the command, but the United States opted to temporarily base it in Germany. The mission of AFRICOM was to provide humanitarian assistance, civic action, professional development of militaries, and natural disaster response. The command was also meant to operate bilaterally via regional institutions such as ECOWAS and multilaterally via the African Union.

Fah traced the roots of American militarization in Africa to the Special Forces Group which was created by the Pentagon in the 1990s to engage in special operations in Africa. Prior to the development of AFRICOM, the increasing American military presence in Africa was noticeable. For example, the East African Regional Security Initiative was established to combat terrorism in East Africa. To achieve this aim, thousands of soldiers were stationed in Djibouti.

The militarization which the Bush administration and successive administrations have pursued has created more instability in Africa. One example of this was Ethiopia's invasion of Somalia, which was supported by the Bush administration. The invasion was not only costly for Ethiopia, but it created more instability in Somalia. Moreover, as Fah noted, AFRICOM provided training and weapons to "phantom, failed, corrupt, and undemocratic regimes." This was merely a continuation of the policies of the Cold War period. During the period of the Cold War, the United States was willing to support brutal regimes in the name of combating communism. The problem with providing support for such regimes in the name of security in Africa is that these regimes are often the very source of the insecurity in Africa. Rather than promoting effective governance to improve security in Africa, the United States engages in the flawed policy of arming the very forces which create instability.

Fah noted that the militarization in Africa has led to creating a culture of violence in Africa through the proliferation of weapons and training local armies. The result is that hostage taking for ransom and the development of rebel groups have increased. Politicians, police officers, and military officers are sometimes engaged in these activities.

The issue of providing training to the forces which create instability came up during a congressional hearing in which Representative Matt Gaetz questioned General Michael Langley who serves as the commander of AFRICOM. During the hearing, General Langley stated that the training program was based on core values. In response to this, Representative Gaetz asked if those values were shared with Mamady Doumbouya who led a coup in Guinea. He was trained by AFRICOM, but General Langley stated that he could not identify him when shown a photo of Doumbouya along with American service members, although the general did make the interesting admission that Doumbouya shared the same core values. The photo was taken just months before Doumbouya led the coup in Guinea. Gaetz added that the coup leader in Burkina Faso was also trained by the United States.

Gaetz posed this question. "Why should U.S. taxpayers be paying to train people who then lead coups in Africa?" This is an important question which exposes the nature of American military intervention. This policy obviously does nothing to help taxpayers, yet at the same time it also does little to help the African nations where these coups take place. During the exchange, it was apparent that General Langley struggled to address the issue of American trained soldiers who lead coups. What was also telling was that the general did not even have the information on how many American trained soldiers have led coups in Africa.

Part of the problem is that these American trained soldiers are often able to take advantage of the political instability in their nations. Guinea and Burkina Faso are both nations which have had histories of political instability and coups in the past. Both nations also have a history of the military being utilized to oppress the civilian population in service of a brutal dictatorship. The aim of AFRICOM has not been to break this cycle. AFRICOM has actually contributed to the problem by providing training without regard for the political history of nations such as Guinea and Burkina Faso.

Apart from the fact that American military presence in Africa has contributed to the instability in Africa by training coup leaders, there is also the danger that America's military presence has posed to the Americans who are sent to serve in African nations. For example, there was an incident in which four American soldiers were killed in an ambush in Niger. The ambush was recorded and the recording was retrieved by ISIS, who then released the video for propaganda purposes. The troops were not only ambushed, but they were not properly equipped to protect themselves. At the time that they were attacked, they were driving an unarmored SUV. Representative Marc Veasey was puzzled as to why the troops were sent on such a dangerous mission without the necessary equipment to protect themselves.

To return to Fah again, Fah called for a coordinated Pan-African policy to halt American imperialism in Africa. Fah noted that Muammar Gaddafi of Libya opposed AFRICOM, but that other African leaders have not posed the same resistance. As was noted before, the president of Liberia went so far as to offer Liberia as a base for AFRICOM. Fah noted that this Pan-African task force should also "publicly shame opportunistic African leaders who ally themselves with imperial policies to serve their individual interests." Since the end of colonialism, Africa has struggled against this opportunistic class of leadership.

Terrorism is a serious concern for African nations which must be addressed. The problem with America's attempts to address this issue is that American involvement in Africa is often presented in humanitarian terms, but, as Malcolm had exposed since the 1960s, America's concerns have never been humanitarian. Fah stated that "Africa already contains many volatile regions. The US militarization will worsen instability, sustain insecurity and undermine peace-building efforts." This is precisely what has happened. Not only has the American militarization worsened the problem of security in Africa, but African leaders have exploited this concern over terrorism to garner American support and sympathy. An example of this is the government of Togo which has engaged in the tactic of labeling activists as terrorists.

Note:

Gilbert L. Taguem Fah, "Dealing with Africom: The Political Economy of Anger and Protest," *The Journal of Pan African Studies*, vol.3, no.6, March 2010.

BIRTH OF A NATION

The United States of America was the product of the European colonization of what came to be known as the "New World." The European settlement of the Americas had important global implications. The discovery led to the emergence of the colonial powers of Europe. It led to the slave trade, which began the process of the European exploitation and underdevelopment of Africa. It led to the destruction of the Native American nations which existed in the New World prior to the European colonization of those lands.

Not only are the roots of the United States to be found in the process of colonization, but the roots of the United States can also be found in the struggle between England and France over dominance in the Americas. The conflicts between France and England extended into the North American colonies where the British and French fought over land and trade routes. In 1689, the War of the League of Augsburg broke out in Europe. This war was one in which England and other European nations fought against France. The war became known as King William's War in North America. This reflected the fact that the colonists felt that the monarchy was dragging the colonies into a war which they were forced into. A few years after King William's War ended, Queen Anne's War began. The King William's War and the Queen Anne's War were also complicated by the involvement of Native Americans.

The final in the series of conflicts between the British and the French over the colonies in North America was known as the French and Indian War. Prior to the war, George Washington was sent to claim a portion of Ohio for Virginia. In the process, Washington's forces surprised a detachment of French troops and killed their leader. This sparked the war.

For seven years England and Prussia fought against France, Spain, Austria, and Russia. This conflict has been described as being the first world war because France and England were both global powers at this point, so the war was fought on many different fronts around the world.

In North America, the Native Americans were also involved in the war. The war became known as the French and Indian War because the British fought the French and their Native American allies, but the British had their own Native American allies in the war as well. The Iroquois Confederacy sided with the English in the war. Their objective was to assist the British to keep the British from taking more of their land.

Britain won the war, but the war was a very costly one. To make up the costs of the war, Britain raised taxes on the American colonists. It was already noted that the colonists were not pleased by the fact that they were being dragged into the conflicts between England and France. These wars were already unpopular among the colonists, but the colonists were outraged by the taxes which were being levied against them. The colonies eventually decided to declare their independence and a war followed. The American colonies were fighting for their independence, whereas the British Empire was fighting to maintain control of its colony.

France supported the American cause in the war. Though Louis XVI was initially opposed to entering into a treaty with the United States, a treaty was signed in 1778. The alliance between France and the United States was significant for the American cause in the war and played a role in America's victory over England.

George III wanted to continue the war in order to retain control of the American colonies, but this position was becoming unattainable. Public opinion in Britain was never very eager in support of the war. The war finally came to an end in 1783 when a peace treaty was signed between the parties involved in the war. Shortly after the treaty was signed, the nations of Europe recognized America's independence.

Following independence, American struggled with the question of governance. The colonies were governed under the Articles of Confederation. The problem was that this was not sufficient to establish centralized power. States began to compete with each other for trade with foreign nations. To address this problem, delegates of all the states met in Philadelphia in 1787 and formed a convention. After four months, the convention resulted in a new constitution. Under the new constitution, George Washington was elected president and John Adams was vice president.

Washington was inaugurated in 1789. His vision was to command the respect of the world. Establishing the United States' legitimacy to the powers of Europe was of particular importance given that the new nation was still vulnerable. The United States was in debt from the Revolutionary War and trying to reconcile with England. There were also conflicts with the Native Americans.

The Treaty of Paris which ended the war also extended American territory. The problem was that Native American nations were not represented at the signing of the treaty and did not believe that they were bound by the treaty. Moreover, the British continued to maintain forts in the area and supported Native American nations to counter the American expansion. These tensions led to the Northwest Indian War. During the war, the United States army suffered one of the worst defeats in its history. At the Battle of the Wabash, America lost more than 95% of its soldiers in the battle. This defeat forced Congress to raise funds for a better trained force. This newly trained force managed to defeat the Western Confederacy in 1795.

Prior to this war, there was some attempt to ease these tensions. In 1787, the government drafted the Northwest Ordinance which affirmed that the American government would respect the rights of the Native American population. It stated that Native American "lands and property shall never be taken from them without their consent." Arthur St. Clair, who fought in the Revolutionary War, was made governor of the Northwest Territory. He was also instructed by Congress to make treaties with the Native Americans if he needed to. The hostilities made a treaty necessary. In 1788, St. Clair met with delegations from six Native American nations to discuss a treaty. St. Clair refused to accept their desire to change the land boundary. St. Clair's position was that Britain had ceded the lands to the United States. He also informed the Native American delegates that the United States desired peace, but was willing to go to war if necessary.

The American policy at the time was to buy land from Native Americans, but the issue for the Native Americans was not merely being compensated for their lands. Native Americans were upset that the American government assumed that it had rights to their lands and offers to pay for the land did little to alleviate this. There was also an increase in hostilities on the frontiers. The government initially did not act against the Native Americans. This inaction caused citizens on the frontier to lose faith in the government's ability to protect them. The citizens sought to protect themselves by indiscriminately attacking Native Americans, including the Miami and Shawnee who were not particularly hostile towards the citizens on the frontier. Governor St. Clair wrote to Washington to explain that the people of Kentucky cannot be expected to submit "to the cruelties and depredations of those savages". These conditions made war between the American government and Native Americans inevitable.

Interestingly, there were some voices who denounced the American policy of expansion. One writer, who used the pseudonym "Anti-Pizaro" wrote: "What better right have we to march through the centre of their country, than Great-Britain would have to march a body of troops through the centre of the United States?" This remark was interesting because it demonstrated that the United States was acting no differently towards the Native Americans than the British had acted against America. Another critic of the war effort wrote that "it is our interest to promote friendship and harmony with all the world, and not to sacrifice our young men and our money, to acquire territory by war, while so much land remains unsettled, and which courts our cultivation under the auspices of peace." There were others in the public who supported the war as well.

The Northwest Indian War was an important one in America's history. As noted before, during the war, the American army suffered a horrible defeat at the Battle of the Wabash. The failure to defeat the Native Americans placed the federal government in jeopardy of being seen as being unable to protect its citizens. At the time Washington was already dealing with the political tensions between the emerging Federalist and Democratic-Republican political parties. Washington did not want party alliances to divide America and he avoided aligning with either party. Even so, Washington was in agreement with the Federalist view, which desired to create a strong standing army to protect the nation.

The Northwest Indian War took place as political debates were taking place about the creation of a standing army and about the powers of the federal government. Some critics of the war saw the war as a ploy by the Federalists to give the government more power. This is precisely what happened. In a paper titled "'Under the auspices of peace': The Northwest Indian War and its Impact on the Early American Republic, Melanie L. Fernandes wrote: "In this way, the events of the Northwest Indian War ultimately contributed to determining the role of the federal government in the early republic. With their demands for protection, American citizens on the frontier inadvertently conceded to a more centralized, more powerful government." The war also led to the development of a standing army.

In "The First AUMF: The Northwest Indian War, 1790-1795, and the War on Terror," Adam Mendel argued that the Northwest Indian War was the precursor to the War on Terror's Authorization for the Use of Military Force (AUMF). Mendel noted that the War of Terror which was launched after the attacks of September 11, 2001 was a war without a specific state or groups of states. Moreover, the battlefield of this war had no defined location or limitations. AUMF states that "the President is authorized to use all necessary and appropriate force against those nations, organizations, or persons he determines planned, authorized, committed, or aided the terrorist attacks that occurred on September 11, 2001, or harbored such organizations or persons, in order to prevent any future acts of international terrorism against the United States by such nations, organizations or persons." The AUMF effectively allows the president to engage in military actions without a formal declaration of war.

Mandel argued that the roots of the AUMF can be found in the Northwest Indian War Authorization which was a preventative measure to allow the president to use force to protect inhabitants of the frontiers of the United States. Mandel noted that the Northwest Indian War Authorization did limit the president's powers by defining Native Americans as enemies, but did not state which ones. The lack of specificity gave Washington the authority to engage in military action even against Native Americans who were not hostile to the United States. Divisions of war powers did remain, however. Washington's actions were bound by Congress. The Northwest Indian War was a war which expanded the power of the federal government and led to the creation of a standing army.

The American Revolution would not be the last war between America and the British Empire. A second war took place known as the War of 1812. Native Americans found themselves fighting on both sides of this conflict. The Creek Nation joined the British in the War of 1812 to fight the Americans. These Creeks were known as "Red Sticks." The lower Creeks decided to align with the United States during the war instead. In the scramble to colonize the Americas, Native Americans were caught up in the conflict, often on different sides of the conflict between the European colonizers. The United States was born out of the European colonization of the Americas. The same process which gave birth to the United States also led to the eventual destruction of the nations which the Native Americans had established before.

The Revolutionary War also had an influence on the Dutch colonies in the West Indies. Britain complained that during the war, Dutch settlements in the West Indies were used as depots to supply the enemy with provisions and contraband. This led Britain to declare war in 1780. The Dutch were charged with giving secret assistance to France and the rebel colonies, as well as making a secret treaty with the Americans. The States General replied in 1781 by stating that "if ever the annals of the world have furnished an instance of a free and independent state being attacked by an enemy, in the most unjustifiable manner, and without the least appearance of right or equity, by a neighboring power allied for a long time, and bound by ties founded on the basis of common interest, it is without doubt the Republic of United Netherlands, which finds itself in that case with His Majesty the king of Great Britain and his Ministers."

Following the war, Britain temporarily occupied Berbice, Essequibo, and Demerara. The occupation lasted for a few months until France and the Netherlands were able to seize control of the colonies. The Dutch regained power in 1784 and moved the colonial capital to a location which they named Stabroeck. The capital would later become Georgetown. Britain would seize control of territory from the Dutch once again in 1796. At the time, France had occupied the Netherlands. Britain declared war on France and, in 1796, Britain sent troops from Barbados to occupy the Dutch colonies. Demerara and Essequibo were once again under British control from 1796 to 1802. The colonies were temporarily returned to the Dutch, but when the war between Britain and France resumed, Britain seized control of Berbice, Demerara, and Essequibo. All three territories were formally ceded to Britain in 1814. The colonies were united into British Guiana in 1831. British Guiana became independent as Guyana in 1966.

The British seizure of the Dutch colonies had lasting implications for the region many generations later when a territorial dispute arose between Guyana and Suriname. In 1969, Suriname sent troops into the disputed territory, but they were repelled by the Guyanese army. The tensions continued into the 1980s when Suriname's leader blamed Guyanese immigrants for the poor state of Suriname's economy. Both Guyana and Suriname also detained each other's fishermen for fishing in the disputed area.

The loss of the North American colonies was a blow to the British overseas empire, but the seizure of Dutch possessions in South America demonstrated that the British Empire in the Americas continued to expand itself territorially. This expansion was also done within the context of the rivalry among the colonial powers. Britain waged war against the Dutch and the French.

The revolutionary ideals of some of the American Founding Fathers were not extended to black people. A clear example of this is the case of Thomas Jefferson, who not only was a slave owner, but also someone who opposed the revolution in Haiti. In a paper titled "The Color of Counterrevolution: Thomas Jefferson and the Rebellion in San Domingo," Michael Zuckerman wrote about Jefferson's opposition to the revolution, which included failing to act when the French were massacring black people. Zuckerman wrote: "Jefferson never did demur at the senseless slaughter, so long as it was directed against the blacks." Not only this, but Jefferson refused to acknowledge Haiti's independence. When Jean-Jacques Dessalines wrote to Jefferson to express a desire for trade relations, Zuckerman noted that Jefferson "did not even deign to reply."

Zuckerman suggested that the victorious American rebels had departed from the principles for which they battled the British, but it was more than this. Jefferson's opposition to Haiti was an early indication that America's racist domestic policy extended to its foreign policy. The generations of American presidents who came after Jefferson would continue this as well. In defeating the British Empire, the United States took its first steps to becoming a powerful military empire of its own. This was a process which took several years to develop, but the seeds of this development were already planted in the early years of the republic. The success of the American Revolution was one which had a profound impact on shaping the New World. The success of the revolution obviously led to the formation of a new nation and a significant loss of territory for the British Empire, but as I have shown here, the immediate impact of the revolution also influenced developments in other parts of the New World, such as the loss of Native American territory in North America and the conflict between the British and Dutch over Guyana.

3

ON WESTERN CIVILIZATION AND THE BIRTH OF WHITE IDENTITY

Western civilization is a rather interesting topic to address because views on this topic are shaped by the perspective one uses to judge what is known as civilization. Obviously, Western civilization has given birth to many great technological advancements, many great philosophical concepts, and many great examples of art. At the same time, it is also true that Western civilization has been responsible for many great atrocities as well. The statement here is not unique to Western civilization. Western civilization is not the only civilization which has committed atrocities, but I mentioned the atrocities to make the point that the topic of Western civilization can be a complex one because of these two conflicting realities of what Western civilization has been.

I am an African who was born in a former European colony. I state this at the onset to make the point that my very existence is rooted in the historical legacy of Western colonialism. I was born in Guyana and Guyana itself is a product of this legacy of colonialism. Western civilization has left an undeniable global impact on peoples across the world, yet this has not always been a positive impact. My African ancestors were stolen from their African homelands and enslaved in the Americas. I also have Amerindian ancestry. Amerindians were dispossessed of their lands as European colonizers took control. I have Indian ancestry as well. Indians were not only colonized, but my Indian ancestors were brought to Guyana as indentured laborers where they endured brutalities as well. Flowing through my blood is a lengthy history of abuse which was carried out by Europeans.

I am not suggesting that Europeans were the only ones to have ever done bad things in history. Africans waged wars on each other which often resulted in death and destruction. Most of the Africans who were captured and enslaved in the Americas were sold by other Africans. Amerindians also waged wars on each other, as did Indians. War, conquest, and slavery are human traits which are not unique to European societies. I want to state this early on, so critics of my position cannot accuse me of trying to propagate the view that the various ills of Western civilization are unique only to Western civilization.

I am also not denying the great things which Western civilization has produced, yet I also have to deal with the reality that as an African from a former colony, Western civilization has never been my civilization. I come from a people who have been victims of Western civilization. I come from a people who have suffered the worst aspects of Western civilization. This was the point that Malcolm X made about being an African in America. He stated that African Americans have not enjoyed the fruits of Americanism. Rather, they have only known the thorns. This has been the general situation of African people where Western civilization is concerned. The lofty ideals about democracy, liberty, and the rights of man have never been extended to us.

Among some Westerners there has been an attempt to distance Western civilization itself from the crimes of colonialism. M. Mannoni, for example, wrote that European civilization and its best representatives are not responsible for colonial racialism. To this, Frantz Fanon quoted Francis Jeanson who noted that certain French citizens prided themselves in keeping a distance from colonialism. Jeanson noted that it was the "blind indifference" of French citizens which allowed thugs to carry out the deeds which they did. Colonialism is Western civilization. There is no way to separate the two. Colonialism was carried out not only by the leaders of Western civilization, but also through citizens who prided themselves in keeping their distance from the crimes committed by their government.

Before I get deep into the discussion about Western civilization, I think it is first necessary to state what I mean by Western civilization. Western civilization refers to a collection of the nations which emerged in Europe. As European settlers moved to the Americas, they also brought their culture and worldview with them, which expanded Western civilization beyond the geographic location of Europe. The concept of Western civilization is essentially one which seeks to create a unifying identity for the diverse ethnic groups and nationalities which originate in Europe. The concept is also one which sets the West apart from the rest of the world. The history of Western civilization is one which is filled with conflicts and clashes between various Western states, so it is not as though the West has always been united, but the concept of a collective Western civilization is how the West has set itself apart from the rest of the world. This became especially necessary during the age of colonialism when Western states sought to conquer the rest of the world.

The concept of Western civilization is also related to the concept of race. Humans have always recognized differences in physical traits and cultural traits, but race is a concept which emerged within Western civilization during the age of colonialism to justify the Western colonization of people who were not deemed to be white. White itself represented the physical appearances of Europeans who recognized that the complexions of others around the world were much darker than their own. Out of this concept of race came racism, which was built on the notion white people were a superior race and that people should be defined by their racial identity. Out of racism emerged systems such as Jim Crow and apartheid, which upheld white supremacy at the expense of black people who were deemed to be inferior.

It is important to note here that racism may have been one of Western civilization's negative aspects, but racism in Western civilization was not a feature which was present in its early Greco-Roman roots. Frank Snowden demonstrated that in ancient Greco-Roman society, there was no prejudice associated with skin color. Snowden explained that "both Greeks and Romans, notwithstanding a few concepts and ideas sometimes misinterpreted as anti-black in sentiment, had the ability to see and to comment on the obviously different physical characteristics of Ethiopians without developing an elaborate and rigid system of discrimination based on the color of the skin." Color prejudice in Europe did become more noticeable. In one of his lectures, Eusi Kwayana noted that in William Shakespeare's play, *The Merchant of Venice*, a man from Morocco seeks to marry a woman named Portia. Much of their interaction was centers on the complexion of the Moroccan man, who asks Portia to mislike him not because of his dark complexion. The Moroccan man fails in his attempt to marry Portia because he selects the wrong casket. This causes Portia to remark, "Let all of his complexion choose me so." Kwayana mentioned this to show that prejudice based on skin color did exist in Europe before racism became institutionalized.

James Sweet argued that racial prejudice was introduced to Europe by the Moors when the Moors had conquered Iberia. As Sweet noted, Arabs developed their own racist views against African people. Sweet argued that "many Iberian Christians had internalized the racist attitudes of the Muslims and were applying them to the increasing flow of African slaves to their part of the world." This seems plausible, but my focus here is not so much on where racism in Western civilization emerged from. My point is that racism was not a feature of Western civilization in the early development of Western civilization. Racism became more prominent in the 1500s and onward.

The notion of racial superiority has been connected to the concept of Western superiority. Sam Francis expressed this view when he stated: "The civilization that we as whites created in Europe and America could not have developed apart from the genetic endowments of the creating people, nor is there any reason to believe that the civilization can be successfully transmitted by a different people." According to Patrick Buchanan, Francis was "suggesting Western civilization was superior and that only Europeans could have created it."

The question is why would such a suggestion need to be made? There is no question that white people created Western civilization, but it has never been enough for Westerners to feel content with the civilization which they created for themselves. There has always been a sense of superiority over other civilizations which has driven a desire to conquer other civilizations and to impose Western cultural norms on those conquered people.

This sense of superiority was also reinforced through denying the historical achievements of others. An example of this was the civilization of Great Zimbabwe in Africa. Its historical achievements were attributed to Phoenicians to avoid giving credit to African people. This view was challenged by Peter Garlake. This brought Garlake into conflict with Ian Smith's government.

Smith hired individuals to challenge Garlake's conclusions. Garlake was forced into exile in 1970 simply for daring to write the truth about the history of Great Zimbabwe. In an obituary for Garlake titled "Peter Garlake (1934-2011), Great Zimbabwe and the politics of the past in Zimbabwe," Innocent Pikirayi wrote that "Peter Garlake enjoyed considerable international recognition for the high quality and impact of his recent research, all of which indicated his standing as a leading international scholar." This was also precisely why the government of Rhodesia opposed his work.

One point which caught my attention upon revisiting Buchanan's work was his claim that the genocide in Rwanda and Burundi represented the "long and bloody history" of the Tutsi and Hutu people. Buchanan was mistaken. The history of the Tutsi and Hutu was not long and bloody at all. In fact, prior to European colonization, the dividing line was between Rwanda and Burundi, not Tutsi and Hutu. The tribal conflict was one which was instigated by the colonial powers. I make this point here to show that in the process of spreading its civilization to other people, the colonial powers created a great deal of instability and conflict. This is not to suggest that Africans were living in utopian societies before Europeans arrived, but colonialism certainly did no favors for Africa.

One of the worst examples of this was in the nation which would become known as Namibia. The Germans committed genocide. For several years, Germany did not even acknowledge the genocide nor did Germany offer an apology. Germany has also refused to pay reparations for the genocide. The genocide in Namibia was followed by the genocide of the Jews in Germany many years later. This is the product of a civilization which creates a distinction between superior people and inferior people who are worthy of being eliminated.

African people have often pondered on the roots of this racist and violent behavior. Elijah Muhammad claimed that white people were created to be a race of devils by a scientist named Yakub. Dr. Bobby E. Wright offered a more scientific explanation by suggesting that European behavior reflected an "underlying biologically transmitted proclivity" which was rooted "deep in their evolutionary history." Dr. Frances Cress Welsing argued that racism was motivated by a fear of white genetic annihilation. She argued that white people are not only a global minority, but that they are also genetically recessive. This view would certainly explain the white supremacist opposition to miscegenation—although some white supremacists advocated for miscegenation to eliminate the African population. Welsing also argued that white racism specifically targeted black males because black males posed a threat to white genetic survival.

In *How Europe Underdeveloped Africa*, Walter Rodney, utilizing a Marxist analysis of history, traced the roots of racism in Europe to slavery and the emergence of capitalism. He noted that the enslavement of African people was not done for racist reasons, but rather that racism developed as a means to rationalize the enslavement of African people. As the capitalist system developed, Rodney noted that racism became an integral part of the capitalist mode of production. Rodney was also careful to point out that it would be too sweeping a statement to suggest that all racial prejudice in Europe derived from the enslavement of Africans and the exploitation of other non-white groups. The example he gave was anti-Semitism in Europe, which predated capitalism. This would suggest that racial prejudice in Europe became part of the mode of production due to colonialism and the emergence of capitalism, but that within Western society there was already a tendency towards extreme prejudice towards other groups.

The idea of race itself is not so much the problem. Physical differences exist. The problem with white supremacy is that white supremacists believe that differences suggest that there must be inferior and superior races. On his hajj to Mecca, Malcolm X shared the profound experience of worshiping alongside white people. Malcolm had believed Elijah Muhammad's teachings that white people were devils by nature, but his experience in Mecca brought him in contact with people who were physically white, but to them being white represented incidental characteristics. Malcolm contrasted this with white identity in American society, in which white means "boss." White within a white supremacist society is not merely an incidental physical trait, but a social status which represents power and domination.

As I will demonstrate here, race as a concept is one which is not only biological, but cultural as well. It is for this reason that roots of Western civilization and the roots of white identity can be traced to a process of historical development in Europe by which Europeans or white people came to develop a sense of a collective identity. This sense of a shard white identity was one which distinguished white people and Western civilization from the other peoples and civilizations of the world. To be white and to be a Westerner then not only defines Europeans as a group in relation to each other, but it also defines Europeans as a group in relation to the rest of the world which fell outside of the category of white.

Greco-Roman civilization forms the basis of what is known as Western civilization. It is for this reason that to understand Western civilization, one must understand ancient Greece and Rome. I stated earlier that what is known as Western civilization generally refers to the nations of Europe, but Greece and Rome were part of the Mediterranean world which expanded beyond Europe to include North Africa and West Asia. This interaction with these societies did shape Greece and Rome in important ways. This is also significant because the proponents of this notion that Western civilization represents a superior civilization would have to acknowledge that the roots of Western civilization did not emerge in isolation from other civilizations in the world, particularly those in North Africa and Western Asia.

George M. James argued in *Stolen Legacy* that Greek philosophy was stolen from the Egyptians. His aim in this book was to challenge the view that black people are "backward in culture and have made no contribution to civilization". I maintain that James may have been overstating the case to claim that Greeks stole their philosophy from the Egyptians, but I do think the point does stand that Egyptian civilization predated Greek civilization and that Greek society was hostile to philosophers. I do not think the Greek hostility towards philosophers necessarily indicates that the philosophers were preaching alien ideas which they took from Africa, but it does indicate the level of hostility which Western societies have often displayed towards new ideas which challenge the existing status quo. James noted: "Only a brief study of history is necessary to show that Greek philosophers were undesirable citizens, who throughout the period of their investigations were victims of relentless persecution, at the hands of the Athenian government. Anaxagoras was imprisoned and exiled; Socrates was executed; Plato was sold into slavery and Aristotle was indicted and exiled; while the earliest of them all, Pythagoras, was expelled from Croton in Italy."

Socrates was sentenced for committing the crime of not believing in the gods of the city and for introducing new divinities. He was also accused of corrupting the youth. Socrates' crime was that he dared to introduce new ideas which challenged the existing ideas. Socrates was made to kill himself by drinking poison, which he apparently did cheerfully.

It was not Socrates alone who was persecuted for his teachings. As James pointed out, Plato was sold into slavery and Aristotle was exiled. This is indicative of the fact that Western civilization has historically been hostile to new ideas. In prior writings, I have mentioned Giordano Bruno being killed by the Catholic Church for his scientific views. Bruno was arrested and charged with blasphemy. After a seven year trial, Bruno refused to recant his views. He was sentenced to death on January 20, 1600. Bruno was gagged so that he could not speak. He was then burned alive at the stake.

Ancient Greece was a collection of independent city-states. In *The Mediterranean World in Ancient Times*, Eva Matthews Sanford explained that the city-states "contrasted with the oriental monarchies, in which the city was subordinate to the royal power, and with the less civilized peoples who did not develop politically beyond a tribal organization." Sanford also noted that not all Western states developed in the same manner that the Greek city-states did. Epirus, for example, maintained a government of tribal kings. In this essay I draw a lot from Sanford's book because it provides a chronology of the history of civilizations in the Mediterranean world of which Greece and Rome were part of. Sanford also does a great job at detailing the social and political organization of Greece and Rome.

Within the city-states, aristocracies emerged. The aristocracy was to represent "the rule of the best," although the aristocracy began to break down as wealth began to overshadow birth. In some cases, men of ordinary birth were able to accumulate wealth through industry and commerce. Thus, aristocracy gave way to oligarchy, in which political rights were based on wealth rather than birth. What followed was political unrest which resulted in individuals seizing control of their cities and ruling as what became known as tyrants.

Aristotle defined tyranny as monarchy which ruled in the interest of the monarch alone without any regard for the community. Sanford noted that tyrants still depended on popular support against the opposition of the former rulers. The tyrant needed to ensure that he had soldiers to carry out a military coup if necessary. Tyrants were also known to increase their wealth by seizing the estates of aristocrats. Sanford noted the specific case of Orthagoras, who led a farmer's revolt against the aristocracy and established the longest uninterrupted tyranny in Greek history.

Athens stands out among the Greek city-states for its democratic government. Solon was a statesman in Athens who was appointed to resolve the economic and political crisis in Athens. Solon engaged in constitutional reforms which assisted the poor. This included cancelling all debts. Not only were all those who had been enslaved for debt freed, but enslavement for debt was prohibited. It was noted that Solon did not establish Athenian democracy, but his reforms prepared the way for it by giving people more power. Solon also held the view that the "people will follow its leaders best if it is neither given excessive liberty nor subjected to undue oppression."

It was the reforms of Cleisthenes which led to the emergence of democracy in Athens. Cleisthenes was a tyrant who played a leading role in Hellenic politics. He became the most powerful man in Athens following a period of strife. He also reformed the political structure of Athens by breaking up old factions. A council of 500 known as the boule was put in place as well. Fifty of its members were chosen by a lot from each of the ten tribes to serve for an annual term. Any Athenian citizen might be called to preside over the general assembly of the senate.

In addition to Athens, Sparta was another powerful Greek city-state. Sparta became a wealthy state following the conquest of Messenia. The land of Messenia was allotted to the helots who tilled it for the Spartans. The Spartan system of government was one in which two kings were chosen from the two royal families.

Women in Sparta enjoyed more freedom than women in most other Greek cities, although they rarely saw their husbands—the condition of women in most Greek societies was reflected in Aristotle's *Generation of Animals*, in which he stated females are deformed males. Sparta was a warrior society in which from the age of seven, boys were raised in military bands. Cowardice was abhorred in Spartan society. A man who displayed cowardice in battle was stripped of citizenship. Spartan mothers were free to kill their sons for being cowardly.

The Greek conflict with the Persian empire was an important conflict in Greece's history. The Greek city-states were disunited, but the threat posed by the Persian Empire forced the city-states to unite against a common enemy. The Persian dynasty was founded by Achaemenes. In time, the Persian state expanded through conquest and during the short reign of Cambyses, Persia annexed Egypt.

The conflict between Greece and Persia was sparked when the Ionian Greeks rebelled against Persia in 499 B.C. Aristagoras led this revolt. This revolt was put down by the Persians, despite the support that it received from Athens and Eretria. After suppressing the rebellion, Darius decided to send a punitive expedition to Greece. Greek and Persian forces clashed in 490 B.C. at the Battle of Marathon. This battle was a victory for the Athenians who were able to repel the Persians.

After Marathon, Darius' attention turned to Egypt where a revolt had broken out. Darius died in 486 B.C. and was succeeded by Xerxes who was occupied with subduing Egypt and Babylonia. Greece was given a ten year respite before having to confront the Persian Empire again in 480 B.C. The Greeks ultimately defeated the Persians.

One of the most significant moments in the conflict between the Persians and the Greeks was the battle at Thermopylae. This battle is notable for the stand made by Leonidas and his 300 Spartan warriors. These warriors, along with about 6,000 other Greek soldiers, stood up against a larger Persian army under the leadership of Xerxes. The Persians won the battle, but the Greek forces inflicted heavy casualties on the Persian forces. Herodotus reported that Xerxes lost so many men in the battle that he hid his dead so that no one could see how many Persians were killed by so few men. The stand which Leonidas and his Spartan warriors made not only came to represent what a Spartan warrior should be, but Leonidas became a symbol of Western freedom. This is why Sir William Golding wrote: "A little of Leonidas lies in the fact that I can go where I like and write what I like. He contributed to setting us free."

The Greek victory over the Persians was made possible by the unity of the Greek city-states, including Athens and Sparta. The unity produced by this war was not to last, however. This is demonstrated by the Peloponnesian War which was fought between Athens and the Peloponnesian League which included Sparta. The sessions of the Peloponnesian League were hosted in Sparta and Sparta also commanded the army of the league. The first Peloponnesian War began in 460 B.C. This conflict ended with the signing of a peace treaty in 445 B.C. War broke out again between the Peloponnesians and Athens. The Peloponnesian League ultimately prevailed over Athens in the second war.

Isocrates, who was a Greek orator, stands out for his advocacy of Greek unity. He believed that the role of Athens was the proper leader of this envisioned union. He saw interstate rivalry among Greek city-states as being ruinous. In his view, unity was needed for "the most necessary and righteous war which we wage in alliance with the Hellenes against the barbarians, who are by nature our foes and are eternally plotting against us." Isocrates eventually turned to Philip to undertake the effort of uniting the Greeks. Phillip was a Macedonian leader who was able to unite Greece under his authority. Phillip was eventually assassinated and he was succeeded by his son Alexander.

Alexander, who became known as Alexander the Great, emerged as one of history's great conquerors. He ascended to the throne of Macedonia following the assassination of his father and proceeded to build a large impure. Alexander's conquests included taking control of Egypt, which had been under Persian rule. Alexander accepted the crown of Upper and Lower Egypt, and was enthroned as pharaoh under the protection of Horus. Alexander was viewed as the son of Amun, whom the Greeks identified with Zeus. Alexander was addressed as the son of Zeus Amun. That

Alexander embraced the religion of Egypt is interesting given the fact that the European colonial powers which colonized Africa many centuries later would impose their own cultural traditions on Africans rather than embracing African cultural traditions in the manner which Alexander did.

Alexander died in 323 B.C. The empire which he built fragmented. The significance of Alexander the Great in European history is that he was the first great conqueror to emerge out of Europe who built a massive empire. Western civilization has given rise to a number of massive empires. This tradition began with Alexander the Great who expanded his empire into Asia and Africa. The empire which Alexander built would later be surpassed by the size of Rome.

As was noted, the Greeks and Romans did not perceive themselves as being white nor did they display the type of racist attitudes which would later emerge in the West. What the racist colonial empires of the West did draw from Greece and Rome— apart from the intellectual, cultural, and political traditions of Greece and Rome—was the drive for aggressive imperial expansion. This is what Alexander the Great was engaged in and it was what the Roman Empire was engaged in.

Rome was initially ruled by kings until the republic was established in 509 B.C. The republic was established by a bloodless revolution which expelled Tarquin the Proud. The senate in Rome served as the chief governing body of the republic. Two consuls were elected annually from the patrician families. Each consul held absolute authority, which included being able to have any citizen summarily executed or scourged. Each consul was also given the authority to veto the action of the other. In times of a political or military crisis, a dictator was appointed and given absolute authority over the two consuls. The dictator gave up power when the crisis was over.

The term dictator now carries a negative connotation because dictators tend to be leaders who have absolute power, which they abuse at the expense of their citizens. The Roman concept of dictatorship was that in times of extreme crisis, the dictator would temporarily seize power to resolve the situation. The dictator was not meant to have absolute power for life, but this is what dictatorship eventually came to be for many societies which have had dictators. As will be demonstrated, even in Rome itself the notion of having temporary dictators allowed room for the development of an empire which supplanted the republic.

The republic in Rome eventually came to an end due to the internal struggles over power in Rome. Julius Caesar joined with Crassus and Pompey to form what became known as the First Triumvirate. Together, the three men dominated Rome. The trio formed a temporary union to achieve their goals. Together, they secured a consulship for Caesar in 59 B.C. along with Bibulus. Caesar's status also increased following his conquest of Gaul, which further expanded Roman territory.

The Triumvirate eventually broke up. As Caesar was involved in his campaign in Gaul, Pompey was made the sole consul by the senate in order to restore order in Rome following the fights between Clodius' followers and rivals hired by Milo. By this time, Crassus had been killed in combat. As Pompey's political influence in Rome increased, Caesar found himself in political trouble after he was declared a public enemy. When this news reached Caesar, he decided to cross the river Rubicon. Marching an army into Roman territory was an act of war. The civil war which followed resulted in Caesar seizing power in Rome. He was granted dictatorship for ten years in 46 B.C. and then for life in 44 B.C. Caesar also had the right to express his opinion first in senatorial debates, to make war and peace without consulting the senate, and he was given complete control over the treasury.

Caesar's rule came to a violent end. The assassination of Caesar not only impacted Rome, it had implications for Egypt as well given that Caesar had a relationship with Cleopatra VII, which produced a child. Following Caesar's death, Cleopatra returned from Rome to Egypt and met Mark Antony in Syria. Cleopatra aligned herself with Mark Antony.

Following Caesar's assassination, his grandnephew Octavian rose to power in Rome and eventually became the first emperor in the history of the Roman Empire. He eventually clashed with Mark Antony over power in Rome. Octavian's forces defeated Antony's forces. Antony committed suicide and Cleopatra did the same. Following this, Egypt was annexed by Rome and came under

Octavian's control.

Octavian was given the name Augustus by the senate. He was also called the principate. Augustus was granted greater powers. Augustus claimed that he had restored the republic by transferring his power to the senate, although the power of the senate had been reduced. Augustus carried out a purge of the senate and reduced its size. Augustus also controlled foreign policy and treaties.

The Roman republic developed as a response to one-man rule which had been overthrown. The problem was that the republic still left space for one individual to seize power and rule as a dictator. As I stated previously, this was intended to be a temporary position, but Caesar exploited this position to make himself dictator for life. Caesar's dictatorship signaled the decline of the republic and the transition towards empire.

Nero, who began his rule in 54, was one of the most infamous emperors in the history of the Roman Empire. One of the most infamous moments of his rule was a fire which had destroyed much of Rome. Nero was accused of having set the fire himself. To shift the blame, Nero blamed the fire on Christians. Nero's conduct came to typify a leader who is inactive and complacent in addressing a serious crisis. This is why Malcolm X had compared John F. Kennedy to Nero because of Kennedy's inaction when it came to dealing with the race problem in America.

Under Nero's rule, the empire experienced rebellions. There was one in Britain which was led by a woman named Boudicca. The Roman towns in London were sacked and as many as 70,000 Romans were killed. There was also a Jewish uprising. Nero was more interested in the arts than in maintaining the military dominance of the empire.

In 65, a plot to overthrow Nero was exposed and the conspirators were executed. This was not the last attempt to remove Nero. In 68, Julius Vindex gained support among the Gauls who were tired of the burden of taxation and debt. Vindex was defeated, but the revolt spread. Galba revolted as well. Realizing that he lacked support, Nero died at the hands of one of his servants, although rumors that Nero was still alive persisted.

The period following Nero's death was one of instability. Galba became the new emperor, but he was murdered. The throne was given to Otho who was then defeated by Vitellius' troops. Vitellius was then overthrown and the throne was given to Flavius Vespasian. All of this took place within the span of a year.

Nero opposed Christianity, but Christianity eventually spread in Rome and became the dominant religion. In the early years of Christianity in Rome, Christians were viewed as a Jewish sect which strayed from the norms of Judaism. Christianity was also met with hostility from the Roman emperors. Nero executed Christians in Rome after the great fire which he blamed them for. In 303, Diocletian issued decrees which deprived Christians of their rights as citizens and ordered the destruction of their churches. In time, Christianity found acceptance from Constantine who not only restored the civil rights of Christians, but he also built churches.

Christianity came to supplant paganism as the dominant religion in Rome. The Roman emperors themselves began to root out paganism. This created a situation in which followers of the pagan religions were forced to defend their faith. A statesman named Symmachus, who led a movement to restore the altar of Victory which had been removed from the senate house, opposed rigid monotheism which did not allow each to practice their own customs. He stated: "There is no single road by which we may arrive at so great a mystery." In the end, the Christian influence prevailed. Edicts were put in place to confiscate the salaries of pagan priests and to ban sacrifices. Those who were outspoken in their pagan beliefs were excluded from office and from the army.

Prior to the acceptance of Christianity, Roman society had worshiped a supreme sky god known as Jupiter, who was known as Zeus to the Greeks. The story of Zeus was attested in the poems of Homer. Zeus was the leader of all the gods. These gods were to be appeased through rituals and sacrifices. The Greeks also believed that great heroes went to the Elysian fields when they died, whereas most men went to Hades.

The historian John Henrik Clarke argued that Europeans did not have the temperament for Christianity. Erich Fromm made a similar point when he argued that Christianity was at odds with the Greek and Germanic tradition of celebrating great conquerors. Whereas Greek religion told stories of great heroes and conquerors, the story of Jesus was the story of a martyr who sacrificed his life for the benefit of others. It is not as though Greek religion was without examples of martyrs. There was the tale of Prometheus, who was subjected to a cruel punishment by Zeus for taking fire away from the gods to give it to human beings. This can be viewed as an act of sacrifice because what Prometheus did caused him to be punished even though humanity ultimately benefitted from his action. Generally speaking, however, Greek religious tradition was one which favored heroic conquerors, which is why there was a separate afterlife for heroes as opposed to ordinary people. In Christianity, everyone is equal before God when it comes time for judgment in the afterlife. Those who enter heaven in the Christian religion are not great warriors and heroes, but those who lived a righteous life.

Greco-Roman culture formed the basis of Western civilization, but Western civilization as we know it to be really did not come into being until after the spread of Christianity into Europe. Christianity provided a stronger sense of cultural connection in Europe because it united Europe under a common religion. This religion also helped to set the West apart from the rest of the world. Christianity even became a tool in the process of colonial conquest. Africans were viewed as being heathens who needed to be saved through Christian conversion by the European colonizers.

Theodosius was the last emperor to rule over a unified empire. Theodosius came to power at a time when the Goths were posing a danger to Rome. In 376, Valens permitted the Goths to settle under the protection of the Roman Empire. They were also promised supplies, but this promise was not fulfilled. The Goths, who were facing starvation, began to plunder Rome. When Valens attacked, his army was defeated. Theodosius was made emperor and he managed to subdue the Goths. Theodosius died in 395, leaving two sons who were each given one half of the empire. Arcadius was given the eastern part and Honorius was given the west. The empire remained whole and all edicts were issued in the name of both emperors.

The western portion of the empire eventually collapsed after years of a slow decline. One of the signs of this decline was that "barbarian nations" who were looked down upon by the Romans eventually came to form a major part of the Roman army. Rome found itself being unable to sustain the large empire which it had established. The eastern portion became what is known as the Byzantine Empire. The difference between east and west was as much cultural as it was geographic. The language of administration in the east was Greek, rather than the Latin of the West. The religious doctrines of the two differed as well, with the Orthodox Greek Church having a doctrine which diverged from the Latin Catholics.

The emperor Heraclius managed to defeat Persia and regained control of Syria. The Roman control of Syria was not to last long, however. Sanford noted: "At the very moment of Heraclius' great victory, the first bands of Arabs, inspired by the teachings of Mohammed, the inability of their land to support its growing population, and the ambition of their leaders, began raids which were to result in the conquest of a larger territory than Rome had ever ruled."

The emergence of Islam posed a serious challenge to the dominance of Western civilization. Muslims took control over the regions which were previously under the rule of the Romans. Sanford noted that the Syrians welcomed the Arabs who provided relief from Byzantine oppression. Sanford presented this as a situation in which the "Semites recovered sovereignty in the eastern world […]." Sanford also noted that by the middle of the eight century the former territories of the Roman Empire were split between the Byzantine Empire with its capital at Constantinople, the Abbasid Caliphate, and the Franks. All three of these powers drew from the Greco-Roman world for their literature and science. Arab scholars translated the works of the Greek philosophers and scientists.

In time, the spread of Islam encroached on Europe itself. In 711, Moors from North Africa seized control of Spain. Muslim rule in Spain was to last several centuries. In 1453, Constantinople fell to the Turks. The conquest of the Ottoman Turks also had a significant impact on trade in Europe because it blocked eastern trade routes.

The period from the fall of the Roman Empire to the 1492 discovery of the Americas was a period of decline and stagnation in Europe. This was a political decline in the sense that Western Europe did not have a state which matched the military might of the Roman Empire of the past. Europe also confronted the threat of Islamic invasion from the West and from the East. In the West, the Moors managed to seize control of Iberia. In the East, the Byzantine Empire fell to the Turks.

The Roman Empire provided a strong centralized power in Europe. Following the fall of Rome, feudal kingdoms emerged in Europe. Under the feudal system, peasants worked for landlords in exchange for protection. Most of these peasants were serfs who were bound to estates and obligated to serve their landlords. Within this system there was a significant disparity between the wealthy and the poor. The Catholic Church was also an institution which had significant power and authority in Europe at this time.

In a paper titled "The Black Death, an Unforeseen Exchange: Europe's Encounter with Pandemic Sparked an Age of Exploration," Camryn Franke noted that in the centuries prior to the Black Plague, "Europe became prime for a pandemic". The factors which made Europe prime for a pandemic included a massive population increase, urbanization, unsanitary living conditions, and inadequate healthcare. Franke explained: "Many Europeans lived in unsanitary and squalid conditions. People in cities lived in close contact and interacted with disease vectors like rodents and waste." These poor conditions were partly related to the fact that when the Western Roman Empire fell, infrastructure crumbled. Waste ran through the streets due to lack of running water and sewers. Yet another factor which contributed to the plague was the Hundred Years' War between England and France which lasted from 1337 to 1453. During this war, soldiers often encountered disease and returned home to spread it.

In 1347, the plague spread to Eastern Europe. From the east it then spread north and west into Europe. The plague killed millions and led to a collapse in the social order. Entire villages were wiped out by the plague. The plague was especially harmful for the lower class in European society. Giovanni Boccaccio explained that the lower class and most of the middle class received no care and attention, so almost all of them died. It was estimated that one third of the population in Europe perished due to the plague.

The plague also led to significant social changes. As the labor supply declined, peasants realized that they could demand higher wages. In England, King Edward III tried to quell these demands by issuing the Statute of Laborers which required every able-bodied unemployed person under the age of sixty to work for anyone who wanted to hire him. This failed to stop the peasants' demands, however.

Peasant uprisings continued in Europe. Eventually, peasants managed to secure increased wages. This caused serfdom to disappear in many places in Europe. Serfs, who were no longer tied to a landlord, could leave for another who would hire him. The freedom of the workers to leave to find other work resulted in many manors collapsing.

The plague led to the weakening of the feudal system. It also led to a weakening of the Catholic Church's power. After the plague, medical practices improved. More individuals also turned to independent practitioners. Prior to the plague, healthcare was operated by the Catholic Church, but following the plague there was an increase in healthcare options outside of the Catholic Church. Apart from this, the plague also raised questions about the Catholic Church's inability to protect people from the plague. It led to increased mistrust of the Catholic Church, which eventually resulted in religious reformations.

The Black Plague devastated Europe, but it also led to social changes in Europe which weakened the existing feudalistic system. These social changes also contributed to the Renaissance and the age of exploration for Europe. There was an economic transformation as well. As the feudal system weakened, Europe developed mercantilism which was a system based on using exports to increase national wealth. Mercantilism served as the precursor to capitalism.

Sanford pointed out that even after Rome fell, the idea of empire itself persisted. There was a belief that imperial power in the West merely transferred to the Franks when Charlemagne was crowned in 800 and then by Otto the Great in 962, which began the history of the Holy Roman Empire. Constantinople was identified as the Second Rome and Moscow positioned itself as the Third Rome. Sanford noted that even after Napoleon ended the Holy

Roman Empire in 1806, the title persisted in central Europe until the 1917 revolution in Russia and the 1918 revolution in Prague.

Greece and Rome also shaped the early formation of the United States. Greek and Latin were taught in nine Colonial Colleges, which demonstrated how strong the interest in Greece and Rome were in the American colonies. Thomas Jefferson and John Adams admired the achievements of Greece and Rome. Adams believed that Sparta should have been the model for the United States to follow. One of the most obvious points of influence was that the United States adopted the republicanism of Rome.

The importance of understanding the roots of Western civilization and white identity is because these concepts formed the basis of the colonial world order. This is a world order which placed Western civilization at the top, whereas all others were regulated to being colonial subjects who were exploited for the benefit of the dominant colonial power.

The supposed moral and cultural superiority was backed by the technological superiority of the West. It was this technological superiority of the West which allowed the West to conquer and colonize Africa. The technological superiority of the West and its desire for military dominance became a shortcoming during the World Wars. I shan't go into the details about the World Wars other than to state here that the military aggression and rapid advancement in military technology which enabled the Western powers to establish colonial empires around the world eventually resulted in two extremely destructive wars among the European powers which resulted in the deaths of millions. I do not deny the many great achievements of Western civilization, but I do believe they should be weighed against the negative impact as well. For African people, in particular, the impact has been overwhelmingly negative.

4

SLAVERY AND RACE

Slavery was an important economic institution in the European settlement of the New World. Slavery provided a source of free labor for European planters in the New World. Out of the economic system of slavery came a social system based on race. This social system was designed to uphold the plantation economy by classifying labor and social relations based on race. Those who belonged to the white race occupied a position of power, whereas the black race was regulated to slavery. The aim of this essay is to explore the way that the concept of race not only shaped the development of the New World, but also how the idea of race impacted African people as well.

The slave trade not only helped to enrich Western societies, but it transformed the African societies which were impacted by the trade. It was observed that it was not unusual for a headman in Sierra Leone to have 200-300 slaves, while some of the Muslim rulers had between 700 and 1,000 inhabitants in their "slave towns." Walter Rodney noted that in most cases "their status was far removed from chattel slavery, but the fact remains that social relationships had been profoundly altered in the direction of disprivilege and unfreedom during the period of contact with Europeans, and the Atlantic slave trade bears the major share of the responsibility."

The wars in Africa helped to provide a supply of captives to be enslaved. An example of this is that the Mane would recruit some Sapes as captives, but sell as many as possible to keep the population manageable. Farma was a Mane ruler who died in 1606. It was noted that during his rule, it was not unusual to have twenty or thirty vessels loading slaves at any given time. The slave trade itself provided an incentive for such wars. It was reported by English slave traders in the 1580s that Farma would obtain hundreds of slaves on request by embarking on a campaign.

Wars of conquest were an aspect of the state formation process in Africa. These wars often produced a significant captive population. One example of this is the emergence of the Akwamu

Kingdom. Under the rule of Ansa Sasraku, Akwamu engaged in a policy of imperial expansion. The result of this expansion was that Akwamu seized control of Great Accra. Akwamu also brought the Ladokou Kingdom under its control. The captives who were produced by Akwamu's military campaigns were marched to the state's capital district. There they would labor as slave cultivators. Some of the elite captives were ransomed, whereas others were ritualistically killed. Women captives in war were made to leave their homes to join the conquering group. They were assimilated as slave laborers and wives. War captives who were not absorbed into the existing slave population in Akwamu were led to the coast where they were sold. Little Popo was also known to be a warlike kingdom which engaged in the slave trade. Guns which were acquired from the slave trade helped to establish Little Popo as a military power in West Africa.

Stephanie Smallwood gave some idea of how the slave trade impacted African society. Smallwood argued that slavery and slave trading was likely already established throughout much of pre-colonial West Africa before the arrival of the Portuguese, but the arrival of the Portuguese transformed the existing slave trade. Smallwood explained: "The Portuguese had not introduced slave trading in African regions where no such commerce had existed prior to their arrival. But through the commerce they did introduce, they helped initiate a dramatic and abrupt shift in the scale of slave trading." This shift created "institutionalized markets for people" and reduced those people to commodities.

The extent to which there was an existing slave trade is difficult to ascertain. Forms of domestic slavery certainly existed in pre-colonial West Africa, but it does not appear that this was a universal practice. Walter Rodney noted that there were regions in Africa where absence of reference to any forms of local slavery would suggest an absence in the practice of slavery itself. What we do know is that the European presence incentivized slave trading. War captives who would otherwise be assimilated or killed now had commercial value and were sold to European buyers.

European traders themselves would incite conflicts for the purpose of increasing the number of captives which they purchased. The Bijagos were known as a fearsome group who engaged in raids which produced captives who were sold to European buyers. So brutal were the Bijagos that it was reported that they would set fire to the huts in a village and if the occupants came out fighting, they were cut to pieces. When European slavers found few or no slaves among the Bijagos, they would insist that the lack of slaves was a stain on the name of the Bijagos. These appeals to the honor of the Bijagos were done to incite them to bring more captives to be sold.

The Beafadas were among the groups who were attacked by the Bijagos, but the Beafadas themselves were engaged in slave raids. This demonstrated that the victims of the slave trade could just as easily be victimizers as well depending on the situation. Such conflicts were ultimately most beneficial to the European slave traders who acquired captives from these wars. The African ruling class and slave traders benefited in that they obtained European goods for selling captives to the Europeans. As a whole, however, the slave trade was destructive to African society. Rodney explained that the slave trade "proved entirely detrimental to African society, which was the weaker party." Indeed, slavery weakened African societies, while allowing Western nations to build profitable businesses and industries. An example of this is the role slavery played in the development of JP Morgan Chase.

The slave trade was detrimental for Africa because the wars to acquire the slaves were fought in Africa. As was already noted, even some of the groups which sold captives could themselves become victims of the slave trade. Whereas wars in Africa were fought over political power and control of wealth, the slave trade created an incentive to wage wars and engage in raids solely for the purpose of acquiring captives. This created a vicious cycle of war and instability which European traders and slave owners profited from. The more wars which were waged, the more slaves Europeans were able to acquire.

Apart from the economic ramifications of slavery and the slave trade, this historical event also had profound social implications. The enslavement of African people, as well as the subjugation of the indigenous population, resulted in the creation of a social structure of racism which placed white people above other races of people. Racism is also the reason why the European treatment of the captives which they bought differed from the African treatment of war captives. As was noted, captives who were not killed were assimilated into African societies. Within the racial societies of the New World, there was no hope for assimilation for African people who were considered to be an inferior people. Even those who became free were still limited by the fact that they were African.

Race as a social classification was of little prominence or significance in European and African societies prior to the colonization of the Americas. Ancient societies recognized that physical differences existed among humans from different regions of the world, but no political or economic significance was attached to these physical differences. This is not to suggest that forms of prejudice did not exist, but there was no institutionalized system of racism in Western society prior to the European colonization of the New World.

The system of white supremacy which Europeans constructed was one which varied from colonial society to colonial society. In the United States, for example, the one-drop rule developed as a means to classify anyone with a drop of African blood as being an African in the United States. This was not the case in countries such as Brazil or South Africa where mixed race individuals were treated differently than those who were black. The conception of white identity differed as well. For example, the Portuguese in Guyana were not regarded as being white because they came to Guyana as indentured laborers. White as an identity developed as one which was related to power. In colonial Guyana, the Portuguese did not have power as the British did, so they were not viewed as being white within that context. The Portuguese faced discrimination as well in Guyana because they did not fit into the construct of being white in Guyana.

Jews provide an interesting example of the concept of white identity in colonial societies. Jews were a group which had historically faced persecution in Europe for their religion. This persecution did not prevent Jews from participating as slave owners within the colonial economy, however. Some Jews also developed racist attitudes towards African people. This was a case in which a group which had been oppressed in Europe was in a position of power and dominance over African people, which further demonstrated the nature of racial hierarchy in colonial societies.

Jews were expelled from Spain in 1492 and were subsequently barred from settling in any of the new Spanish colonies in the Americas. Jews did settle in other parts of the Americas, however. Max J. Kohler noted that hundreds of Jews left Holland to settle in Brazil in 1624. Jewish settlers in Brazil came to make up the largest number of those who were transplanted from Holland, with the exception of those who worked for the Dutch West India Company. The Jewish settlers in Brazil worked as traders. The Dutch were forced to quit Brazil in 1654 after the Portuguese seized Pernambuco. Some of the Jewish settlers who left Brazil made their way to New York.

Slavery was a business in the New World and Jews were involved in that business. Kohler pointed out that "every New York family of any wealth or comfort held slaves, and in keeping and even in dealing in them the Jews were neither better nor worse than the Christian inhabitants." Kohler further explained that Jews in New York were involved in the slave trade as well. Kohler found a record of "Simon the Jew" who was waiting for the arrival of his slave ship from Guinea.

Jews in the United States also displayed some of the discrimination towards African people which was typical of the era. Bertram Wallace Korn noted that "Jewish congregations would not accept Negro members." Korn further noted that the Charleston Beth Elohim constitution of 1820 accepted proselytes only if "he, she, or they are not people of colour."

Even though there were Jews who were slave owners and who engaged in discrimination against African Americans, Jews also continued to experience discrimination themselves. This exposed the complexity of the system of white supremacy. Though white Jews were white enough to find themselves in a position of dominance over African people, there were still segments within the white population which viewed Jews as outsiders and enemies. In Germany, the Nazis were so extreme in this view that they resorted to massacring the Jews.

Nazism itself arose out of the same racist logic which developed in the New World, which is why it is hardly surprising that the racist ideology of the Nazi regime was met with sympathy from racists in America. Madison Grant held the view that there would be an imminent racial conflict between whites and the non-white people of the world. Grant also criticized the wealthy classes for introducing African slaves and Asian immigrants to the detriment of common people. Lothrop Stoddard, who was influenced by Grant's work, was a proponent of eugenics. He also maintained a favorable view of the Nazi government in Germany.

In time, the United States found itself at war with the Nazi regime in Germany. Even though the two nations were at war, there was still a mutual understanding that both nations were committed to the maintenance of white supremacy. This is demonstrated by the fact that German prisoners of war were treated better than African American soldiers were. The white supremacist ideology of the West was such that even though Western states clashed among each other over political power, there was still a sense of a shared racial identity.

David Walker, who was an American abolitionist, was one of the early critics of the white supremacist system which enslaved and brutalized African people. In his *Appeal*, Walker asserted that the disunity of Africans in the United States was the reason why they remained oppressed by white people: "Yea further, when I view that mighty son of Africa, Hannibal, one of the greatest generals of antiquity, who defeated and cut off so many thousands of the white Romans or murderers, and who carried his victorious arms, to the very gate of Rome, and I give it as my candid opinion, that had Carthage been well united and had given him good support, he would have carried that cruel and barbarous city by storm. But they were disunited, as the colored people are now, in the United States of America, the reason our natural enemies are enabled to keep their feet on our throats."

Walker's call for unity could be seen as an early example of what would come to be known as Pan-Africanism. Walker's book was addressed to the colored citizens of the world. He was writing not for an American audience alone, but for a global African audience. As the previous quote demonstrated, Walker also drew much inspiration from Hannibal's struggle against Rome. He saw

Hannibal as an African warrior who was engaged in a war against a European foe, which was not unlike the situation of Africans during slavery who also confronted a struggle against European enslavers. Whether or not Hannibal was a black man is debatable, but Walker clearly identified with Hannibal because he saw a connection between Hannibal's fight against the Romans and the African American fight against American slave owners.

Walker believed that the Lord would give black people a Hannibal. He believed that this liberator which the Lord would provide to black people should be one who would receive support from his people. Walker was also clear in his view that there would be retribution for the suffering which white people inflicted on their slaves: "The whites want slaves, and want us for their slaves, but some of them will curse the day they ever saw us. As true as the sun ever shine in its meridian splendor, my colour will root some of them out of the very face of the earth. They shall have enough of making slaves of, and butchering, and murdering us in the manner which they have."

Walker also noted the brutality of slavery was such that the white slave masters prevented enslaved Africans from practicing the religion of Christianity. He stated: "The Pagans, Jews and Mahometans try to make proselytes to their religions, and whatever human beings adopt their religions, they extend to them their protection. But Christian Americans not only hinder their fellow creatures, the Africans, but thousands of them will *absolutely beat a coloured person nearly to death, if they catch him on his knees, supplicating the throne of grace.* This barbarous cruelty was by all the heathen nations of antiquity, and is by the Pagans, Jews and Mahometans of the present day, left entirely to Christian Americans to inflict on the Africans and their descendants that their cup which is nearly full may be completed."

The point that Walker made about religion is an important one for understanding race. The European slave masters were Christians, yet in their view race was a more important classification than religion was. Africans who converted to Christianity were not viewed as brothers and sisters in Christ by the European slave masters. For the Christian slave master on the plantations, Christianity became a tool to advance white supremacy.

Africans like Walker utilized religion for their own racial purposes. Whereas Europeans saw religion as a tool which helped to impose their dominance, Africans like Walker believed that the redemption of African people was divinely ordained. Walker was not alone in this view. Nat Turner's rebellion was premised on his belief that he was being divinely guided to rebel against slavery. Leonard Howell and Elijah Muhammad are other examples of this. This theological approach of viewing African people as chosen people of God was a reaction to the racial oppression which was inflicted on African people by white racists and has managed to inspire great acts of resistance on the part of oppressed black people.

Race has been so pervasive in Western societies that it has not only influenced religion, but politics as well. In the United States' political system, which has historically been dominated by two parties, we find that both parties may have ideological disagreements, but they both uphold white supremacy. Frances Butler Leigh wrote: "The Northerners take it for granted that every negro must be Republican, because the Republicans released them from bondage; they seem to forget that since the war the Republicans have really done nothing for the negroes, nor in any way fulfilled the many promises they made to them." Not only this, but Republicans were responsible for making a deal with Democrats in 1877 which gave the White House to the Republican, Rutherford Hayes. After a closely contested election in 1876, the two parties held a discussion in which the Democrats agreed to recognize Hayes as the president and Hayes in turn pulled federal troops from the South. This deal ended Reconstruction and restored Democratic control in the South. The deal was also a betrayal of the black people who supported the Republican Party.

President Hayes himself apparently did not think too highly of black people. George Campbell traveled to Washington on the same train with President Hayes and his wife. Based on his exchange with the president, Campbell wrote: "The President takes a very favourable view of the position and prospects of the negro. He thinks the present race of negroes are not equal to white men; but then, according to his views, the qualities of mankind are very much a matter of climate. Whether white or black, he thinks men are inferior in hot climates. The American blacks have not yet had time to develop higher human qualities nor to acquire much land, but he hopes they will."

In Campbell's view, President Hayes held a "favourable view" of black people, yet Hayes still believed that black people were not equal to white people. In Hayes' view, this was not based on an inherent inferiority. Hayes argued that this inferiority was the result of the climate, yet he still believed that there was inequality nevertheless. And this was regarded as being a "favourable view" of black people.

This inequality was further imposed through the criminal justice system. Marc Mauer explained: "The exclusion of felons from the body politic derived from the concept of 'civil death' that had its origins in medieval Europe. Such a designation meant that a lawbreaker had no legal status, and also had dishonor and incapacity imposed on his or her descendants. The concept was brought to North America by the English in the Colonial period. After the Revolution, some of the English common law heritage was rejected, but the voting disqualifications were maintained by many states." The purpose of this exclusion was to punish criminal offenders, but in the United States this policy took on a racial component given that America's anti-drug policies disproportionately targeted African Americans who were then disenfranchised and lost their ability to vote.

Mauer also noted that laws to prevent citizens from voting can be traced to the founding of the nation. Originally only wealthy white male property holders could vote. This excluded women, African Americans, and those who did not own property. Mauer noted that over time the barriers to voting were removed, with the exception of felons. This is due to the concept of "civil death" which was mentioned before. This has allowed for the continued disenfranchisement of African Americans. Mauer noted that in 2002 it was estimated that 13 percent of African American males were disenfranchised.

After the end of the Civil War, the South implemented a number of policies to prevent African Americans from being able to vote. This included a poll tax and literacy requirements. The situation was not much better in the North, where only six

Northern states allowed African Americans the right to vote. Race was a fundamental aspect of the societies which developed out of the system of slavery in the New World and laws which restricted the voting rights of Africans were simply yet another one of the methods utilized to secure the dominant position of Europeans while keeping African people suppressed.

Selected References:

Adam J. Ondo, "Little Popo: The sociopolitical and economic erosion of a port town," 2014.

Bertram Wallace Korn, *Jews and Negro Slavery in The Old South 1789-1865*, 1961.

David Teather, "Bank Admits it owned slaves," *Guardian*, Jan. 21, 2005.

David Walker, *An Appeal to the Colored Citizens of the World*, 1830.

Marc Mauer, "Disenfranchisement: The Modern-Day Voting Rights Challenge," *Civil Rights Journal*, 2002.

Max Kohler, "Phases of Jewish Life in New York Before 1800," *Publications of the American Jewish Historical Society*, 1894, No. 2 (1894), pp.77-100

Sir George Campbell, *The American People or The Relations Between the White and the Black*, 1889.

Stephanie Smallwood, *Saltwater Slavery: A Middle Passage from Africa to American Diaspora*, (Harvard University Press, 2008).

Walter Rodney, *A History of the Upper Guinea Coast, 1545 to 1800*, (Oxford University Press, 1970).

5

MY VIEWS ON SOCIALISM

As a Pan-Africanist, my interest in socialism comes from the fact that socialism is an ideology which had an important role within the Pan-African movement, particularly during the Cold War. Many Pan-African leaders, activists, and scholars embraced socialism as an alternative to capitalism. The reason for doing so was the perception that capitalism was an exploitative system which upheld the very colonial system which Africans were struggling against.

By the 1960s, socialism had become a significant aspect of the anti-colonial struggles which were being waged around the world. This was something which Malcolm X recognized and confronted. Malcolm was someone who became critical of capitalism, although it seems that it would be more accurate to state that Malcolm was an anti-capitalist, rather than a socialist. He never publicly embraced socialism or labeled himself as a socialist, but he was interested in socialism since he recognized that it was an ideology being embraced by nations which were gaining their independence. Malcolm explained: "I've had an opportunity to do a lot of it in the Middle East and Africa. While I was traveling I noticed that most of the countries that had recently emerged into independence have turned away from the so-called capitalistic system in the direction of socialism. So out of curiosity, I can't resist the temptation to do a little investigating wherever that particular philosophy happens to be in existence or an attempt is being made to bring it into existence."

Countries which were coming out of colonialism were rejecting colonialism and the capitalist economic system which sustained colonialism. These nations also looked to nations which had launched successful revolutions such as Russia and China. There was Cuba as well. Marcus Garvey never became a socialist, but he recognized the importance of the Russian Revolution in 1917. In the 1960s, Malcolm was also coming to recognize the significance of the socialist anti-colonial struggles which were being waged around the world.

Malcolm had never reached a point where he fully embraced socialism. When questioned on which economic system he wanted, Malcolm stated that he did not know, but he was flexible. He also added: "It's impossible for a white person to believe in capitalism and not believe in racism. You can't have capitalism without racism. And if you find one and you happen to get that person into a conversation and they have a philosophy that makes you sure they don't have this racism in their outlook, usually they're socialists or their political philosophy is socialism."

Based on Malcolm's response, it seemed that Malcolm was critical of capitalism, but he also was not ready to fully embrace socialism as a solution. I would argue that this was partly related to Malcolm's unwillingness to tie himself to any dogma since he had previously broken from the dogmatic program of the Nation of Islam. Malcolm was critical of capitalism, but he also kept an open mind about alternatives. For this reason, he sought to better understand socialism, but he did not fully commit to socialism because he still wanted to retain some degree of ideological flexibility.

Malcolm's ideological flexibility was demonstrated by his position on Black Nationalism. Nationalism had been something which Malcolm had advocated for. He looked to the nationalist struggles in Africa to support his view that African Americans needed to adopt nationalism as well. Malcolm explained that he later was forced to rethink his views on Black Nationalism when he realized that framing nationalism around blackness would alienate Arab revolutionaries who were not black. Malcolm was developing an internationalist position which recognized that the revolutionary struggle against colonialism was not being fought by black people alone. Malcolm also softened his views on white people playing a role in the black struggle. He maintained that he would not accept white members in his organization, but he was no longer as dismissive of white support as he had been in the past.

Malcolm rejected the doctrine of the Nation of Islam which saw white people as a race of devils who were condemned to be destroyed by God because it was in their nature to be wicked. Such a position obviously does not lend itself to support for unity among people of different races. The Nation of Islam saw the African American struggle purely in racial terms. In their worldview, white people were devils and black people were the people of God who had been led astray by white people.

After leaving the Nation of Islam, Malcolm was more open to the idea of working unity among all people, although Malcolm was clear that he felt that black unity must come first before black people could unite with whites. Malcolm also believed that black people needed to free themselves, rather than having white people lead their liberation struggle.

Much like Malcolm, I also have a hesitancy to fully embrace socialism. I recognize that capitalism is a system which is heavily flawed, yet many of the socialist ideologies which emerged in response to capitalism have often proven to be unsatisfactory. Socialists themselves have often clashed on what socialism truly is and how it should be applied. I have not been one to attach myself to any particular ideology, but I think those who profess to be socialists do have to contend with the problem of how to define socialism and what a successful socialist revolution would look like.

Socialism is a broad term which really encompasses a number of different ideologies and approaches, some of which are at odds with each other. Generally speaking, socialism advocates for community control of the means of production. This could mean co-operatives in which the means of production are collectively controlled by the workers or it could mean state control of the means of production. Whereas capitalism promotes individual accumulation of wealth through profiting from the labor of the working class, socialism advocates for a wider distribution of wealth so that the wealth will not be concentrated in the hands of a few.

The general pattern in socialist states has been that socialism was carried out via state control of the means of production. State ownership of the means of production is, in theory, a type of socialism because it places control over the means of production in the hands of a government which is controlled by the masses. This does raise the question of precisely who controls the government and this gets into the critique of Stalinism. The critics of Stalinism denounced Joseph Stalin for creating a brutal dictatorship and cult of personality around the idea of communism. In this case, the state was not used as an apparatus to represent the masses of working people in Russia, but rather as an apparatus to further the agenda of a dictator and the bureaucracy which emerged under that dictatorship. In theory, however, the government in a socialist state is meant to serve as a representative of the working class.

The Russian Revolution of 1917 was the historical event which popularized socialism as a revolutionary political force which challenged the exploitative nature of capitalism. Russia's revolution also helped to popularize Marxism, which is a historical and economic theory based on the writings of Karl Marx and Friedrich Engels. Marxism helped to influence and inspire revolutionary struggles around the world.

In my view, Marxism works as a method for historical analysis which can be used to understand the nature of the relationship between social organization and modes of production. Marxism also explains how changing modes of production create changes in a society's social organization. Marx documented these changes in Europe's history. He pointed out that Europe started with communalism. This was a stage in which property was collectively owned. This was followed by slavery in which slaves worked for their masters. This was then followed by feudalism. Unlike slaves, the feudal serfs were not the property of the master. The serf worked on land which belonged to a manor or estate. When the manor changed hands, the serfs remained and continued to work for the landlord. Finally, came capitalism in which machines generated the greatest wealth in society. Capitalism was also marked by greater freedom and social mobility for the laborers. Whereas slaves belonged to slave owners and serfs belonged to estates, workers in the capitalist system are free to pursue work for whomever will hire them. Of course, this freedom to seek work is still restricted by the fact that the bourgeoisie in the capitalist system retains ultimate control over a worker's destiny, but the worker in capitalism has more freedom than the slave and the serf had.

Yet another feature of capitalism is greater division of labor. Division of labor refers to the separation of tasks within the economic system. For example, a teacher performs the task of educating students. Teachers are individuals who specialize in providing education. This is a different task than a musician who specializes in making music and who serves the function of providing entertainment. This is also different from the factory worker who is trained to perform the task of working in a factory to produce goods. The task of the factory worker is different from the farmer who is trained in producing food.

Division of labor ensures the effective management of a given economy by ensuring that individuals are paid to perform the tasks which they are skilled at performing. These different tasks are necessary to sustain the economic system as a whole. For example, farmers produce food so that the factory worker does not need to worry about growing his own food. This creates specialization, which means that an individual professional can specialize as a worker in his or her field without having to worry about managing other aspects of the society.

The author Bryan Ward-Perkins explained that civilizations are very complex and that everyone relies on the comfort which this complexity gives us. He gave the example of sitting in a room with good heating and an internet connection. He noted that these things were basic to his existence and yet it takes a very complex social organization to sustain this. He also noted that hundreds of thousands of people are involved in sustaining this complex social organization. This network of specialization is what makes it possible for Ward-Perkins to sit in a heated room with an internet connection. I mention this to make the point that capitalism was more than a mere shift in production. The emergence of capitalism resulted in a complex form of social organization which can only be sustained by specialization and division of labor.

In Marx's view, capitalism was to follow the same fate as slavery and feudalism. Though capitalism provided greater freedoms for the laborer and provided technological advancements which improved quality of life, Marx believed that capitalism would eventually fall and that a new system would emerge. Marx envisioned that the working class would rise up and overthrow the capitalist ruling class to produce a new society. This new society would be a communist society in which the workers themselves had control over the means of production.

As I stated, I think Marxism works as a tool for analysis because Marx studied European history and drew his conclusions from that study. Marxism as an ideology for revolutionary struggle has often not led to the creation of the type of communism which Marx envisioned. Part of this is due to the inherent limitation in Marxism. By this I mean that Marx's views on revolution and the creation of a communist society were largely theoretical. He obviously had never successfully overthrown the capitalist class and replaced it with the dictatorship of the proletariat. Marx described why a revolution to overthrow capitalism would happen, but it was not clear precisely how this revolution would be brought about and what it would look like.

Marx and Engels envisioned that this revolution would happen in the developed capitalist nations of the world. In *Principles of Communism*, Engels explained that the revolution will happen in "all civilized countries" including England, America, France, and Germany. Engels also defined communism as "the doctrine of the conditions of the liberation of the proletariat." The proletariat as a class originated from the industrial revolution in England. As it would turn out, socialist revolutions which were inspired by the doctrine of Marxism would not succeed in the industrialized capitalist nations. Instead, they took place in nations such as Russia, China, Cuba, Ethiopia, and in other nations which were not advanced industrialized capitalist states or "civilized countries" as Engels put it.

The Soviet Union was the first experiment in organizing a socialist revolution. The success of the revolution in Russia helped to spread socialism globally. The fall of the Soviet Union subsequently was a massive blow to socialism globally. By the end of the Cold War, socialism itself was on the decline. I have noted in other writings that a number of political leaders in Africa and the Caribbean abandoned socialism by the end of the Cold War.

There are several reasons for why the Soviet Union collapsed, but I would argue that the fundamental problem was that Marx's vision for a great proletariat revolution throughout Europe never came. Lenin explained that his view was: "Either revolution breaks out in the other countries, in the capitalistically more developed countries, immediately, or at least very quickly, or we must perish." He continued: "In actual fact, however, events did not proceed along as straight a line as we expected. In the other big capitalistically more developed countries the revolution has not broken out to this day." Lenin was forced to adopt the view that "the socialist republic can exist—of course, not for a long time—in a capitalist surrounding." Lenin was correct that a socialist republic could not exist long in a capitalist surrounding. The Soviet Union perished after a prolonged Cold War with the United States.

Nikolai Bukhari wrote that: "The victory of the Western proletariat will make it possible to heal in a planned way the economic wounds of Russia with highly developed West European techniques." This victory never happened, which resulted in the Soviet Union adopting capitalist reforms under Lenin's New Economic Policy. This move towards "state capitalism" demonstrated the difficulties in sustaining a socialist republic under the conditions which Lenin was confronted with.

Lenin was perhaps too ambitious in organizing a revolution in Russia before the proletariat revolution in developed capitalist nations broke out, although if he had waited for a revolution in the developed nations then his chance for revolution would have never arrived. The ideal condition which the Russian Revolution needed to survive was not met, which meant that so long as the Soviet Union existed as a socialist state, it was viewed as a threat to be eliminated by the capitalists. Had the proletariat revolution taken place, capitalism would have been smashed at its core and the type of healing which Bukhari wrote about could have become a possibility for Russia, but this was not to be the case.

Within the Pan-African context, socialist revolution had meant something different than it had for Marx. As was explained, Marx saw capitalism as a particular stage of Western Europe's historical development which would eventually be supplanted by another stage. For African people, capitalism was not a stage in our historical development, but a system which was imposed as part of the colonial process. We found ourselves being victims within a capitalist system which we did not create and which did not emerge out of our societies. China confronted a similar problem given that China also did not arrive at capitalism through its own internal process, yet Mao Zedong believed that a socialist revolution in China was necessary to combat the foreign capitalist influences in China.

One serious challenge which socialism has confronted is that the concept itself is a broad one. Even if we focus specifically on Marxism as being a particular socialist ideology which envisions a revolution which will overthrow capitalism, we would have to acknowledge the various different ideologies which sprang from Marxism. This would include Marxism-Leninism which is derived from the ideas of Vladimir Lenin, Stalinism from Joseph Stalin, and Trotskyism from Leon Trotsky. These schisms are not unlike the various schisms one finds in different religions in which different interpretations of the same foundational text leads to different approaches, which at times can even come in conflict with each other.

The differing Marxist ideologies can further be demonstrated by the split between China and the Soviet Union. This split demonstrated that the two leading Marxist nations of the world could not reach a common ideological agreement among themselves. The tensions between China and the Soviet Union had a larger international impact as well. For example, as Mongolia continued to strengthen its ties with the Soviet Union in the 1960s, Mongolia's relationship with China worsened. China cut off aid to Mongolia and trade decreased. There was also some concern that China was aiming to claim some of Mongolia's territory. When Mongolia experienced economic problems in the 1960s, part of the blame was placed on China's decision to withdraw economic and technical assistance.

The tension between the two nations became so serious that more than 100,000 Soviet troops were placed in Mongolia in the early 1970s. By this point, Mongolia's criticisms of China had intensified because of the number of Chinese military exercises which were being carried out along the frontier. China demanded the withdrawal of Soviet troops as a condition for the normalization of relations between China and the Soviet Union.

The ideological nature of the split between the Soviet Union and China can be demonstrated by Henry Winston's book *Strategy for a Black Agenda*. Winston's ideological support for the Soviet

Union led him to denounce China. In his book, Winston argued: "One reason many honest radicals find it difficult to recognize Maoist great power nationalism is because China was preyed upon by foreign powers (not only Western white capitalist powers, but also non-white Japanese imperialism) for over one hundred years. For this reason, many people mistakenly place China among the oppressed nations of the 'third world.'"

Winston continued to note that China did experience forms of external domination which were experienced by most of the peoples of Africa, Asia, and Latin America, but he also argued that what China experienced was qualitatively different from other oppressed nations. This point is true in that China's experience with external domination was not as severe as what most African nations experienced with colonialism.

Winston's argument is that even as China was experiencing external oppression, China itself remained an oppressor nation. To support this point, Winston noted that the concept of Han racial supremacy in China existed for over 2,000 years. In Winston's view, Maoism is based on the revival of Han chauvinist traditions. He further accused Mao of betraying the right of self-determination for the non-Chinese nations and nationalities in China. Instead of self-determination, these nations were given regional autonomy. He noted that this autonomy was undermined by having these areas also being administered by Han Chinese.

The purpose of Winston's book was to promote Soviet propaganda. The book itself was filled with a lot of misleading claims, but I mention Winston's book here to show how serious the ideological division between the Soviet Union and China became.

I am willing to defend the socialist tradition within the Pan-African struggle as a tradition which opposed colonialism and capitalist oppression. Of course, the socialist tradition is not a flawless one, but I am certainly willing to defend the socialist tradition against capitalist apologists for Western imperialism against African people around the world.

The apologists for the capitalist system are usually very quick to point to the flaws and sins of socialism while also downplaying some of the problems with capitalism. An example that I can point to is an article titled "Socialism 509" by Kenneth Hilborn. Hilborn criticized Marxism as an ideology which was incapable of upholding human rights because Marx believed in class struggle which would only end when the capitalist class was abolished. Noting that capitalists are human too, Hilborn concluded that Marxism would require the denial of the rights of capitalists to freedom. He wrote: "For Marxists to champion the right of capitalists to liberty, and thus to property, would be just as much a repudiation of their own doctrine as it would be for Nazis to uphold the right of Jews to equal status in society." The comparison is an extreme one, although not an entirely inaccurate one since Marxists do aim to eliminate the capitalist class. Of course, it is equally true that capitalists have often failed to champion the right of socialists to liberty. During the Cold War, America's foreign policy was often ruthless in its attempt to defeat communism around the world.

Hilborn was viewing the topic purely from an intellectual standpoint, which is why he wrote: "The Right, with its commitment to economic freedom, has been right all along; the socialist Left (under whatever name) was, is and always will be wrong." I would argue that a complex issue such as capitalism or socialism cannot be reduced to a matter of who is right and who is wrong. I state this because I think leaders who have embraced socialism have managed to accomplish some important achievements, but this is something which proponents of capitalism will always reject purely for ideological reasons. The idea that the Right has been right all along on its commitment to economic freedom would also suggest that the support of brutal dictatorships during the Cold War or the overthrow of democratically elected leaders was right and that such actions were necessary for economic freedom. This is not a position which I would agree with at all.

The reality is that in pursuit of economic freedom, capitalism has often trampled on the rights of other nations to choose their own path. Kwame Ture, who was a socialist, was highly critical of the United States for punishing Cuba because Fidel Castro rejected America's "bourgeois democracy." The reality is that the United States has a long history of meddling in the affairs of nations where the leaders have pursued socialist paths of development.

This is the point which Hilborn and others will not acknowledge. Economic freedom for the United States' government has typically meant the freedom to act in ways which support American imperialism. Those who fail to do so are confronted with the military might or the economic might of the American government.

In my view, this debate is neither an intellectual one nor an ideological one. For me, this question of capitalism or socialism should be rooted in looking at actual policies and how these policies impact the lives of ordinary individuals. In terms of improving quality of life, I would argue that socialism has never been a complete failure and that capitalism has never been a complete success.

In conclusion, socialism is not an ideology which I would assign to myself. At the same time, I also do not view socialism as being a great evil or a great threat to the world that it is often made out to be. For the colonized world, socialism seemed to be a practical alternative to the capitalist exploitation of the colonial powers. Among some Pan-Africanists, socialism was also appealing because of the connection between the ideals advocated by socialism and the communal nature of African societies.

6

FROM ANTI-COLONIALISM TO NEO-COLONIALISM IN AFRICA

Nationalist movements emerged in Africa to confront the system of colonialism. James Coleman noted that "the drive behind African nationalism in many instances is not the consciousness of belonging to a distinct politico-cultural unit which is seeking to protect or assert itself, but rather it is the movement of racially-conscious modernists seeking to create new political and cultural nationalities out of the heterogenous people within the artificial boundaries imposed by the European master ..."

What Coleman was noting here was that in the struggle against colonialism in Africa, it was necessary to develop new national identities. The pre-colonial political formations and identities in Africa had been transformed due to colonialism. The nationalist movements in Africa were reactions to these new formations. This is a point which Julius Nyerere made in one of his speeches in which he noted that Tanzania was a nation which he created. The nations in Africa were born out of the nationalist, anti-colonial struggle which sought to liberate Africa from colonial rule.

In *Africa Must Unite*, Kwame Nkrumah wrote that a number of political demonstrations and strikes took place throughout Africa prior to World War II. During the 1940s, many organizations were formed, such as the National Council of Nigeria and the Cameroons, as well as the Nyasaland National Congress. In the Gold Coast, Nkrumah formed the Convention People's Party. Nkrumah noted that these parties acted as unifying forces in Africa. In Nkrumah's view, the C.P.P. represented the ordinary, common folk of Ghana. He contrasted this with the opposition party which was supported by lawyers and other conservative professionals who did not understand the new mood of the people.

Nkrumah had previously served as secretary of the United Gold Coast Convention (U.G.C.C.). Nkrumah stated that the leaders of

55

the U.G.C.C. were frightened to learn that Nkrumah had spearheaded a mass movement. He explained: "They had wanted me to build up a movement whose ranks would not question their self-assumed right to political leadership, but would nevertheless provide a solid enough base for them to pose as the national champions in pressing for constitutional change. It was when the leaders of the U.G.C.C. demanded I get rid of the mass following I had built up, that I withdrew from their secretariat, and formed the Convention People's Party."

Nkrumah was describing a conflict which would become more pronounced in the post-colonial period. During colonialism, there arose a class within the African population which managed to carve out a comfortable living for themselves as professionals within the colonial system. This was the class which seized power following the formal end of colonialism. This new neo-colonial class continues to enjoy a degree of comfort as the African masses continue to struggle.

The roots of this neo-colonial class can be traced to the development of colonialism in Africa. There were various Africans who aligned with and supported colonialism for one reason or another. Bishop Samuel Ajayi Crowther in Nigeria, for example, defended colonialism because it brought Christianity to Africa. This is an example of the fact that some Africans embraced colonialism. The nationalist leaders in Africa were generally opposed to colonialism, although many of these nationalist leaders were themselves highly influenced by colonialism. The result was that these leaders opposed colonialism, but also kept the colonial system in place once in power. These anti-colonial leaders would prove themselves to be little more than opportunists who fought colonialism so that they could replace the colonizers as exploiters of the African masses.

In Ghana, Nkrumah sought to pursue a path of socialist development to guarantee full employment, good housing, equal educational opportunity, and cultural advancement for all. Nkrumah believed that the government had to "play the role of main entrepreneur in laying the basis of the national economic and social advancement." In Nkrumah's view, to turn the country over to private interests would be an act of "betraying the trust of the great masses of our people for the greedy interests of a small

coterie of individuals, probably in alliance with foreign capitalist."
It was indeed foreign capitalists who overthrew Nkrumah in a
coup. The United States and other Western powers would not
tolerate any attempt to transform Africa through socialism,
especially in the 1960s as the United States was waging its
ideological struggle with the Soviet Union.

That the nationalist movements in Africa at the time embraced
socialism is hardly surprising considering that many African
leaders recognized that capitalism formed the economic basis of
the very colonial system which they had fought. For leaders such
as Nkrumah, socialism promised an alternative path of
development which was different from the exploitative capitalist
system. It was also the case that African leaders who opted to
embrace socialism did not all share the same vision regarding what
socialism in their respective nations was to look like. There were
others who rejected socialism, as well.

In some circumstances, the nationalist struggle in Africa was
one in which Africans were forced to wage an armed struggle
against the colonial powers. This was the case in the Portuguese
colonies. Amilcar Cabral from Guinea-Bissau emerged as one of
the most notable of the African nationalist leaders who were
engaged in armed struggle. Like Nkrumah, Cabral was a socialist.
He also received aid for his nationalist struggle from socialist
nations. A report from the American Department of State from
February 1, 1973 noted: "Under Cabral's direction since 1956, the
PAIGC developed into the most successful insurgent force facing
the Portuguese. Cabral depended heavily on Soviet and Cuban
military assistance, but remained politically moderate, and had
been receiving increasing economic and political assistance from
the Scandinavian countries and a number of international
philanthropic organizations." This report was produced after
Cabral's assassination on January 20.

The same report noted that the Portuguese condemned the
assassination of Cabral and denied any complicity in the
assassination. The assailants themselves claimed in their
confession that they were working for the Portuguese and that
Portugal was willing to grant independence to Guinea-Bissau on

the condition that the dissidents kill Cabral.

What is also notable about Cabral's struggle is that Cabral used Guinea as a base of operations. He was supported in his fight against colonialism by Sekou Toure, who was the president of Guinea. This is an example of the fact that these nationalist struggles in Africa were also Pan-African in nature as well. As nationalist leaders struggled to liberate and develop their own nations, there was also a recognition of the fact that the struggle for independence was a transnational struggle since colonialism itself was a transnational project.

The nationalist movement in Africa was one which not only sought to redefine national identities in Africa, but also to redefine the African identity itself. One limitation of this effort was the fact that after independence, African nations opted to retain the existing colonial borders. This became a source of conflict and disunity in Africa.

The anti-colonial effort in Africa became connected to the Pan-African movement which envisioned the unification of African people. In Africa, Pan-Africanism not only unified African nations in the struggle against European colonialism, but it also connected African nations to African descendants outside of Africa. This can be exemplified by Haile Selassie of Ethiopia who became a leading Pan-African figure among the leaders of his generation.

Apart from his support of liberation struggles in Africa, Haile Selassie also welcomed Africans from throughout the Americas to Ethiopia. Haile Selassie set aside land in Shashamane for Africans from the Americas to resettle. The first to settle on this land were Helen and James Piper, who were from Montserrat. The two supported Ethiopia during the war. They were also Garveyites as well. In Ethiopia, James earned a living teaching carpentry in Addis Ababa. Helen received an administrative position at the airport. In the 1960s, the Pipers began building a house for Reverend William Hillman from Georgia. Hillman heard about Shashemene at a Malcolm X meeting and decided to relocate to Ethiopia with his wife.

In the 1960s, the Pipers were challenged by Gladstone Robinson. Robinson was born in America to a Barbadian father and a Cherokee mother. Robinson eventually became a Rasta and moved to Ethiopia where he challenged the authority of the Pipers and fought to get a piece of land for himself. Gladstone was not the only prominent Rasta to settle in this land. A Jamaican Rasta named Noel Dyer emigrated to England and walked to Ethiopia. It took him a year and three months before he arrived. He was the first of many Jamaican Rastas to settle in Shashemene. After Haile Selassie was overthrown, Rastas in Ethiopia found themselves being marginalized by the government because of their religious beliefs. The local authorities regularly seized the photos of Haile Selassie which Rastas displayed. Following the fall of the Derg regime in 1991, Rastas settling at Shashemene resumed.

In 1948, an African American artist named Mayme Richardson performed at Haile Selassie's palace. Richardson expressed the following view about being in Ethiopia: "Yes, I was completely overcome by the spirit of freedom, untrammelled freedom! I was at home once more with my people. I felt happy, secure and moved. It was indeed the land of my heritage." Haile Selassie thanked her for her performance. He also told her: "No one could hear you sing and interpret the songs of such a great race without being deeply moved and touched. They are indeed soul stirring and borne out of hearts praying and fighting for freedom. I recognize the kinship between American blacks and our own people." These experiences in Ethiopia touched Richardson so much that he became an organizer for the Ethiopian World Federation, which had been founded in New York in 1937. The purpose of this organization was to gather support for the Ethiopian war effort. The purpose in mentioning Ethiopia and Haile Selassie is to demonstrate the extent to which Pan-Africanism helped to shape the politics of certain African nations.

Ethiopia also had an important role in the formation of the Organisation of African Unity (OAU). Selassie, like Nkrumah, was a proponent of Pan-African unity. This was displayed in 1960 when Selassie visited Ghana. At the end of the visit a communique was issued which declared that Ghana and Ethiopia agreed that a union of African states should be pursued. Nkrumah noted that President Abdulla Osman of Somalia expressed similar views when he visited Ghana in 1961.

Uniting Africa was no easy task. Cameron Duodu noted this in a piece for *New Africa* entitled "The Birth Pangs of the OAU." Duodo pointed out that Africa split into two blocs known as the Monrovia Group and the Casablanca Group. As Nkrumah attempted to resolve the differences between these two groups, he was also confronted with the aftermath of the assassination of Sylvanus Olympio. Given the antagonism between the two men, it was suspected that Nkrumah was behind the coup. Nkrumah himself was removed from power in a coup as well, as was Selassie. The anti-colonial movement in Africa was a success in the sense that it did manage to liberate African nations from colonial rule. The problem was that many of the nationalist leaders became neo-colonialists in the post-colonial period. Political conflict and instability also led to a number of coups throughout Africa.

Nkrumah denounced imperialism and neo-colonialism as threats not only to Africa, but to world peace. He also argued that Africa's independence and unity would contribute to world peace. Unfortunately, the neo-colonial powers were committed to sustaining their control over Africa. Maintaining control often meant keeping Africa divided.

In his book, *Fate of Africa*, Martin Meredith explained that the 1980s became known as the "lost decade" because of the economic crisis that many African nations confronted. African nations became so crippled by debt and mismanagement that they were unable to maintain public services such as roads, railways, water, and power supplies. Civil service salaries eroded as well. These problems were combined with a brain drain as well.

To raise funds, African states turned to the International Monetary Fund and the World Bank. This allowed neo-colonialism in Africa to become further entrenched. The loans came with stipulations which placed greater burdens on the struggling masses. The International Monetary Fund and World Bank required governments to devalue their currencies, remove subsidies, and deregulate prices. Jerry Rawlings of Ghana was among the leaders who accepted these structural adjustment plans. By the 1980s, Ghana's economy was struggling. It was under these conditions that Rawlings implemented reforms. The result was that Ghana's debt more than doubled between 1983 and 1988.

More than 30 years after Nkrumah had led Ghana into

independence, Ghana's economy continued to struggle. In some ways, the challenges which confronted Rawlings were the same challenges which confronted Nkrumah, who turned to the World Bank to help finance his projects. Decades later, Ghana was still trapped in the cycle of digging itself deeper in debt in an effort to develop itself. Ghana's case indicated the extent to which the nationalist movement of the 1950s which led to Ghana's independence gave way to neo-colonialism. Nkrumah clearly understood the threat which this new form of colonialism posed to Africa. Unfortunately, few African leaders shared Nkrumah's concern. Many of them became willing servants of the new neo-colonial order.

7

ON THE TACUMA OGUNSEYE CONTROVERSY IN GUYANA

I wish to state from the beginning that I found Tacuma Ogunseye's remarks to be troubling and reckless. I am referring to remarks which Ogunseye made at a rally in which he spoke about Africans complaining about being oppressed. He pointed out that Africans are the majority of the army and the police, so they have most of the guns in their hands. Ogunseye then stated: "Anytime we turn those guns in the right direction, it is over."

Now, Ogunseye did not say to put the guns down or to use those guns to protect the community. He said to turn them in the right direction, which implies that the guns needed to be pointed at the government. Given the history of political and racial violence in Guyana, I felt that the statement was a reckless one and it was rightfully condemned as such. President Irfaan Ali criticized Ogunseye's remarks. He denounced the statement as one which promoted racism, hate, and terrorism. The remarks were also denounced by the attorney general, Anil Nandlall.

David Hinds of the WPA later tried to clarify that the WPA was criticizing rogue police officers and members of the army. Hinds also stated that Ogunseye's remark was a statement that the police and army must not turn their guns against people in the community who are fighting for liberty. In his defense of Ogunseye, I think that Hinds was being a bit disingenuous. The controversy is not that Ogunseye told the armed forces not to turn their guns against the community. The problem was that he told them to turn their guns in the "right direction". He did not state which direction was the "right direction", but it did appear that he was calling for them to aim their guns at the government. The statement was framed as a response to those who were complaining about being oppressed in Guyana. Hinds himself expressed the view that the PPP was using the armed forces for political purposes, so Hinds did not try to hide the fact that the remarks were intended to be directed at the government.

62

That the controversial remarks came from Ogunseye is not totally surprising. Ogunseye is someone with a history of taking extreme positions. This was a point which Freddie Kissoon made in the December 11, 2018 edition of *Kaieteur News* in an editorial titled "The Political Culture of Activists Like This Man is Destructive." Kissoon wrote: "If you go through the list of parties that produced activists that have achieved some national publicity over the past fifty years, from small outfits to major organizations, none has birthed someone so driven by race, crass political mentality and opportunism as Ogunseye."

Kissoon also criticized Ogunseye for his position on the unrest in Buxton. He pointed out that Ogunseye supported the gunmen. Kissoon noted that the only member of the WPA who publicly condemned Ogunseye's position was Eusi Kwayana. Kwayana wrote in his book, *The Morning After*: "Tacuma Ogunseye whom I have called Brother Tacuma for some thirty years, has described the story of Buxton as a liberation struggle. At no time in our long association have I disagreed more with him…I have attacked what he now supports or justifies."

Kissoon also mentioned that Ogunseye was banned from speaking on behalf of the African Cultural and Development Association (ACDA) and was chastised by ACDA for hate speech after he gave a speech in which he called for Africans to remove the PPP government. The point here is that Ogunseye is someone with a history of making such reckless remarks which incite controversy. This was not the first time that he has done so.

I do respect Ogunseye as a political activist who has been part of the struggle for change in Guyana for many decades as a member of the WPA, but I also recognize that his work has been hindered by this tendency to make extreme pronouncements which incite controversy, but do little else. The call for the security forces in Guyana to turn their guns in the right direction accomplished little more than creating a backlash from various segments of Guyanese society. It also placed the PNC in a difficult situation. The WPA formally left the APNU+AFC coalition after the coalition lost the election, but the WPA has remained aligned with the PNC, which is why Aubrey Norton was invited to speak at the

WPA's rally with Ogunseye.

Norton defended Ogunseye's right to free speech, but he did not agree with the language. Norton remained critical of the PPP, while also distancing himself from the remarks from the WPA. Norton obviously did not want to join with the PPP in condemning Ogunseye's remarks, yet he also could not afford to allow himself or the PNC to be associated with such remarks.

The free speech issue is a delicate one in Guyana. Following the remarks which Ogunseye made, he was arrested and charged with one count of inciting racial ill-will in Guyana. The Alliance for Change (AFC) criticized the PPP for its treatment of Ogunseye, which the AFC stated was an act of humiliating Ogunseye. The party also stated that the government was trying to drive fear in opposition activists. Ogunseye himself was confident that there was no case against him.

The AFC also stated that the fragility of Guyana's democracy was made even more fragile by this kind of treatment of a citizen. I am inclined to agree. Ogunseye's statement was reckless, but I am not sure that what he said was so dangerous that it warranted him being arrested in the manner that he was. I understand the need to send a strong message that such rhetoric would not be tolerated in Guyana, but it does raise the question of where does the government set the limit for what is and is not regarded as criminal speech. This is especially important in a nation such as Guyana with a history of governments acting to suppress free speech.

Gail Teixeira, the PPP Minister of Governance and the Minister of Parliamentary Affairs, accused the government of David Granger of carrying out the most racist policies which Guyana had experienced since Burnham's government. Meanwhile, Anette Ferguson, a member of the opposition, stated that there is racism in Guyana and the PPP government was engaged in racial discrimination.

The PPP and the PNC have blamed each other for racism in Guyana. The truth is neither party has moral authority where Guyana's politics are concerned. It is unfortunate that the WPA also seems to have lost some of its moral authority as well given its history as a party which has struggled against both the PNC and PPP at various points of its existence.

Ogunseye's remarks were not the first time that a member of the

WPA made remarks which were denounced by the government. When Hinds told onlookers at a rally that they should undermine the government, he was denounced by Vice President Bharrat Jagdeo. Jagdeo criticized the call from Hinds and claimed that Hinds did nothing when Afro-Guyanese were suffering. Jagdeo was being a bit disingenuous given that Hinds was in fact very critical of the APNU+AFC government when they were in power, so it is not that Hinds was so distracted by his "cushy job" that he did not notice the suffering of African Guyanese. Jagdeo did raise a valid point, however, when he noted that it was the state's responsibility to take care of those who became sick with COVID. This is why Hinds' call to undermine the government could become underproductive given that citizens rely on services from the very government that they are being told to undermine.

Historically, the WPA has never held political power in Guyana, but the importance of the party was that it operated as a political entity which spoke out against the abuse of power and which urged for the unity of the working people in the country. The WPA fought against Burnham's dictatorship in the 1970s and 1980s. In the process of doing so, the WPA entered into a coalition with the PPP which would help the PPP to take power. After the PPP came to power, the WPA found itself fighting against the corruption and racism of the PPP administration. In this fight against the PPP, the WPA joined a coalition with the PNC which brought the PNC into power. The period from 2015 to 2020 really exposed the limitation of the WPA as an opposition party which has a history of helping to defeat the party in power, but which has never been able to seize power for itself. In both scenarios, the PPP and the PNC effectively used the WPA to take power and then discarded the WPA after having seized power.

I was sympathetic to the position which the WPA found itself in when the coalition was in power. I also respected the fact that members of the WPA—including Ogunseye—were willing to speak out against certain acts by the government which they disagreed with. The problem for the WPA is that after the electoral defeat in 2020, the party has been reduced to urging those who attend their rallies to resist the government, but the WPA itself has little chance of winning an election on its own.

As for the call to point guns in the right direction, I will state here that it is not that I am opposed to political revolution or armed rebellion, but I also understand that these are solutions which are not to be taken lightly. As I pointed out, Guyana is a nation which has a history of politically and racially motivated violence. This violence has not led to any significant political transformation. For example, the "liberation struggle" which Ogunseye supported in Buxton resulted in needless bloodshed. The "liberation struggle" liberated nothing. The political violence in Guyana has been such that when the WPA opposed Burnham's dictatorship in the 1970s and 1980s, Ogunseye admitted that he was among the members within the party who armed themselves in self-defense against the brutality of the PNC.

In cases where armed rebellion does become necessary to force political change, there is also serious concern about the military leading the rebellion. This is a cause for concern because it is often the case that when the military decides to overthrow a government, the military then installs itself in power. I am not sure if Ogunseye even considered the implications of what would happen if the military in Guyana did decide to turn its guns against the government and overthrow the government. Violent struggle is not something which should be taken as lightly as Ogunseye has taken it.

As critical as I have been of Ogunseye's speech, I also wish to make it clear that this is not intended to be a defense of the PPP government. One of the unfortunate consequences of Ogunseye's speech was that it provided an opportunity for the PPP to present itself as a party which is trying to unify Guyana. In the past, I have been critical of President Ali for not being willing and honest enough to confront the PPP's own history of dividing Guyana. Denouncing Ogunseye allowed the PPP to give the appearance that they are trying to bring unity to Guyana when this is not the case at all.

I do agree that Ogunseye's arrest raised concerns about the issue of free speech in Guyana. I also think it raised concerns about the extent to which the PPP is truly committed to ensuring justice in Guyana. One of the reasons why I felt that Ogunseye's remarks were reckless was because Guyana had experienced an outburst of violence over the shooting death of Quindon Bacchus. Reports about his age were conflicting, but Bacchus was in his twenties at the time he was shot and killed by police. Protesters took to the streets to make their anger known. The protests turned violent as vendors were beaten and had their property destroyed. The damages were reported to have been in the millions. The destruction left some of the vendors concerned about how to earn money to support their families. One victim noted that he was beaten before his van was set on fire.

I do not condone this type of violence. Attacking vendors did nothing to achieve justice for Bacchus, but I understand the frustrations of the protesters. After Bacchus was buried, Dexter Todd, the attorney representing Bacchus' family, called for structural changes within the Guyana police force so that another young man would not be killed by the police. Unlike Ogunseye who appeared to call for more violence, Todd called for structural change.

Bacchus' name came up again when Nigel Dharamlall resigned. Dharamlall served as the minister of local government and regional development within the PPP government. Dharamlall was accused of raping and sodomizing a sixteen-year-old girl. Dharamlall was represented by Nigel Hughes who was prepared to defend the minister against these allegations. In response to protesters who demanded that Hughes drop Dharamlall as his client, he stated that the "system has to work." The point he was making is that the system in Guyana is one in which everyone who is accused receives representation. As Hughes explained, everyone deserves a fair trial. As it turned out, Dharamlall would never get to a trial.

Dharamlall resigned without having to face the rape charges in court. Protesters expressed their view that the resignation of the minister was not justice. One protester also expressed disappointment with President Ali because he did not fire the accused minister. At the protest, a member of parliament named Ganesh Mahipaul noted that Bacchus had been murdered. He also mentioned other examples of individuals who were killed and did not receive justice. What made matters worse in my opinion was the fact that Dharamlall had been accused of harassing a woman the year before, so this had not been his first incident. There was also a situation in which Dharamlall made a vulgar remark towards a parliamentarian named Natasha Singh-Lewis. Members of the opposition called for sanctions and the expulsion of Dharamlall after he made his remark. Dharamlall was someone who had a history of mistreating women, but the PPP tolerated this behavior from him until he was charged with a serious offense.

The perception in Guyana is that under the PPP government those like Bacchus cannot get justice while a minister like Dharamlall can be accused of raping a teenage girl and is allowed to resign without having to go to trial over his actions. I mention this topic to show that Guyana has serious issues which are much greater than Ogunseye's remarks. I have been critical of what Ogunseye stated, but I also recognize that Ogunseye and Hinds are reacting to what they view as an immoral and oppressive government.

8

THE LONG WALK CONTINUES

In an interview with Dr. Gnaka Lagoke of the Revival of Pan-Africanism Forum, Farida Nabourema spoke about Nelson Mandela's legacy. In the interview Nabourema listed some of Mandela's accomplishments. Among the accomplishments which Nabourema listed included building homes to take people out of townships, providing free healthcare to pregnant women, and scholarships for students. She also noted that even though Mandela achieved things which so many African leaders had failed to achieve, many Africans still viewed Mandela as a failure and a traitor.

The view of Mandela being a traitor comes from the fact that when he took power in South Africa, there was not a radical transformation of South Africa's society. Dr. Lagoke praised Mandela for his leadership qualities, but he also expressed the view that Mandela compromised too much. John Henrik Clarke explained: "Mandela came into power with whites owning 87% of the land. They still own 87% of the land. Mandela probably doesn't even control his own chauffeur." This remark demonstrated the extent to which Mandela compromised.

What was very telling was that in his autobiography, *A Long Walk to Freedom*, Mandela acknowledged that he eventually outgrew his Africanist outlook. Meanwhile, the emergence of the Black Consciousness Movement (BCM) produced a new generation of Africanists who were militant and angry. They wanted a nonracial society, but they also rejected any white assistance in their struggle. Mandela recognized these views as being much like the views that he held at the founding of the ANC Youth League. Mandela believed that the members would eventually transcend the strictures of Black Consciousness. He believed that their concentration on blackness was exclusionary.

Mandela was correct that Black Consciousness offered no program of action. The aim of the BCM was to offer a psychological rehabilitation for black people. It developed in the vacuum left by the banning of the ANC, the Pan-Africanist Congress (PAC), and the Communist Party. Steve Biko noted that the banning of the PAC and ANC led to a political emasculation of the black population. This created a situation in which white people were the main participants in both the oppression of black people and the opposition to that oppression. Biko understood that black people needed to work out their own program and to do this black people needed to defeat the psychological feeling of inferiority. He noted that white people also needed to defeat their psychological feeling of superiority.

The BCM's primary focus was addressing this issue of psychological inferiority. Biko and others also formed the South African Students Organisation (SASO) to create a positive value system for black people by challenging the cultural dominance of Europeans. Biko believed that SASO was effective at motivating black people to speak out against the racism in South Africa. The government reaction to this was just as brutal as the reaction had been to the ANC and the PAC, but this did not deter Biko.

The aim of SASO was explained in the May/June 1972 edition of the newsletter. In that edition, B.A. Khoapa explained: "In the past Black students and others tried to liberate white people as a means of their own liberation. Black students are liberating themselves directly, thereby forcing white students to begin to confront themselves and their own institutions." Khoapa also accused "white liberals" of being cowards who only stand behind "the Blacks who are being routed by the police." Khoapa further explained: "The process of engaging in self-liberation and collective liberation has predisposed Blacks to overcome any tolerance which they might have for white oppression: to resist any tendency to emulate white men as an end in itself."

In addition to criticizing the role of white liberals in the struggle and asserting the need for self-liberation, SASO also promoted Black Consciousness as an aspect of the liberation struggle. Strini Moodley wrote that Black Consciousness rejected white values which attempted to make black people hate themselves. Moodley argued that Black Consciousness restored his "psychological humanness." Most importantly is that Moodley noted that Black Consciousness did not call simply for a change of government, but "for an injection of new values, of new attitudes and a more compassionate regard for society."

The BCM represented a renewed sense of militancy in South Africa which Mandela himself had moved away from. It was not only Mandela. The ANC Youth League itself moderated its nationalism after the death of Anton Lembede. This was demonstrated by the ANC's charter which stated that "South Africa belongs to all who live in it, black and white, and that no government can justly claim authority unless it is based on the will of the people..." Mandela noted that some members objected to the charter "as being a design for a radically different South Africa from the one the ANC had called for throughout its history." Mandela saw the charter as a revolutionary document, but others in the ANC felt otherwise. Some of these members rejected the ANC's multiracialism and its Freedom Charter. They decided to form the PAC. The PAC took its inspiration from Lembede's nationalism. Mandela described some of the members of the PAC as friends, including Robert Sobukwe.

Mandela was sympathetic to the Africanist position which advocated for ethnic pride while rejecting white assistance, but these were views which he held in the past as a member of the ANC Youth League. He had moved towards what he believed was a less exclusionary vision for South African society. Mandela did not reject violent struggle, however. He recalled an exchange with editors of the *Washington Times*. The editors asserted that Martin Luther King had never resorted to violence. Mandela defended himself by noting that South Africa was a police state, not a democracy like the United States. Mandela also affirmed that he was a Christian and that even Christ used force to expel moneylenders from the temple.

The ANC came to power in 1994. The election was a profound occasion for Mandela who had struggled tirelessly for many years just for the people of South Africa to earn the ability to vote in a truly democratic election. For this Mandela deserves credit. He oversaw the peaceful transition from apartheid to democracy. It seemed that Mandela himself felt that his mission had been accomplished because he resigned after one term.

When Mandela stepped down, he was replaced by Thabo Mbeki. Whereas Mandela adopted a policy of nonracialism, Mbeki's policy was more "Africanist" in nature. This included developing a program for the economic advancement of black people in South Africa. This shift in direction alienated the white members of the ANC. Mbeki was more direct in speaking to racial inequality in South Africa, but under his leadership it was becoming obvious that the ANC was dominated by corrupt leadership who were interested in their own self-enrichment.

Mbeki's support of Robert Mugabe in Zimbabwe also caused some controversy. Mbeki pointed out that the only reason why Britain was criticizing Mugabe's land reform policy was because "white people died and white people were deprived of their property." This was true. Britain had no problem ignoring the violence which Mugabe's government had unleashed on Africans, but the same could be said of Mbeki who also did not raise any concerns over what Mugabe's government was doing to African people in Zimbabwe.

Martin Merdith argued that Mbeki's support for Mugabe "sullied the reputation of the ANC," but the support for Mugabe was also typical of the nature of post-colonial African politics. Leaders who once fought colonialism were now joined together as exploiters of African people. The colonial system in Zimbabwe and South Africa remained in place, even though white rule was replaced with black rule.

Mbeki's presidency was also marked by conflict within the ranks of the ANC. Two factions emerged. One was led by Mbeki and the other was led by Jacob Zuma. Zuma, who joined the ANC in 1959 and was imprisoned with Mandela in 1962, was himself caught up in corruption scandals in the ANC. He was implicated in taking bribes and was even charged of rape—keep in mind that rape has been such a serious issue in South Africa that South Africa became known as the rape capital of the world. Zuma admitted to having sex with the woman, but he denied that he raped her. He also infamously remarked that he took a shower after having sex with his accuser to protect himself from contracting HIV.

Despite the corruption allegations, Zuma was elected president. Many delegates voted for him just to remove Mbeki. Zuma himself was forced to resign after a scandal filled presidency. Zuma's resignation demonstrated just how significant the problem of corruption within the ANC had become. This was a problem which traces its roots back to 1994 when the ANC first came to power under the leadership of Nelson Mandela. Meredith explained that when ministers that Mandela appointed "proved incompetent or corrupt, he rode to their rescue out of loyalty rather than sack them." This sense of loyalty also led Mandela to retain close ties to Muammar Gaddafi and Fidel Castro. Meredith noted that these ties were likely to deter Western investors, but Mandela would not abandon those who supported him in his struggle. The problem with Mandela's sense of loyalty was that it led him to defend corruption in situations where he should have punished officials in the government. The unwillingness to address the incompetence and corruption within the ANC was certainly one of Mandela's failings when he was in power.

Mandela reflected on the struggle against apartheid by stating: "The policy of apartheid created a deep and lasting wound in my country and my people. All of us will spend many years, if not generations, recovering from that profound hurt. But the decades of oppression and brutality had another, unintended effect, and that was that it produced the Oliver Tambos, the Walter Sisulus, the Chief Luthulis, the Yusuf Dadoos, the Bram Fischers, the Robert Sobukwes of our time—men of such extraordinary courage, wisdom, and generosity that their like may never be known again." Unfortunately, individuals of their like were not the type of individuals who took power in South Africa. The long walk to freedom which Mandela described continues in South Africa, but the struggle is not against apartheid. The struggle is against the opportunists who betrayed the struggle. I would not classify Mandela as one of the traitors, but I do think he can be faulted for compromising too much and not doing enough to address the problem of corruption in the ANC.

9

THE GREAT SUDANESE RELIGIOUS REFORMER

Mahmoud Muhammad Taha was born in Sudan in 1909 or 1911 in a town known as Rufa'a. The precise year of his birth is not certain. Taha's mother died in 1915 and his father died in 1920. He was raised by relatives in a nearby village. Taha graduated in civil engineering from the Gordon Memorial College—this college later became the University of Khartoum. Taha briefly worked for Sudan Railways, but Taha's involvement in the independence movement led to difficulties with his employer and the colonial government, which led him to resign to start his own engineering business.

Taha's early education shaped his religious and political views. Taha came from a religious family and received instruction in the Qur'an. He also read the writings of Karl Marx, Vladimir Lenin, and other political thinkers. Taha became involved in the Graduates Congress which was established in 1938. The purpose of this organization was to advocate for Sudan's independence from Anglo-Egyptian rule. Taha advocated for the establishment of a Republic of Sudan.

In 1945, Taha founded a political group which was known as the Republican Party. Taha's anti-colonial political activity resulted in him being imprisoned twice. During his second imprisonment in 1946, Taha began the process of engaging in a profound religious transformation. After being released in 1948, Taha went into seclusion and prayer for three years.

During the period of seclusion, Taha spoke to a few. He also allowed his hair to grow out. Taha fasted as well. His wife Amna Lofti brought him plates of simple food. Amna Lofti refused to leave her husband, despite being urged to do so by her family. Taha, who was once a successful professional, was viewed by some as a madman. For three years, Taha remained in his hut, leaving only to take a swim in the Nile. He emerged in 1951 with a new vision of Islam.

Taha developed a new interpretation of the Qur'an which was moderate in comparison to those who promoted a dogmatic form of Islamic law. The Qur'an was revealed to the Prophet Muhammad in two phases. The first phase was in Mecca and the second phase was in Medina. In Taha's view, the first phase represented Islam in its perfect form. He expressed this view in his book, *The Second Message of Islam.* In this book, he argued that the lives of early Muslims in Mecca represented the "supreme expression of their religion and consisted of sincere worship, kindness, and peaceful coexistence with all other people."

The second phase in Medina represented a period of time in which Muhammad and his followers had been forced to migrate to Medina following the persecution they faced in Mecca. In Taha's view, it was during this period in Medina that "the verses of compulsion by the sword prevailed." Taha argued that Muslims were forced to adapt to the reality of life at a time when "there was no law except the sword." It was in Medina where the first Muslim state was developed. Here Muslims lived with Jews and Christians under a charter in which non-Muslim communities had to pledge their submission to Muhammad. The Jewish tribe of Banu Qurayiza later violated the terms of the charter by siding with enemy forces who were invading Medina. Muhammad retaliated by punishing that Jewish tribe. This incident demonstrated the situation which confronted Muhammad and his followers who worked to defend their state from external and internal threats.

Taha held the view that the Meccan verses represented the ideal version of Islam and could only be revived when humanity reached the stage of being able to accept these verses. In Taha's view, the second message of Islam would be higher and better than the first message. This was a controversial message which resulted in Taha being charged with apostasy by his critics. In 1968, the High Court of Khartoum ruled that Taha was an apostate from Islam, though the court lacked the power to enforce actual sanctions against Taha. It was not until the transformation of the legal system in 1983 that Taha could be punished for the crime for which he was accused.

Taha sought to live the values which he preached. He was

known for living a very simple lifestyle and his Republican Brotherhood maintained a very informal structure. One follower named Naim recalled that Taha's followers would see the fruit of his teachings in his personal lifestyle and in his attitudes. Taha was so devout in his religious belief that one man recalled that in 1954, Taha's son vanished in the Blue Nile. Taha's reaction was, "he's gone to a kinder father than I am."

Taha was not merely a religious leader. He took political positions, such as his involvement in Sudan's independence struggle against Britain. Taha called for peace and normal relations with the state of Israel. Taha also addressed social issues, such as the treatment of women in Sudanese society. Taha preached the equality of women, which was demonstrated in the role which women played in the leadership of the Republican movement which Taha led.

The Republican view of women subjected the movement to criticisms and even insults. Women in the movement were harassed, which included having their hair or clothing pulled. Women in the movement became political prisoners as well. Taha's daughter Asma and other sisters in the Republican movement were among the first female political prisoners in Sudan. Asma explained that while the Republican sisters were in prison, they saw the struggles which women in Sudan endured. Some of the women were in prison because they killed their husbands in self-defense.

Asma was also actively engaged in recruiting women for the movement. This was done by talking with women about their problems and how the Republican movement would address those problems. Some of the women complained about being beaten for thinking about joining the Republican movement, which further demonstrated how unpopular the movement was in Sudan. Some of the women who were recruited came from the Sudan Communist Party.

Taha held the view that marriage is the "accurate test of social equality." Taha's own marriage provided a model for Republicans. One significant aspect of Taha's Republican movement is that its members were discouraged from engaging in polygamous marriages. This aspect of the movement is fascinating considering that polygamy is not only allowed in Islam, but it is also an aspect of many African societies as well. In Taha's view, polygamy was not acceptable. Even so, some exceptions were made. Men who were already in polygamous marriages were welcomed in the Republican Brotherhood since it was considered unfair to force them to get a divorce to join the Republicans. Taking a second wife was also considered acceptable in instances where the first wife was infertile. The Republican ideology held the view that marriage should provide complete equality for women.

Verse thirty-four of chapter four of the Qur'an dictated that men are to be protectors of women because they are physically stronger than women, whereas women are expected to be obedient to their husbands. Malcolm X explained Islam's view on gender roles in his autobiography when he stated that "Islam has very strict laws and teachings about women, the core of them being that the true nature of man is to be strong, and a woman's true nature is to be weak, and while a man must at all times respect his woman, at the same time he needs to understand that he must control her if he expects to get her respect." Senator Sani of Nigeria went even further by using Islam to justify his opposition to gender equality in Nigeria. Taha's organization challenged the role traditionally assigned to women in Islam.

Taha was executed in 1985 for his teachings. Taha refused to recant his views. He defended his position by stating that the September 1983 laws violated Sharia and Islam—Taha called these laws the September Laws to disassociate these policies from Islamic law. He believed that the Sudanese government actually distorted Islam with their policies. A reporter named Judith Miller gave the following description of Taha's execution: "When they saw him, many in the crowd leaped to their feet, jeering and shaking their fists at him. A few waved their Korans in the air. I managed to catch only a glimpse of Taha's face before the executioner placed an oatmeal-colored sack over his head and body, but I shall never forget his expression: His eyes were defiant; his mouth firm. He showed no hint of fear." Taha refused to make a final statement. He simply smiled as a bag was slipped over his head before he was executed by hanging. The four others who were convicted with Taha were forced to recant his teachings on national television after he was executed.

Taha's conviction for apostasy was later overturned after his daughter Asma brought a case to Sudan's Supreme Court. The ruling not only overturned Taha's conviction, but his marriage was restored. According to the law in Sudan, a Muslim woman could not marry a non-Muslim man, so when Taha was convicted for apostasy, his marriage was nullified.

In his article for the *New Yorker* titled "The Moderate Martyr," George Packer argued that Taha's ideology was significant given the terrorism caused by Islamic fundamentalism—the type of terrorism which was responsible for the September 11th attack in the United States. Taha's vision of Islam was not one of a religion which should be imposed through terror and violence, but a religion which promoted peace and harmony among Muslims and non-Muslims alike. Packer contrasted Taha's teachings with that of Sayyid Qutb. Qutb was an Egyptian religious teacher who advocated jihad and the overthrow of secular Arab states. Qutb was hanged in 1966 by Gamal Nasser's government. Osama bin Laden was among those who studied Qutb's writings.

The significance of Taha's religious message was not simply that it provided an alternative to the type of Islamic fundamentalism which produced violent extremists, but it also challenged the attempt to suppress Sudan's African identity in favor of an Arab one. Alison Ayers noted that the Arabist project in Sudan embraced the narrative of the colonial intelligentsia that "civilization in Sudan had been mainly an exogenous affair, narrowly a product of 'Arab' immigration and intermarriage and broadly an outcome of 'Arabization' of the indigenous population of Sudan". Ayers also noted that successive parliamentary and military regimes sought to "define Sudanese national identity along Arab-Islamic lines" by equating Sudanese national identity with Arab culture.

The Arabization of Sudan was a factor in the conflict in Darfur. The Sudanese government sided with Arab pastoralists in their conflict with the tribes in Darfur. The conflict became a full-scale war in which the government backed a campaign of ethnic cleansing which was designed to drive the local population in Darfur from their lands. This included bombing villages from the air, slaughtering villagers, and raping women. The conflict in

Darfur became known as the worst humanitarian crisis in the world. Hundreds of thousands were killed as a result of the conflict. Millions more were displaced.

Taha was a Muslim, but he identified as an African. Steve Howard, who first met Taha in 1982, noted that Taha had firmly identified himself as an African. Taha was noted to have remarked, "I am an African. I like the night, the scent of *buhur* (incense), the hot weather." On another occasion, Taha explained, "We are black or Negro." He also wrote in his book *Religion and Social Development* that Africa was the first home of man. Howard came to realize that the ones who opposed Taha were "also the ones engaged in the suppression of Sudan's African identity." The suppression of African identity in Sudan was such that Howard was told by Dr. Asma Adbelhalim that Sudanese who came to Ohio University to study in the African Studies Program came to understand for the first time that they were African.

Taha's Islamic vision is one which promoted a vision of Islam which was more moderate, but also tolerant of non-Muslims in Sudan. Taha did not believe in imposing Islam on the non-Muslim population in Sudan. He also believed that non-Muslims should be granted equal rights. Taha declared: "It is not enough for a citizen today merely to enjoy freedom of worship. He is entitled to the full rights of a citizen in total equality with all other citizens. The rights of southern citizens in their country are not provided for in sharia but rather in Islam at the level of fundamental Koranic revelation." Taha's vision did not prevail in Sudan. What prevailed was the hardline Islamist position which sought to impose an Arab identity on Sudan. This was overseen by Hassan al-Turabi. Turabi was a religious leader who gave asylum and assistance to bin Laden and other Al Qaeda members. He was also responsible for the execution of Taha. According to Gaafar Nimeiry, he ordered the execution of Taha at the urging of Turabi. Nimeiry claimed that Turabi told him that Taha was trying to unite with the left to remove Nimeiry from power.

After the coup in 1989, Turabi assisted the new regime which was led by Omar al-Bashir. Turabi, who was labeled as "the pope of terrorism", eventually fell out of favor with Bashir. Turabi was expelled from the government. He was also imprisoned multiple times. Turabi was later forced to admit that the Islamists were wrong for failing to adhere to the principles of democracy and human rights. Turabi began to preach a moderate version of Islam, though he continued to denounce Taha as an apostate. Further proof of the failures of Islamic fundamentalism in Sudan was the fact that Bashir himself was later overthrown following mass protests in Sudan.

Cornel West explained that Taha conceived Islam "as a holistic way of life that promotes freedom—the overcoming of fear—in order to pursue a loving and wise life". He also compared Taha to other historical figures such as Gandhi, Martin Luther King, and Nelson Mandela. West's remark demonstrated Taha's legacy as a religious reformer who used Islam to advocate for freedom and democracy.

Further Reading:

Abdullahi Ahmed An-Na'Im, "Mahmud Muhammad Taha and the Crisis in Islamic Law Reform: Implications for Interreligious Relations," *Journal of Ecumenical Studies*, 25:1, Winter 1988.

Alison J. Ayers, "Beyond the Ideology of 'Civil War': The Global-Historical Constitution of Political Violence in Sudan," *The Journal of Pan African Studies*, vol.4, no.10, January 2012.

George Packer, "The Moderate Martyr," *The New Yorker*, September 3, 2006.

Steve Howard, *Modern Muslims: A Sudan Memoir*, 2016.

Sylvia Chika Ifemeje, "The 2016 Rejection of Gender and Equal Opportunities Bill in Nigeria: A Critique"

10

EDWARD WILMOT BLYDEN AND THE CHALLENGES OF CHRISTIANITY IN AFRICA

Edward Wilmot Blyden is one of the most important figures in the history of the Pan-African movement. Blyden, who was born in the Danish West Indies, relocated to Liberia and became an advocate for emigration to Liberia. He believed that it was the duty of Africans throughout the Americas to return to Africa to develop Liberia.

W.E.B. Du Bois argued that Blyden was perhaps Liberia's greatest citizen. Blyden was certainly a man who expressed the noble aspirations which Liberia represented, but Blyden displayed the cultural challenges which Liberia confronted as well. Blyden's life also represented the challenges which Africans confronted regarding the effort to spread Christianity in Africa.

In Blyden's view, Africa remained "in its primitive simplicity and barbarism, contributing nothing to the well-being of mankind." He also expressed the view that this did not represent an inherent inferiority on the part of Africans, especially since Europe's history demonstrated that some European nations had failed to sustain a certain level of development. Blyden noted: "Look at the peasantry of many of the countries of Europe. Why are they so far down in the scale of civilization? And look at those countries in the south of Europe, Turkey, Greece, Italy, Spain, and Portugal, which formerly flourished, and contained within themselves all the learning and wisdom that existed in the world. They have sadly degenerated. They are comparatively insignificant."

The point which Blyden was making is that a people's level of civilization is not something which is inherently rooted in them, but is based on circumstances. As such, he argued that Africa's comparative lack of development with Europe was due to "differing circumstances." Blyden was confident in Africa's ability to develop itself. He stated: "Africa will furnish a development of civilization which the world has never yet witnessed."

Blyden noted that all people feel a pride in their ancestral land and complained that descendants of Africa "speak disparagingly of their country". He continued to note: "It is a sad feature in the residence of Africans in this country, that it has begotten in them a forgetfulness of Africa—a want of sympathy with her in her moral and intellectual desolation, and a clinging to the land which for centuries has been the scene of their thralldom." Blyden even quoted a European observer who noted that the African in America "makes a thousand fruitless efforts to insinuate himself among men who repulse him; he conforms to the taste of his oppressors, adopts their opinions, and hopes by imitating them to form a part of their community. Having been told from infancy that his race is naturally inferior to that of the whites, he assents to the proposition, and is ashamed of his own nature. In each of his features he discovers a trace of slavery, and, if it were in his power, he would willingly rid himself of every thing that makes him what he is."

Blyden also held the view that slavery provided "some very important advantages" to black people in America, though he noted that this has been at the expense of black manhood. He acknowledged that slavery dragged black people "into depths of degradation" and taught "cringing servility". Even though Blyden acknowledged the harsh nature of slavery in the Americas, he also believed the slave trade was transporting Africans from "a land of barbarism to a land of civilization".

Blyden expressed the view that those who returned to Liberia were fulfilling a divine plan to introduce Christianity and civilization to their "benighted brethren." Based on this view, he argued that Liberia became a center which radiated the light of Christianity. He also noted that there were fifteen thousand "civilized and Christianized Africans" working to introduce the Gospel among millions of "barbarous men." The language which Blyden uses here demonstrates unequivocally that Blyden saw the mission of the returnees as being one of not only spreading Christianity to the natives, but also introducing "civilization" to them. Blyden's concept of civilization was a very Eurocentric one. This was a fact which Blyden himself did not hide. He boasted about the English culture in Liberia. He also boasted that Liberia "resisted the influence of heathenism." He also mentioned efforts to "civilize and Christianize" the "dark land".

Blyden was so sure in his view that Africa was a dark land that he believed that missionary work in Africa would be easier than in Asia because Africans "have no system of religion protected by the sanction of a hoary antiquity; so that the work of evangelization need not be commenced by the slow process of undermining ancient and venerable systems of belief." He described missionary work in Africa as being "more constructive than destructive." This was because Blyden did not believe that there were existing religious systems or cultural practices in Africa which were worthy of note. He described Africa as a "moral desert", which really indicated just how much Blyden believed that traditional African societies were lacking meaningful religions. He noted that for thousands of years "has African been without a knowledge of God." The reality is that God does exist in traditional African religious beliefs, but Blyden dismissed the indigenous African concept of God because it did not match the Christian understanding of God. He also dismissed the achievements of Egyptian civilization by claiming that they "were destitute of the true wisdom."

Blyden expressed the view that Africans could only hope for a glorious future because they lacked a glorious past. He explained: "As a race we have been quite unfortunate. We have no pleasing antecedents—nothing in the past to inspire us. All behind us is dark, and gloomy, and repulsive." Here he was expressing the view that Africans are a people with no history of note.

One progressive aspect of the establishment of Liberia was that it suppressed the slave trade within the territory in which Liberia was established. Blyden himself noted that some of the natives professed indifference to the laws of Liberia and that sometimes slavers would purchase slaves on Liberian territory. He further pointed out that it became necessary to wage war to convince some of the local chiefs that Liberia had the power to compel them to obedience. The attempt to end the slave trade in Liberia was a positive development, but it also served to further entrench the notion that native Africans needed to be brought under the guidance of the "civilized Africans" who settled in Liberia.

Blyden appeared to have completely accepted the racist depictions of Africa as a land filled with a barbarous people who were lacking a true culture, religion, and civilization. Even though he maintained such views, Blyden denied that a distinction between the colonists and the aborigines in Liberia existed, but he did acknowledge that the idea came from "the fact that the aborigines of a country generally suffer from the settling of colonists among them." Even so, Blyden maintained that the settlement of Liberia was not like other examples of colonization in history. He gave examples such as the Israelites exterminating the indigenous population of Canaan and the European colonies in the Americas. Blyden argued that it would actually be "suicidal" for Liberia to keep the natives aloof from the settlers. His desire was to incorporate the natives.

The reality is that tensions between America-Liberians and the native population in Liberia persisted precisely because the native population remained aloof from the America-Liberian population. This was not only due to cultural differences, but also due to the fact that the America-Liberian population maintained its privileged positions by restricting the political participation of the natives. The economic power of the natives was restricted as well. In 1839, trade was restricted to only six America-Liberian ports. The restriction upset local African chiefs. Natives also turned to armed resistance against the Liberian government to resist against the impositions on their trade.

Liberia was not only confronted with the existing tensions between its own population. There was also the ever-present challenge which Western imperialism posed. When Liberia became independent, the United States refused to recognize Liberia's independence. Liberia was also confronted with threats from England and France, as Du Bois noted: "No sooner was the independence of Liberia announced than England and France began a long series of aggressions to limit her territory and sovereignty. Considerable territory was lost by treaty, and in the effort to get capital to develop the rest, Liberia was saddled with a debt of four hundred thousand dollars, of which she received less than one hundred thousand dollars in actual cash."

In time, Blyden's views on religion changed to the point where he argued that Islam "is the form that Christianity takes in Africa."

It would appear that Blyden became less concerned with Christianizing Africa as he came to view Islam as a religion which was better suited for Africa. Blyden claimed that with Islam "Africa is safe at least from physical destruction" and he provided the fate of Native Americans in North America as an example of the type of destruction he referred to. This was an interesting remark considering that the spread of Islam in Africa was at times very destructive and violent, but what mattered to Blyden was that Islam was a religion which was not attached to the type of brutalities which European Christians had inflicted on Africans and others.

Islam also offered a universal appeal which Blyden did not find in Christianity. Blyden would note that Islam became the faith of members of "all known races" and that "Christianity has never been able thus to unite distinct and dissimilar races." Blyden gave the example of a proposal which was made by a European missionary named Rev. J. Thomas. Thomas suggested that there should be Indian Bishops in the Church of England. Blyden noted that forty years later no attempt had been made to appoint any Indian Bishops. Blyden lamented that "Christendom is getting farther and farther away from the idea of brotherhood." Whereas Islam seemed to have united the races, Blyden believed that Christianity was moving away from the idea of brotherhood. Blyden's views were a response to the racism of white Christians. Blyden pointed out that in the United States, many white Christians were troubled by the importation of an African Episcopal Church because white Christians would not endure any equality of black and white in Church or in State. Blyden did not perceive the same prejudices in Islam.

Blyden described Christianity as having become "the monopoly of Europe." Blyden noted that the manner in which the Christians of Europe behaved was contrary to the message of Paul, who was sent to evangelize Europe. Blyden noted that Paul told the Europeans: "There is neither Jew nor Greek, there is neither bond nor free, there is neither male nor female; for ye are all one in Christ Jesus." According to Blyden, European Christians seem unable to grasp the universal message which Paul gave them.

Apart from the universal appeal of Islam, Blyden also believed that the religion of Islam protected Africans against the undue ascendency of Arab peculiarities. Blyden mentioned that educated African Muslims quote the Koran which explains in chapter nine that Arabs are most stout in their disbelief and hypocrisy. Blyden explained that the importance of this passage is that it protected African Muslims against having an undue reverence for Arabs. Blyden also quoted Mr. Lane Poole who noted that Muhammad "in part destroyed the Arab when he created the Muslim." The reason why Blyden mentioned this is because, in his view, Islam is not a religion which asserts the supremacy of Arabs. He expressed the view that Islam actually held a very critical view of Arabs.

Europeans also had prejudices and misconceptions about Islam in Africa. Blyden noted that European writers on the topic of Islam in Africa tended to view it as "an imitation if not caricature of Islam in Arabia," but Blyden challenged this notion by pointing out that Europeans who commented on Islam in Africa actually knew very little about the topic. Blyden also challenged assertions that Muslims in Africa were hostile to Europeans and Christians by noting that Muslims in Africa are "peaceable, tolerant, and nonpolitical in their aspirations."

Blyden's support for Islam in Africa was not necessarily a rejection of Christianity. He argued that Muhammad's teachings "agree with the belief of Christendom as expressed in the Apostles' Creed." Much like Christians, Muslims believe in God, the maker of heaven and earth. Muslims also believe that Jesus was born of the virgin Mary and that he ascended into heaven, though they reject that Jesus is God's son and that he rose from the dead. It would seem that in Blyden's view, Islam was similar enough to Christianity so that it was not a "pagan" religion—it was not the "heathenism" which Blyden denounced. Yet Islam's differences from European Christianity were appealing to Blyden who began to recognize the problems with European Christianity.

Blyden's shifting views on religion demonstrated a sense of disillusionment with the racism of white Christians. Blyden still held Eurocentric notions of civilization. In his view, Western culture still represented the standard of civilization which Liberia should strive to emulate, but he also came to recognize the need to look for something outside of European Christianity.

Watson Omulokoli wrote about the quest for an authentic African Christianity. This is no easy task given that the widespread introduction of Christianity into Africa came as the result of European missionary activity which was also connected to Western notions of civilization and culture. As Omulokoli noted, European missionaries took Christianity to Africa "clothed in Western European garb." Omulokoli further noted the need to dress Christianity "in African clothing if it is to be of any lasting significance to the indigenous peoples."

Omulokoli further argued that it was not always the case that Africans accepted the "warped Gospel" which was given to them. Indeed, there were attempts to Africanize Christianity. A most notable example of this was Mojola Agbebi, who was formerly known as David Vincent Brown. He not only cast off his European name, but European clothing as well. Agbebi denounced European Christianity as "a dangerous thing". He also described "American civilization" as a snare and its Christianity as a counterfeit.

Agbebi was not alone in his effort to develop a form of Christianity which was independent from European dominance. In 1888, the Native Baptist Church in Nigeria formed as a response to the European domination of churches. Willie Mokalapa founded the Ethiopian Church. Mokalapa and his followers protested against the discrimination of European missionaries. The disillusionment with European Christianity also led to the formation of new religions movements. In Kenya, John Owalo formed an independent church in 1910 after he left the Catholic Church, the Scottish Mission, and the Anglican Church. Owalo proclaimed himself to be a prophet and denied the divinity of Christ. His new religion managed to attract thousands and he managed to build his own primary school. In 1913, the Mumbo cult movement developed in Kenya. Its founder Onyango Dande explained that the Christian religion is "rotten" and that all Europeans were enemies. The colonial government worked to suppress Dande's movement.

Some Africans used Christianity as part of the anti-colonial movement which sought to liberate Africa from colonial domination. One of the most prominent examples of this was John

Chilembwe, who led a revolt against British colonial rule. Blyden certainly recognized the racism of European missionaries, but he also could not envision an anti-colonial movement. Even as he advocated Islam as a religion which would protect Africans against undue ascendency of European peculiarities, Blyden also believed that European colonial rule was a benefit for Africa.

Blyden acknowledged: "Wrongs have been committed by Englishmen upon the natives—cruel things have been done." Blyden was not completely ignorant about the cruelties inflicted by the colonial powers, yet Blyden continued to maintain the view that colonialism in Africa had a generally positive influence on Africa's development. Though Blyden was critical of certain aspects of European imperialism, he could not bring himself to totally abandon the view that European colonialism was a progressive force for Africa. He explained: "The possibilities for European commerce in West Africa are practically unlimited, and England has done more than any other nation to create, foster, and develop commerce in that country, and England will, as is justly her due, reap most of its rewards in future." This demonstrated the extent to which Blyden was willing to praise colonial policies in Africa, while only giving minimal acknowledgment of the cruelties of colonial policy in Africa.

Omulokoli stated: "If Christianity is truly universal, as we allege it is, then it must recommend itself to every culture in an amicable way, while at the same time transcending the limitations of the particular cultural sct-up. The man in Australasia, in the Americas, in Europe, and in Africa should be comfortably Christian without surrendering his own cultural distinctives to any other culture but that of Jesus Christ." This is a difficult task because, as noted before, the spread of Christianity throughout much of Africa came as a result of European missionary activity. It is also difficult because Omulokoli cautions against developing an African Christianity which is so overlaid with African culture that it fails to meet the test of a true Christianity. Even so, the question of culture is not one which can be easily removed from the discussion around Abrahamic religions in Africa, particularly given the legacy of colonialism in Africa. Blyden attempted to resolve this problem by looking to Islam rather than Christianity, but Islam too comes with its own cultural assumptions rooted in the fact that Islam emerged out of Arabic culture.

One of the areas in which the Arabization of Africa through the religion of Islam has displayed itself is in Mauritania where a very strict interpretation of Islamic law which reduced the majority Haratin ethnic group to slaves of the Arab-Berber ethnic group. Slavery in Mauritania—which also allows for women, and even girls, who are enslaved to be sexually abused—is justified by the country's religious law. Biram Dah Abedi, who has advocated for an end to slavery, noted that he had been jailed numerous times simply for opposing these laws. This shows that Islam in Africa has not been without some problems of its own.

References:

A. Abu Boahen (editor), *General History of Africa VII: African Under Colonial Domination 1880-1935*, (University of California Press, 1985).

Biram Dah Abeid's 2016 keynote speech at the Trust Women Conference.

Edward Wilmot Blyden, *Liberia's Offering*, 1862.

___*West Africa Before Europe*, 1905.

Watson Omulokoli, "The Quest for Authentic African Christianity," *East Africa Journal of Evangelical Theology*.

W.E.B. Du Bois, *The Negro*, 1915.

11

ON SIR SERETSE KHAMA

The adverse impact of colonialism in Africa was not simply that colonialism ruthlessly exploited and abused African people to enrich the colonial powers of Europe. Part of the process of exploitation included indoctrinating the minds of the colonized Africans with the cultural lifestyle of the colonial powers. This was done to better assist the process of establishing colonial control over Africa.

This brings me to Sir Seretse Khama, who was the first president of Botswana. He is an interesting figure in Africa's history because he stands out as one of the better political leaders in post-colonial Africa. He was not a dictator who oppressed and murdered his people to stay in power. Rather than wasting money on prestige projects, Khama was noted for investing in improving his country's infrastructure, healthcare and education. Botswana has also remained one of the more politically stable nations in Africa. Khama was also among the most thoroughly colonized of the post-colonial leaders in Africa.

Khama decided to marry a white woman named Ruth. This upset his uncle Tshekedi who was outraged that his nephew would marry a white woman and make her queen. It was not only his uncle who opposed this marriage. All of the churches in London refused to marry them. They were forced to marry through a civil ceremony. The marriage also had serious political implications as well. The racist regime in South Africa pressured the British government into banishing Khama and his wife.

Britain claimed that Khama's marriage without the consent of his tribesmen displayed lack of leadership qualities. Khama's exile was upheld in the House of Commons in a vote of 308 to 286. The leader of the British Labor Party criticized Winston Churchill's failure to oppose the racial policies of South Africa's government. Khama was offered a job in Jamaica, but he turned it down, claiming, "I would not take bread from any Jamaican's mouth."

The exiling of Khama caused disturbances as the Bamangwatos rioted and refused to pay taxes until their chief was allowed to return home. Khama finally returned home in 1956, only after agreeing to relinquish claims to his father's throne. He later was elected and became the first president of Botswana when the nation became independent.

Khama's marriage to a British woman exposed two realities. Firstly, it exposed the racism of British colonialism in Africa. The British government exiled Khama simply because of who he had married. Moreover, no church in England would marry the couple. It also exposed Khama's own deep personal identification with Britain. His decision to marry a white British woman represented Khama's own deep attachment to Britain. The attachment was such that he had even been knighted in 1966. Despite the fact that Britain had exiled him from his own country because of his marriage, Khama still accepted knighthood from his colonizers.

As noted before, Khama can be regarded as being among the better leaders in Africa in that he was not a brutal dictator who encouraged widespread corruption within his nation. Under his leadership, Botswana progressed and remained stable, but Botswana also retained the colonial model. This meant that Botswana's wealth was largely generated through selling its diamonds to De Beers which benefited more from the diamonds than the average citizen in Botswana does. This is a situation which Kenneth Good described as "negative peace."

Selected References:

"A Happy End for Prince Seretse and Ruth," *Ebony* 1966.

Ameila Cook and Jeremy Sarkin, "Is Botswana the Miracle of Africa? Democracy, the Rule of Law, and Human Rights Versus Economic Development," *Transnational Law & Contemporary Problems* Vol. 19, Spring 2010.

"Seretse Khama Spurns Jamaican Job," *Jet* April 10, 1952.

The London Gazette, September 23, 1966.

12

WHITE AND BLACK SEPARATISTS

James Baldwin's criticisms of the Nation of Islam are worth noting because although Baldwin disagreed with the ideology which the Nation of Islam preached, he acknowledged the truths of what the Nation of Islam stated. In an article for *The New Yorker* titled "Letter from a Region in My Mind," Baldwin wrote: "I, in any case, certainly refuse to be put in the position of denying the truth of Malcolm's statements simply because I disagree with his conclusions, or in order to pacify the liberal conscience. Things are as bad as the Muslims say they are—in fact, they are worse […]."

One conclusion which Baldwin certainly disagreed with was the Nation of Islam's position on racial separation. Elijah Muhammad preached the separation of the races. In this the Nation of Islam found commonality with white supremacist organizations which also preached racial separation. Baldwin noted that during a Muslim rally, George Lincoln Rockwell of the American Nazi Party contributed twenty dollars to the cause. Upon receiving the donation from Rockwell, Malcolm expressed how "glad" he was to have Rockwell there. Baldwin added that Rockwell "and Malcolm X decided that, racially speaking, anyway, they were in complete agreement." Baldwin also added: "The glorification of one race and the consequent debasement of another—or others—always has been and always will be a recipe for murder."

Baldwin seemed to have been making the error of conflating the racial separatism of the Nation of Islam with that of the American Nazi Party. The difference is that the Nazi Party was the product of the murderous ideology of Adolf Hitler, whereas the Nation of Islam was a response to America's violence against black people. The point to be understood here is that the racial separatism of the American Nazis and the Black Muslims were born out of different realities. Even so, the two organizations were united in their opposition to race mixing.

One of the most controversial aspects of the Nation of Islam was its teaching that white people are devils. This makes it all the more interesting that Rockwell was not only welcomed by the

Nation of Islam, but invited to speak as well. This event was recalled by Rockwell in the first issue of *The Stromtrooper*, which served as the American Nazi Party's paper. Rockwell mentioned that he and the others were welcomed by the Fruit of Islam, which he described as Elijah Muhammad's "impressive" storm troops. Elijah Muhammad spoke at the occasion. Rockwell stated that Elijah Muhammad stated that the black man should not want to mix with the white man and should not beg for integration. After Elijah Muhammad spoke, Rockwell was invited to speak.

Rockwell described his address as follows: "I told them, I believe and the American Nazi Party believes, that the black man has had a rotten deal in America, and, even though we have no intention of mixing with them, we do not want to hurt them." He added that he was cheered and applauded by black men who were supposed to be "hate men". Rockwell concluded his address with a Nazi salute and a shout of "Heil Hitler!"

Rockwell commented that a "very rich Negro" spoke on behalf of the NAACP and that this eventually was "filled with hate at the sight" of two groups working in harmony for a common goal. This comment by Rockwell was interesting because he presented the work of two separatist groups as being an example of "harmony", which further demonstrates the point that black and white separatist groups were able to find a common cause in their shared belief in racial separation.

Not all of the Muslims were receptive of Rockwell. In Elijah Muhammad's speech he acknowledged that he had his ministers stand up because he did not believe that they should sit and hold their hand when Rockwell was telling the truth. That "truth" as Elijah Muhammad saw it was that Rockwell was a white man who encouraged black people to do for self, which was the very thing which Elijah Muhammad preached. Indeed, as Baldwin stated, the Nation of Islam spoke the truth about how bad the racial situation in America was. In the view of Elijah Muhammad, Rockwell was a white man who told the truth. Unlike white liberals who preached integration, but did not practice it, Rockwell was honest about his desire for racial separation.

One of the consequences of Malcolm leaving the Nation of

Islam was that he was no longer connected to the racial separatism of Elijah Muhammad. This also changed his relationship with Rockwell. In the past, Malcolm welcomed Rockwell's support for the Nation of Islam, but after leaving the Nation of Islam, Malcolm sent a message warning Rockwell that there would be maximum retaliation if he or any of his "Ku Klux Klan friends" harmed Martin Luther King. Malcolm still maintained some disagreements with King's methods, but what was most important to him was protecting King and others from white supremacist violence. Malcolm's views on self-defense had not changed after he left the Nation of Islam. He still believed that black people had a right to defend themselves if attacked. What did change was that Malcolm, now free of Elijah Muhammad's influence, no longer recognized a common cause between himself and Rockwell.

13

HISTORY AND THE BIBLE

The Bible mentions real historical events and individuals, which can often make it difficult to distinguish what is historical in the Bible from what is not. It would perhaps be most accurate to view the Bible as a mythological historical narrative which combines history and myth as a means to convey religious messages and teachings.

It would appear that the intention of the Bible itself was not be viewed as a historical book necessarily. An example which supports this point is that Genesis offers two different creation stories, which contradict each other. In the first story, God created the creatures of the earth before creating men and women at the same time (Genesis 1: 21-27). In the second story, God created man first, then the creatures of the earth, and then God created woman from one of the man's ribs (Genesis 2: 7-22). The purpose of these two stories is not historical accuracy given that the two accounts differ. The purpose of these two stories is to establish that God is the creator of the earth. The second story goes further to tell the tale of humankind's act of rebellion against God by showing how the first two humans—Adam and Eve—disobeyed God.

The entire narrative of the Old Testament continues from the story of Adam and Eve by showing how man's rebellion against God continuously led to suffering. The Old Testament particularly focuses on the Hebrews, who become God's chosen people. The history of the Hebrews given in the Old Testament continues this theme of rebellion against God. The roots of the Israelite kingdom in the Bible begin following the Hebrew exodus from Egypt. This story is told in the Book of Exodus.

The exodus of a large number of Hebrews out of Egypt is not attested in Egyptian records, which makes it difficult to corroborate the Bible's account. What also makes it difficult to corroborate the Bible's account is that the Bible itself does not list the names of any of the pharaohs mentioned in the Book of Exodus. Similarly, no pharaohs are mentioned by name in the

Book of Genesis either. This would suggest that these stories are not meant to correspond to any particular period in Egypt's history and that the pharaohs mentioned in these stories are symbolic representations of the power of Egypt, rather than references to any actual pharaohs who ruled over Egypt.

That the pharaoh at the time of the exodus is unnamed is also noteworthy given that the Bible makes it a point to name historical rulers who conquered and oppressed the Israelites. The Bible states that Hazael of Aram oppressed Israel (2 Kings 13:22) and Shalmaneser of Assyria is stated to have attacked Hoshea of Israel (2 Kings 17:1-6)—interestingly, 2 Kings 17 mentions that Hoshea had attempted to enlist the aid of So of Egypt, marking an example where an Egyptian ruler is mentioned by name in the Bible. The domination of Nebuchadnezzar of Babylon is mentioned as well. The Bible states that Nebuchadnezzar attacked Jerusalem (Daniel 1:1-2). There is also a story in the Bible in which Nebuchadnezzar captured three Hebrews—named Shadrach, Meshach, and Abednego—and had them thrown into a furnace to be burned alive, but the Bible states that the three Hebrews were saved by an angel sent by God (Daniel 3). The point here is that rulers who oppressed the Israelites are mentioned by name in certain parts of the Bible, but the pharaoh who oppressed the Israelites and opposed Moses is not named.

The lack of historical evidence of a mass exodus led by a man named Moses does not suggest that the story itself has no basis in historical events. There are a number of theories which explain the historical roots of the Exodus story. One of which was provided by the Jewish historian, Flavius Josephus. Josephus stated that many of the Hebrews left Egypt when the Hyksos were driven out. This would suggest that the Hebrews arrived in Egypt when the Hyksos were in power, but left when Egyptians regained control. This could mean that the pharaoh "who knew not Joseph" who is mentioned in the Bible was a reference to the fact that a new dynasty came to power in Egypt after the Hyksos were expelled. In *Moses and Monotheism*, Sigmund Freud proposed that Moses was an Egyptian priest during the time of Akhenaten and that the Hebrews developed their monotheism from Akhenaten's monotheistic religion. Freud also argued that the Hebrew custom of circumcision was taken from Egypt as well. The Bible explains that circumcision was part of the covenant between God and Abraham, which demonstrates the importance of this custom to the religious practices of the Hebrews (Genesis 17:11-14).

Here I would propose yet another theory. There is an Egyptian inscription which took place during the reign of Merneptah, who came to power after the death of Ramesses II. It was recorded that Merneptah put down a revolt in Palestine and the pharaoh boasted that "Israel is laid waste and has no seed." The destruction of Israel due to an Egyptian attack is not mentioned in the Bible, but it is possible that the Exodus story is meant to represent a period in Israel's history when the Israelites endured suffering due to Egypt. The Bible mentions that the Hebrews built the capital city of Ramesses II (Exodus 1:11), so it may be possible that the enslavement of the Hebrews mentioned in the Bible is a reference to a time when Israel was under the domination of the Ramesses II and his successors.

From a religious aspect, what is important about the Book of Exodus is not the historical nature of the story, but what the story represents. The Book of Exodus represents the beginning of the fulfillment of God's covenant with the Hebrews. In the story, God leads the Hebrews out of slavery in Egypt and they begin their journey to the promised land. This journey is also of religious significance because the early examples of Israel's rebellion against God take place during this period. This is displayed when the Hebrews create a golden calf to worship (Exodus 32). God was enraged by this and Moses had to intercede to prevent God from unleashing his wrath on the very people that God led out of slavery in Egypt.

The unfaithfulness of the Hebrews caused them to wander in the wilderness for forty years. Twelve explorers are ordered by Moses to explore the land of Canaan (Numbers 13). Some of the explorers claimed that the Canaanites were too powerful to be defeated. This caused the Hebrews to rebel (Numbers 14). They complained that they should have died in Egypt, rather than in the wilderness. God is enraged and Moses again has to intercede on behalf of his people. God is convinced by Moses to forgive the Hebrews, but God also stated that the Hebrews would have to wander the wilderness for forty years before they could see the promised land.

It is important to note that the Hebrews are not God's chosen people because they are inherently more moral than the other nations mentioned in the Bible. Rather, God chooses the Hebrews to place upon them the challenge of being an example of morality for the rest of the nations. God instructs the Hebrews to be not like the Egyptians or the Canaanites (Leviticus 18: 1-3). God further instructs the Hebrews not to sacrifice their children to him as the Canaanites had done to their gods (Deuteronomy 12:31). The punishment for those who engaged in child sacrifice is death (Leviticus 20:1-5). This opposition to child sacrifice is displayed in Genesis 22 when God instructs Abraham to sacrifice his son Isaac. This is done to test Abraham's loyalty, but God ultimately instructs Abraham not to sacrifice his son and to sacrifice a ram instead.

Throughout the Old Testament, the Hebrews frequently break their covenant with God by worshipping other gods. This is demonstrated shortly after the Hebrews enter the land which was promised to them by God. Moses was the man who led the Hebrews out of Egypt, but he never saw the promised land. Instead, it was Joshua who brought the Hebrews to the promised land. The Book of Judges recounts that Joshua died and in time a generation of Hebrews who did not know of God rose up (Judges 2:7-10). The Israelites abandoned God and instead worshipped alien gods such as Baal (Judges 2:12-13).

According to the Bible, Israel was ruled by judges, but in time the Israelites demanded to have a king like other nations (1 Samuel 8). Despite acknowledging the unfaithfulness of the Israelites, God allowed them to have a king. Saul is selected as Israel's first king (1 Samuel 9). Saul eventually fell out of favor with God when God commanded him to slaughter the Amalekites. Saul decided to spare Agag who was the king of the Amalekites. Saul's army also spared the best sheep and cattle. After this, God expressed to Samuel regret for making Saul king because Saul has disobeyed God's instructions (1 Samuel 15). David is then anointed by Samuel (1 Samuel 16:1-13).

Saul's failure to follow the command of God does have consequences which are mentioned later in the Bible. It is mentioned in Psalm 83 that the Amalekites join in a plot against the people of Israel. Esther 3 mentions that a man named Haman issued a decree on behalf of the Persian ruler Xerxes to kill all of the Jews after a Jewish man named Mordecai refused to kneel before Haman. Haman was a Agagite, which meant that he was a descendant of the Amalekite ruler Agag. Why this is significant is that Saul's failure to kill Agag resulted in Jews being placed in danger by one of Agag's descendants.

David is of significance here because of the discovery of an Aramaic stele in Tel Dan in 1993. Two more pieces were found in 1994. The stele made reference to Jehoram being a king of Israel and Ahaziah of Judah being a member of the House of David. This confirmed the existence of an Israelite kingdom whose kings were descendants of David. Moreover, the stele confirmed the existence of Jehoram and Ahaziah who are both mentioned in the Bible. The author of the stele claimed to have killed Jehoram and Ahaziah, which confirmed that both men were violently killed as the Bible claims. Hazael has been identified as the author of the stele, which appears to contradict the Bible's narrative which states that Jehu was the one who killed Jehoram and Ahaziah. This apparent contradiction could perhaps be explained by a possible alliance between Hazael and Jehu. This alliance is alluded to in the Bible. The Bible notes that Jehu's revolt against Jehoram happened after Jehoram was wounded in battle with Hazael (2 Kings 9). The Bible also states that anyone who escaped Hazael's sword would be executed by Jehu (1 Kings 19:17). The implication of the last passage is that Hazael's enemies are also Jehu's enemies. The alliance between Jehu and Hazael was likely also responsible for the death of Ahaziah of Judah, who was killed by Jehu's men according to the Bible's account (2 Kings 9).

David, like Saul, also fell out of favor with God after David committed adultery by having sex with a woman named Bathsheba. David impregnated Bathsheba, which was a grave sin considering that she was married to a man named Uriah. David arranged to have Uriah killed in battle so that he could marry Bathsheba. David was aware that he had sinned, but tried to cover this sin by killing Bathsheba's husband and taking her for himself (2 Samuel 11).

The rest of David's reign was marked by tragedy. First, the

child that he had with Bathsheba was killed by God as punishment for David's sin (2 Samuel 12:16-19). The situation for David became worse when his son Amnon raped his daughter Tamar. Absalom, who was another one of David's children, ordered his soldiers to kill Amnon to avenge the rape of their sister (2 Samuel 13). Absalom later led a revolt against David (2 Samuel 15:1-13).

The tragedies which impact David's life were punishments for the sin of killing Uriah and taking his wife (2 Samuel 12:7-12). God explained that as punishment, he would raise evil within David's own household. This included taking some of David's women and giving them away so that they would have sex in public. God declared that what David did in secret would be done to David in front of all of Israel. This punishment comes when Absalom, David's rebellious son, had sex with David's concubines in public for all of Israel to see (2 Samuel 16:22). It is worth noting here that Absalom's actions were in violation of the law which prohibited a son from having sex with his father's wife (Leviticus 18:8). This is such a grave offense that a son who has had sex with his father's wife is to be put to death (Leviticus 20:11). Here this act is done purely to cause humiliation to David.

When David died, the throne was given to his son Solomon. What is curious about Solomon's reign is that the Bible explains that Solomon made a peace treaty with the pharaoh of Egypt by marrying his daughter (1 Kings 3:1-2). Once again, the pharaoh here is unnamed, but the implication of the marriage seems to suggest that there was some sort of political alliance between Israel and Egypt. This marriage was also consistent with Solomon's love of foreign women. Solomon married women from other nations as well, despite the fact that the Hebrews were commanded not to intermarry with foreign women (1 Kings 11: 1-5). In addition to the daughter of the pharaoh, Solomon also married women from Moab, Ammon, Edom, Sibon, and the Hittites. Solomon loved women so much that he had 700 wives and 300 concubines. These women led him away from worshiping God to the point that Solomon had built a place for Chemosh, the god of Moab (1 Kings 3: 7). Solomon's love for women is even mentioned in the *Kebra Nagast*, which states that the Queen of Sheba was impregnated by Solomon. The Bible makes no mention of any sexual relations between Solomon and the Queen of Sheba, although Solomon impregnating the Queen of Sheba would certainly be consistent with how he is portrayed in the Bible.

The stories of Saul, David, and Solomon demonstrate that the rulers of Israel failed to obey God's commands and were punished for doing so. Even after the united Israelite kingdom is split up, the people of Israel and Judah continue to displease God with their actions (Jeremiah 32:30).

What is interesting to note is that in Exodus, God rescued the Hebrews from slavery in Egypt, but the fate of Josiah demonstrated the fall of the Hebrews in the eyes of God. The Bible states that Josiah was the ruler of Judah who became the ruler at the age of eight. By the age of 12, Josiah pursued a policy of purging all of the idols in Judah (2 Chronicles 34:1–4). Josiah's dedication to God was a contrast with his father Amon who was described as being a wicked ruler who worshipped idols and was eventually assassinated by his own officials (2 Kings 21: 19-24). Josiah realized that God was angry at the people of Israel for failing to act in accordance with God's law and sought to remedy the situation (2 Chronicles 34:21). The problem is that even Josiah too would act against God.

The Bible explained that Josiah was killed in battle after he decided to go to war with Necho of Egypt—yet another example of an Egyptian ruler being mentioned by name. What is interesting about the Bible's narrative is that before the battle, Necho warns Josiah that God is on Necho's side and if Josiah fought Necho, then God would destroy Josiah (2 Chronicles 35: 20-27). Josiah, who up until this point is portrayed as a man who was completely devoted to God, apparently decided to rebel against God to fight Necho. It is also curious that Necho, the ruler of Egypt, is portrayed as being on God's side. This would appear to be a reversal of the situation presented in Exodus in which the Hebrews were on the side of God and the Egyptian ruler was punished for opposing God.

A slightly different account of Josiah's death is mentioned in 2 Kings 23:29-30. In that passage, it is stated that Josiah is killed by Necho, but there is no mention of Josiah being in opposition to God nor is there any mention of Jeremiah composing laments for

Josiah in this account. The tragedy of Josiah's death is worsened by the Bible's claim that Josiah's son Jehoahaz did evil in the eyes of the Lord (2 Kings 23: 30-34). Jehoahaz was subsequently placed in chains by Necho, who also imposed a tax on Judah. The Hebrews who had escaped Egyptian domination due to the power of God found themselves once again under the domination of Egypt because they had turned away from God.

As noted before, the Bible is a text which does contain references to real historical individuals and events, although it is often difficult to determine precisely what in the Bible is historical and what is not. Ultimately, for those who practice the Abrahamic faiths, the importance of the Bible is not that it is a source of history, but that it is a source of religious guidance. Though the story of the Hebrews in the Bible is a political story about the creation and eventual fall of the Israelite state, the fall of the Israelites in the Bible is also told as a tale of morality; a tale about a people who were punished for turning away from God.

Selected References:

Avraham Biran and Joseph Naveh, "The Tel Dan Inscription: A New Fragment," *Israel Exploration Journal*, Volume 45, No. 1, 1995.

George Steindorff and Keith C. Seele, *When Egypt Ruled the East*, (The University of Chicago Press, 1957).

John Coleman De Graft-Johnson, *African Glory: The Story of Vanished Negro Civilizations*, (Black Classic Press, 1986).

Sigmund Freud, *Moses and Monotheism*, 1937.

William Leo Hansberry, *Pillars in Ethiopian History*, (Howard University Press, 1981).

14

ON THE OVP IN GUYANA

The importance of the Organization for the Victory of the People (OVP) in Guyana is that it is a political party which represents a revolutionary and anti-colonial vision which has been lacking in the politics of Guyana. Forbes Burnham and Cheddi Jagan are two political leaders in Guyana's history whom I have been critical of, yet there is no denying that both men were individuals who took strong anti-colonial and anti-capitalist positions. One could argue that they pursued policies which may have contradicted their socialist ideologies, but there is certainly no denying that they took anti-colonial positions.

Gerald A. Perreira, who was the founding leader of the OVP, is someone who comes out of this anti-colonial tradition in Guyana's politics. Perreira explained that the OVP was launched in 2015 on the birthday of Forbes Burnham because of how much Burnham's vision influenced Perreira. Perreira was a member of the Young Socialist Movement within the PNC, so his earliest experience in politics in Guyana came as a member of the PNC under the leadership of Burnham.

As a Pan-Africanist, the Pan-African movement in Guyana has posed the particular challenge of how to reconcile the obvious differences between those who are influenced by Burnham and his vision for Guyana versus those who come out of the tradition of Walter Rodney and the Working People's Alliance. Rodney and Burnham were both Pan-Africanists, but the two men were in political opposition towards each other. What makes reconciliation between the two traditions especially difficult is the repressive nature of Burnham's government which resulted in the death of Rodney. Perreira is among those who hold the position that Burnham did not kill Rodney. I am among those who differ with such a view.

My purpose here is no to repeat my disagreements with Perreira on this question of who was responsible for the death of Walter Rodney or the nature of Burnham's government. The aim of this short piece is actually to express my admiration for Perreira and the OVP for representing the anti-colonial tradition in Guyana's politics. One area where I certainly do agree with Perreira is that the PNC has lost its direction. The PNC, like the PPP, abandoned socialism in favor of what Perreira referred to as the neo-liberal capitalist model of development. In an article titled "Socialism Is A Superior System to Capitalism," which was published by *Kaieteur News* on September 2, 2017, Perreira explained: "Both the PNCR and PPP have long abandoned the vision and ideology of their founding fathers." Perreira explained that this is unfortunately not uncommon. He explained: "Many a great leader, after passing away, is still eulogized by their founding parties, even though those parties have abandoned the vision they started out with. It happened in Egypt after Nasser, in Ghana after Nkrumah, and sadly in Azania (South Africa) after Mandela."

Perreira made the point that his vision of socialism is not one which comes from "Soviet-style Communism," which he describes as a "destructive parody of socialism." Perreira locates his socialism in non-European traditions. He further argues that Christianity and Islam represent religions which are opposed to the vices which capitalism encourages.

What the OVP represents is a vision for Guyanese society which is located outside of the typical neo-liberal capitalist model which has continued to fail nations such as Guyana. Perreira is a socialist whose vision for Guyana is one in which Guyanese society breaks with the Western model of neo-liberal capitalism and embraces an economic model which empowers the people of Guyana. On this point I am in full support of Perreira and the OVP. Guyana needs a break with the neo-liberal model. Rather than advancing the visions of Jagan and Burnham, the two dominant political parties in Guyana have actually regressed politically.

15

THE BLACK PRESIDENT

The election of Barack Obama in 2008 was a significant moment if for no other reason than he was the first black president in American history. The tears which Jesse Jackson shed on that day were a testament to what Obama's victory represented to black people who witnessed the election of a man who looked like them. Obama's election was significant for other reasons as well. After eight years of George W. Bush's presidency, Obama represented optimism and a sense of change. This feeling was encapsulated by his campaign slogan, "Yes we can!"

The eight years before Obama were difficult. There were the terrorist attacks on September 11, 2001. This was followed by wars in Iraq and Afghanistan. The invasion of Iraq was premised on the notion that Sadaam Hussein was holding weapons of mass destruction. No such weapons were found, however. Obama also took office during an economic crisis which was the result of an economic crash which happened during Bush's presidency. Apart from these problems, there was also the fact that Bush simply was not a captivating leader. He tended to make gaffes and was a bit awkward in public. All of this set up the stage for Obama to launch a campaign centered on change. It was not simply change in the sense of a change in the racial identity of the president. He offered change from eight years of ineffective governance. He offered a change in the way that politicians related to the American people.

That Obama represented a break with the old political order served him well during his campaign. During the Democratic primary, Obama criticized Hillary Clinton for the money which she took from lobbyists and for her support of NAFTA. Obama also criticized the fact that Clinton had voted in support of the invasion of Iraq. In this regard, Obama was able to present himself as the purer candidate of the two because he was not connected to lobbyists nor had he supported policies which were harmful for America. Obama enjoyed a similar advantage over John McCain, who was the Republican nominee for the presidency. McCain seemed out of touch with the economic realities of America. He insisted that the fundamentals of the economy were strong. McCain also spoke of the economic progress which was made during Bush's presidency. McCain could state this because he was doing so well for himself that when asked how many houses he had, McCain did not even know. He had so many houses that he forgot how many he owned!

Obama prevailed over Mitt Romney in 2012 because, like McCain, Romney seemed like another comfortable politician who could not relate to the struggles of the ordinary American voter. Obama did not present this perception, however. Obama seemed to have been a political leader who was concerned with wealth inequality in America. Obama was certainly concerned about the influence of money in politics. He criticized the Supreme Court's ruling in *Citizens United v. FEC*. He saw this ruling as a blow to the effort to rein in corporate influence in politics, although Obama's expressed concern about the role of lobbyists and the role of big money in politics was undermined by his own policies. Despite signing an executive order to restrict lobbyists, Obama made exceptions to his own policy to include former lobbyists. This included appointing William Lynn as the deputy Defense Secretary. Lynn was a lobbyist for a defense contractor named Raytheon.

Obama's willingness to include lobbyist in his administration was a sign that his administration would not be as tough on Wall Street as some of his supporters may have hoped. Cornel West, who endorsed Obama during the campaign and stated that Obama had the vision for America, became one of Obama's most vocal critics. He denounced Obama as being a "black puppet" for Wall Street and even stated that Obama had a fear of free black men because Obama was raised in a "white context". There seemed to be some degree of personal animosity because Obama never thanked West for West's endorsement nor did West receive a ticket to the inauguration. Even so, West did raise legitimate points regarding the struggles of working people under Obama's presidency.

There was also the question of race. After all, Obama was the first black president and he experience racism for this reason. There were those who doubted that Obama was truly born in

America. Donald Trump was among those who raised these doubts. The intention was obviously to suggest that Obama was an illegitimate president who was not truly an American. To McCain's credit, he did not seek to discredit Obama in this manner. When confronted by a woman who suggested that Obama is an Arab, he responded by stating that Obama is a decent man. This was not Trump's approach, however.

There was also a moment involving Chris Matthews, who, after listening to Obama give a speech, stated that he forgot that Obama was black for an hour. The remark was apparently intended to convey Matthews' view of Obama being a "post-racial" president. The suggestion of Obama being a post-racial president is problematic in itself. How could a post-racial president truly exist in a racist society? Matthews himself certainly did not have a post-racial view of Obama given that he stated he forgot that Obama was black for an hour. Apparently, when the hour was over, Matthews went back to noticing Obama's race.

Obama himself preferred to avoid the topic of race. When Jimmy Carter suggested that the animosity towards Obama was due to his race, White House Press Secretary Robert Gibbs responded by explaining that it was not Obama's view that the criticism that he received was due to the color of his skin. The reaction of the White House was typical of Obama's approach of avoiding the topic of race.

The interesting aspect of Trump's campaign is that polling data showed that Trump had a larger percentage of African American votes in 2016 than Romney and McCain had when they ran. The percentage was still much lower than it had been for other Republican candidates of the past, but the slight increase demonstrated the degree to which African American voters had become dissatisfied with the Democratic Party.

Part of Trump's appeal to African American voters was the frustration with the way that the Democratic Party had treated African Americans. This was especially an issue in 2016 given that Clinton had supported the 1994 crime bill which was signed by her husband when he was president. In response to the issue of crime in America, the 1994 crime bill was passed. The bill was meant to address the issue of crime in the African American community. The problem with the bill was that its harsh measures ended up having an adverse impact on the lives of some African Americans. Edward Douglas, for example, was sentenced to life in prison after three drug convictions. The law was meant to address the problem of violent crime, but in doing so it also targeted drug offenders who were not violent criminals. Douglas was later released due to a criminal justice reform law which was signed by Trump. The legacy of the 1994 bill was that it expanded mass incarceration in America and this was a bill which was signed into law by a Democratic president.

Obama was in a difficult situation in which some white people would have never accepted him for who he was, yet he also faced criticism from segments of the black community who felt dissatisfied with Obama's handling of racial issues in America. There was a sense that not enough had been done to address racism in America during Obama's presidency.

Obama's relationship with Africa has also been shaped by the view that he had not done enough for African Americans. During a visit to Kenya, Obama spoke of rights for homosexuals and compared their struggle to the civil rights struggle in America. Obama was well-received in Ethiopia and Kenya, but there were those who rightfully noted that Obama should be concerned about the suffering of black people in America. This was reported by the BBC in an article titled, "Young Africans to Obama: 'Clean your own house first'". As the headline indicated, the view was that before Obama lectured Africa on human rights, he should have ensured the safety and rights of African Americans.

When asked about Obama's legacy, Glen Ford argued that Obama's presidency demonstrated to black people that appeals to power were ineffective and that what was needed was a mass movement "from below". He saw this as a "second coming" of a mass movement which had not been seen in America in forty years. In Ford's view, Obama belonged to what he referred to as the black "mis-leadership" class. This class included the likes of Jesse Jackson, who was booed when he went to Ferguson. Ford saw this a victory of the movement because it delegitimized the leaders like Jackson and others who seek to collaborate with the powers that be.

What was apparent in 2016 was that there was a prevailing sense that not enough had changed during Obama's presidency. Obama explained that he understood the frustrations of the Occupy Wall Street protests, but what did understanding these protests mean to Obama given that he was given $400,000 from Wall Street for a speaking engagement? Obama's appeal as president was his apparent sympathy with the American people, yet he also displayed the distance from the American people which led to the type of frustrations seen by the Occupy Wall Street protesters. There is not only a sense that wealth inequality is a serious problem, but that America's political leaders are poorly positioned to confront the problem because of their close ties to Wall Street. Obama demonstrated this the money he took from Wall Street.

The disappointment with Obama's presidency gave Bernie Sanders and Donald Trump a certain appeal among those who were frustrated with the political system. They both represented an apparent break with the status quo. Clinton, however, struggled with the fact that she had worked in the Obama administration and she represented the status quo. When Obama ran against Clinton, he had used Clinton's ties with lobbyists as a point of attack. Clinton's ties with the establishment continued to represent a problem for her. One of the issues which came up when she was running was the disclosure that she had been given over $600,000 for three speeches she gave for Goldman Sachs. Clinton dismissed this by stating she gave speeches to lots of groups. When questioned about how much she was paid, Clinton drew laughter from the crowd by stating, "that's what they offered." Sanders pointed out that while Clinton was being paid for her speeches, he was working on legislation to break up the fraudulent operators who were responsible for the recession.

There was also the matter of the intervention in Libya. Obama admitted that the aftermath of the intervention was his worst mistake of his presidency. Clinton could not own this mistake because it would have obviously hurt her politically, so she took the position of trying to defend her role in the intervention while also shifting the blame on Obama. On the debate stage, she attempted to justify the intervention by stating that it resulted in

Libya hosting two elections. She also pointed to the experts who were sent to Libya to help establish a government in Libya. When Sanders pointed to the unintended consequences of regime change, Clinton distanced herself from the intervention in Libya by stating that it was Obama's decision. It may have been Obama's decision, but Clinton publicly joked about the demise of Gaddafi, which indicated her approval. The situation was not so funny when the American embassy in Libya had to be evacuated due to fighting in Libya between rival militias. It was not only Sanders who seized on the opportunity to criticize Clinton. Trump also criticized the result of intervention in Libya.

In the view of some, Obama should be remembered as one of the worst presidents in the nation's history. Ben Quayle stated publicly that Obama is the worst president in history. This view was repeated by Donald Trump. When Obama stated that Trump was "unfit" to serve for president and that he was "woefully unprepared", Trump responded by stating that Obama was maybe the worst president in American history.

Is Obama the worst president in the history of America? In the discussion of worst presidents ever, Warren G. Harding's presidency comes to mind. It was rumored that Harding was having extramarital affairs and even had a child with one of these women. The biggest issue with his administration were those whom he appointed. He appointed his political supporters to positions in the government. These men became known as the "Ohio Gang." The most notable scandal which came out of Harding's administration was the Teapot Dome scandal in which Albert Fall enriched himself after taking bribes from two oil companies. For this, he was imprisoned, becoming the first member of a presidential cabinet to be sentenced. Jess Smith, who was the aid to the attorney general, was exposed for selling illegal permits to bootleggers who were selling alcohol. Charles Forbes, who was charged with overseeing the development of veterans' hospitals, took bribes from construction companies.

I specifically point to Harding's scandal filled presidency because of Trump's own scandalous record. One need only look at the Trump University scheme which marketed itself as a school to educate students on how to become successful. The university later closed and then faced lawsuits from former students who felt misled by the university. This was the man whom the American people elected as president.

Outside of questionable business decisions, Trump's candidacy also divided the Republican Party. Trump refused to support fellow Republicans Paul Ryan and John McCain in their primaries. There was also the fact that Trump's past support for Democrats was well-known. Trump praised the presidency of Bill Clinton and had donated money Hillary Clinton's campaign. Trump's defense of his past support for Democrats was to point out that he had also donated money to Republican politicians as well. Trump had even given money to some of the opposing candidates during the Republican primary. This gave the impression that Trump was a man with no political loyalties. Trump reinforced this view when he refused to pledge not to run as an independent if he lost the Republican nomination.

Obama was correct. Trump simply was unfit for office. This is the man who promised to build a wall on the border with Mexico and to have Mexico pay for the wall. How this was to be accomplished was not clear, but not that the details mattered to Trump. Facts did not matter either. Trump lied so frequently that the *New York Times* was forced to add footnotes to correct remarks which were made by Trump and Trump's press secretary. The dishonesty and paranoia which Trump cultivated among his followers resulted in a violent attempt to overturn the election results in 2020 when Trump lost. Trump refused to concede defeat and claimed that the election had been stolen.

For African Americans who wanted to see a black man hold the office of the presidency, Obama filled the role and he filled it well. By this I mean that Obama carried himself honorably. His presidency was nothing like Bush's calamitous presidency and certainly nothing like Trump's presidency. For this, I can honor Obama. I also agree with the critics that Obama had not done enough to create meaningful change either. He promised change, but his presidency merely upheld the status quo.

16

THE TRIPLE HERITAGE IN AFRICA

Abrahamic religious faiths have helped to shape the experiences of African people. For example, a number of prominent leaders were Christians. This included Harriet Tubman, Martin Delany, Nat Turner, Sam Sharpe, Marcus Garvey, and Anton Lembede to name a few. These were men and women who drew inspiration from Christianity in their struggle for freedom. Christianity became a dominant religion in Ethiopia when Ezana of Axum embraced the religion. Kaleb, who ruled several years after Ezana, was such a staunch defender of the faith that around 520, he invaded Yemen to oust a Jewish ruler named Yusuf Asar Yathar for persecuting the Christian population. Ethiopia's Christian tradition and Ethiopia's historical link to the Solomonic dynasty of the Bible was a significant influence on the development of the Rastafarian movement in the Caribbean. In "Blackman Redemption," Bob Marley sang about how Haile Selassie of Ethiopia descended from the root of King David. In this song, he was singing about this link between Ethiopia and Solomon.

In his book, *The Souls of Black Folk*, W.E.B. Du Bois gave the following description of his first experience with a Negro revival: "The black and massive form of the preacher swayed and quivered as the words crowded to his lips and flew at us in singular eloquence. The people moaned and fluttered, and then the gaunt-cheeked brown woman beside me suddenly leaped straight into the air and shrieked like a lost soul, while round about came wail and groan and outcry, and a scene of human passion such as I had never conceived before."

Du Bois also explained that the "Negro church of to-day is the social centre of Negro life in the United States, and the most characteristic expression of African character." He continued to note: "Take a typical church in a small Virginia town: it is the 'First Baptist'—a roomy brick edifice seating five hundred or more persons, tastefully finished in Georgia pine, with a carpet, a small organ, and stained-glass windows. Underneath is a large assembly room with benches. This building is the central club-house of a community of a thousand or more Negroes. Various organizations meet here,—the church proper, the Sunday-school, two or three insurance societies, women's societies, secret societies, and mass meetings of various kinds. Entertainments, suppers, and lectures are held beside the five or six regular weekly religious services. Considerable sums of money are collected and expended here, employment is found for the idle, strangers are introduced, news is disseminated and charity distributed."

The observations made by Du Bois demonstrated the importance of the church as not only a place of religious worship, but as an institution which served the needs of the community. Many years later, in his book *The Falsification of Afrikan Consciousness*, Amos Wilson made a similar point about the role of the church in the life of black people. He explained: "So the church is not separated from money and economics by any stretch of the imagination. This means that we, as Black people, have the right to redefine the Church in ways that advance our interests, not only economic interests, but social, political, and many other interests in our lives." Wilson continued to note that there were examples of churches which were creating housing.

These quotes from Du Bois and Wilson show that the church became a very powerful institution in the lives of African Americans. The church institution among African Americans was one which emerged during slavery. One of the earliest examples of a prominent black preacher was George Liele, who was born in 1750. His master Mr. Sharp was a deacon in a Baptist church. Liele himself was a Baptist who came to prominence as a Baptist missionary. He founded the first Baptist church in Savannah and then went to Jamaica to establish the first Baptist church there.

Another early black preacher was Andrew Bryan, who was often persecuted for his teachings. It was stated: "Their evening assemblies were broken up and those found present were punished with stripes. Andrew Bryan and Sampson, his brother, converted about a year after him, were twice imprisoned, and they with about fifty others were whipped. When publicly whipped, and bleeding under his wounds, Andrew declared that he not only rejoiced to be whipped, but would gladly suffer death for the cause of Jesus

Christ, and that while he had life and opportunity he would continue to preach Christ." Bryan would not be deterred from his preachings. He represented the determination of many black Christian preachers to sustain their faith in the face of racism.

Islam has also shaped Africa's history. The ruling class of prominent kingdoms such as Mali, Songhai, Kanem-Bornu, Sokoto, and Fouta Djallon all embraced Islam. The 1835 Malê Revolt in Brazil was a revolt led by enslaved Muslims. The Nation of Islam rose to prominence as an Islamic organization in the United States. Out of the Nation of Islam came prominent voices in the African American struggle such as Elijah Muhammad, Malcolm X, Muhammad Ali, and Louis Farrakhan. Mahmoud Muhammad Taha of Sudan stands out as a prominent anti-colonial leader. He was a Muslim religious leader as well. I cite some of these examples to show how Christianity and Islam have shaped the history of Africans at home and abroad.

Ali Mazrui stated that Africa's religious tradition was a "triple heritage". By this he was referring to the historical influence of Christianity and Islam, as well as the numerous traditional African religions. The purpose of this essay is to show how these three traditions can be compared and contrasted with each other.

Christianity and Islam are Abrahamic religions. Abrahamic religions refer to religions which worship the God of the Bible who revealed himself to Abraham. The Abrahamic faiths all perceive God as not only the being who created the universe, but as a being with very human feelings such as jealousy and anger. The wrath of the Abrahamic God is seen throughout the Bible. For example, when Joshua seized Eglon, he killed everyone in the city. He did the same to Hebron, where the Bible states that Joshua killed everyone and left no survivors (Joshua 10:34-37). These violent actions are carried out with the approval of God. The God of Abraham in the Bible is described as being compassionate, forgiving, and slow to anger, yet God also does not leave the guilty unpunished (Exodus 34:6-7). God is also described as being jealous and vengeful (Nahum 1:2). The God of Abraham is in fact so vengeful that he was willing to wipe out most of the human population to punish humanity for its evil (Genesis 6).

It may seem difficult to reconcile this depiction of a loving God with a God who is willing to engage in and condone such destructive violence, but the Bible continually presents God's wrath as being in response to human disobedience of God, beginning with Adam and Eve. The message of the Old Testament is that humanity's suffering has been caused by disobedience to God. This message is conveyed through the rise and fall of Israel. Though the Israelites are God's chosen people, their continued disloyalty to God causes their downfall. It also causes many of them to be brutally punished by God. For example, in Numbers 11:1-3, God kills some of the Israelites who complain about him. Moses had to intercede and pray to God to make God stop.

The strict nature of God in the Old Testament is demonstrated in the Book of Leviticus which sets forth laws for the Hebrews to live by. Chapter 20 of Leviticus deals with punishments for the violations of these laws. In this book, it is commanded that men who engage in adultery should be put to death along with the woman that they committed the act with; men who have sex with their father's wife should be put to death with the wife; men who marry a woman and her mother must be burned in a fire with the two women; and men who have sex with animals must be killed along with the animal. The laws are meant to uphold strictest form of sexual morality among the Hebrew people by imposing death for violating such morals.

Of the punishments in Leviticus, the most controversial would be the command that men who engage in sex with other men must be put to death, which is found in Leviticus 20:13. The reason why I state this is the most controversial is that this has formed the basis of the very violent oppression which homosexuals have endured from Christians. Prior to the spread of Christianity in Europe, same-sex behavior was generally tolerated in Europe. This changed with the spread of Christianity. Justinian was a Christian emperor who closed the philosophical schools in the Greek cities because he regarded them as relics of paganism. Justinian also brutally punished men who engaged in homosexuality. Alfonso X of Spain ordered that sins against nature were to be punished by castration and stoning. In 1206, France outlawed homosexuality. Those who violated this law could have certain body parts removed or even be burnt alive at the stake.

Christianity has also resulted in similar prejudices against homosexuals in Africa. For example, Robert Mugabe, who was a Christian, denounced homosexuality as a Western import. A commentator named Kendall countered this view by arguing that homophobia and Mugabe's Christianity were both Western imports to Africa. The reality is that even in some pre-Christian African societies, homosexuality was viewed negatively. For example, among the Shona people, the term *kutamba chete* (just playing) was used to describe same-sex activities. Marc Epprecht explained that: "'Just playing' among Shona adults in the normal circumstances of precolonial life was almost certainly very rare, highly disapproved of, and almost never talked about. Indeed, homosexuality in adults (as opposed to adolescents) seems to have been regarded as a form of witchcraft, an otherwise inexplicable exception to the normal moral order. Children were sternly warned to stay away from men rumored to do such things (although absolutely not told why)." Epprecht further noted that for a woman to avoid heterosexual marriage, that woman had to become a healer or a prophetess. Otherwise, women were expected to engage in heterosexual marriages. The point here is that there was already a negative view of homosexuality in some parts of Africa even before the colonial influence and spread of Christianity, but it is also important to note that in African societies there generally was not the same level of violent persecution against homosexuals prior to the spread of Abrahamic religions in Africa.

Kwame Ture quoted Sekou Toure, who stated: "*À chaque peuple sa culture.*" This means that each people have their own culture. In Ture's view, the nature of Africa's culture was one of tolerance and that the persecution of homosexuals was really a European problem rooted in Europe's culture of intolerance. Ture noted that the tolerance for homosexuality among African people was such that even ministers of the Nation of Islam such as Malcolm X and Louis Farrakhan spoke of James Baldwin with respect though Baldwin was a homosexual. Even though African cultures have tended to be tolerant regarding homosexuality, African nations which have been influenced by Abrahamic religions have adopted a more intolerant view of homosexuality, hence why homosexuality was criminalized in certain African nations.

The harsh nature of these laws in Leviticus should be seen in terms of the continued disobedience which the Hebrew people displayed towards God. These measures were meant to discourage sinful activities from among the Hebrew people, but despite of the harsh punishments which were imposed, the Hebrew people would continue to violate the terms of their covenant with God, as well as violating some of the strict laws which God imposed on the Hebrews.

The rejection of God by the chosen people is a theme which continues in the New Testament as well. The Gospels themselves are explicit about the fact that Jesus' message of salvation was unpopular among some of the Jews of his day. Jesus was nearly killed in Nazareth for pointing out that no prophet is ever accepted in his hometown. He was forced to escape through a crowd to avoid being thrown off a cliff (Luke 4:14-30). On another occasion, some Pharisees tried to entrap Jesus by asking him if it was lawful to pay taxes. They were hoping that Jesus would say no so that they could have Jesus arrested (Matthew 22:15–22).

Jesus finally was arrested and was brought before Pontius Pilate. The account of what happened next differs slightly among the four Gospels. In Luke's account, Pilate sent Jesus to Herod since Jesus was from Galilee, which was under Herod's jurisdiction. Neither Pilate nor Herod found any basis to charge Jesus, but the Jewish crowd insisted that Jesus should be crucified and so Pilate granted their demand (Luke 23:1-25). In Mark's account, Pilate orders for Jesus to be executed in order to satisfy a Jewish crowd which shouted for Jesus to be crucified (Mark 15:1-15). In the account of the crucifixion given in Matthew, Pilate washed his hands in front of the crowd to display that he is innocent in killing Jesus and that Jesus' execution was the responsibility of the crowd (Matthew 27: 22-25). In John's account, the Jewish leaders insisted that Jesus must die because he violated Jewish law by claiming to be the Son of God. In John's account, Pilate tried to save Jesus, but the Jewish crowd shouted that if Pilate let Jesus go then it would mean that Pilate was opposed to Caesar. The crowd rejected the notion that Jesus was their king, explaining that they had no king but Caesar (John 19:7-

16). These four accounts differ in some respects, but they all demonstrate that Jesus was crucified because a Jewish crowd demanded it.

The Jewish rejection of Jesus serves as a continuation of the rejection of the prophets in the Old Testament. By sending Jesus, God is once again providing Jews with an opportunity to be redeemed, but they once again reject God. This rejection is displayed in a very brutal manner with the death of Stephen. Stephen was a follower of God who faced opposition from a synagogue of Jews. They falsely claimed that Stephen had spoken against God and seized him. A false witness was also brought against Stephen (Acts 6:8-15). In defense of himself, Stephen denounced his accusers by pointing out that the Jews had rejected Moses (Acts 7:39). He continued to denounce his accusers of being just like their ancestors who persecuted the prophets (Acts 7:51-52). Stephen was subsequently stoned to death. As he died, Stephen prayed that God forgive those who were stoning him (Acts 7:54-60).

The Qur'an is also similarly critical of Jews for their rejection of Jesus. Despite identifying Jews as people of the book, the Qur'an is critical of the Jews for rejecting the prophets of God, including Moses and Jesus (Qur'an 2:87-92). Unlike Christians, Muslims do not believe that Jesus is the son of God who was killed and resurrected, but Muslims do believe that Jesus was born of Mary and is the Messiah (Qur'an 3:42-45). Muslims also believe that Jesus will come again (Qur'an 43:61-64). For Christians and Muslims, the fate of the Jewish people serves as a warning about disobedience to God.

The murder of Jesus represents the continuation of the religious theme of the Jewish rejection of prophets, but it also reflected the politics of the day as well. Jesus was killed not only because of the Jewish crowd which rejected him, but also because his message was perceived as being in opposition to Caesar, which is why it was the Roman state which oversaw Jesus' execution. Based on the accounts of the Gospels, Pilate knew that Jesus was innocent and had the power to release Jesus, but he had Jesus executed anyway.

Christianity emerged out of Judaism with a new message of redemption and salvation. Whereas the Old Testament tells the story of a people who were punished for turning against God, the New Testament is a story of salvation brought to humanity through the sacrifice of Jesus. The story of Jesus' death and resurrection is central to the doctrine of Christianity, for Christians believe that it was due to this sacrifice that humanity was saved. Romans chapter five explains that Jesus' death saved humanity from God's wrath— here again we see the theme of God's wrath. Jesus' sacrifice is also rooted in the Jewish tradition of symbolic sacrifices. For instance, in the Old Testament, Aaron places his hands on a goat and confesses over the goat all of the sins of the Israelites. The goat is then released in the wilderness, symbolizing that the goat is carrying away the sins of the Israelites (Leviticus 16:21-22). This is where the concept of a scapegoat comes from. The scapegoat is made to carry the burden for issues which the goat itself did not cause. Jesus became the scapegoat, who was sacrificed to redeem humanity of our sins.

After Judaism and Christianity then came Islam. Islam drew from both Judaism and Christianity. Like Jews, Muslims believe in a strictly monotheistic religion which views God as a singular entity, rather than a trinity. Christianity teaches that the God of Abraham exists as three distinct entities: the Father, the Son, and the Holy Spirit (Matthew 28:19). Islam teaches that God is indivisible (Qur'an 112:1) and Jesus was no more than a messenger for God (Qur'an 5:75). Like Christians, Muslims developed a universal religion which was meant for the salvation of all of humanity. Whereas Judaism is a religion which is centered around the covenant between God and his chosen people, Christianity and Islam came into the world as universal religions for all of humanity.

The introduction of Islam into Africa did produce certain social changes. Among the Bamum people, Islam was introduced under the rule of King Njoya. Njoya accepted Islam rather than Catholicism and Protestantism because Islam allowed for marriage to many women. Catholic and Protestant clergymen advised Njoya to divorce his wives to marry only one woman, but he refused. Islam did not interfere with the Bamum practice of polygamy, but Islam did alter other marital traditions. In Bamum society, marriages were arranged by a women's parents. The introduction of Islam allowed women to choose their own husbands. The introduction of Islam also put an end to the Bamum trade of palm wine since Muslims were forbidden from consuming alcohol.

Under Bamum tradition, all those who were not part of the royal family were regarded as slaves of the ruling class. A member of the ruling class could freely kill an ordinary citizen and seize their property. The introduction of Islam resulted in certain protections for ordinary citizens. For example, Njoya banned the practice of burying a king with living people because this was regarded as a form of slavery. Njoya also abolished the practice of having men carry the king because he felt that this was a form of slavery. Such protections were not extended to non-Muslims, however. The Bamum Muslims believed that selling non-Muslims into slavery was not a sin because the non-Muslims were infidels.

Christianity and Islam present themselves as divinely revealed absolute truths which must be spread throughout the world for the salvation of others. As such, believers of these religions are called to proselytize to convert others so that they too may find salvation through these faiths. In the Bible, Jesus commands his disciples to make disciples of all nations (Matthew 28:16-20). The Qur'an also encourages Muslims to invite others to join the religion (Qur'an 16:125). To be clear, both religions are opposed to forced conversion. In Matthew 10:14, Jesus told his disciples to depart from those who refuse to listen to their words. He did not command his disciples to impose their wills on those who did not listen. The Qur'an (Qur'an 2:256) states that there is to be no compulsion in religion. Chapter 109 of the Qur'an states, "My religion is for me and your religion is for you." Even so, these commands have not stopped adherents of these faiths from forcibly converting others. An example of forced conversions being carried out was in the Ottoman Empire, which maintained an infantry corps of boys who were captured and forcibly converted to Islam. This forced conversion was not only done to spread the religion of Islam among those who were under Ottoman rule, but to also ensure that the boys became effective soldiers for the Ottoman Empire.

The history of violent extremism from Christians and Muslims led John Henrik Clarke to denounce these religions as "male chauvinist murder cults, brought into countries by invaders, foreigners, fakers, and fools." He also stated: "Every new belief system or religion that was brought into Afrika, ultimately did Afrika more harm than good." Clarke did clarify that his issue was not with religion itself, but with how religions have been misused: "I'm not preaching against the religion. I'm preaching against the misuse of it, and the lack of understanding of it."

Of Islam, Clarke stated: "Islam did not have to be an endorser of slavery." This quote stood out to me given that the Qur'an actually encourages the freeing of slaves (Qur'an 2:177). The Qur'an also commands that slave girls are not to be forced into prostitution (Qur'an 24:33). The Qur'an does not outright abolish slavery, but it did encourage slave owners to be more humane in the treatment of their slaves, which would indicate that in the early formation of Islam there was a sense that the practice of slavery needed to be reformed in a way which was more humane. Even though Clarke saw religion as being more harmful for Africa than helpful, he still expressed the belief that religions could be used as a tool for good: "I believe in all religions that are honest. I think all religions can be and should be instruments of liberation. I grant that every person has the right to use it, other than to be misused by it."

The call to convert others certainly contrasts with West African religions which value secrecy where religious knowledge is concerned. As Anne Bailey noted, "a systematic set of creeds and sacred scriptures is often absent, or at least unavailable to the general public." An example of the secrecy involved in African religion is the Yewe cult of the Ewe people. Those who are initiated perform a ritual in a secret compound and only those who have a special password are permitted to enter. Initiates undergo a period of training which lasts several months and during this time they are kept separate from their family. The outside public is only given some elements of the cult so as to attract new members. One of the reasons why individuals joined the Yewe cult was the freedom which the group offered. For example, women who wanted to escape an arranged marriage would join the Yewe cult to gain more freedom in selecting a partner.

African religions tend to be more tolerant, so in African religions one does not find too many examples of the type of religious violence which is more commonplace in the history of Christianity and Islam. For example, the lengthy history of prejudice against Jews in Europe was rooted in religious discrimination. This prejudice against Jews was demonstrated in 1492 when the Spanish monarch issued the Alhambra Decree. This decree gave Jews the choice to either convert to Christianity or to leave Spain. This would represent yet another example forced conversion.

Yet another difference is the approach to prophets. Abrahamic religions are largely based on the messages of religious prophets who came to preach the message of God. The messages of these prophets are to be found in the holy books, which are the Bible and the Qur'an. Some of the most prominent prophets are Moses who led the Hebrews out of slavery in Egypt, Samuel who was an early king maker for the Israelites, Jeremiah who cautioned the Hebrews that their exile in Babylon was punishment from God, and Daniel who rose to prominence in the court of Babylon as an interpreter of dreams. Muslims regard Muhammad as the last prophet of Allah.

African religions by contrast did not produce religious prophets whose teachings formed the basis of the core religious beliefs in African religions—it was already noted that African religions tended not to have a systematic set of creeds. This is not to suggest that Africans did not have prophets or prophecies. An example of a prophet in African religions which I have written about was a Xhosa leader named Nongqawuse. Nongqawuse called on the Xhosa people to kill their cattle and plant no crops. The purpose of this was to revitalize the Xhosa nation, but it resulted in people starving to death. This was a case in which the preachings of a self-professed prophet became destructive to the nation. In Xhosa society, the executions of prophets were carried out to check the influence of prophets who could undermine the power of the ruling class.

African religions have been sometimes identified as being animistic due to the belief that objects such as trees contain spirits. As Mary Kingsley explained: "To the African there is perhaps no gap between the conception of spirit and matter, animate or inanimate. It is all an affair of grade—not of essential difference in essence." European observers referred to African religion as juju (from the French word joujou, which means doll) and fetishism (from the Portuguese word feitiço and the Latin word factitious which referred to a magically artful). These terms conveyed the view that African religions were defined by the African veneration of objects such as trees and idols. Kinglsey observed that Africans not only believed that objects had spirits, but also that spirits within these objects could be weakened or killed. One example she gave was that some Africans would place rubbing medicine on a weapon to strengthen the spirit within the weapon.

Many African religions also believe in a powerful divine creator, though they are not strictly monotheistic in that they also venerate spirits and other less powerful deities. The Yoruba, for example, view Olorun as the creator of the universe. The Yoruba people also believe in Orishas which are spirits which are also venerated by the Yoruba people. Whereas God in the Abrahamic tradition is directly involved in human affairs, Olorun does not concern himself with the affairs of men, so the Yoruba look to the Orishas as intermediaries. The Akan people refer to God as Nyame. Nyame is also worshipped through intermediaries known as the abosom. Similarly, the Oromo people refer to God as Waka and believe that the ayana are spirits which serve as meditators between humans and Waka. Among the Fon, Mawu-Lisa is the creator deity, but they also believe in other deities such as Legba. In Vodun ceremonies, Legba is invoked and offered a sacrifice, which is often a chicken or a goat.

Unlike the Abrahamic religions, God in most African religions does not play an active role in human affairs, as the following quote indicates: "Most classical African religions involve belief in a supreme being who created the world and its inhabitants but who then retired from active intervention in human affairs." Apart from a belief in spirits, African religions often view ancestors as the link between the world of the living and the world of the divine. They also view ancestors as intervening in daily affairs.

Religion in Africa was often connected to the political power of the ruling class. The pharaohs of Egypt, for example, were viewed as god-kings who had a connection to the divine. George

Steindorff explained: "From time immemorial the Egyptian king had been considered the lord of the world. He was held to be the embodiment of the falcon-god Horus [...]." Amenhotep III, in particular, was worshipped as the "living image of Re on earth". The role of the pharaoh in Egypt was not only that of a political leader, but a religious leader as well. The pharaoh participated in religious festivals and oversaw the building of temples which were dedicated to the gods. The pharaoh was also expected to uphold Maat, which was the Egyptian concept of justice.

The pharaoh of Egypt was viewed as a divine figure, but religion in Egypt was somewhat decentralized in that each city, town, and village had its own local god. Akhenaten later challenged the polytheistic nature of Egyptian society when he introduced a monotheistic religion centered around the worship of Aton.

In the religion of the Bushongo people, the world was created by Chembe (God) who is called Bumba. Much like the pharaoh of Egypt, the ruler of Bushongo was viewed as a divine figure as well, being dubbed "God on earth." The ruler of Oyo was also seen as having a connection to the divine. Samuel Johnson stated: "The person of a King is regarded as sacred. Kings are venerated as gods, indeed many of them have been actually deified [...]." An example of a deified king was Shango, who was a ruler of Oyo.

That religion in African societies was used as a means to uphold the power of a ruling monarch demonstrated the political nature of religion in Africa. The political nature of religion is to be found in the Abrahamic traditions as well. After all, God's promise to the Hebrew people was land of their own where they would build a kingdom of their own. Religion, whether traditionally African or Abrahamic, is not only spiritual, but it is also deeply rooted in the politics and the culture of a people. This is demonstrated in the genealogy of Jesus which is given in Matthew 1 and Luke 1. The genealogy is listed to show that Jesus descended from the lineage of David. This is significant because Luke 1:26-33 clearly demonstrates that Jesus is to take the throne of David and to rule over Jacob's descendants. Jesus comes from royal lineage and is stated to be the king of the Jews (Matthew 2:2).

The political aspect of religion was apparent in the European colonization of Africa. This is demonstrated by Robert Pickering

Ashe who wrote *Chronicles of Uganda*. In that book, Ashe presented Islam as a hostile rival to the Christian religion, writing that "Christianity calm in the possession of the Light of the World, will patiently await its final triumph. But Muhammedanism will not brook any rival religion, and therefore must either conquer or be strongly held down. It must of necessity try conclusions with the sword. It takes the sword, and must either triumph or perish with the sword."

In Ashe's view, Islam was not only a theological rival, but a political one as well for Ashe believed that there was a risk in introducing a large number of Muslims into Uganda because of the danger of "a coalition between those of the same religion against native Christians and Europeans alike." This concern was warranted as the British in Uganda did face resistance from Muslims who were led by a Muslim named Selim Bey. Selim Bey was hired by the British colonial government to serve them in Uganda, but Selim Bey mutinied.

Religion also shaped the politics of Buganda. In his book, Ashe noted that Mutesa was hostile towards Islam. Mutesa initially welcomed Arab traders and even learned to read the Qur'an, but he later became hostile towards the religion. Ashe noted that whereas Mutesa was hostile towards Islam, Mutesa's son Mwanga became hostile towards Christianity. The hostility that both leaders displayed towards these religions was not hostility towards the religions themselves, but a hostility rooted in a concern that these religions would be used to undermine the authority of Buganda's ruler. Ashe held the view that Mwanga "had allowed himself to fall completely under the influence of Arab traders and the old heathen chiefs." The reality is that Mwanga was just as cautious of the Muslim influence in his kingdom as he was of the Christian influence. Both Mutesa and Mwanga seemed to have recognized that foreign religious influences posed a threat to their traditional authority.

According to Ashe's account, Mutesa admitted to a missionary named Mackay that he did not personally believe in the deities of Buganda, but he could not oppose the influence of his queen mother and the chiefs. It could have possibly been the case Mutesa made such a statement to Mackay as part of an effort to win over Christian support as a means to check the Islamic Arabic influence while Mutesa also maintained the traditional religion in Buganda to secure his position in power. Whatever the case may have been, Ashe's book does demonstrate how Christianity, Islam, and the "heathenism" of Buganda maintained an uneasy coexistence with each other as each belief system contested for influence.

Much like Christianity and Islam, African religions also have their own conceptions of the afterlife. As stated before, ancestors were believed to intervene in the lives of the living. Some African religions even believed that ancestors were reborn. The Yewe cult among the Ewe people, for example, believe that when a member of the cult dies, that member is reincarnated within the family. Among the Yoruba people, this belief in the return of the ancestors is expressed in traditional names such as Babatunde (father returns) and Yetunde (mother returns). The concept of reincarnation does not exist in Abrahamic religions because Abrahamic religions believe that every individual represents a unique soul which lives and dies once. Hebrews 9:27 affirms that humans die but once. The understanding of some of the West African religions which believe in reincarnation is that ancestors are reborn within the same family through the birth of children. This is true in a sense, since the same genetic code which produced a child's ancestors is replicated within the newborn child. For this reason, the birth of a child is, in a sense, the return of an ancestor. Some Africans held the view that spirits passed into animals, as this example given by Mary Kinsley noted: "The Doctor told me he once knew a man whose plantations were devastated by an elephant. He advised that the beast should be shot, but the man said he dare not because the spirit of his dead father had passed into the elephant."

A common trait of African and Abrahamic religions is a desire to understand the world. This is one area where science and religion have clashed. Science concerns itself with what can be objectively proven through testing and experimentation, whereas religion operates on the basis of faith in the unseen and the unknown. The Hebrew word for faith is "emunah," which also means "certainty." This conveys the sense that having faith means having a degree of certainty in that which one cannot prove.

Followers of Abrahamic religions are called to have faith in the word of God and the teachings of the prophets, though the followers have not seen God (John 1:18)—it is curious that the New Testament states that no one has seen God given that Jacob was stated to have seen God in the Old Testament (Genesis 32:30). Faith in the Abrahamic tradition is so powerful that Jesus tells his followers that having faith like a grain of a mustard seed would be enough to move a mountain (Matthew 17:20).

The importance of faith in the Bible is demonstrated in the story of Job which is found in the Book of Job. In this story, God allows Satan to test Job by inflicting hardships upon him. Job loses his wealth, his children, and his health, but Job remained steadfast in his faith in God, however. For retaining his faith, Job was rewarded by being given more than he ever had before. Job's faith in God and the reward which he reaped is also mentioned in the Qur'an (Qur'an 21:83-84). Job not only came to represent strong faith in God, but also patience, as demonstrated by the Mighty Spoiler's reference to being more patient than Job in his song "Money in the Bank."

In the Qur'an, a clear distinction is made between believers and unbelievers. Chapter 9:23 instructs believers to not choose allies who are disbelievers. Chapter 2:221 instructs that believers are not to marry women who are polytheists until they become believers. The same passage also states that it is better to be a slave who believes than to be a free unbeliever for the unbelievers can only lead believers into the fire. These verses indicate just how important belief in Allah is.

In Christianity and Islam, a fiery punishment is the fate which awaits the non-believer. Revelation 21:8 states that those who lack faith or belief in God will be punished in a fiery lake along with cowards, murderers, and the sexually immoral. Chapter 2:39 of the Qur'an states that the disbelievers will become residents of the fire where they will remain forever. Chapter 98:6 states that not only will disbelievers from the people of the book burn in hell, but so too will polytheists.

Huey Newton stated: "Religion, perhaps, is a thing that man needs at this time because scientists cannot answer all of the questions. As far as I am concerned, when all of the questions are not answered, when the extraordinary is not explained, when the unknown is not known, then there is room for God because the unexplained and the unknown is God." Indeed, God and religion explain what man has struggled to explain and, as Newton noted, "as soon as the scientist develops or points out a new way of controlling a part of the universe, that aspect of the universe is no longer God."

It is true that African religions have practices and traditions which are rooted in unscientific superstitions. One backwards aspect of African religious practice was the tradition of twin killing. This was done out of the ignorant belief that twins were a bad omen since the birth of twins could not be scientifically explained by the societies which engaged in such practices. Concerning the previously mentioned prophecy of Nongqawuse, one commentator stated that superstition was "the black man's weakness". I would certainly argue that traditional African religious practices are at their worst when they inflict suffering and death to uphold superstitious ideas and beliefs, such as the belief that twins must be killed because they represent a bad omen.

Scientific knowledge certainly does dispel the more fantastical and superstitious aspects of religion, but science does not replace the philosophy of religion. Religions are not simply about believing in the supernatural. They often strive to provide a code of morality for a people to live by. This is not to suggest that religious belief is a necessity for one to be moral, but that religions concern themselves with how humans ought to behave and treat each other. The Qur'an, for example, described humanity as being touched with evil save for those who not only pray, but who give their share of wealth to the poor (Qur'an 40:19-25).

Christianity and Islam promote a system of celestial reward and punishment where those who are deemed worthy enough may enter an eternal paradise in the afterlife. Those who are wicked are punished for their actions in the afterlife. The concept of heaven and hell in Christianity and Islam demonstrate this system of reward and punishment. Both the Bible and the Qur'an refer to a fiery place of punishment where sinners are sent to suffer after they die. The concept of being judged in the afterlife was found in African religions as well. For the Egyptians, Osiris served as the judge of the dead. The Yoruba people also have a concept of judgement in the afterlife as well. This is expressed in the adage, "Whatever we do on earth we shall give an account therefor at the portals of heaven." It should be noted here that the concept of judgement in the afterlife is not universal across Africa. In the worldview of the Bafia people there was no afterlife, which meant no punishment in the life after death.

In the view of Erich Fromm, which was expressed in *To Have Or To Be?,* the preoccupation with the afterlife is rooted in the human striving for immorality. He wrote that "since we know by experience that we shall die, we seek for solutions that make us believe that, in spite of the empirical evidence, we are immortal." Fromm also argued that the desire to be famous is rooted in the quest for immortality as well. Whereas many religions believe in an immortal life after death, Fromm argued that history also became a substitute for heaven because fame guaranteed a bit of immorality. Whereas heaven in Christianity and Islam gives meaning to our lives because it ensures that if one lives a righteous life one is rewarded with paradise, fame ensures that if one if one's life has a great enough impact then that life will be remembered long after the individual is gone.

As Fromm noted, there is no empirical evidence of life after death. Obviously, the religious believe in life after death because faith compels them to believe in an afterlife which they cannot prove empirically just as faith compels the believer to believe in a divine being which cannot be proven empirically. This here is where Newton's point about God being the unexplained becomes important. The concept of an afterlife and the existence of a human soul implies that human consciousness can exist independently of a living human body. This is precisely an experience which some individuals have reported.

Those who have experienced near death experiences (NDEs) have reported having at out of body experience in which they report looking down upon their own lifeless body. Other aspects include seeing a light, going through a tunnel, meeting deceased relatives, seeing a being of light, and having a life review. After years of researching NDEs, Pim van Lommel concluded that consciousness was not located in the brain, but rather existed independently of the brain. This was because those who had NDEs were experiencing consciousness at a time when there was no brain activity.

Lommel's research is not empirical proof of life after death given that he was reporting on the experiences of those who came close to dying, but did not actually die. The reason why I mention Lommel's work in this context is to raise the point that the concept of an afterlife which is found in many of the world's religions is similar to what those who have experienced NDEs have described, which suggests that belief in an afterlife is rooted in actual experiences which individuals have had with coming close to death and meeting those who have already died. This is yet another example of religion attempting to explain what science has not yet been able to explain.

The point made thus far has been that African religions and Abrahamic religions are similar in certain aspects, even though there are many differences as well. As Mazuri noted, there is a triple heritage in Africa due to the influences of these religions. This triple heritage has not been an easy balance, however, given the previously mentioned drive by some Christians and Muslims to forcibly impose their religions on others. This balance is further complicated by the reality that Christianity and Islam in Africa were often introduced by European and Arab imperial forces which sought to subjugate African people and impose an alien culture in Africa. As such, Africans who have embraced these religions have at times become alienated from their own culture. Even so, there is no denying the significant impact which these religions have had on African people.

17

MIA MOTTLEY'S PAN-AFRICAN VISION

In 2017, when I hosted the first meeting of the Movement for Restoring the African Mind, one of the examples of uprisings on the part of African people which I mentioned were strikes which were taking place in Barbados. Unions were protesting against the austerity measures which were being implemented by the government. This was in July. In September there was a situation in which the Caribbean Broadcasting Corporation and the Barbados Workers' Union reached an impasse over a pay dispute which resulted in workers going on strike.

The protests demonstrated the mood of Barbados at the time. The people were ready for change and change came in 2018 when elections were held. The result was the election of Mia Mottley. The victory of Barbados Labour Party was no surprise to analysts who recognized the unpopularity of the government. What was somewhat surprising was that the Barbados Labour Party won all of the seats in the House of Assembly, which resulted in absence of the opposition. Mottley was reelected again in 2022. Her party again won all of the seats.

Following being reelected, Mottley acknowledged that her colleagues asked her how she was able to retain so much support from the people during the middle of an International Monetary Fund (IMF) program. She explained that she found a "sweet spot" which matched the will of the people with development by creating an environment in which Barbadians were willing to share the burden of adjustment together and were willing to share the "bounty of accomplishment" together.

Part of what has made Mottley so popular among the people of Barbados is her Pan-African and anti-colonial vision. This vision was displayed in a speech she gave in Ghana on June 19, 2023. She began by noting that this was an emotional moment for her because she remembered those who were stolen from Ghana and taken to Barbados. She recognized that she was representing the legacy of Pan-Africanism from those who came before her. This included Dr. Courtney Blackman, who served as the first governor of the Central Bank in Barbados. Mottley noted that he spent time in Ghana.

In her speech, Mottley spoke about the need to build economic connections between the Caribbean and Africa. She also spoke about utilizing unity to confront the challenge imposed upon African people by colonialism. She explained that the blame for the absence of connectivity can no longer be placed on the colonizers, but on those who are in power. In stating this, she acknowledged that it has to be the responsibility of African and Caribbean leaders to bring about unity.

Mottley's vision was further demonstrated not only by the fact that under her leadership the infamous statue of Horatio Nelson was finally removed, but that Barbados also became a republic. Both moves were necessary steps towards the decolonization of Barbados, a nation which was known as "Little England" due to its ties to the colonial master. The removal of the Nelson statue was something which was encouraging to activists such as David Comissiong and David Denny. Mottley's political success in Barbados, I would argue, demonstrates the appeal which her anti-colonial Pan-African vision has for the masses in Barbados.

Mottley represents the revolutionary spirit of the Pan-African movement, although Mottley herself is hardly a revolutionary, nor does she present herself as such. This very topic came up in a tribute which Mottley delivered for Bobby Clarke following his passing. Clarke was a political activist whom Mottley had great admiration for. She acknowledged that Clarke worked to ensure that the citizens of Barbados lived more comfortably.

In her speech Mottley noted that she came from a politically active family, so she was exposed to politics at an early age. She recalled that one of her earliest memories was the debate over the public order act which was designed to suppress the work which Clarke and Elombe Mottley were doing. Mottley also recalled seeing Maurice Bishop in her parents' house, with his head bandaged—this was no doubt the result of injuries Bishop sustained for his opposition to Eric Gairy's government in Grenada. Mottley explained that within her family, there were rebels who fought the establishment and those who became part of the establishment. Mottley expressed the belief that she took the best of both positions. This was an acknowledgement on Mottley's part that she was neither a rebel who sought to fight the establishment, nor was she unsympathetic to the radical calls for change. Mottley also acknowledged that as a politician she was forced to deal with "probabilities," whereas activists like Clarke were free to fight for "possibilities."

Mottley's tribute to Clarke was profound in that it was an acknowledgement that she was restrained in ways that a political activist such as Clarke was not. Mottley's polices in Barbados did not represent a break with the neoliberal policies which have stifled Caribbean nations such as Barbados. Mottley herself has acknowledged that she has had to navigate this reality. She did this with a degree of success during her first term, but there are obvious contradictions in Mottley's politics given that she has attempted to assert her anti-colonial vision within the framework of the very institutions which have worked to suppress that anti-colonial, Pan-African vision. Even so, one must grant Mottley's genuine belief in her vision and her belief that her pragmatic approach is, at least at the present moment, the most effective way to carry out her vision.

18

ON THE LENINIST VANGUARD PARTY

Leon Trotsky explained: "Marxism is a method of historical analysis, of political orientation, and not an ensemble of decisions prepared in advance. Leninism is the application of this method in the conditions of an exceptional historical epoch." Marxism-Leninism emerged as a synthesis of the ideas of Marx and Lenin. One of Lenin's important contributions to Marxist theory was concept of the Leninist vanguard party. This was a party which was designed to represent the interests of the working class. Huey Newton explained that the main purpose of "the vanguard group should be to raise the consciousness of the masses through educational programs and other activities. The sleeping masses must be bombarded with the correct approach to struggle and the party must use all means available to get this information across to the masses."

In theory, the vanguard was to do as Newton stated. It was to raise the consciousness of the masses. In practice, however, the vanguard was sometimes utilized for opportunistic purposes. This can be demonstrated by Ethiopia's example. After seizing power in Ethiopia, Mengistu Haile Mariam was initially hesitant to form a vanguard party, but one was eventually formed as a response to the armed opposition which the regime faced. When the vanguard party in Ethiopia was formed, it was dominated by former military personnel. This was contrary to the wishes of the Soviet Union, which urged the Ethiopian government to establish a vanguard party in the first place. The vanguard party was implemented solely to protect the Derg regime from counterrevolutionary efforts, not to guide the masses in the revolutionary struggle.

As it would turn out, the Derg was not interested in guiding any socialist revolution at all. Dawit Giorgis, who served as a minister for Mengistu, noted that senior government officials began to wear designer clothes from European tailors. They also lived in the best homes, had the best cars, and consumed the best champagne. Mengistu himself began to use fancy imported cars. As the Derg regime in Ethiopia preached Marxism-Leninism, its government officials lived lavishly at the expense of the Ethiopian peasantry. As all of this was taking place, a great deal of Ethiopia's resources was also wasted on combating the Eritrean secessionist effort which Ethiopia was losing. In 1988, in the span of two days, the Eritrean rebels killed and captured about 18,000 Ethiopian troops. Ethiopia's example demonstrates that far too often, Marxism-Leninism resulted in the emergence of totalitarian states in which the leadership exploited the masses under the justification of building a socialist workers' state.

The implosion of the revolution in Grenada raised questions about vanguardism among those within the Caribbean Left. These were concerns which were raised even before the implosion. For example, in 1982, Tim Hector had urged Maurice Bishop to break with vanguardism, but Bishop refused. Bishop declared: "Our revolution is not going to get bogged down in any ism or schism." The unfortunate reality is that this is precisely what happened to the revolution in Grenada and this ism schism resulted in Bishop being killed.

The New Jewel Movement (NJM) which seized power in Grenada was organized as a vanguard political party. Marxist-Leninist ideals were instilled in the masses through worker education programs. The programs were not well-received by everyone in Grenada, however. Some complained that the hours conflicted with Sunday church. Others complained that the concepts were taught as theories that were disconnected from the lived experiences of the people of Grenada. One worker stated that he wanted to learn more about his future as a worker in Grenada, but he didn't "care about that fellow Marx".

Part of the effort to build a vanguard party meant establishing party control over workers' efforts in Grenada. The revolutionary government supported unions, but also ensured that trade unions were controlled by the party. Bishop stated that five of the eight leading trade unions were under the leadership and control of members of the party.

Ultimately it was an internal conflict within the party in Grenada which resulted in the revolution unraveling. In

Contributing to Rethinking: Issues in the Communist Movement, Barry Chevannes admitted that the Workers Party of Jamaica (WPJ) was wrong on Grenada. Chevannes also noted that focusing on organizing the party without also being involved in the life of the people was a recipe for creating bureaucratic apparatchiks who are cut off from the people. Rupert Roopnarine of the Working People's Alliance of Guyana explained that the revolution in Grenada engaged in "making the majority within the vanguard a fetish and ignoring the majority among the masses".

Black Stalin's "Ism Schism" further demonstrated the lessons learned from Grenada. In the opening line of the song Black Stalin declared: "Grenada, Grenada the black man thanks you/Grenadians teach me my biggest lesson". The lesson was not to team with any ism. This was a profound statement from an artist who was so supportive of the revolution in Grenada that he received a letter of appreciation from Maurice Bishop. Stalin also joined Sparrow and Brother Valentino to put on a benefit performance to donate the proceeds to the government in Grenada.

In the case of Cuba, the established Marxist-Leninist ruling party did not offer space for any organizational efforts outside of the ruling party. This was an observation made by William Lee Brent when he was living in Cuba. Brent was a former member of the Black Panther Party who was expelled from the Party following his involvement in the robbery of a gas station. Brent decided that the best thing to do was to leave America. He decided to go to Cuba because Cuba "reportedly, had eliminated racism and welcomed all revolutionaries, regardless."

Brent skyjacked an airplane and forced the plane to land in Cuba in 1969. Brent subsequently spent nearly two years in prison on the suspicion that he was an American spy. In an interview with *Democracy Now!*, Brent stated: "There are no organized dissident groups operating in Cuba. There's no propaganda from any dissident groups. There is no black liberation movement going on in Cuba. I think there should be one all over the world. And every place that they got two black people, I think there should be a black liberation movement." He also noted the lack of a feminist movement in Cuba as well. Everything went through the Women's Federation.

As stated before, in theory the Leninist vanguard party exists to serve the interests of the masses. In practice, the vanguard party does pose the danger of being exploited by opportunists. It also poses the danger of the party being so focused on building the vanguard party that it alienates itself from the masses or stifles independent organization among the masses. This is not to suggest that opportunism and the alienation of the masses are necessarily unavoidable outcomes of building a vanguard party, but these are problems which have emerged.

19

IVAN VAN SERTIMA REVISITED

It is no secret that I have been critical of Ivan Van Sertima's book, *They Came Before Columbus*. In critiquing Van Sertima's work, I also want to make it clear that I am not completely dismissive of the idea that Africans could have sailed to the Americas before Christopher Columbus did. Van Sertima was not even the first person to posit such an assertion. In the 1800s, Martin Delany wrote: "And among the earliest and most numerous class who found their way to the New World, were those of the African race. And it is now ascertained to our mind, beyond a peradventure, that when the continent was discovered, there were found in Central America, a tribe of the black race, of fine looking people, having characteristics of color and hair, identifying them originally of the African race—no doubt being a remnant of the Africans who, with the Carthaginian expedition, were adventitiously cast upon this continent, in their memorable excursion to the 'Great Island,' after sailing many miles distant to the West of the Pillars of Hercules."

It was not clear which excursion Delany was referring to in the abovementioned quote or even which tribe he was referring to. The lack of clarity certainly makes it difficult to verify the claim which Delany made. It is possible that an excursion from Africa could have arrived in the Americas, but the reality is that there is little historical documentation which proves that Africans did manage to arrive in the Americas and this is my main critique of *They Came Before Columbus*. It is possible that Africans could have sailed to the Americas, but we simply do not know. As I have noted in prior critiques of *They Came Before Columbus*, Abu Bakr II of Mali left to sail the Atlantic Ocean, but he never returned home, so no one knows what became of him. Christopher Columbus' voyage was known to Europe because he returned to Europe. His voyage subsequently resulted in the establishment of connections between Europe and European settlements in the Americas. Purposed African voyages, however, are always based on the claim that Africans managed to sail to the Americas, but never returned back and never established connections. This is certainly demonstrated in the quote from Delany in which Delany explained that these African travelers were "discovered" in Central America. This would imply that the existence of these people was not previously known to those outside of Central America. Delany certainly does not suggest that this black tribe maintained any connection with Africa once they arrived in Central America.

Flawed though Van Sertima's claims may be, I do not think the entirety of what he argued should be dismissed insofar as it may very well have been possible that Africans sailed to the Americas. I certainly hope that my critiques of *They Came Before Columbus* are not seen as an attempt to inveigh against the premise that anyone but Europeans could have sailed to the Americas.

I also recognize that Van Sertima's work was part of the larger effort to challenge the narrative of Columbus being a great explorer. This is precisely what H. Rap Brown did when he wrote: "He was so dumb. He was trying to get to India. Did you ever see where India is on the map." The point Brown was making was that Columbus ended up in the Caribbean by accident. In making this statement, Brown was challenging the glorification of Columbus. Van Sertima went even further by suggesting that Columbus was not even the first explorer to sail to the Americas. Van Sertima's argument may have been flawed, but he did make an important contribution to the study of Africa's history simply for daring to posit the possibility that Africans could have reached the Americas before Columbus did.

20

A REVOLUTION BETRAYED IN NICARAGUA

In August 1986, President Daniel Ortega of Nicaragua headed a delegation to Burkina Faso. He was invited for an official dinner in which he was presented with Burkina Faso's highest award by Thomas Sankara. Sankara also made remarks during the occasion. In his speech, Sankara affirmed the common interests between Nicaragua and Burkina Faso, including their membership in the Group of 77 and the Nonaligned Movement. He also noted that he and Ortea had chosen to condemn colonialism, neocolonialism apartheid, racism, Zionism, and other forms of aggression. It was not Sankara alone who supported Ortega's government in Nicaragua. Maurice Bishop's government sent its internationalist brigade in Nicaragua to launch a literacy campaign.

This support for the government of Nicaragua came at a time when the nation was facing destabilization efforts led by the United States. The American government was providing funding for a violent rebel movement which was seeking to overthrow the government of Nicaragua. In 1986, Congress approved $100 million in military and other assistance for the contras, which indicated the degree to which American politicians were supporting the destabilization effort. Congress supported the contras in part out of a fear of being perceived as being too "soft on Communism". Ortega's decision to visit Moscow was also a factor in shaping congressional opinion on funding the contras.

The Sandinista government came to power in Nicaragua after overthrowing the dictator Anastasio Somoza in 1979. The Sandinista movement was supported by various segments of Nicaragua's society including peasants, artisans, intellectuals, and religious leaders. The revolution in Nicaragua which was led by Ortega was backed by a mass movement which transformed Nicaraguan society. In 1986, the government adopted a new constitution which established separation of powers, incorporated human rights declarations, and outlawed the death penalty.

Unfortunately, the gains of the revolution were not to last.

Nicaragua was facing a heavy burden due to the American supported contra rebellion. The war became a drain on Nicaragua's economy. To end the war, it was agreed that the contras be allowed to participate in the 1990 election. What followed was the shocking defeat of Ortega. The people of Nicaragua were tired of war and felt that the only way to end the conflict was to vote for the opposition. Even those who were sympathetic to the Sandinistas voted for the opposition to avoid conflict.

For 16 years Ortega remained in the opposition as Nicaragua was led by presidents who implemented neoliberal policies which dismantled the social and economic policies of the Sandinista era. Ortega remained in opposition until he won in 2006. Prior to the 2006 election, Ortega found himself reconciling with former political opponents in order to build up support. This included Cardinal Miguela Obando y Bravo. To demonstrate his change in position, Ortega converted to Catholicism and supported a ban on abortion, even in cases in which the mother's life is endangered. Ortega went even further to select Jaime Morales, a former contra leader, to be his vice president.

The shift in policy worked as Ortega was finally reelected, although he won with less than 40% of the votes. This shift also came with a change in policy. Mónica Baltodano, the leader of a dissident Sandinista organization, charged that Ortega's policies did not differ from previous governments. This was demonstrated by Ortega's decision to sign new accords with the International Monetary Fund, while failing to raise salaries for teachers and health workers.

Ortega's government also began to suppress dissent by harassing critics. Former Sandinistas who spoke out against Ortega's government became targets. This included Ernesto Cardenal, a priest and poet who formerly served as the minister of culture. Ortega had essentially embraced some of his old political enemies and betrayed his old political associates for the sake of regaining power in Nicaragua. By his actions, Ortega demonstrated that maintaining power was of greater importance to him than the ideals of the revolution. Ortega betrayed not only the people of Nicaragua, but also the international allies who supported Ortega in the face of an American destabilization effort. In an article titled "Et Tu, Daniel? The Sandinista Revolution Betrayed," Roger Burbach quoted José Saramago who wrote: "Once more a revolution has been betrayed from within." Burbach also compared Ortega's actions to that of Joseph Stalin's "desecration" of the Bolshevik revolution.

Burbach suggested that Ortega's betrayal reinforces Trotsky's view that revolution cannot survive in one nation alone. He arrived at this conclusion from the fac that it was ultimately the pressure which Nicaragua faced from America's counterrevolutionary efforts which caused the fall of the Sandinista government. There is also a lesson about the importance of commitment to the principles of the revolution. Ortega's betrayal is what happens when a revolutionary leader decides that retaining power itself becomes much more important than the principles of the revolutionary struggle.

21

THE EMPEROR OF HARLEM

Adam Clayton Powell was born in 1908. His father, Adam Clayton Powell, Sr., was the pastor of Abyssinian Baptist Church. Powell decided to follow his father and become a preacher in Harlem. Harlem at the time was deeply impoverished and struggling. Powell sought to address these problems by implementing a number of social services to assist the community. This included opening a soup kitchen, adult education, a mental health club, a job bank, and clothing.

Powell was not only a religious leader. He became a community activist as well. Powell and his church members organized pickets against businesses which refused to hire black people. This helped to provide employment opportunities for black people in businesses where they were previously unable to work. Malcolm X explained in his autobiography: "Adam Clayton Powell made it a big fight. He had successfully fought Consolidated Edison and the New York Telephone Company until they had hired Negroes." Powell also organized a bus boycott. This secured jobs for black drivers and mechanics.

Rev. Calvin Butts, who was himself a pastor of the Abyssinian Baptist Church, explained that, "everything that we are about as African people in terms of our struggle for justice and freedom started in the church." Butts did not believe that there was a separation between the scared and the secular for black America. This was displayed in Powell's own activism. He used the church as a means to mobilize for change.

Mobilizing for change not only meant organizing community aid programs and protesting for change. For Powell, creating change meant involving himself in politics. In 1941, Powell became the first black person elected to the New York City Council. When a new congressional district was created for Harlem, Powell was presented with the opportunity to advance his political career. He decided to run for the seat. In 1944, Powell was elected to the House of Representatives.

Powell proved to be an active legislator. This included putting an amendment on every piece of legislation which provided funding to segregated services. The "Powell Amendment" denied funds to states which segregated its facilities. Powell was also involved in efforts to combat lynching and voting taxes. His efforts resulted in the first black reporter getting into the Congressional press gallery and the first black cadet admitted to the Naval Academy. Powell also advocated for the integration of the army.

After 16 years in Congress, Powell became the chairman of the Education and Labor Committee. Powell's committee passed a number of bills. This included bills to build schools and libraries, as well as training the unemployed and establishing equal pay for equal work. In a span of five years, Powell's committee produced 60 pieces of legislation which were all passed by Congress. Powell's success in Congress made him one of the most powerful men in America.

Despite his success as a legislator, Powell was also a controversial figure as well. Though Powell was a Baptist preacher, he developed a reputation for being a womanizer. Powell's first wife was a show girl named Isabel Washington. Powell's father opposed the relationship because he felt that it was improper for a preacher to marry a show girl, but Powell insisted and married Isabel anyway. This would be the first of Powell's three marriages. Powell then married Hazel Scott, who was a jazz pianist. Powell and Scott lived a lavish life, which included attending shows on Broadway. Powell later divorced his wife and married yet again. This final marriage was to Yvette Flores Diago.

Powell's lavish lifestyle resulted in much scrutiny. In 1952, the Internal Revenue Service charged that Powell was underpaying his taxes. Powell was indicted in 1958 for his taxes. The case against Powell was dropped, but one of his aides was jailed. A second aide was also found guilty for tax evasion. Powell's travels also resulted in public criticism. In 1962, Powell set off for Europe along with two female aides, Corrine Huff and Tamara Wall—Powell would later develop a romantic relationship with Huff which ended when Huff left Powell for another man. Powell's wife was in Puerto Rico where she had just delivered their son. The trip elicited such an outcry that Powell ended the trip early to return home.

Powell openly reveled in the criticism which he received over his conduct. For example, it was known that Powell kept his wife on his payroll. When asked about having relatives on the payroll, Powell stated that it was "very good." Representative John Rankin labeled Powell's election as a disgrace. Powell responded to this by sitting next to Rankin whenever Rankin entered the chamber. It was reported that Rankin moved five times just to avoid Powell. Powell explained that being an irritant served a purpose. It certainly served a purpose for him. Powell would not allow himself to be controlled or tamed. Powell himself once joked that even God sometimes could not control the Negro Baptist preacher.

Powell's defiant attitude appealed to the black community. Julius Lester explained that the community saw Powell as someone who was willing to do battle on behalf of black people. John Henrik Clarke stated that Powell smeared his blackness in people's face. Clarke's remark is interesting considering that when he was in college Powell passed himself off as white before his racial background had been exposed. Once he became a public figure, Powell was unequivocal about his identity as a black man.

Powell's willingness to speak out against racism was demonstrated by his appearance in *The Hate That Hate Produced*. In that documentary, Elijah Muhammad denounced Christianity as a religion of enslavement. He expressed the view that black people are born Muslims by "nature". When asked about this, Powell expressed a critical view of Christianity in America. Despite being a Christian preacher, Powell acknowledged that Christianity in the United States was "determinantal" to solving racial problems in America because of the racial segregation which was practiced by churches in America. Malcolm X, who was also featured in the same documentary, admired Powell. Alex Haley recorded that Malcolm stated that he would think about retiring if there were ten black men like Powell in Washington. In an interview, Malcolm also stated, "Adam Clayton Powell is a remarkable man and has done a remarkable job in fighting for rights of black people in this country." Critical as he was of America's racism, Powell was also willing to defend America internationally. Powell attended the Bandung Conference in 1955. At the conference Powell defended race relations in America and blocked a Chinese effort to have the conference condemn American racism.

For a time, it seemed that Powell was above reproach. He was one of the most powerful political leaders in America. This power was rooted in the unquestioned support he received from the black community, but this support began to erode. Powell had always used his black identity to shield himself against criticisms from the white press, but this could no longer work as black people also began to question Powell. It also did not help matters that Powell would soon face competition for leadership of black America.

The development of the civil rights movement and the emergence of Martin Luther King presented a challenge to Powell's power. Up until this point, Powell benefitted from his position as a dominant figure in black politics, but the civil rights movement brought a new generation of leaders to the fore. It was now King, not Powell, who was viewed as the spokesman for black people in America.

The relationship between Powell and King became a contentious one. When King planned a protest at the Democratic convention, Powell took control of the situation by threatening to leak a story about a homosexual relationship between King and Bayard Rustin. The story was false, but the potential damage to King's reputation was enough to force King to put the plans for the protest on hold. It also demonstrated a vindictive side to Powell. James Farmer stated that Powell was neither moral or immoral, but that Powell was amoral. What Farmer meant by this was that for Powell it was not about doing what was right or wrong, but whatever would serve his purposes politically. In this situation, Powell was willing to smear King with a lie for the purpose of protecting the Democratic Party.

Powell's attitude towards King was a very dismissive one at times. Powell had labeled King as "Martin Loser King." At a press conference, when King's name was mentioned, Powell responded by asking, "Who?" When King's name was repeated, Powell remarked, "I remember him." Powell did express some admiration of King, however. On another occasion, Powell stated that King had done a "yeoman job." Powell also expressed the view that King was going through an agonizing reappraisal given that King did not belong to the "decadent aristocratic colonials" in the civil rights movement. This was an acknowledgment on Powell's part that King was a different type of leader from others in the civil rights movement.

Not only did it appear that Powell perceived King to be a potential threat to his influence in the black community, but there were ideological differences as well. Despite King's position as a leading figure in the struggle against racism, there were those in the community who broke with King's nonviolent approach. These individuals also rejected the integrationist objectives of King and others in the movement. King declared that he would remain committed to nonviolence even if every black person in the United States rejected nonviolence. Not only were black people rejecting nonviolence, but some were even rejecting King himself.

Al Sharpton noted that King was heckled when he came to Harlem. Some in Harlem even threw eggs at him. This demonstrated the resentment which some in the community had towards King. Powell was also among those voices in Harlem who denounced King. Sharpton recalled that during King's last visit to Harlem, Powell referred to King as the "biggest Uncle Tom in America."

Stokely Carmichael, who became an advocate for Black Power, represented a generation of activists who broke with King's approach. Powell fully embraced Carmichael and the Black Power movement. This was demonstrated by a press conference the two men organized together in which it was announced that Powell would join a conference on the topic of Black Power. Whereas King remained committed to nonviolence, Powell defended the militant approach of the Black Panther Party. Powell even used King's assassination to justify why the Panthers took arms as a form of self-defense. Powell also explained that Black Power meant dignity and that it meant "we're going to walk side by side with you or through you." It was not that Powell was opposed to nonviolence. He felt that black men needed to respond to violence with violence for the sake of their manhood. In Powell's view, King simply did not know what Black Power really meant.

Powell connected with the impatience and the militancy of those like Carmichael, the Black Panthers, and others in ways which King did not. Whereas Powell connected to the militancy of the movement, he also lacked King's apparent dedication to the struggle. Julius Lester noted that Powell's lifestyle and womanizing began to seem "tawdry." The womanizing was certainly unbecoming of someone who was a preacher, but Powell hardly seemed to care about presenting a sanctified public image. Powell's self-indulgent behavior was a stark contrast with King whose public image was one of a man who was faithfully committed to struggling on behalf of the black community. Powell's attitude had been to "do no more or no less" than anybody else.

Apart from the challenge to the perception that Powell was the leading spokesman of black America, Powell faced other challenges as well. Powell found himself entangled in a legal situation when, in 1960, a woman named Esther James sued Powell for libel after he claimed that she was a "bag woman." A bag woman referred to someone who delivered money from gambling, prostitution, and drug racketeers to the police. Even though James was a bag woman, she won the judgement. Stokely Carmichael questioned how a poor woman in Harlem could afford five lawyers to bring a case against Powell. The point that Carmichael was making was that there were powerful individuals supporting James' suit as a means of discrediting Powell. Powell himself refused to appear in court and was cited for contempt. The case with James dragged on and in 1966, Powell was given a citation for criminal contempt. Wyatt Tee Walker explained that Powell could have resolved the situation simply by apologizing, but Powell could not bring himself to do so.

Powell, who established a retreat for himself in the Bahamas, began to drink heavily. In spite of this, Powell's political dominance continued as he was elected to his 12th term in the House of Representatives. Other representatives decided to bar Powell from taking his seat in Congress. Rep. Albert Watson from South Carolina charged that Powell was in the Bahamas with a glass in one hand and a woman in the other hand. Watson's remark demonstrated the prevailing negative view that members of the House of Representatives had of Powell. He was viewed as someone who did not take the job as seriously as he should have.

Speaker John McCormack did not seem to believe that the

members of Congress would deny a seat to an elected official. Powell himself seemed unconcerned about the situation. This lax attitude caused Powell to lose support. Powell refused to humble himself and apologize. Powell had become accustomed to flaunting his political power and his lavish lifestyle. To Powell, the issue was racism. He felt that he was too powerful in the eyes of white people who could not accept that he passed 60 bills without being defeated. When it came time for the vote, 363 members voted to bar Powell from taking his seat. Only 63 had voted for Powell. Powell himself was in disbelief that he had been voted out of the seat which he had been elected for. The vote was an emotional blow to Powell who had grown accustomed to political victories.

Martin Luther King asserted that he did not justify Powell's misdeeds, but he also felt that singling Powell out was an act of hypocrisy. Others shared King's view. The perception seemed to have been that Powell was not innocent, but that he should be allowed to take his seat in Congress. Powell still retained enough support that he was reelected to fill the vacant seat. John Henrik Clarke noted that despite the personal misgivings which the black community in Harlem had about Powell, the community still elected Powell to let white people know that it was not their prerogative to select who would represent the community.

Powell was again barred by the House of Representatives until the Supreme Court ruled that Congress had acted illegally in refusing to seat Powell. Powell was finally seated in Congress again, but he no longer had seniority. Powell also spent less time in Congress. He responded to 9 of the 177 roll calls. The view of some in Harlem was that Powell's absences left Harlem without representation. Powell himself was ailing. He spent the last three years of his life battling cancer, though Powell publicly downplayed the severity of his condition and gave the perception that he had beaten his sickness. This was not true, however. In 1970, Powell lost his first election. He died two years later in 1972. John Henrik Clarke had fittingly described Powell as the "Emperor of Harlem." For a period of time, he was.

22

MAP OF THE SOUL

Dr. Murray Stein appeared with Laura London on her "Speaking of Jung" program where he discussed BTS' album, *Map of the Soul: Persona*. That Murray was invited to discuss BTS' album is noteworthy considering that the album was inspired by Murray's own book titled *Jung's Map of the Soul*. The discussion also enforced the reality that the music of BTS often conveys messages which are relevant to Jungian psychology. In this essay, I seek to recap the discussion between Dr. Stein and London regarding some of the themes in BTS' album.

Stein explained that the word persona comes from a word for mask which was worn by actors. Stein continued to note that everyone is an actor in the stage of life. By this, he meant that everyone puts on a persona depending on where they are. Stein noted that people have different personalities for different situations. The example he gave is that a firefighter would behave differently at his job than he would at home with his children. This is because the human personality is complex and there are different aspects to the personality which is displayed in different settings.

Stein's remarks about what the persona represents is important for not only understanding the first song on the album, but the overall theme of the album. The album is essentially about the challenge of understanding oneself and bettering oneself which typically means going beyond the personas which we often hide ourselves behind.

"Persona" is performed by RM, who is the leader of BTS. In the video for the song, the words "shadow," "self," and "ego" are displayed on the board. These words are all related to concepts in Jungian psychology. In the song, RM refers to his anxiety as his shadow because like a shadow, his anxiety follows him wherever he goes. Rather than seeking to distance himself from his anxiety, RM embraces it because he recognizes that it is just as much a part of him as his shadow.

Stein noted that the shadow is typically something one hides,

150

but RM is clearly not hiding his shadow here because he's acknowledging his anxiety. The anxiety is understandable given the position of fame and influence which RM finds himself in due to the success of BTS. In Stein's view, RM's anxiety is related to feeling insufficient or feeling immature. Stein explained that when individuals find themselves in elevated positions which are above where they have been, they can find themselves feeling that they are not up to it, so they have to bluff their way through it. He related this to RM's feelings about having to hide his immaturity while performing on stage because RM is concerned that he cannot handle the fame and success that comes with being a performing artist. In the song, RM also expressed the fear that he is not good enough to tell the truth, that his flaws are all that he has, and that the world is not interested in his clumsiness. Stein notes that these insecurities are what is hidden underneath RM's mask. In this regard, RM's stage persona becomes something which he uses to cover these insecurities. In a speech he gave at the United Nations, RM described himself as a boy from a small village near Seoul. He explained that he was not a famous celebrity. This fame has taken RM all over the world, including to the United Nations. Given RM's background, it would seem rather understandable that he finds himself struggling with this newfound fame.

Stein was also struck by RM's line about being raised up. Stein described this as being almost biblical. This makes sense given that in the Bible, God is often seen as rising up individuals so that they may achieve great things. It is often the case that those who are selected by God come from humble origins. Joseph was sold into slavery in Egypt and found himself in prison in Egypt before he became the vizier of Egypt. King David was a shepherd before he became a renowned warrior and the eventual king of the Israelites. In Stein's view, what raises RM up is "the self". Stein explained that the self can become a source of inspiration for individuals who are feeling down.

In Jungian psychology, the self is the core of one's being. Stein explained that this is who a person is at the time they were born, or even before they are born. This suggests that the self is the most unadulterated version of a human because it represents a human outside of any social influences. The notion of a self which exists before birth does imply a degree of religious sentiment in that it can suggest that a human comes into the world created to be a particular way or is predestined to be a particular way.

In Jeremiah 29: 10-14, the prophet Jeremiah instructs the Hebrews that God has plans for them to free them from their captivity in Babylon after having banished the Hebrews. Chapter 9, verse 51 of the Qur'an explains that only that which God has destined for us can befall us. These verses demonstrate that God within the Abrahamic religious tradition is not just a passive creator, but a being who actively shapes the destinies of his creations. This does not mean that humans have no role in the process. Abrahamic religious traditions also stress that it is the responsibility of humans to seek God and to worship God in order to receive God's blessings.

Applied to BTS, the "self" which existed at or before birth would suggest that the creative ability which drives BTS as performers was something which was inherent to who the members of BTS were at the time of birth or even before it. This is not a passive process for the members of BTS, however. Even though they were born with a particular self, achieving that self required a great deal of work on the part of the members to become successful artists.

It is important to understand that the concept of the self does not exist outside of established social and cultural norms. What this means is that how one views oneself is in some degree related to the established values of the larger society. For example, Western society tends to value fame, money, and power. As such, an individual socialized within these values may come to define self in terms of acquiring fame, money, and power. The emphasis on individual accumulation developed as a product of Western industrialization. This led Jung to conclude that Western man cannot fully understand Eastern systems such as Zen Buddhism. The reason why Jung held this view is that he recognized the differences in cultural values between Western society and the cultural norms expressed in Zen Buddhism. The "self" within Western society is a concept which is connected to one's status or standing in society. It is a self which is focused on the external, rather than the internal.

The problem with seeking external sources to validate the self is that it can result in a deeper identity crisis as the individual fails to find validation through external sources. This is why Erich Fromm noted: "The 'identity crisis' of modern society is actually the crisis produced by the fact that its members have become selfless instruments, whose identity rests upon their participation in the corporations (or other giant bureaucracies), as a primitive individual's identity rested upon membership in the clan." What Fromm explained here is that in the quest for validation through external sources, the individual can in fact lose his or her self.

The next song on the album is "Boy With Luv" (spelt "Luv" rather than "Love"). London noted that Halsey, an American singer, appeared in the video for the song. Stein pointed out that Halsey's inclusion reflected the international reach of BTS. Stein also viewed the inclusion of Halsey as representing an "anima figure." This refers to a "soul figure" who is often from a different culture. For Koreans, an American woman becomes an anima figure who represents their soul figure much in the same way that Europeans had viewed women from other cultures as their Amina figures. Stein pointed out that Wolfgang Pauli, one of Jung's friends, had a Chinese woman as an anima figure and he dreamed of her several times. The concept of an anima figure suggests that the subconscious mind is drawn to things which appear to be exotic.

Stein pointed out that the concept of boy with love was different from a prior song by BTS which described being a boy in love. He explained that being in love implies being controlled by the emotion of love. By contrast, being with love describes a feeling of being in actual control of the love. Rather than being in love, a person who is with love can control the love and bring it with them. Stein explained that a more mature ego is not an ego which is in love, but an ego who possesses love and uses the love as a resource. Stein clarified that the usage of this love is not necessarily about manipulation, but that being with love implied a greater degree of control.

The next song is "Mikrokosmos." The name of this song is based on the concept of microcosm. Stein explained that the theory of microcosm is one which posits that the human being reflects the larger cosmic world. Stein explained that Jung once had a dream while he was ill. Jung dreamt that he saw a star in a pool of water. He realized that in the dream, he was the microcosm reflected in the pool of the unconscious. The pool represented the macrocosm. This dream apparently made Jung feel a sense of well-being.

It seemed that what Jung was experiencing was a sense of belonging to something which was grander than himself. He was dreaming about his connection to the larger universe around him. Stein referred to this as the "individuation process." This is the process in which one realizes that one has an inner self which is not completely dependent on the outside world. A person who develops a sense of being a "star" draws a sense of worth from the self, rather than from others. This relates to the prior concept of being with love, rather than being in love. A person who has developed a strong inner self does not need the love of others for validation or self-worth. Such an individual is then capable of displaying a healthy form of love which is not rooted in a search for self-validation through being loved by others. This individual can exist with love, without needing to be in love.

One of the lines in the song notes that we shine in our own way. This implies that each individual is unique. Yet even though each individual is unique, we are also interconnected. Stein referenced a German philosopher named Leibniz. Leibniz developed the theory that humans are all monads. Each individual is a self-enclosed monad, but that each monad also has a relationship to all of the other monads in the universe. The implication here is that we exist as individuals, but our existence is also connected to the people around us. Each personality is a total individual, yet the individual does not exist in isolation from other individuals. This collection of individuals is ultimately what constitutes the society at large.

Stein described this connection as being a mysterious link. He also expressed the view that the individual monads are harmonized by a force called God. Here Stein is expressing the view that God operates as a force which links everyone together. In Abrahamic religions and other religious traditions, God is the creator of the universe. This means that we are all linked by the fact that we share a common creator and come from a common source. Many religions believe that we are all destined to return to the source from which we come. In Abrahamic religions, this typically means returning before God to be judged for the actions which we undertook during our lives.

An important point which Stein does not mention is what the theory of humans representing interconnected monads means in terms of understanding prejudice and discrimination. If it is true that we are all connected to each other via a force known as God because we share God as a common creator, it would imply that no group is superior to another. Yet the concept of racism and other ideologies which promote discrimination believes just that. These ideologies believe that certain groups of people should be treated adversely because of certain differences, whether the differences be related to skin color, political views, or religious views. This is at odds with the message in "Mikrokosmos."

A point which was not raised in the discussion—not that I would have expected this point to come up—is that Jung himself was a racist. This would suggest that in Jung's quest to understand human psychology, he did not see fit to explore his own racial prejudice or even the very existence of racial prejudice itself. If we are indeed monads which exist as part of a larger, interconnected microcosm, then it would mean that we owe a duty to the other monads in the microcosm to treat them with equal respect and recognition.

It is also interesting to explore the internationalism of BTS' music within this context. BTS is not only international in the sense that the group enjoys international acclaim, but BTS' music reflects very strong international influences from outside of Korean culture. It was noted earlier that Hasley's inclusion represented the international aspect of BTS' music. The internationalism of BTS' music is further demonstrated by the fact that the group draws heavily on Western thought such as the psychological theories of Jung and Greek mythology. An example of the Greek mythological influence is demonstrated in "Boy With Luv". In the song, BTS references the Greek mythological figure Icarus.

BTS also mixes other languages in their music as well. In the song "Home," Stein noted that BTS uses the Spanish word for home, which is *mi casa*. Stein noted that *mi casa* adds a feeling of intimacy because this term describes a humble dwelling, not a palace. There is another song titled "Jamais Vu." Jamais vu is a French phrase which is related to déjà vu. Déjà vu is the experience of being in a new location, but feeling that the new location is familiar. Jamais vu is the opposite situation. It is one in which someone is in a familiar situation or environment, but does not recognize it. Stein noted that this song is a song about struggle. It is a song about someone who has failed to learn the lessons of the past and finds himself making the same mistake again.

Stein noted that one of the lines in the song is "it always hurts like it's the first time." The song describes the condition of not only failing to learn from the mistakes of the past, but it also invokes the feeling that each failure feels new; it feels like jamais vu. Another line in the song describes running again only to fall again. There is a sense of repeated failure, with each attempt ending in the same result. As Stein noted, this is a song about struggle.

Stein also saw the song as being one which describes the struggle with one's self. He explained that this is precisely what therapy focuses on. It is the continuous process of revisiting one's behavior until it becomes easier to recognize such behaviors. To this London added that repetition is the work which Jungian analysts are engaged in. Stein responded by noting that he has worked with some people for thirty years. The point is that we don't arrive at some ideal point and become perfect, so it is a continued struggle. The song itself mentions feeling a sense of shame about being imperfect. Yet as Stein noted, one can never become perfect.

The final song on the album is titled "Dionysus." The title is yet another reference to Greek mythology. Dionysus was a Greek god and, in Greek society, the rites associated with Dionysus were orgiastic in character, which demonstrated the nature of Dionysus himself. Dionysus was also noted for being an invader god who created disruption wherever he went. Dionysus was viewed as foreign god to the Greeks. They initially saw Dionysus as a threat because of the manner in which he disrupted society and overwhelmed those who attempted to resist him.

In Greek mythology, it was believed that Dionysus was killed by the Titans and that he was later reborn. Eva Matthews Sanford compared this rebirth to the cults of Osiris and Isis in Egypt. These cults were also centered around the idea of death and rebirth. Sanford noted that the cults of Osiris and Isis became popular in Greece, which would indicate that the Greeks themselves saw some similarities between their beliefs and Egyptian beliefs. George M. James had argued in *Stolen Legacy* that the Greeks actually took their religious beliefs from Egyptians. James argued: "From the conquest of Egypt by Alexander the Great, the Greeks, who were always attracted by the mysterious worship of the Nile-land, began to imitate the Egyptian religion in its entirety; and during the Roman occupation, the Egyptian religion spread not only to Italy: but throughout the Roman Empire, including Brittany." James further explained that what the Greeks produced was a failed attempt at imitating Egyptian religion: "The Greeks failed to imitate Egyptian conservatism and not only in Egyptian cities, with large Greek population, but in Europe, Egyptian divinities were corrupted with Greek and Asiatic names and mythologies and reduced to vague pantheistic personalities, so that Isis and Osiris had retained very little of their Egyptian origin."

James noted that both Egyptian and Greek religions faded as Christianity spread. Interestingly, the concept of death and rebirth is found in Christianity as well. In the Christian doctrine, Jesus is believed to have been killed and resurrected. This demonstrates the importance of the theme of death and rebirth in the religious life of ancient societies, although Jesus is a much different figure than Dionysus. Jesus advocated for his followers to practice discipline and control. In Matthew 5, Jesus explained that to merely look at a woman with lustful intention is an act of committing adultery with the heart. Jesus further instructed that one should tear out the right eye if the eye causes one to sin for it is better to lose one body part than for one's whole body to be thrown into hell. Whereas Jesus urged against giving in to temptation by sinning with one's thoughts and desires, Dionysus compelled the Greeks to loosen their self-control and to fully embrace their lustful desires.

Stein noted that the Greeks ended up integrating Dionysus into their pantheon of gods. He was given a place at Delphi along with Apollo, who was the god of structure. It is indeed interesting that a god who represented chaos was placed alongside a god of structure, but this is not a conflicting arrangement either given the reality that chaos and structure cannot exist without the other. The Greeks seemed to believe that Dionysus could not be resisted, so the Greeks learned to occasionally celebrate the chaos and intoxication associated with Dionysus while also upholding the order of Apollo.

Stein gave the example of Swiss culture where there is a day called "Fasnacht." On this day, people would dress up in masks and engage in revelry. The next day, no one was supposed to speak of anything that happened on Fasnacht. Stein noted that Jung described this day as a "safety valve" to let out some steam. Stein explained that humans need the release which Dionysus allows. This makes the chaos of Dionysus just as important as the order represented by Apollo.

It is fitting that the album would end with a reference to Dionysus considering that Dionysus represents the breaking down of the persona. In the discussion, Stein spoke of the importance of not being confined to one's persona. As such, he describes Dionysus as the "freer" who encourages individuals to break from their persona, even if it is only a temporary break. Stein saw the closing song as a song which celebrates the freedom which Dionysus offered.

23

ON THE PRINCIPLES OF UNITY

Pan-Africanism is a movement which advocates for unity among African people. It is also important to define what we mean by unity because not all forms of unity are useful or constructive. This was certainly the critique I raised on Khafra Kambon's approach to Pan-African unity which resulted in embracing a dictator like Yoweri Museveni of Uganda. We certainly do need to establish boundaries for when unity is practical or impractical. We cannot unite with everyone in the name of unity, yet there are also situations in which constructive unity might mean aligning with those whom we may have a strong ideological disagreement with.

I will start with Kambon because though I raise this critique of his particular approach to Pan-Africanism, I have tremendous respect for Kambon's work as a Pan-Africanist. Not only was Kambon one of the leading figures of the Black Power rebellion in 1970, but he has played a role in promoting cultural transformation in Trinidad, which included using the annual Emancipation Day celebration in Trinidad as a means to promote culture and history. On one occasion, Kambon used the celebration to speak about the important role that Haiti's rebellion played in ending slavery. Apart from being used as an occasion to promote culture and education on history, Emancipation Day has also served as an opportunity for entrepreneurs to sell their items.

Where I take issue with Kambon's approach to Pan-Africanism is his willingness to unite with neo-colonial regimes which oppress African people and his relative silence on these issues. I quote Horace Campbell who wrote: "One of the cardinal principles of Pan Africanism which emerged at the period of slavery and colonialism was that 'the people of one part of Africa are responsible for the freedom of their brothers in other parts of Africa; and indeed black people everywhere were to accept this same responsibility.' This ideal has been subverted in the OAU by the principle of non-intervention in the internal affairs of member states, thus leading to a conspiracy of silence among most states when African leaders carry out atrocities in their own societies. Many leaders such as Sekou Toure and Idi Amin carried out repression at home while verbally supporting the anti-colonial struggles in Southern Africa." This is the same critique of the OAU that Julius Nyerere raised when he stated: "We protected one another, whatever we did to our own peoples in our respective countries. To condemn a Mobutu, or Idi Amin or a Bokassa was taboo! It would be regarded as interference in the internal affairs of a fellow African State!" Unity must not come at the expense of remaining silent about these types of abuses.

In my view, Pan-African unity has to be more than a mere cultural exercise. There must be a solid political and ideological base for the work that we do, otherwise we may very well find ourselves uniting with those who work against the interests of the African masses. This was precisely the problem which hindered the OAU.

My essay "On the OVP in Guyana" represents this approach of developing constructive unity beyond ideological disagreements. As I stated in that essay, although I disagree with Gerald Perriera's assessment on the conflict between Forbes Burnham and Walter Rodney, I cannot help but admire his principled commitment to the anti-imperialist and socialist vision which Burnham espoused. Perriera could have easily remained in the PNC when the party shifted away from socialism to embrace neoliberalism, but he did not. He remained committed to the vision espoused by Burnham.

Perriera himself is an example of engaging in principled unity despite real ideological disagreements. He was willing to support the A Partnership for National Unity coalition in the 2015 and 2020 elections. Though he disagreed with their politics, he saw the People's Progressive Party as being the principal contradiction because of the type of racist politics which the People's Progressive Party was engaged in. He recognized that keeping the People's Progressive Party out of power was more important than his political disagreements with the coalition.

My disagreements with Perriera over the situation between Walter Rodney and Forbes Burnham were expressed in my essay "Did Burnham Kill Rodney?" What I will state here is that though I disagree with Perriera's positive assessment of Burnham, I understand it. There are times when leaders espouse ideals which the leaders themselves do not necessarily practice. Such was the case with Burnham. Burnham espoused an anti-colonial and anti-imperialist vision which was rooted in socialism. He was also a Pan-Africanist who supported liberation struggles across Africa and who voiced solidarity for the African American struggle. I think Walter Rodney himself accurately summed up Burnham when he pointed out that Burnham promoted many beautiful ideas, but these ideas were corrupted by Burnham's touch.

The same is true of other leaders. Take for example, Elijah Muhammad. That Elijah Muhammad was a religious leader who used his position to enrich himself and to impregnate young women in his organization does not take away from the fact that the message which he preached was a necessary one. The power of Elijah Muhammad's teachings was that it restored the humanity within black people by allowing black people to see themselves as people of God, while rejecting a wicked American society which had brutalized them. This rejection of America also accompanied the controversial teaching that white people were devils, but it was important to get black people to recognize their own humanity. It was also important to get black people to understand the nature of their oppression and to not worship the very people who were oppressing them. That I have disagreements with Elijah Muhammad's teachings and his conduct has not stopped me from recognizing certain positive aspects of the Nation of Islam. For this reason, I can work with brothers and sisters in the Nation of Islam so long as the work is based on building from the positive aspects of what the Nation of Islam teaches.

I understand that critics of the Nation of Islam charge that it teaches a pseudo version of Islam which promotes racial separatism. There is also the charge that the Nation of Islam is a cult. It is true that the Nation of Islam's particular brand of Islam differs in a number of ways from what can be viewed as orthodox Islam, but I would argue that this is precisely the point. The Nation of Islam's brand of Islam reflected the nature of the racist society which black people in America lived in and struggled in.

As for the charges of the Nation of Islam being a cult, I would state that the Nation of Islam does have traits which are typical of religious cults, although I do not think that the Nation of Islam has been as harmful as other cults such as the People's Temple or the House of Israel. The term cult generally refers to a system of veneration which is centered around a particular object. Cults tend to be smaller than established religions. This is often by design as some cults operate in secrecy, with knowledge only being reserved for initiates—this is one aspect of African religious tradition which contrasts with the Abrahamic religious tradition of seeking converts. Cults are not inherently bad, although the term cult does carry a negative connation. The negative connation comes from cults in which veneration is given to a particular religious leader who is seen as either being divine or having a connection to the divine. Such cults seek to elevate the personality of the religious leader in such a way that the leader becomes above question or critique. In some instances, members of the cult are even indoctrinated to act violently in defense of the cult leader. The cult leader, in turn, will often abuse this devotion to exploit the members of the cult. These negative aspects were to be found in the Nation of Islam as well.

The cultish tendencies within the Nation of Islam can be demonstrated by the reaction to Malcolm X publicly disclosing that Elijah Muhammad had fathered children out of wedlock. In the September 11, 1964 edition of *Muhammad Speaks*, Isaiah Karriem published an article to defend Elijah Muhammad. He explained that in the twenty years that he had known Elijah Muhammad, he had never seen anything "but a righteous man." He referred to two of the women who claimed to have had babies by Elijah Muhammad as "prostitutes" who should hang their heads in shame "for putting out such lies on the Honorable Elijah Muhammad." In the same piece, Isaiah Karriem also denounced the "no good Malcolm Little" whom he accused of "lying, scandal, and trying to pull followers away from the Messenger to follow him to his own selfish end."

One must keep in mind that Malcolm's issue with Elijah Muhammad's conduct was not simply that Elijah Muhammad had children out of wedlock, but that Elijah Muhammad attempted to hide his conduct by shaming the women whom he impregnated. In his defense of Elijah Muhammad, Isaiah Karriem sought to further shame these women by denouncing them as prostitutes.

Years later, Louis Farrakhan offered a different type of defense. In defense of Elijah Muhammad, Louis Farrakhan acknowledged that Elijah Muhammad had relations with these women, but he suggested that Elijah Muhammad married the woman that had his children. If these women were the "wives" of Elijah Muhammad, why then would Isaiah Karriem denounce these women as prostitutes? Why would Elijah Muhammad allow his wives to be discredited as prostitutes? The Nation of Islam's defense of Elijah Muhammad went from shaming the women to trying to present them as Elijah Muhammad's wives. This is the type of confusion which emerges within cults because of the fact that devotion to the leader becomes more important than principles and truth. Thus, Malcolm was branded as a hypocrite and a liar for exposing the truth about Elijah Muhammad. The denouncements of Malcolm were taken to an extreme when Thomas Hagan decided to kill Malcolm because Malcolm had "gone against the leader of the Nation of Islam".

As stated, this notion that the cult leader is above critique is rooted in this notion that the cult leader is in some way connected to the divine. It is important to note that according to the Bible, God was never above question. In fact, God is questioned numerous times in the Bible. When God told Abram that he would provide land for him, Abram questioned God (Genesis 15:7-8). When Moses was selected by God to free the Israelites, he questioned why God sent him (Exodus 5:22-23). Joshua, who took over leadership of the Hebrews when Moses died, questioned why God delivered the Hebrews into the hands of the Amorites (Joshua 7:7). The point here is that if God in the Bible was not above question, then anyone who claims to represent God certainly cannot be above question.

There is also the case of Haile Selassie, who was deified by Rastas. Apart from the religious significance which Rastas have attributed to Haile Selassie, they view Haile Selassie as a symbol of Pan-African unity and anti-colonial resistance. In some respects, he did represent those things. It is equally true that Haile Selassie oversaw a brutal and exploitative feudal regime, and that he was largely indifferent to the suffering of his people. Haile Selassie certainly was not God—a reality that Bob Marley struggled with after Haile Selassie died. Yet, I recognize that the positive things which he did influenced Rastas in a very profound way and has helped to shape the anti-colonialism of the Rastafarian movement. As I stated before, sometimes individual leaders espouse ideals which they fall short of themselves. This was true of Burnham and it was true of Haile Selassie as well.

What is especially curious about the Rastafarian religion is that Haile Selassie himself never claimed to be God, though the Rastafarian religion claims him to be God. The religion was founded by Leonard Howell. Howell lived at Pinnacle mansion, referred to himself as "God," and had several wives and concubines. He also oversaw an estate upon which his followers planted cannabis as a cash crop. Cannabis eventually became a popular element of the Rastafarian religious belief. Interestingly, the usage of hallucinogenic plants in religious worship is found in African traditions. The Ben-Riamba was a cult whose adherents were stated to have smoked cannabis as part of their rituals. The Tsonga and Fang people were also noted for using hallucinogenic plants in their rituals.

Howell not only proclaimed Selassie's divinity, but he went so far as to declare that those who "forsaketh" Haile Selassie as "God Almighty" should be cast into hell. Howell was also especially critical of the Roman Catholic Church and he denounced the pope as being the devil. Despite being the founder of the Rastafarian religion, Howell eventually faded into obscurity as the religious movement grew beyond him. Rastafarianism presents an example of what can be viewed as a small cult around Howell and his claims about Haile Selassie being God growing into a larger international religious movement. The movement reached its largest international appeal through the music of popular reggae artists, most notably Bob Marley. I mention Rastafarians here because the faults of Haile Selassie do not invalidate the positive contributions which Rastas have made.

I state all this to state that I can disagree with the ideological views of a brother or sister, but still understand why they hold such views and still appreciate why such views are an important influence for them. It is on this basis that I am able to move forward in unity for the greater good of African people. This is not to suggest that these disagreements should never be discussed or debated. What I am suggesting is that these disagreements should never prevent constructive and meaningful unity.

I understand that such unity is not always easy. It certainly is not for me. After all, I cannot overlook Burnham's role in the assassination of Walter Rodney nor the Nation of Islam's complicity in the assassination of Malcolm X. These things factor into my critique of Burnham's leadership in Guyana and my critique of the Nation of Islam. Even so, I think it is important to develop constructive unity that works towards the objective of African liberation.

24

ON MARTIN LUTHER KING'S AFFAIRS

Rev. Ralph Abernathy created much controversy when he published *And The Walls Came Tumbling Down*. The controversy came from Abernathy's claim that King spent his last night having extramarital affairs with different women. Among those who challenged Abernathy's story was Adjua Abi Naantaanbuu, who was one of the women in question. Naantaanbuu stated that she cooked dinner for King, but she was not as close to King as Abernathy suggested in his book. She further claimed that at no point was she ever alone with King. Naantaanbuu also sued Abernathy for libel over the claims in his book. Naantaanbuu's version of events was supported by Rev. Bernard Lee who also challenged the truthfulness of Abernathy's claims. Others such as Fred Shuttlesworth, John Lewis, and Joseph Lowery pointed out other errors in Abernathy's book. Most shocking to those who knew King was Abernathy's claim that King had a violent altercation with a woman after she confronted him for being with other women.

Part of the reason why Abernathy's book created such a controversy is that the FBI had attempted to discredit King by claiming to have exposed King's infidelities. The view seemed to have been that Abernathy was trying to make money through making shocking, but inaccurate claims about his friend which aligned with the FBI's effort to smear King. It is difficult to know what to make of Abernathy's claims. That Abernathy was King's friend would seem to lend credibility to his claims, yet Abernathy's book was also denounced by those who not only knew King and Abernathy, but who were present for the events which Abernathy wrote about. Abernathy's claims were also met with legal action from one of the women whom Abernathy alleged was with King.

Years later Georgia Davis Powers wrote an autobiography in which she admitted that she had been with King the night before he was assassinated. It would seem that an admission on the part of a woman claiming to have had a sexual relationship with King would appear credible since Powers risked harming her own reputation to make such an admission, but Powers' claims were met with the same type of scrutiny which Abernathy faced. Hosea Williams stated that he had assigned three people to guard King's room on the night in question. He stated that King never left the room and that Powers never entered the room. Williams further added that he traveled with King during the last several months of King's life and King could not have engaged in any intimate relationships without Williams knowing about it.

Abernathy wrote in his book that King was with a black woman who was "a member of the Kentucky legislature" the night before he was killed. Abernathy did not reveal the name of the individual in question, but Powers' account of her relationship with King is an admission of Abernathy's story. Williams charged that Powers was telling the same lie which Abernathy told to sell books. In Williams' view, Abernathy became a Judas and told a lie which ran "Dr. Abernathy insane and finally killed him." Powers asserted that her account was the truth, but Williams was not alone in questioning Powers' version of events. Powers claimed that Andrew Young knew of her relationship with King, but Young claimed that he was not aware of her relationship with King. David Garrow, who wrote a book about King, supported Powers' claim when he stated that he was aware of King's sexual relationship with Powers.

Naantaanbuu was one of the women who was claimed to have had an affair with King. She not only denied it, but took legal action as well. If Williams was correct, then Powers simply used Abernathy's lie to her advantage to publish a book in which she claimed to have a relationship with King which never happened. There is merit in the notion that claiming to have an affair with King would generate more book sales, but it also would have done so at the cost of potentially damaging Powers' own reputation in the same way that Abernathy's reputation was damaged when he published his book. It could be true that Powers simply did not care about any damage to her reputation so long as her book sold, but this does raise the question of why Abernathy would fabricate a story about King being with a black politician from Kentucky.

This seems to be a very specific thing to lie about if the story was not true. Abernathy did not mention Powers by name in his book, but at the time it was known that Powers was the politician whom Abernathy was referring to.

Further adding to the confusion over the competing narratives is that *People* reported in 1989 that Powers was surprised by Abernathy's claim that she had sex with King. She insisted that she visited King at his hotel, but that she merely went there to talk with him, as well as Abernathy and A.D. King. The version of the story which she initially presented contradicted Abernathy's claim. Did Powers initially lie by denying the claim to protect herself or did she later opportunistically decide to lie about having an intimate relationship with King which never happened just to sell her book? One cannot be sure, but Powers' conflicting stories of what happened when she visited King on the night before he was killed does damage her credibility here.

Kwame Ture's remarks are also worth noting in the context of discussing King's relationship with women. Ture stated that one evening, he went to see King with "some nice beautiful things." Ture stated that King had an appreciation for "all beautiful things." Ture did not state that the young women that he took to meet King engaged in any sexual relations with King, but Ture's story does seem to indicate that King was someone who enjoyed the company of beautiful women. This would seemingly add some weight to the claim that King was a womanizer.

Incidentally, it was Ture's own womanizing which ended his marriage to Mariam Makeba. It was published in *Jet* that Ture had denied the reports of their divorce as being "a filthy bedroom rumor circulated by the foe who reflect the capitalist views concerning anyone who disagrees with their policies and tactics." It was no rumor. The two did get divorced and Makeba would recall that what ended their marriage was that Ture had fallen in love with a woman in Guinea.

Manning Marable's biography of Malcolm X was a controversial one for the number of unsubstantiated claims it made, including claims of Malcolm engaging in extramarital affairs while being married to his wife Betty. The issue with Marable's claims is that there was no evidence to support these claims. None of the claims which Marable made are corroborated by anyone who knew

Malcolm. None of the women who Marable claimed that Malcolm was having an affair with admitted to it either.

King's situation is different. In King's case, the claims regarding his infidelities come from someone who was King's friend and who professed to be an eyewitness to these infidelities, as well as from a woman who admitted to being King's mistress. Yet there are also those who knew King who have vigorously denounced the claims around King's infidelity. Interestingly, one of those individuals was King's wife, Coretta Scott King. Her view of this topic is perhaps the most important one of all.

Coretta Scott King's view was that the claims of her husband's adultery were fabricated. She stated that he was one of the most moral persons that she knew and that he struggled to retain the respect that others had of him. It is possible that King was having affairs and that his wife truly did not know. It is also possible that she knew, but would not publicly admit to her husband's affairs to protect his legacy. Even if one of the two previously noted scenarios is true, it is still notable that Mrs. King sought to defend her husband's morality. It would indicate that as King's wife, Coretta Scott King felt that it was important to defend her husband's legacy. After his assassination, Mrs. King continued to promote her husband's legacy. This meant not only invoking him as often as she could with their children, but also by representing her husband's ideals in public. This was how much King meant to her.

Given King's status as a public figure, even actions which he undertook in private may be of interest to the general public. Moreover, King was a religious leader, so there is the issue of religious hypocrisy involving a preacher who seemingly preached one thing while doing something else in private. This was certainly the issue which Malcolm X raised when he discovered that Elijah Muhammad had fathered children out of wedlock. Of course, Malcolm's issue was not only the hypocrisy of Elijah Muhammad's adultery, but that Elijah Muhammad had sought to cover up these affairs by punishing the women who gave birth to his children. This was especially troubling to Malcolm considering that Malcolm had rejected one of his own brothers after his brother was kicked out of the Nation of Islam for carrying on an improper affair. This created a situation in which others were punished for engaging in the very acts which Elijah Muhammad engaged in.

King's case is different. There were no allegations that King had used his leadership position to punish individuals in an effort to cover up his alleged affairs nor were there allegations that King had used his position to punish others for engaging in affairs. This would mean that King's alleged affairs were a moral issue on his part, not a political issue. King was never in a position where he sought to impose any type of moral standards on others. As such, whatever extramarital affairs that he did engage in were a matter to be addressed between King, his wife, and God. This means that to the extent that King did engage in extramarital affairs, he was not only violating Christian ethics (Hebrews 13:4), but he was violating the vows made to his wife.

If one is to accept the view that King did engage in extramarital affairs, then the question becomes to what extent were such infidelities a betrayal of his morals. The person best positioned to address this would be King's wife. As was noted before, her position was that her husband was a very moral man and she did not believe that the claims of his adultery were true. In her book *My Life, My Love, My Legacy*, Mrs. King noted that there were a number of false claims about her husband, including that he had a secret bank account or that he went out cavorting with prostitutes while on a family trip in Oslo. Mrs. King stated that she had no evidence that her husband was unfaithful, nor did she feel that he was. He never became indifferent or cold towards her. Her view of her marriage was: "But as far as I am concerned, our marriage was a very good marriage, and it was like that all the way to the end."

If King was guilty of infidelity, then he had committed a sin and as a Christian his only recourse for such a moral failing would be to seek forgiveness from God. As a husband, even if King did violate his marriage vows through his infidelity, what was most important to his wife was that he remained a caring husband. She acknowledged that her husband was no saint, but what truly mattered to her was that he "helped transform America."

25

THE COMPLEX LEGACY OF JIMMY CARTER

Jimmy Carter recalled that one of the most gratifying moments of his life was when he was on his way to villages in Nigeria. There he saw some of the children holding signs which read, "Watch out, Guinea worm. Here comes Jimmy Carter." Carter was recalling his efforts to eradicate Guinea worm in Africa. It is remarkable that a former president would dedicate his life to such a noble cause.

Carter was indeed a genuine humanitarian who committed his life after his presidency to service to others. Apart from the issue of Guinea worm, Carter undertook other efforts such as upholding democracy in Guyana and speaking out against racism in America. On one occasion, Carter spoke about the issue of racial tensions in America at a Baptist conference. Carter expressed his concern about the resurgence of racism in America. He was especially concerned about the presidential campaign which was taking place in 2016. The concern about racism and racial justice was not simply a domestic concern for Carter. The first time that Carter met Nelson Mandela was in Ethiopia. During their meeting Mandela congratulated Carter because of the fact that Carter's daughter had been arrested three times for protesting against apartheid. Mandela and Carter eventually became friends.

What makes Carter so complex is that these humanitarian actions must be seen against actions which Carter took as president which were less than noble. For example, Carter's friendship with Mandela developed due to the Carter's family's support for the struggle against apartheid, yet when Carter was president, his policies regarding South Africa were criticized by Julius Nyerere because Nyerere felt that America was ignoring calls for meaningful sanctions against South Africa. Carter was also involved in the effort to restore democracy to Guyana after several years of dictatorship under Forbes Burnham, yet during it was during Carter's presidency that American aid to Guyana resumed after aid to Guyana had previously been restricted due to Burnham's policies.

As president, Carter promoted human rights, but his policies were rather inconsistent in this regard. In 1977, Carter curtailed arms sales to Ethiopia over human rights abuses. It was also in 1977 that Carter affirmed his support for Joseph Mobutu's dictatorship in Zaire. Carter described Mobutu as "a friend of ours." That same "friend" was exploiting the poor masses of Zaire, but Carter was willing to overlook the corruption in Zaire to maintain this friendship.

Then there was the matter of Vietnam. When asked if America had a moral obligation to help rebuild Vietnam, Carter's position was that "the destruction was mutual." He continued: "We went there to defend the freedom of the South Vietnamese. And I don't feel that we ought to apologize or to castigate ourselves or assume the status of culpability." Carter concluded: "I don't feel that we owe a debt, nor that we should be forced to pay reparations at all."

Pham Thanh Cong was forced to watch as American soldiers blew apart his mother, sisters, and brother with grenades. Cong survived the blast, but he woke up injured and covered in the flesh of his family members. Cong's family members were among the 504 unarmed civilians who were killed by American soldiers in 1968. Among those slaughtered included children. There was no "mutual" destruction as Carter claimed. The destruction was felt by Vietnamese civilians such as Cong and many others whose lives were destroyed by America's effort to defend freedom in Vietnam. In Carter's view, America was not culpable for these actions since the actions were undertaken in the name of defending the freedom of the very people that American soldiers were massacring.

Carter's remarks regarding America's role in the Vietnam War were hardly the words of a caring humanitarian, but that of a heartless apologist for American imperialism. And that is the complexity of Jimmy Carter. Carter's a man whose humanitarian impulses drove him to undertake causes which benefitted humanity, yet during his time as president, many of Carter's policies demonstrated his willingness to uphold an uncaring empire which asserted its interest at the expense of poor and suffering people in other parts of the world.

26

FRANK SNOWDEN AND THE DEBATE OVER AFROCENTRICITY

In an article titled "Misconceptions about African Blacks in the Ancient Mediterranean World: Specialists and Afrocentrists," Frank Snowden provided his critique of "Afrocentrists." I must begin by posing the following question: is what is Afrocentricity or Afrocentrism? It is a theoretical and methodological approach to the study of African history which was born out of Molefi Asante's book, *Afrocentricity: The Theory of Social Change*. It must be noted here that Afrocentricity is particular to Asante's approach to studying African history, but it is a term which has not been embraced by all. John Henrik Clarke, who was identified by Frank Snowden as being an Afrocentrist, rejected the term because he believed it was a compromise with the word African.

I mention this because I make the distinction between being African-centered and being an Afrocentrist. I view being African-centered as having ideologies and worldviews rooted in the historical and cultural experiences of African people in the same way that being Eurocentric refers to having worldviews and ideologies which are rooted in the historical and cultural experiences of Europeans. I view Afrocentricity as a particular approach to studying African history which was developed by Molefi Asante. Afrocentricity is certainly African-centered, but everyone who is African-centered is not an Afrocentrist. This may seem like a trivial semantical point, but it is important to make this distinction for the purpose of clarity.

Having stated this, Snowden does have some legitimate criticisms of the scholars whom he labels as Afrocentrists in his article. For example, Snowden raised issues with George M. James using "African" and "black" interchangeably in *Stolen Legacy* when describing the Greek geographer Eratosthenes who was a native of Cyrene in North Africa. The population of North Africa was diverse. Though Snowden is critical of Chancellor Williams'

173

claim that "African" and "Ethiopian" were used interchangeably because they meant the same thing, Williams does acknowledge the racial diversity in Egypt, particularly in Lower Egypt.

Frank expressed the view that Afrocentrists engage in the practice of claiming historical figures as being black, even if they were not black. This was something which Chancellor Williams himself critiqued when he criticized those who seek to "blackize" history. Williams certainly was not a scholar who claimed that everyone who lived in North Africa was black.

The debate over the racial identity of the ancient Egyptians is largely centered around how the Egyptians portrayed themselves. Snowden explained: "The art of ancient Egypt frequently painted Egyptian men as reddish brown, women as yellow, and people to the south as black. Ancient Egyptians, like their modern descendants, varied in complexion from a light Mediterranean type, to a light brown in Middle Egypt, to a darker brown in southern Egypt." Snowden also quoted David O'Connor who explained: "Thousands of sculpted and painted representatives from Egypt as well as hundreds of well preserved bodies from its cemeteries show that the typical physical type was neither Negro nor Negroid."

The debate over the racial identity of the ancient Egyptians has centered around the question of whether or not the reddish brown color of the Egyptians represented a racial difference between the Egyptians and the Nubians who were generally depicted as being darker than the Egyptians. A UNESCO report on a debate over the peopling of ancient Egypt noted: "Professor Vercoutter wondered why the Egyptians, if they did regard themselves as black, rarely, if ever, used carbon black in their representations of themselves but used a red colour instead. Professor Diop considered that this red colour was indicative of the black Egyptian race and that the yellow colouring of the womenfolk illustrated the fact, to which attention had been drawn by American anthropologists, that women, in a number of racial groups studied, were, as a rule, of a paler hue than the men."

Snowden argued: "Suffice it to say that the time has come for Afrocentrists to cease mythologizing and to cease claiming, in spite of the copious evidence to the contrary, that Egyptians, Carthaginians, Moors, and other inhabitants of ancient Africa were black or Negroes in the twentieth-century sense of these terms."

The problem with Snowden's claim here is that the "twentieth-century" definition of black actually does include people with lighter complexions. If individuals such as Daniel Hale Williams or Adam Clayton Powell would be classified as black, despite being able to pass for white, then there is no reason to believe that the reddish brown people of Egypt would not be classified as black. As Walter Rodney explained, "according to the white men's way of seeing things, the red and the black populations of Egypt would have been classed as 'coloured' or 'Negro'."

This is not to suggest that all the Egyptians, Carthaginians, and Moors were black. This certainly was not the case at all. Even some of the scholars whom Snowden critiqued did not seem to believe that these groups were entirely black. It was noted that Williams certainly did not have the view that all Egyptians were black. Snowden challenged the view that the Carthaginians, who were descendants of the Phoenicians, were a Negro people. He also criticized Ivan Van Sertima for accepting this view of the Carthaginians. Interestingly, in *They Came Before Columbus*, Van Sertima argued that there were traces of "Mediterranean Caucasoids" among the Olmecs which he suggested probably came from the Phoenicians. This is important to note because it suggests that Van Sertima's position on the issue was not that Phoenicians were all black.

Snowden further noted that the claim of Cleopatra being black was one which was circulated by Joel Rogers. Snowden then continued on to critique John Henrik Clarke's view on the matter. In "African Warrior Queens," Clarke wrote: "More nonsense has been written about Cleopatra than about any other African queen, mainly because it has been the desire of many writers to paint her white. She was not a white woman, she was not a Greek....Until the emergence of the doctrine of white superiority, Cleopatra was generally pictured as a distinctly African woman, dark in color. Shakespeare in the opening line of *Antony and Cleopatra* calls her 'tawny.' In his day, mulattos were called 'tawny Moors.' ... In the Book of Acts, Cleopatra describes herself as 'black.'"

Snowden correctly pointed out that William Shakespeare had no reliable evidence of Cleopatra being black and Cleopatra was not mentioned in the Book of Acts. The idea that Cleopatra would have given a description of herself in the Book of Acts is an odd suggestion considering that Cleopatra was already dead by the time the Book of Acts was written, so she certainly could not have given a description of herself in that book.

As Snowden also noted, Cleopatra was not an Egyptian. She was the last of the Ptolemaic rulers, so she was actually a descendant of a Macedonian dynasty which was established by foreign conquest. Cleopatra's ancestry is important here because Cleopatra's rule did not represent African rule. She represented the foreign conquest of Egypt. Moreover, her relationship to Rome via her connections to Julius Caesar and Mark Antony were a precursor to the Roman domination of Egypt.

Clarke's analysis of Cleopatra may have been terribly flawed, but Clarke was generally correct in his view that Egypt was an African civilization. Clarke argued: "When you look at Egypt and the Nile Valley, the Nile river stretches 4,000 miles into the body of Afrika. There's no way possible, even if the Egyptians were white, there is no way possible they could have built that civilization without other parts of Afrika playing a role in it." The UNESCO report noted that some of the scholars involved in the discussion recognized the African nature of Egypt's culture: "Professor Leclant, for his part, recognized the same African character in the Egyptian temperament and way of thinking. In his opinion, however, the unity of the Egyptian people was not racial but cultural."

Snowden wrote in his conclusion that "blacks have already been misled and in many ways confused by the kinds of inaccuracies and omissions I have illustrated, but the damage to future generations will be incalculable if the present Afrocentric trend continues. The time has come for Afrocentrists to cease mythologizing and falsifying the past."

Snowden is correct in that the scholars whom he critiqued did have inaccuracies in their scholarship, so his concern was not unwarranted. The problem with Snowden's critique is that he was operating from a narrow view of blackness in the ancient world. This produced the opposite problem of creating a general narrative that none of the Egyptians were black.

Notes:

Chancellor Williams, *The Destruction of Black Civilization*, (Chicago: Third World Press, 1987).

Frank Snowden, "Misconceptions about African Blacks in the Ancient Mediterranean World: Specialists and Afrocentrists," *Arion*, Third Series, Vol. 4, No, 3, 1997, pp. 28-50

Ivan Van Sertima, *They Came Before Columbus*, 1976.

Kwaku Person-Lynn, "On My Journey Now: The Narrative and Works of Dr. John Henrik Clarke, The Knowledge Revolutionary," *The Journal of Pan African Studies*, vol.6, no.7, February 2014.

The Peopling of Ancient Egypt and the Deciphering of Meroitic Script, United Nations Education, Scientific, and Cultural Organization, 1978.

Walter Rodney, *The Groundings with my Brothers*, (Frontline Distribution International, 1969).

27

THE LABOUR MOVEMENT AND SELF-GOVERNMENT IN THE CARIBBEAN

In 1865, Paul Bogle led the Morant Bay rebellion in Jamaica. Bogle was a Baptist deacon who was relatively successful. He owned land and was able to vote at a time when many Jamaicans were unable to vote due to the large voting fee. Despite Bogle's relative success, he still felt compelled to struggle for better living conditions in Jamaica. The roots of the rebellion began when Bogle attended a trial for two men. One of the men was imprisoned for trespassing on an abandoned plantation. One of the members of Bogle's group in court protested and was arrested. Bogle and his supporters responded by attacking some police officers.

Following the assault on the police, an arrest warrant was issued for Bogle and others. The police who arrived to arrest Bogle were met with resistance from the locals who fought the police and forced them to retreat. The conflict continued when Bogle and his supporters went to a court house, armed with weapons. This resulted in a confrontation in which the group set fire to the court house and other buildings. The colonial government finally sent troops to capture Bogle. Bogle was subsequently placed on trial and executed.

For his role in the rebellion, Bogle became a national hero in Jamaica. He became viewed as a martyr in the struggle for black rights in the Caribbean. I start with mentioning Bogle's rebellion to demonstrate that the end of slavery in the Caribbean was not the end of the struggles for freedom on the part of the citizens of the Caribbean who continued to live under the neglect and oppression of British colonial rule.

Bogle's rebellion brought about a change in the local politics in Jamaica as well. A commission was sent to investigate the situation, which resulted in Governor Edward Eyre being dismissed from his position. Following the uprising, Britain established direct rule over Jamaica. The new government consisted of the Legislative Council and the executive of Privy Council. The legal structure in Jamaica was also reformed to match

English common law.

The demands for self-government in Jamaica intensified in the 1930s. Alexander Bustamante, who formed the Jamaican Trade Workers and Tradesmen Union, emerged as a populist leader following the 1938 labour riots in Jamaica. It was also in 1938 that Bustamante's cousin Norman Manley formed the People's National Party (PNP). By 1940, the PNP adopted a socialist ideology and joined the Socialist International. Not to be outdone, Bustamante formed the Jamaica Labour Party (JLP) in 1942 as a political rival to the PNP. When Jamaica became independent in 1962, Bustamante served as the nation's first prime minister.

Much like in Jamaica, the roots of Trinidad's move towards self-government can also be traced to the labour movement of the 1930s. Captain Arthur Andrew Cipriani emerged as a prominent labour leader in Trinidad after he formed the Trinidad Labour Party. This party had a close communication with the British Labour Party. Cipriani was a white man, but Eric Williams argued that he was "devoid of racial antipathy and prejudices." This is demonstrated by Cipriani's ability to draw support from Indians in Trinidad. C.B. Mathura wrote that he was called "foolish" for urging Indians to join the Trinidad Labour Party. Cipriani enjoyed a very successful political career, which included being elected to Legislative Council in 1925 and also being elected as the mayor of Port-of-Spain on several occasions. In these offices, Cipriani struggled against racial discrimination and advocated for better rights for workers.

The 1930s saw the emergence of Tubal Uriah Butler as a prominent labour leader in Trinidad. By this time, Cipriani's more moderate approach did not appeal to workers. Butler himself had been expelled from the Trinidad Labour Party. Williams noted that although Butler had become a national hero, he "proved inadequate to the task either of forming a political party or of organising the oilfield workers". Williams also noted that Butler was defeated in the 1946 elections in which, according to Williams, Butler had "perhaps stupidly" contested a seat in Port-of-Spain. One observer stated of the 1946 elections: "The trade unions did not consolidate into a cohesive political entity. The labor vote fragmented, as blacks and East Indians divided and as racial slurs became a common part of campaign rhetoric." Williams continued to note that as Butler's political light dimmed, Dr. Patrick Solomon rose to the fore as a leader in the movement towards self-government. Solomon formed the West Indian National Party with David Pratt, who was from Grenada. Solomon would also struggle to find lasting political success as his West Indian National Party did not effectively function as a party and his Caribbean Socialist Party was even less successful.

Williams concluded that "Cipriani, Butler and Solomon laboured, each in his own way in the vineyard, only to produce the barren fruit of Albert Gomes." Williams wrote that "Butler ended up in sonorous platitudes, not all of them intelligible, in the Legislative Council, in which he lost his seat in the 1961 Elections." In Williams' view, by 1956 the "depressing situation" in Trinidad was revitalized with the formation of his People's National Movement. Solomon came out of retirement to join this political movement.

It was the People's National Movement under Williams' leadership which managed to successfully achieve self-government for Trinidad, yet this too was not enough. The 1970s saw the emergence of a Black Power movement in the Caribbean which challenged post-colonial governments throughout the region. In *Eric Williams and the Making of the Modern Caribbean*, Colin Palmer noted: "Although conditions in Trinidad and Tobago were not an exact replica of those that existed in the United States, some of Black Power's principles applied. The dispossessed groups in the nation were black and brown, and economic power, in large measure, continued to wear a white face."

The Black Power movement in the Caribbean demonstrated that Bogle's struggle remained relevant still because the black masses remained oppressed. The labour movements in Jamaica and Trinidad did make important strides in terms of advocating for the rights of workers and for self-governance, but these movements were limited in their own ways. In Jamaica, the contests for power between the JLP and PNP would continue into the post-colonial period, producing violent results. Of the 1980 election, a report from the 2012 *Jamaica Observer* titled "The bloody general election that changed Jamaica" noted: "The 1980 poll, though, saw

844 people murdered, by police official statistics, a figure that political analysts believe—due to the limitations and challenges in recording criminal activities at the time—was higher." As Eric Williams noted, the labour movement in Trinidad did produce prominent political figures, but none of them proved to be up to the task of organizing an effective political party. The PNM did manage to accomplish this under Williams' leadership, but Williams himself faced criticism due to the fact that his policies failed to effectively alleviate the suffering of the poor in Trinidad.

28

THE HOUSE NEGRO AND THE FIELD NEGRO

Malcolm X spoke about the "house Negro" and the "field Negro." The house Negro lived in the house next to the master. It was because the house Negro lived in relative comfort that the house Negro was willing to fight to protect the master and the master's property. The field Negro, on the other hand, worked in the field and was treated horribly. Malcolm noted that whereas the house Negro was willing to defend the master, the field Negro hated the master and was willing to do whatever he could to escape his conditions.

It should be noted that there were numerous examples of those who worked in the house engaging in acts of resistance and rebellion themselves, so it was not always the case that those who labored in the relative comfort of the house always sided with the slave master. In his book, *Rebels and Runaways*, Larry Eugene Rivers noted that poison was one of the means by which slaves rebelled against their masters. This was such a concern that in 1829, Florida lawmakers enacted a law which stated that "any slave or free negro or mulatto" would suffer death for preparing any poison with the intent to kill. It would have been the slaves who worked in the house and prepared the meals for their masters who were best positioned to administer poison.

Malcolm did make the important point that it is often the case that those who live in relative privilege and comfort have no incentive to rebel. They may even defend the oppressor. What Malcolm was referring to were states of mind among those who are oppressed. Malcolm saw the "Uncle Tom" integrationist leaders as being modern day house Negroes who are so aligned with the master that they are willing to defend the master's house. Malcolm viewed himself as a field Negro who had little interest in integrating into the house of the slave master.

29

AMERICA'S INDIFFERENCE TO BLACK SUFFERING

The violent death of Tyre Nichols at the hands of Memphis police officers offers yet another reminder of the reality of what life is like for black men in America. The video which was released demonstrated that even as Nichols was arrested and on the ground, officers continued to beat him by kicking him in his head. Afterwards he was held up to be beaten by a baton and punches. There was no need for such acts of violence against him as Nichols had already been detained, but such is the savage nature of the American judicial system.

The unfortunate reality is that violent deaths such as this have not only become too commonplace in America, but there is also an indifference to such acts of police violence against black men. This has historically been a problem in America, dating back to slavery when enslaved Africans were frequently beaten. The white abolitionist John Rankin published open letters on the topic of slavery in a local newspaper. Of these letters, Saidiya Hartman stated: "By providing the minutest detail of macabre acts of violence, embellished by his own fantasy of slavery's bloodstained gate, Rankin hoped to rouse the sensibility of those indifferent to slavery by exhibiting the suffering of the enslaved and facilitating an identification between those free and those enslaved." Hartman also quoted Rankin who stated: "We are naturally too callous to the sufferings of others, and consequently prone to look upon them with cold indifference, until, in imagination we identify ourselves with the sufferers, and make their sufferings our own."

Rankin was correct about the indifference to suffering. Unfortunately, it is often the case that racists lack the imagination to identify with the sufferers when the sufferers are black. That the officers who were involved in beating Nichols to death were black as well means very little given that within a racist system is often the case that black people internalize the values of the racist

183

system and end up becoming part of the system of abuse, rather than challenging the system. Black people can also become indifferent to black suffering. This indifference allows individuals to actively participate in inflicting the suffering or watching as the suffering takes place without making a serious effort to stop it.

30

RASTAS AND BABYLON

In his song "Chant Down Babylon," Bob Marley sang about burning down the system of Babylon, which he described as an evil system which caused men to watch their dreams and aspirations crumble in front of them. Peter Tosh, who was formerly a member of the Wailers along with Bob Marley, explained that Babylon "is where they tell you that everything that is wrong is right, and everything that is right is wrong." Denouncing Babylon has been a central aspect of Rastafarian theology. Ennis Edmonds described Babylon as follows: "At the highest level of generality, Babylon portrays the forces of evil arrayed against God and the righteous (Hail Selassie, Rastas, and the poor). These evil forces, however, are not metaphysical entities; rather they are human attitudes and activities that are out of touch with the divine-natural order."

For Rastas, Babylon also represents the system of Western colonialism which has historically oppressed African people. Babylon also includes who are perceived as acting in service of this system to keep black people oppressed as well. For Rastas in Jamaica, this has included political leaders. Rastas have referred to politics as "politricks" to emphasize the deceitful nature of Jamaica's political leaders.

Given that the theology of the Rastas is rooted in the Bible, to understand the significance of what Babylon represents to Rastas one must understand the significance of the biblical Babylon. In the Bible, Babylon is depicted as a powerful kingdom which destroys Jerusalem and takes the Hebrews into exile. The Bible presents this period of exile as God's punishment because the Hebrews had been disobedient and strayed away from God. The first chapter of the Book of Isaiah, for example, describes Israel as a sinful nation which had rebelled against God. The Babylonian rule over the Hebrews is described as being very destructive. 2 Kings 25: 8-10 states that Nebuchadnezzar set fire to God's temple and to all of the houses in Jerusalem. After this, the Babylonian army destroyed the walls around Jerusalem.

The Bible is also clear that the oppression of Hebrews by Babylon is not to last. Isaiah 13 declares that Babylon will be destroyed by God much like Sodom and Gomorrah were. This destruction did not occur as Babylon surrendered to Cyrus of Persia without the nation being destroyed. The rise of Persia was also an important development for the Hebrews as it was during this time that the Hebrews were allowed to return from exile. They were also able to rebuild Jerusalem with Persian help. The Persians worshipped a God known as Ahura Mazda, but the Persians did not impose their worship on their subjects, so the Hebrews were free to worship their God. Cyrus' willingness to accommodate the Hebrew return to Jerusalem is recounted in the first chapter of the Book of Ezra, in which it is stated that God had moved Cyrus to build a temple for him in Jerusalem in Judah. Ezra further stated that Cyrus returned the items which Nebuchadnezzar had taken away from Jerusalem.

Babylon appears in the New Testament as a symbolic representation of rebellion against God. Revelation 17:5 makes mention of "Babylon the Great" which is described as a mother of prostitutes and abominations. For Rastas, Babylon also became a symbol of oppression, which must be opposed at all costs.

31

A RESPONSE TO E.A. BUDGE

When addressing the legacy of colonialism in Africa, it is important to make the distinction between the type of colonial conquests which foreign powers engaged in and the type of colonialism which African states engaged in. The political systems which existed in African societies prior to colonialism certainly were systems in which class differences did exist and this ensured that access to resources were not equal, yet commoners were typically not totally deprived of basic needs either. Mungo Park noted that "the natives have no want; and although the common class of people are but sparingly supplied with animal food, yet this article is not wholly withheld from them." What Park observed was that commoners in West Africa were not totally starved and malnourished, even though they did not necessarily have the same access to certain foods as the ruling class may have had.

Throughout Africa there were examples of societies which were ruled by an aristocracy. The chapter that I wrote on the Xhosa resistance against European colonial rule demonstrated that Xhosa society was one which was ruled by an aristocracy. This aristocratic class often waged violent struggles with each other for power, but even with their rivalries the aristocratic class protected each other. This was demonstrated when Matwa was injured by a commoner and that commoner was subsequently tortured by Maqoma despite the fact that Maqoma and Matwa were rivals.

Even though there was a class hierarchy within Xhosa society, the masses were not so far removed from those in power that the ones in power lived in luxury as the masses starved. Xhosa culture was generally a very hospitable culture and Xhosa chiefs did not have absolute power. Chiefs who ruled poorly were removed from power. The Xhosa people offer but one example, but there are some other examples that I can point to which show that class structures in Africa did not result in complete deprivation for the masses.

In the process of colonizing African people, we were brought into an alien system. This alien system was a capitalist system which not only ruthlessly exploited African people, but which introduced new class distinctions which differed from what had existed in Africa prior. This capitalist system was developed out of a historical process in Europe where class distinctions were already more antagonistic than they were in Africa due to the nature of European society. I am not suggesting that all African rulers were upstanding. The very fact that certain African states had systems in place to remove poor rulers demonstrates that this was far from the case. Within the capitalist system, it would appear that corrupt and ineffective leadership has become the norm.

The existence of a ruling class did not mean that the masses of African people were so thoroughly exploited so as to remain trapped in the direst forms of poverty. This was a development which was brought about by colonialism in Africa. Colonialism eroded existing social structures and replaced those structures with a very ruthless form of capitalist exploitation. This ruthless system was inherited by African leaders in the post-colonial era. The result has been the birth of a class of leaders who live lavishly at the expense of the masses and have little concern for the well-being of the masses.

I make all of this clear to demonstrate that the political systems which existed in pre-colonial Africa were built on the same degree of exploitation which the systems of foreign invaders were built on. Having stated this, I now wish to address a claim made by E.A. Budge. Of Nastasenen's raids, E.A. Budge noted: "Cattle, women, and gold were three things desired by the Nubian king five hundred years before Christ, and it is interesting to note how closely his views on the matter resembled those of Muhammad Ali, twenty-four centuries later!" The point that Bugle was making was that long before Muhammad Ali was implementing slave raids in Sudan, the Kushite ruler Nastasenen was doing the same thing.

Nastasenen's raids were no doubt violent and destructive for those who were impacted, but there is an important distinction to draw between those raids and that which Muhammad Ali engaged in. To understand the distinction, one must understand the nature of Muhammad Ali's rule in Egypt.

Muhammad Ali was appointed as the Ottoman viceroy in Egypt, although he later tried to break away from Ottoman rule to establish himself as an independent ruler in Egypt. To do so, he recognized that he would have to strengthen Egypt's military and economy. This Muhammad Ali did through implementing a number of reforms. He expanded agriculture and industrial development. Among his military reforms included the creation of an Egyptian fleet to engage in combat at sea as well.

Muhammad Ali's reforms came at the expense of the masses in Egypt. Many peasants and artisans died of hunger as the government of Egypt pursued policies which built up the power of the army. In response to this, some fled to Syria. Others rebelled. The Egyptian government responded to this by demanding the return of those who fled. The Egyptian government also suppressed popular uprisings. Muhammad Ali's system of administration was one which was brutally exploitative of the Egyptian peasantry and was even more abusive towards those in the Sudan who were subjected to slave raids from Muhammad Ali's state. This was a level of exploitation and brutality towards ordinary people which simply was not matched in Kush. Budge himself acknowledged the problems with Ottoman rule when he explained: "Misgovernment, monopoly extortion, and oppression were the accompaniments of Turkish rule...Every official plundered..." The brutalities of Muhammad Ali's rule were an extension of the exploitation which accompanied Ottoman rule.

Further Reading:

Helen Chapin Metz, ed. *Egypt: A Country Study*. Washington: GPO for the Library of Congress, 1990.

Vladimir Borisovich Lutsky, *Modern History of the Arab Countries*

32

AHAMDU AND THE DUPLICITOUS NATURE OF COLONIALISM

One of the justifications of colonialism was this notion of the Pax Colonica or the idea that colonialism brought peace and stability to African states which were in conflict prior to the establishment of colonialism. The reality is that prior to the onset of colonialism in Africa, there were conflicts due to the expansion and maintenance of certain states. The colonial powers benefited from some of these conflicts by not only exploiting the division, but also taking advantage of the fact that internal conflicts weakened the ability of certain African states to engage in stronger resistance. J. Thornton noted that some African states which fought against colonialism were also faced with constant revolts due to the fact that "by and large the leadership of the states, exploitative and tyrannical as they were, did not possess the legitimacy to go to the country and carry on the wars."

An important point to be made about European colonialism in Africa is that it was often framed as a civilizing mission, but the reality is that the objective of colonialism was power and the exploitation of African people. There was also a great deal of dishonesty in how Europeans approached their dealings with African states. Take for example the Tukulor Empire which was established by Al Hadj Umar. Umar was succeeded by his son Ahmadu. That Ahmadu was in a precarious situation is demonstrated by the fact that he entered into an alliance with France. Ahmadu was in a weak political position given that he was in conflict with his brothers who challenged his authority. Making a deal with the French allowed Ahmadu to receive the weapons that he needed, but the problem was that the French had no interest in honoring the terms of the agreement.

Ahmadu did manage to quell the rebellion of his brothers in 1874. In 1880, Ahmadu negotiated a treaty with Captain Gallieni. The terms of the treaty allowed the French to build and maintain trade routes in Ahmadu's empire and in turn the French would recognize the sovereignty of Tukulor. The treaty was never ratified, however. In 1881, the French began their invasion of Tukulor. Ahmadu initially failed to engage in direct military resistance against the French. He still had to contend with rebellion within his own state. In 1884, Ahmadu launched an attack his on brother Moutaga, who was the king of Kaarta. Ahmadu was also contending with a Bambara rebellion in the district of Beledugu.

In the case of Ahmadu we see how internal divisions within African states served to benefit the colonial powers. Ahmadu was mainly preoccupied with suppressing rebellion to offer direct military resistance to the French. He attempted to negotiate with the French, but the French had no intention of honoring their word because their primary objective was the conquest of Tukulor. To further this objective the French even went so far as to aid the Bambara rebels. Ahmadu was aware that the French were supporting the Bambara rebels when he agreed to sign the Treaty of Gori in 1887. This placed Tukulor under French protection and the French agreed not to invade his territories. The French later violated the treaty by resuming their attack on the Tukulor fortress.

Part of the reason why Pan-Africanists advocate for African unity is due to the recognition that internal divisions and conflicts weakened the African response to foreign threats. Some African rulers themselves recognized a common interest in defending Africa from the colonial powers of Europe. For example, the Nama leader Hendrik Witbooi expressed the view that the "different kingdoms and regions" in Africa "reflects only a trivial subdivision of Africa." He understood that the need for Africa to retain its independence was greater than the divisions which existed. Witbooi's rival Maherereo who led the uprising of the Herero people wrote to Witbooi to urge joint action against the Germans. Maherereo called for all of Africa to fight the Germans.

33

THE CHALLENGES OF ARAB UNITY

Gamal Nasser came to political prominence in 1952 as one of the leaders of the revolution in Egypt. Nasser. Nasser was a socialist who proclaimed the Arab Socialist Union as the sole political party in Egypt. As part of his socialist vision, Nasser nationalized all private banks, insurance companies, and several shipping companies. Nasser's socialist vision was at odds with organizations which promoted political Islam, however. Among such organizations included the Muslim Brotherhood, which was founded in 1928 by Hasan al Banna. The organization developed a reputation as one which was willing to use violence to achieve its goals. This has included assassinations. Nasser's government accused the Muslim Brotherhood of being involved in a plot to assassinate Nasser in 1954.

Nasser was also a leader who espoused Arab unity. In his attempts to foster such unity, Nasser faced a number of setbacks. In 1958, the political leaders of Syria expressed their interest in forming a union with Egypt. Nasser agreed, although he was initially skeptical. This skepticism was warranted as the union between the two nations was short-lived. Nasser's "socialist decrees" which called for widespread nationalization was opposed by Syrians who feared that Nasser's vision would end Syria's economic independence. The union ended when army officers staged a coup and declared Syria's separation from Egypt. An attempted union with Yemen also failed. Nasser found that unifying Arab states was a difficult task. Not only had unions with Syria and Yemen failed, but the monarchs in Saudi Arabia and Jordan opposed Nasser. Nasser viewed these monarchs as reactionaries who were a threat to Arab unity.

Muammar Gaddafi, who came to power in 1969 via a military coup, saw himself as a successor to Nasser's vision. This included promoting socialism and Arab unity. In Libya, Gaddafi encountered challenges of his own from religious leaders who differed with Gaddafi's unconventional approach to Islam. For example, Gaddafi had declared the Qur'an was the sole guide to

Islamic law. In doing so he also challenged the authenticity of the hadith as a basis of Islamic law. Those imams who openly resisted Gaddafi's socialist changes were replaced by imams who were more compliant with Gaddafi's vision. Gaddafi found himself in conflict with the Muslim Brotherhood and other radical groups such as the Holy War and the Party of God.

Under Gaddafi's leadership, Libya pursued failed attempts at mergers with different Arab states. In 1972, the Federation of Arab Republics was formed. This federation included Libya, Syria, and Egypt. This union was not to last. In 1974, there was a merger of Libya and Tunisia, but this did not last either. There was also a union with Syria in 1980, but it existed only on paper as neither side was willing to surrender its sovereignty. An attempted union with Morocco dissolved when Morocco hosted Israel's prime minister in 1986.

Gaddafi once complained that "it is ironic to see that Americans and Soviets, who are not of the same origin, have come together to create united federations, while the Arabs, who are of the same race and religion, have so far failed to realize the most cherished goal of the present Arab generation." The issue was that beyond a shared language and religion, there was little else to unify the Arab world. There certainly was no shared ideological vision. The socialist vision promoted by Nasser and Gaddafi were not widely accepted by other Arab leaders. Their socialist visions were especially opposed by religious extremists such as the Muslim Brotherhood.

Arab states were also not united on geopolitical matters. As was noted, Libya's union with Morocco dissolved over Morocco's willingness to host the Israeli prime minister. Gaddafi also fell out with Anwar Sadat when the latter journeyed to Jerusalem. Gaddafi, who opposed peaceful relations with Israel, wanted the isolation of Egypt. Gaddafi similarly fell out with Iraq and Saudi Arabia. In 1980, when Iran and Iraq went to war, Libya gave its support to Iran. This broke Libya's relations with Iraq and Saudi Arabia. The fact that the Arab League supported the intervention in Libya which overthrew and killed Gaddafi further demonstrated the challenges Gaddafi confronted with unifying the Arab world.

34

MARTIN LUTHER KING AND ABRAHAM JOSHUA HESCHEL

In a paper titled "Theological Affinities in the Writings of Abraham Joshua Heschel and Martin Luther King, Jr.", Susannah Heschel recalled the bond between Martin Luther King and Abraham Joshua Heschel. This bond between two men, who marched together for civil rights, signaled a high point for the relationship between Jewish people and African Americans. Susannah Heschel noted: "Today, looking back from a generation more accustomed to African-American leaders such as Louis Farrakhan, King's closeness to Heschel seems beyond belief." Indeed, by the 1990s the relationship between the Jewish community and the African American community was not what it appeared to be during the civil rights movement, although even in the 1960s there were tensions, which shall be elaborated on.

King and Heschel were not merely civil rights advocates, but they were religious leaders as well. This helped to shape the affinity that the two men had for each other. Their bond was such that King was invited to speak at Heschel's sixtieth birthday. That Heschel was a Jew and King was a Christian did not interfere with this bond at all. In fact, King had expressed great respect for Judaism. In 1949, he wrote: "Jesus was a Jew. It is impossible to understand Jesus outside of the race in which he was born. The Christian Church has tended to overlook its Judaic origins, but the fact is that Jesus of Nazareth was a Jew of Palestine." King continued to note: "There is no justification of the view that Jesus was attempting to find a church distinct from the Synagogue." Heschel had a similar respect for Christianity. He stated in 1964 that Jews "ought to acknowledge the eminent role and part of Christianity in God's design for the redemption of all men."

King's point about the Jewish origins of the Christian Church is an important one given the historical persecution which Jews have endured due to the Christian Church in Europe. The fact is that Christianity emerged from Judaism. Not only was Jesus a Jew, but the first Christians were Jews who prayed in Hebrew. This is logical considering that the doctrine of Christianity is rooted in the belief that Jesus is the fulfillment of God's promise to the Jews in the Old Testament. Jews would have been the first group to understand the importance of Jesus as a fulfillment of God's divine promise. Despite this, the early Christian hostility was rooted in the view that Jews not only rejected Jesus, but that they were responsible for killing Jesus.

The accounts of the gospels do state that it was a Jewish crowd which called for Jesus to be crucified, but a proper reading of the Bible would clearly indicate that there were Jews who rejected Jesus, while there were others who accepted him as their messiah. Of course, Christians who persecute Jews as an act of revenge for the murder of Jesus have missed the point of Jesus' teachings entirely. Upon being crucified, Jesus asked God (the Father) to forgive those who crucified him for they knew not what they were doing (Luke 23:24). Jesus did not curse the men who killed him, but pleaded that they may be forgiven.

In Europe, laws were implemented to bar Jews from owning land and holding public office. Jews were also excluded from guilds and were forced into segregated communities later known as ghettoes. In 1095, when Pope Urban II called for the First Crusade to capture Jerusalem in order to seize it from Muslim rule, thousands of Jews were also slaughtered by the crusaders as they made their way to Jerusalem. Martin Luther launched the Protestant Reformation by denouncing the Catholic Church. When Jews refused to join Martin Luther's movement, he denounced Jews. He called for their synagogues to be destroyed and their houses be burned. The distrust of Jews was so profound that Jews were even accused of causing the Black Plague in Europe and accused of using the blood of children in ritualistic sacrifices.

The prejudice against Jews in Europe lasted for several centuries. As was noted, this prejudice was rooted in the notion that all Jews were responsible for killing Jesus. As the power of the church in Europe weakened due to the Enlightenment, prejudice against Jewish unfortunately remained. What was once a prejudice rooted in religious belief developed into a prejudice based on the conspiracy that Jews were conspiring to use their money to take over the world. In Russia, Jews were blamed for the assassination of Alexander II in 1881. For many years after, Jews in Russia became the target of violent attacks. This prejudice would have particularly disastrous consequences in Germany with the emergence of the Nazis. Adolf Hitler blamed the Jews for many of the world's ills. The Nazis began to segregate Jews from the non-Jewish population. This segregation led to an eventual massacre in which an estimated six million Jews were murdered by the Nazi regime.

The historical persecution which Jews endured also helped to forge a bond during the civil rights movement of the 1960s. Much like Jews, African Americans had endured persecution and discrimination. There was also a spiritual bond which dated back to the days of enslavement, as enslaved Africans identified their plight with the plight of the Hebrews of the Bible who were enslaved in Egypt.

As was noted, even though there were Jews such as Heschel who actively supported the civil rights movement, tensions did exist in the 1960s as well. The tensions between African Americans and Jews were rooted in the view that there were Jews who benefited from financially exploiting African American communities. Jewish racism against African Americans was an issue as well, which is something which Heschel had addressed. In her essay, Susannah Heschel also noted that Heschel did not support Jewish opposition to affirmative action in the 1970s.

There were also tensions over Israel. Leaders such as Kwame Ture and Louis Farrakhan denounced the Israeli treatment of Palestinians. Malcolm X was also critical of Zionism. He stated: "Zionism is even more dangerous than communism because it is made more acceptable and is thus more destructively effective." This was not a view shared by King. King not only expressed the view that Israel had a right to exist, but he also asserted that Israel was "one of the great outposts of democracy in the world."

King's support for Israel seemed to have been rooted in his view that Jews, being a historically oppressed people, needed a homeland of their own to protect themselves. This is not an unreasonable position, but those leaders who opposed Zionism did so due to the fact that the creation of Israel resulted in the displacement of the Palestinian people. They were also critical of

Zionism's connection to Western imperialism. Leaders such as Malcolm X, Kwame Ture, and Louis Farrakhan expressed a greater solidarity with Arabs who were oppressed under European colonialism than with the Zionists who aligned with European colonialism to acquire territory in Palestine.

The friendship which King and Heschel enjoyed was one which was rooted in a mutual commitment to justice. This commitment led both men to take strong positions against the Vietnam War, even though both men faced resistance for doing so. Heschel co-founded an organization called Clergy and Laymen Concerned About Vietnam in 1965. He considered it blasphemous to speak about God while remaining silent on Vietnam, but other Jews did not agree. Some members of the Jewish community expressed concern that Heschel's criticisms of the Vietnam War would endanger American support for Israel. Civil rights leaders in the African American community expressed a similar concern that King's position on the war would result in President Lyndon Johnson withdrawing some of his support for civil rights.

King certainly differed with Whitney Young, who expressed the view that "the greatest freedom that exists for Negroes . . . is the freedom to die in Vietnam." It was easy for Young to state this considering he was not one of the individuals who was sent to die in Vietnam. Moreover, such a statement displayed a complete disregard for the Vietnamese who were killed as a result of the war. King and Heschel did not share this disregard for those who were being killed due to the war. Heschel stated: "The blood we shed in Vietnam makes a mockery of all our proclamations, dedications, celebrations. Has our conscience become a fossil, is all mercy gone? If mercy, the mother of humility, is still alive as a demand, how can we say yes to our bringing agony to that tormented country? We are here because our own integrity as human beings is decaying in the agony and merciless killing done in our name. In a free society, some are guilty and all are responsible. We are here to call upon the governments of the United States as well as North Vietnam to stand still and to consider that no victory is worth the price of terror, which all parties commit in Vietnam, North and South. Remember that the blood of the innocent cries forever. Should that blood stop to cry, humanity would cease to be." Of the war, King stated: "If America's soul becomes totally poisoned, part of the autopsy must read Vietnam…A nation that continues year after year to spend more money on military defense than on programs of social uplift is approaching spiritual death."

King and Heschel enjoyed a beautiful friendship which was rooted in a common respect for each other's religious beliefs and a shared commitment to justice. This relationship was not representative of the larger relationship between the African American and Jewish community, however. By the 1960s the tensions between the two communities were becoming apparent.

35

FIDEL CASTRO: A BLACK WHITE MAN?

In his song "Message of '70," Chalkdust sang: "Socialism some say no/Some still hate Fidel Castro." Chalkdust was referring to those in the Caribbean who rejected socialism and Fidel Castro due to their attachment to colonialism. The song itself was a critique of those who have failed to receive the revolutionary message of the 1970 Black Power uprising in Trinidad.

That Chalkdust would defend Castro in his song is a reflection of the stature which Castro held as a political figure in the Caribbean, especially during the era of Black Power. Kwame Ture once described Fidel Castro as one of the blackest men in the Caribbean. This was a rather curious remark considering that Castro was a white man, phenotypically. Walter Rodney elaborated on this point by noting that whereas Ture was free to visit Cuba, he could not visit Trinidad or Jamaica despite the fact that both nations were led by black men. Rodney explained that white power was the power of whites over blacks, and that Castro challenged white power in Cuba. This is what made Castro "black" where Ture and Rodney were concerned. It was not that Castro was a black man, but that his policies challenged white domination over black people.

Castro did in fact do a great deal to challenge white power, but I would argue that Castro did not go far enough in challenging white power in Cuba because he saw the fight against racism in Cuba in terms of a class struggle against capitalism. He was really working to dismantle capitalism and to the extent that dismantling capitalism meant challenging white power, Castro did so, but not enough was done in Cuba to empower the black population because black empowerment was never Castro's vision. Even so, one must grant that Castro's policies were certainly much blacker than many of the black Caribbean leaders at the time.

36

RELIGION AND MORALITY

Muammar Gaddafi was a socialist, but his particular socialist vision rejected the atheism promoted by communists. In Gaddafi's view, communists could not be trusted because they had no fear of divine punishment and as such were free to break their word. Gaddafi developed an ideology known as the Third Universal Theory, which was heavily influenced by his Islamic faith. Religion was central to Gaddafi's ideological worldview. F.M. Sheldon expressed a similar view, arguing: "Historically the best morals have been connected with the best religion, and in my judgment, a continued advance in morals is impossible apart from religion."

The question is does morality exist without religion? Does it exist without a belief in God? What is certainly beyond dispute is that belief in God does not make one moral. This can be demonstrated in Romans 2 in the Bible where Paul noted that the very Jews who brag about having God's law also regularly break God's law by stealing and committing adultery. He went so far to note that Gentiles denounce God because of the actions of Jews who believe in God.

Belief in God alone does not make one moral. I would also argue that one does not need to believe in God or a divine being to avoid engaging in actions such as stealing and murder. One does not need to have a religion to display a basic sense of morality, though it is also true that morality is subjective. Actions which one may regard as immoral may not necessarily be regarded as immoral by another. The importance of religion as a tool to instill morality comes from the fact that religions provide a standard for upholding morality. An example of this would be the Ten Commandments which were given to Moses. These were laws which instructed the Hebrews on how to behave and which actions to avoid engaging in.

In an article titled "Business Principles in Christian Work," Lucien Warner argued that business principles should not include misrepresentation or cheating because such actions go against the principles of Christianity. Warner also cited the Bible to support the notion that business principles which are rooted in Christian work should include no waste, no duplication, and that for 100% of effort put forth there should be 100% of the results. Again, it is not that one cannot understand such principles without the Bible, but that those who read the Bible and who strive to live by the message preached by Christ have a standard of morality to live by. For believers, the Bible and the Qur'an offer a guide for morality. Problems do emerge when believers make it their mission to impose their religious standards of morality on others, although that is a separate matter.

37

AS AMERICAN AS CHERRYPIE: THE CASE OF JAMIL AL-AMIN

Jamil Al-Amin, who was formerly known as H. Rap Brown, emerged as a civil rights leader who represented a rejection of the nonviolence of Martin Luther King and others within the civil rights movement. Al-Amin had famously declared that violence is as American as cherrypie. In his autobiography Al-Amin stated: "Ever since Ed and I have been active in the Movement we've always carried our guns. I've always had the utmost confidence in me and the gun. Give me a gun before you even give me somebody to work with. A gun won't fail you. People will. I found that out early."

Al-Amin's views on guns and self-defense placed him at odds with other members of the Student Nonviolent Coordinating Committee (SNCC). He recalled that when he was arrested in Alabama on a concealed weapon charge, members of SNCC debated over whether to get him out of jail. They didn't and his brother Ed put up his bond. To defend his position, Al-Amin stated: "America doesn't rule the world with love. It rules with guns, tanks, missiles, bombs, the Army, Air Force, Navy and the Marines. When america fights a nonviolent war; I'll become nonviolent."

At the time there were ideological disagreements within the movement over the question of nonviolence. There were those in the civil rights movement who promoted nonviolent acts of civil disobedience as a means to combat racism. Others felt that African Americans had the right to defend themselves against acts of racial aggression, even if doing so required violent self-defense. Al-Amin belonged to the latter group.

Al-Amin became affiliated with SNCC through his brother, Ed. Ed was part of an organization known as the Nonviolent Action Group (NAG). Al-Amin spent his summers in Washington D.C. with Ed. During this time, he read W.E.B. Du Bois, Frederick Douglass, Marcus Garvey, and Richard Wright. It was during this time that Al-Amin also met Stanley Wise, who would later be elected as the Executive Secretary of SNCC.

Al-Amin was eventually elected to be the chairman of NAG. In this capacity, Al-Amin worked to close the division between college educated black people and the brothers in the street. He noted: "Negro college students have always felt themselves to be better than the brother on the block." It was also during his time with NAG that Al-Amin was invited to the White House where he met with President Lydon B. Johnson. Al-Amin recalled that he thought so little of the meeting that he stole everything that he could from the White House.

Al-Amin eventually joined SNCC. Much like Kwame Ture (then known as Stokely Carmichael), Al-Amin brought a more militant and revolutionary attitude. He also rejected nonviolence. He acknowledged that nonviolence might have been tactically correct at one time to get sympathy for the movement, but he believed that it ultimately did not work. Al-Amin also supported SNCC's efforts to create a Black Panther Party, which was meant to be an independent political party for African Americans. Al-Amin recalled that the "oldline" leaders and ministers opposed the Black Panther label. The label was also opposed by a leader named Mr. Gilmore who "was still in that integration bag".

Al-Amin's position on nonviolence was also connected to his criticism of America's foreign policy. Much like Malcolm X had done, Al-Amin denounced the fact that black people were expected to remain nonviolent in America, while also being drafted to engage in acts of violence on behalf of the United States. He explained: "We must refuse to participate in the war of genocide against people of color: a war that also commits genocide against us. Black men are being used on the front lines at a disproportionate rate. Forty-five percent of the casualties are Black. That's genocide! We cannot let our Black brothers fight in Vietnam because we need them here to fight with us. If we can die defending our motherland, we can die defending our mothers."

Al-Amin's views were not only controversial, but they also made him a target. Al-Amin was arrested on a number of occasions. It was while he was serving a prison sentence for armed robbery that Al-Amin converted to Islam. Al-Amin emerged from prison as an Islamic religious leader. Al-Amin was later convicted for killing a sheriff deputy. The shooting happened on the same night that the sheriff deputies came to serve a warrant on Al-Amin for missing court over a traffic charge.

Al-Amin's supporters have criticized the conviction, pointing out the inconsistencies in the evidence, such as statements that the assailant had been shot, although Al-Amin was not shot. The outcome was perhaps no surprise to Al-Amin, who had stated in his autobiography: "I anticipate one day, however, that I will be arrested and there will be no legal procedure any lawyer will be able to use to secure my release."

38

PIRATES OF THE AMERICAS

That Peter Tosh denounced "the pirates Christopher Columbus and Henry Morgan" as being representatives of the system of Babylon which keeps African in Jamaica oppressed is a reflection of Tosh's own understanding of the historical forces which shaped the colonial nature of Jamaican society.

Christopher Columbus was not only the man who ushered in the age of European colonialism through his discovery of the Americas in 1492, but he actively participated in constructing the first colonial society in the New World. The first Spanish colony was established on the island of Hispaniola. From the beginning, the Taino people were mistreated and abused. In response to the seizure of their food and the abuse of their women, they rebelled and were defeated. Columbus, who ruled the colony as governor until 1499, attempted to end the more serious abuses, but this simply amounted to a milder form of exploitation in which settlers were provided with land and with natives to labor on the land. This system, known as repartimiento, did little to alleviate the suffering of the natives.

Colonialism in the Americas, and elsewhere in the world, was justified based on the belief that Europeans possessed a superior civilization which needed to be diffused to the rest of the world via colonial conquest. The problem is that this was not the case at all. In an essay titled "Education in Ecuador: Philosophical Culture During the Colonial Period," Julio Endara argued: "The conquest of America was, beyond doubt, a very unfortunate accident. In particular, the empire of the Incas, whose degree of civilization seems to have attained a respectable height, under the pressure of exceptional circumstances, was subjected to the dominion of an ignorant power hampered by prejudices and difficulties."

Endara also noted that the religious tolerance of Incan civilization "had reached the noblest and most magnanimous point; for the beliefs of the conquered peoples were respected, nothing more being demanded..." This was not how European colonial

205

powers approached their dealings with those whom they conquered. Endara also noted the "socialistic" aspects of Incan civilization in that there were no rich and no poor. Endara continued to note that in their greed for treasure, the Spaniards "destroyed even the last vestiges that were of positive value".

European colonialism was also marked by a struggle for power and territory among the colonial powers themselves. Britain seized control of Jamaica in 1655. Jamaica became a hotbed of pirates and smugglers. It was also used as a base of operations for British vessels. It was the Jamaican governor William Henry Lyttleton who dispatched war ships against Nicaragua in 1762. Nicaragua at the time was under Spanish rule. The British were ultimately defeated and forced to return to Jamaica. This was the system of piracy in Jamaica which Tosh decried.

39

TRADITION AND RELIGION IN ETHIOPIA

Abrahamic religions have historically been religions which were intolerant of differing religious views. The Hebrews of the Old Testament were commanded to worship no other gods but Yahweh. Leviticus 19:31 also warned the Hebrews against turning to mediums as a means to communicate with spirits. Judaism, Christianity, and Islam all promote a strict adherence to the worship of the God of Abraham. This has traditionally left little space for tolerance towards other religions, although there have been examples of a synthesis between Abrahamic religious beliefs and other practices. This can be demonstrated in Ethiopia.

One of the features of Christianity in Ethiopia was the manner in which it adopted itself to the local culture. This demonstrated a degree of tolerance for non-Christian religions. Walter Rodney noted that even "when converting 'animists' to Christianity, it respected their previous culture and adopted part of it." An example which Rodney noted is that whereas the priests in Europe used Latin, even though Latin was unknown to the common people, the church in Ethiopia used Ge'ez and Amharic. To further illustrate the religious tolerance in Ethiopia, Rodney noted that "when the Jews and Muslims were overcome militarily, they still had a place in the social, political and economic life of Ethiopia."

Christianity remained the dominant religion in Ethiopia due to being the religion that was traditionally practiced by the monarchy of Ethiopia, but, as Rodney noted, other religions were largely tolerated as well. For example, the government of Haile Selassie retained Muslims courts which handled family and personal disputes in accordance with Islamic law. It was also sometimes the case that Muslims in East Africa handled matters based on customary law. For example, in some parts of Eritrea the practice of treating land as the property of a clan was a break with the Islamic principle of dividing property among one's heirs.

Belief in spirits is an aspect of Ethiopia's traditional religious beliefs which were incorporated into the beliefs of Christians and

Muslims. These spirits, which are known as zar, can either be malevolent or benevolent. There are also protective spirits known as adbar. These protective spirits can either be male or female. Yet another traditional belief which was also incorporated in Christianity and Islam is the belief in the evil eye, known as buda. To protect against evil eye, one must wear amulets or invoke the name of God.

40

THE FRENCH CONQUEST OF ALGERIA

Napoleon I of France expressed a great deal of interest in seizing control of Algeria. In 1808, he sent a military engineer named Major Buten to engage in a topographical survey of Algeria to prepare for the conquest of the territory. This plan was never executed, however. Defeats in Spain and Russia prevented this, but French interest in conquering Algeria remained.

The effort to seize control of Algeria was undertaken by Charles X. On June 14, 1830, a French army landed near Algiers to begin the process of seizing Algeria. In the ensuing battle, France lost 400 men to the 10,000 which were lost by the Turks. By July, the French troops managed to enter Algiers. General de Bourmont declared that the whole kingdom would surrender within fifteen days. He made this announcement prematurely as it would take decades of fighting for France to finally subdue Algeria.

The resistance in Algeria was led by Abd el-Kader. Kader was born in 1808. His father was the head of a religious brotherhood known as Kaderiya. Prior to the French occupation, Kader made his pilgrimage to Mecca. He had also visited Egypt where he was impressed by the reforms undertaken by Muhammad Ali. By 1832, Kader was elected to lead the struggle against French occupation.

Utilizing guerrilla warfare, Kader managed to engage in a fierce resistance of French troops. He was so successful in his resistance that by 1834, France agreed to negotiate with the rebels. This led to the Desmichel Treaty in which France was willing to acknowledge Kader's control of most of western Algeria.

The peace was not to last. In 1837, the French captured the city of Constantine. Ahmed Bey, who was leading the resistance, was forced to retreat. Kader's leadership was requested to assist the struggle in Constantine. For this, Kader was accused of violating the peace treaty and a war was declared against him. Kader was driven out of Algeria and took refuge in Morocco where he continued the struggle.

France finally captured Kader in 1847 and sent him into exile.

Kader spent some time in France before settling in Damascus where he died in 1883, at the age of 75. Kader's exile in Damascus is notable for his support of the local Christian population. In 1860, a group of Muslim fanatics organized pogroms to massacre the Christian population. Kader defended Christians during the massacre. The defeat of Kader brought nearly all of Algeria under French control, but this did not bring an end to Algerian resistance. Throughout the 1850s, France encountered rebellions throughout Algeria.

Uprisings persisted into the 1870s as well due to the poor conditions under which Algerians lived. Between 1868 and 1870 there was a famine which killed a large number of Algerians. There was a mass uprising in 1871, which was led by Muhammad el-Mokrani. The uprising was also motivated by news about the Paris Commune, which made its way to Algeria. The Paris Commune also helped Mokrani's uprising as France was unable to dispatch troops to Algeria. When the Paris Commune was finally defeated, France was finally able to crush Mokrani's uprising. The uprising was finally put down in 1872.

Frantz Fanon's work helped to highlight the brutal nature of French colonialism in Algeria. Fanon, who was born in Martinique, first traveled to Algeria during World War II. Fanon had enlisted to support the French cause in the war. Fanon was transferred to Algeria after undergoing basic training. From Algeria, Fanon was sent to France where he engaged in combat and was wounded. By 1945, Fanon returned to Martinque where he decided to continue his education.

Fanon developed an interest in psychiatry. After he passed his exam in 1953, Fanon applied to work in Blida, Algeria. It was in Algeria that Fanon came to witness the harsh reality of French colonialism. The Arab quarters in Blida was known as "nigger town". Fanon also witnessed acts of medical malpractice, as doctors would administer saline solution or distilled water to Arabs, while claiming that they were providing penicillin or vitamin B.

It was during his time in Algeria that Fanon also came to support the efforts of the Front de Libération National (FLN). In 1955, a state of emergency was declared against the FLN. Fanon decided to hold meetings at the hospital with FLN members. Fanon also began treating some of the rebels who experienced psychoses which were trigged by violence and torture. Fanon's support for the FLN forced him to resign from the hospital. He was later expelled from Algeria and was forced to relocate to Tunis. In exile from Algeria, Fanon traveled throughout Europe and Africa to speak in support of the FLN. The abuse and mistreatment which Fanon witnessed in Algeria compelled him to support the Algerian struggle for liberation.

For the French colonizers, Algeria served as a market for French goods and as a source of raw material. The economy of Algeria was structured in such a way that the French sold their goods at the highest prices possible in Algeria and in return received agricultural raw materials at the lowest price possible. Algeria also became a location for European settlers. Land which was seized from Algerians was given to settlers. These settlers were also provided with schools, shops, and hospitals which were paid for at the public expense. As the colonial administration saw that the needs of the European settlers were met, the Algerians who were subjected to colonialism remained neglected and exploited.

41

FROM NONVIOLENCE TO VIOLENCE

Discriminatory policies were already in place in South Africa prior to 1948, but when Afrikaner Nationalists came to power in 1948, they implemented a system known as "apartheid." Nelson Mandela described apartheid as a new term, but an old idea. This new system segregated various facets of life in South Africa, including residence, education, and employment. Mandela explained that the "often haphazard segregation of the past three hundred years was to be consolidated into a monolithic system that was diabolical in its detail, inescapable in its reach, and overwhelming in its power."

Mandela recalled that the victory of the National Party came as a shock to everyone in South Africa. He and Oliver Tambo barely even discussed the question of a government led by the Nationalists because it was not expected, but the Nationalists prevailed. Mandela was dismayed by the result, but Tambo welcomed it because it allowed Africans to know exactly who the enemies were.

Many years after the implementation of apartheid, Malcolm X expressed a similar view to that of Tambo when he commented on the difference between racism in America and South Africa. He stated: "America is worse than South Africa, because not only is America racist, but she also is deceitful and hypocritical. South Africa preaches segregation and practices segregation. She, at least, practices what she preaches. America preaches integration and practices segregation. She preaches one thing while deceitfully practicing another."

Daniel Malan's new Nationalist government wasted little time with implementing its racist vision. Within weeks, the new government pardoned Robey Leibbrandt, who had organized uprisings in support of Nazi Germany. In 1949, a bill which barred sexual relations between white people and non-white people was passed. Another bill labeled all South Africans by their race. In response to this, the African National Congress (ANC) launched its "Program of Action". The program had been drafted by the ANC Youth League. This program marked a shift in the ANC's direction. Up until this point, the ANC had always worked within the law, but the new program called for boycotts, strikes, protests, and other disruptive activities.

The new direction was opposed by Dr. Alfred Xuma. Mandela recalled that he and Tambo had a very tense exchange with Xuma on the matter which resulted in Xuma showing them out of his house. Xuma was subsequently voted out of his position and Dr. James Moroka became the new president-general of the ANC. This new radical direction would have profound implications for the struggle against apartheid in South Africa. As the ANC was moving in a more radical direction, the government of South Africa had become more repressive. The government passed an act which outlawed the Communist Party, but the act was so broad that it also outlawed even mild acts of protest.

As the repression of the government became more severe, Mandela publicly declared that nonviolence was a useless strategy. For this Mandela was reprimanded. Mandela accepted the censure, but he held firm to his belief that nonviolence was not a solution to the problem. Mandela viewed nonviolence as a strategy, not a moral principle. He recognized that nonviolence as a strategy was no longer effective in the face of such brutal government repression.

Mandela was premature, but in the end the ANC did abandon the principle of nonviolence. It was decided that the ANC would form an armed wing of the party known as Umkhonto we Sizwe or MK. Mandela explained: "A freedom fighter learns the hard way that it is the oppressor who defines the nature of the struggle, and the oppressed is often left no recourse but to use methods that mirror those of the oppressor. At a certain point, one can only fight fire with fire." This remark spoke to the necessity of using violent tactics against the apartheid regime in South Africa.

Despite his willingness to abandon the tactic of nonviolence, Mandela was aware of his own limits as someone who had no prior military experience or training. Mandela recruited Joe Slovo and through Slovo he enlisted the support of white communists who were already engaged in acts of sabotage. The MK also recruited Jack Hodgson, who was a World War II veteran. To further prepare, Mandela read books by and about revolutionary figures such as Che Guevara, Mao Zedong, and Fidel Castro. He also read Menachem Begin's *The Revolt* and studied the history of wars in South Africa.

The ANC's shift away from nonviolence demonstrated the limits of a strict adherence to nonviolence as a tactic. This was a reality which Mandela understood. Malcolm, who was mentioned previously, understood this reality as well, which is why he was so critical of the civil rights movement's insistence of utilizing nonviolence as the sole strategy to combat racism in America.

It should also be noted that violence is not without its consequences. Mandela expressed horror over the fact that civilians were killed in a car bomb explosion which was carried out by the ANC in 1983, but he also acknowledged that such accidents are an inevitable consequence of violent resistance. Mandela also firmly maintained that although violent resistance was necessary to protect against the abuses of the apartheid regime, the only lasting solution in South Africa must be a peaceful one.

42

THE INTERNATIONAL NATURE OF THE STRUGGLE AGAINST APARTHEID

The struggle against apartheid in South Africa was not simply a struggle which was waged by Africans in South Africa. The struggle against apartheid in South Africa was part of the larger liberation struggle being fought across Africa. In Rhodesia, where Africans were confronted with white minority rule as well, the African National Congress was established in 1957 as a mass movement. Joshua Nkomo was selected as the ANC's leader. By 1959, the ANC was banned in Rhodesia. In 1960, the nationalist leaders launched a new organization known as the National Democratic Party (NDP). The NDP was eventually banned, which resulted in the creation of the Zimbabwe African People's Union (ZAPU). ZAPU itself was banned in 1962. The ANC viewed the liberation struggle in Rhodesia as an extension of the struggle in South Africa. Whereas Ian Smith's government received the support of South Africa's Defense Force, the ANC allied itself with ZAPU.

Other struggles were being fought in Angola, Mozambique, and Namibia. It was precisely because of the international nature of the liberation struggles in Africa that the government of South Africa pressured neighboring states into withdrawing their support for the ANC. The pressure forced some of these states to capitulate. In 1982, Swaziland signed an agreement to expel ANC personnel from its territory. Lesotho made a similar agreement in 1983. In Angola, South Africa supported a rebel group known as UNITA in an effort to destabilize the government of José Eduardo dos Santos. Santos' government had provided support for the struggle against apartheid, as well as Namibia's independence struggle. In 1981, South Africa's Defense Force launched Operation Protea, in which thousands of troops were sent to invade Angola. This demonstrated the extent to which Angola's support threatened the apartheid regime in South Africa.

In the United States, TransAfrica helped to launch the "Free South Africa Movement" which advocated for an end to apartheid. TransAfrica was formed in 1977 by Randall Robinson. TransAfrica played a prominent role in rallying American support for anti-apartheid efforts in South Africa. An example of this was when Robinson appeared with Desmond Tutu at a demonstration in front of the South African embassy in Washington D.C. in 1986. Jesse Jackson and Rosa Parks also supported anti-apartheid initiatives with TransAfrica.

The struggle against apartheid also captured the attention of African musicians in the Americas. Rap artists such as Run DMC, Kool Herc, Kool G Rap, Public Enemy, and X Clan also used their music to denounce apartheid. Mandela's plight especially became a central focus for a number of reggae artists who used their music to express support for the struggle against apartheid. The songs which called for Mandela's release included Sugar Minott's "Mandela," Brigadier Jerry's "Mandela for President," Carlene Davis' "Welcome Home Mr. Mandela," and Sister Carol's "Mandela's Release." Peter Tosh not only denounced apartheid in his music, but in his actions as well. In 1986, Tosh was arrested and beaten at an anti-apartheid march in front of the British consulate in Kingston.

The oppression of Africans in South Africa and Nelson Mandela's imprisonment outraged Africans around the world. This support for South Africa's liberation struggle highlighted the impact that Pan-Africanism as a global movement has had in advancing the struggles for liberation of African people. The end of apartheid in South Africa was not merely a triumph for South Africans. It was a triumph for Africans everywhere.

Further Reading:

Itibari M. Zulu, "TransAfrica as a Collective Enterprise: Exploring Leadership and Social Justice Attentiveness," *The Journal of Pan African Studies*, vol.13, no.1, August 2020

Martin Meredith, *The Fate of Africa*, (Public Affairs, 2011).

Nathaniel Murrell, William Spencer, and Adrian McFarlane (editors), *Chanting Down Babylon: The Rastafari Reader*, (Temple University Press, 1998).

Thomas Collelo (editor), *Angola: A Country Study*. Washington: GPO for the Library of Congress, 1991.

43

THE ENDURING LEGACY OF CONFUCIUS

Gilbert Reid argued that Confucianism "contains minute instructions on political science." This statement demonstrates part of why Confucianism has been such a prevailing ideology in East Asia. That Confucius' teachings concerned itself with political science is no surprise given the time period that Confucius lived in. During his lifetime, China was divided into warring states. Confucius sought to bring order to the chaos by traveling throughout China to advocate that rulers lived virtuously and cared for their people. The rulers found little use for these teachings, but Confucius was able to attract thousands of students.

Given the state of turmoil in China at the time that Confucius began his teachings, it should be no surprise that Confucius concerned himself with how rulers ought to govern. Reid noted that "Confucius places all the emphasis on the character of the ruler. To have peace in the country, the people must be loyal, but to be loyal, they must first of all have confidence in their king, and this confidence depends entirely on the worth of the king." In Confucius' view, confidence in the ruler was a more important aspect of governance than even having an army or sufficient food. In his view, "without the confidence of the people, there can be no government." In Confucius' view, the personality of the ruler is so important that he stated: "The moral power of the rulers is as the wind, and that of the people as the grass. Whithersoever the wind blows, the grass is sure to bend."

In response to a noble who asked him what should be done to inspire a feeling of respect and loyalty from the people, Confucius responded that the people must be treated with seriousness and kindness. Confucius' view was that a good king inspired loyalty, which then eliminated the need for revolution. Confucius also stated: "Advance the upright and set aside the crooked, then the people will submit. Advance the crooked and set aside the upright, then the people will not submit." Concerning what constitutes a good government, Confucius explained that a good government is "when those who are near are made happy and those who are far off are attracted."

Confucius' ideas were not accepted by the rulers in China during his lifetime, but his ideas were accepted by the state during the Han Dynasty. Confucian ideals would remain dominant in China until the Opium War in 1839. This began what was known as the Century of Humiliation for China. It was during this time that Confucian ideals came under question and not without good reason. Confucius emphasized the importance of rulers displaying certain values in order to maintain harmony, but in time this emphasis on harmony was used to entrench social hierarchies which led to China's stagnation. During the Song Dynasty, Confucianism was used to emphasize hierarchy and absolute obedience. The neo-Confucianist doctrine which developed caused China to stagnate. Chunjuan Nancy Wei argued that Confucian China "would be doomed in its first encounters with the West."

Confucian values also helped entrench a rigid social hierarchy. Confucius stated: "Let the ruler be ruler, the minister minister, the father father, and the son son." This was meant to bring about harmony by allowing every member of society to understand their particular role and act accordingly. Out of this desire for a social structure with clearly defined roles developed a social system which developed certain hierarchies and expectations. For example, Confucian values taught that a young man's duty was to be filial to his parents and respectful to elders. Confucian teachings also established other hierarchies. For example, women were expected to be subjugated to men. The inequality in gender relations was demonstrated by the fact that a wife who killed her husband faced a harsher punishment than a husband who killed his wife. This hierarchy was one which placed certain burdens on women, as well as subordinates and inferiors. Lu Xun described this system as a "man-eating" one.

It became apparent that for China to progress, the old Confucian ideals needed to be challenged or done away with. This is precisely the task which was undertaken by Mao Zedong and his Communist Party. Whereas the Kuomintang Party under the leadership of Chiang Kai-shek attempted to revive Confucian values, the Communist Party under Mao Zedong's leadership sought to suppress Confucianism. In its place was Mao Zedong Thought, which was influenced by Marxism-Leninism.

Karl Marx, who co-authored *The Communist Manifesto* with Friedrich Engels, argued that the system of capitalism which developed in Europe was one which was destined to be overthrown and replaced by a communist system. In a short book titled *Principles of Communism*, Engels described communism as "the doctrine of the conditions of the liberation of the proletariat." In the same book, he described the proletariat as a class which lives entirely from selling its labor. He further explained that the proletariat originated out of the industrial revolution in England.

Marx and Confucius shared a common concern for the well-being of people. They differed on how this was to be achieved, however. Whereas Confucian ideals emphasized harmony, Marx put forward the view that human history was a history of class struggles. In Marx's view, the liberation of the oppressed working class of Europe necessitated a revolution which would overturn the existing world system. The question of revolution is where the two ideals diverge.

It was stated that Confucianism could be blamed for the fact that in 2,000 years, China experienced more than fifty large scale rebellions, as well as local rebellions which took place annually. Confucius apparently supported rebellious movements. Mencius went further by supporting the murder of bad rulers. So, it certainly was not the case that Confucianism endorsed maintaining a bad leader in power, yet, from a Marxist perspective, it is perhaps true that Confucianism did not go far enough in calling over the overthrow of the class in power. Confucianism advocated for a rebellion against poor leaders, while also upholding the existing feudal system. This is why Reid made the point that it is difficult to gauge the teachings of Confucianism on the matter of revolution because conservative Chinese tended to speak of Confucius as supporting existing governments, whereas revolutionists viewed Confucius as a friend of the revolution. The reality is that both positions are accurate. Confucian ideals did support existing governments to the extent that those governments cared for the masses, but where governments failed to do so then those governments were subject to revolutionary overthrow.

Mencius, who was a disciple of Confucius, was also concerned with the values of rulers. In his view, if a ruler was a good man and ruled in a benevolent manner, then he would be respected and his country would prosper. By contrast, a bad ruler would cause his country to suffer and he would be overthrown. Mencius expressed: "Only the man who possesses benevolence ought to be placed in high office. A man without benevolence in high office will disseminate wickedness among all people." He continued to explain that when those above do not regulate themselves according to fixed principle and if those below do not have laws to follow, then "inferiors will violate the penal laws." In such a situation, Mencius stated that such a country can only last through good luck. In Mencius' statement we once again see a concern with how those in power ought to act and how failure to act in accordance with a particular standard influences the masses.

Mencius also held the view that righteousness was more important than profit. In the Works of Mencius, King Hui asked Mencius about profit, to which Mencius replied by stating: "When righteousness is put last, and profit first, no one will be satisfied till he has snatched all." He expressed the view that if people focused too much on profit there would be a scramble for profit. Mencius was not unconcerned about financial matters, however. He argued that people had a right to purpose their own welfare through works such as farming and handicrafts. He also advocated for equitable taxation and the prevention of famine.

Whereas Marxists see revolution in terms of overturning a system to replace it with another system, Confucian ideals were less concerned with changing the system and more concerned with replacing poor rulers. Mencius expressed the view that rulers who are cruel will be killed and their kingdom will perish with them. He supported this viewpoint by noting that the Hsia, Shang, and Chou dynasties all ended due to lack of benevolence.

Here Mencius was describing the concept of the Mandate of Heaven, which states that the rulers of China are only able to rule when power is bestowed upon them by Heaven. He explained that Heaven does not speak, but that Heaven makes itself known through conduct and deeds. Mencius expressed the view that the people are the most precious and important of all, so to get possession of the peasant people is to become the Son of Heaven. To receive this mandate, a ruler must win the acceptance of the masses and to maintain this mandate, a ruler must demonstrate benevolence. Confucius stated that there were only two ways, the way of benevolence and the other way was without benevolence.

Confucius and Marx shared similar concerns about the conditions of the poor, but they expressed different solutions to the problem. These differences, which have been noted, became relevant to Mao's vision for pursuing socialist revolution in China. Mao, who was born in 1893, came from a background which was steeped in tradition. As a child Mao practiced Buddhism. He also memorized the Analects and the Four Classics. Mao eventually became drawn to the example set by Lenin's revolution in Russia. Mao also understood the need for applying Marxism to China's particular conditions.

Mao was not initially hostile to Confucian ideals. He confessed in 1936 that he visited and paid homage to the grave of the "sage". In a speech in 1938, Mao stated: "We should sum up the history from Confucius to Sun Yat-sen and take with us the valuable legacy. This is important for guiding the great movement of today." After Mao came to power in 1949, he took a more critical approach to Confucius, though he maintained that there was "some truth" in his teachings. Mao's hostility towards Confucius was on full display during the Cultural Revolution. Confucian temples, sites, and relics were destroyed.

Mao's opposition to Confucius was consistent with his Marxist-Leninist worldview. As noted before, Confucian ideals did encourage rebellion against poor governance, but those ideals also helped to sustain the feudal system in China. Confucianism may have questioned the authority of poor rulers, but the ideology did not question the social structure of Chinese society. As was noted, Confucianism even became the state ideology of the ruling class to help maintain its rule. In Mao's view, transforming China meant transforming the existing feudal structure which was maintained by Confucianism.

Wei noted that Marxism was not a particularly appealing philosophy for the Chinese. This was precisely the reason why Mao felt that a cultural revolution was necessary. Marxism presented a worldview which was alien to Chinese culture, so the aim of the Cultural Revolution was to overturn the old ways to create a new national culture. It was an ambitious effort, but one which was very disastrous for Chinese society.

Mao ultimately failed in suppressing Confucianism in China. Following Mao's death, subsequent leaders in China openly embraced Confucius. For example, President Jiang Zemin appeared at a celebration of Confucius' birthday in 1989. The open acknowledgment of Confucius was part of a larger shift away from many of Mao's policies. Deng Xiapoing developed the approach of "allowing some to get rich." The idea that some in society would become rich while others remained in poverty was the very thing which Marx had denounced, but this was to be the direction of the Chinese Communist Party after Mao died.

Mao's successors sought to avoid the problems caused by Mao's policies. President Hu Jinato spoke about developing a socialist market economy. He also spoke about zheteng. This is a Chinese phrase which refers to a person who fritters around by doing the same thing over again, but without producing any good results. Wei described this as a perfect description of Mao's various programs to address poverty in China.

Despite these obvious reversals, the Cultural Revolution did help to ensure that there was not a total shift away from Marxism in China. Wei noted that "Marxism has failed in Russia and Eastern Europe, but in China it has been absorbed into the traditional culture." Wei further explained that Sinicized Marxism and Confucian traditions shared important similarities which allowed the two to coexist. In this regard, the Cultural Revolution could be viewed as a success from the standpoint of allowing Marxism to continue to exist in China, even as Chinese society engaged in reforms, although the reforms themselves are certainly at odds with the end goal of Marxism, which is to create a communist society in which workers control the means of production.

The importance of Confucius in post-Mao Chinese society is that Confucius advocated for harmony through hierarchy, obedience, and respect for authority. These were the very features which Mao opposed, yet for the Chinese government such an ideology is useful for addressing protests or what the Chinese government refers to as "mass incidents". Whereas Mao opposed Confucius, Kim Il-Sung in North Korea embraced Confucius because he also recognized the usefulness in using Confucius to maintain government hierarchy and to discourage rebellion. Confucius served other political purposes for the Chinese government beyond helping to impose authority. Reg Little observed that the Confucian culture of China gave China a unifying political, social, economic, and spiritual influence. Little argued that this Confucian culture presented a stronger influence than the major Abrahamic religions. This is the enduring legacy of Confucius.

References:

Chunjuan Nancy Wei, "From Mao Back to Confucius: China's Approaches to Development and Peace," *Journal of Global Development and Peace*

Gilbert Reid, "Revolution as Taught by Confucius," *International Journal of Ethics*

44

PROPHETS AND CREEDS

H.G. Wells explained that "the oldest empires in the world were religious empires, centering upon the worship of a god or a god-king. Alexander was treated as a divinity and the Caesars were gods in so much as they had altars and temples devoted to them and the offering of incense was made a test of loyalty to the Roman State." Wells noted that in such societies if a man offered his sacrifice and bowed to the god, "he was left not only to think but to say practically whatever he liked about the affair." Wells contrasted the old religions with the "creed religions." The creed religions concerned themselves not only with what men did, but also with what men believed. The creed religions also bred an intolerance of other faiths. John Coleman De Graft-Johnson noted: "All ideas were suspect, and founders of new faiths stood in danger of being exterminated. This was indeed the age of intolerance [...]."

What Wells termed as "creed religions" was not a wholly new concept by the time that Christianity emerged. Christianity's insistence of the worship of its deity to the exclusion of other deities and religions was a feature which existed in Judaism, although Judaism did not seek to convert others. The aim of Judaism was not to spread the worship of Yahweh to others, but to ensure that the Jews, Yahweh's chosen people, remained faithful to the god of their ancestors. This faith in God was so important that the first command of the Ten Commandments stated that the Jews were to have no strange gods before Yahweh. This was a command which the biblical Hebrews struggled to follow, however. The Old Testament is largely the tale of the Hebrew rebellion against God.

The Israelite rebellion against God is demonstrated by the story Jezebel in the Bible. Jezebel is introduced as the wife of the Israelite ruler Ahab in the Book of Kings. The Bible mentions that Ahab did more evil in the eyes of the Lord than any king who came before him. This was because Ahab married Jezebel and then began worshipping Baal. He went so far as to establish an altar for

Baal. As he was worshipping an alien god, Jezebel worked to silence the prophets by killing them. A man named Obadiah decided to protect some of the prophets from Jezebel's wrath.

Here we see that Ahab made the same mistake which was made by Solomon before him, which was marrying a foreign woman and adopting the worship of her god. In the Bible, they both meet a violent end. Ahab was killed in battle. Jezebel was killed after being thrown from a tower under the orders of Jehu (2 Kings 9). Jehu then orders that all of the royal princes be killed (2 Kings 10). In total, seventy princes were killed and their heads placed in baskets which were sent to Jehu. Jehu went even further by killing the remaining members of Ahab's family, as well as his close friends and priests. After killing Ahab's family, Jehu then proclaimed that he planned to hold a sacrifice to Baal. This was a trick to assembly the servants of Baal so that Jehu could kill them as well. Despite slaying the worshippers of Baal, Jehu also failed to upkeep the first commandment. Baal was removed, but idolatry remained in Israel as Jehu failed to remove the golden calves (2 Kings 10:29).

In the Old Testament, the inability to remain faithful to God and the worshipping of idols is used as an explanation for the constant suffering of the Israelites. In the Bible, the Israelite connection with God begins with Abraham, whom the Bible assert was a descendant of Noah. Abraham enters into a covenant with God in which God blesses Abraham and his descendants. In fact, the nation of Israel, according to the Bible, is named after Abraham's grandson, Jacob who was later given the name Israel.

The unfaithfulness of God's chosen people is a theme which persists throughout the Old Testament, as well as the punishment for this unfaithfulness. The unified Israelite kingdom which existed is broken up as a punishment for this unfaithfulness to God. In the end both kingdoms were conquered, with the Babylonians conquering Judah and the Assyrians conquering Israel. Eva Matthews Sandford noted that the separation of the two kingdoms helped in the development of the concept of a religion which transcends national boundaries: "The separation of Israel and Judah after the death of Solomon was the occasion for a remarkable development in Hebrew religion. For both kingdoms continued to worship Yahweh, who now became the national deity of two independent and rival powers. This was a significant advance toward the idea of a universal and international god whose power transcended territorial boundaries and was not confined to a single political unit." The concept of an international god was developed more fully with Christianity and Islam.

One area where Christianity and Islam differ from Judaism is that the two are universal religions which seek to convert all of humanity. Judaism is not a religion which seeks to convert others, but the implication of the Old Testament is that God's plan was to bless humanity through his chosen people. Yahweh in the Old Testament is the creator of all humans, but he only presents himself as the god of the Israelites to whom he reveals himself. It is clear that the intention is the redemption of all of humanity through the Israelites, however. The Bible explains that God selected Abraham to bless the people of the world through him (Genesis 12:1-3). For Christians, this promise is fulfilled through the birth of Christ, who is a descendant of Abraham. In the view of Muslims, it was Muhammad who revealed the true universal religion which humanity is to follow.

Muhammad was born around 571. Muhammad was born into a poor, but well-respected family. He eventually married the widow of a rich merchant in Mecca. Mecca at the time practiced a religion which centered around the worship of a goddess named Allat. Muhammad was to radically transform the religion of Arabia when he began to preach about the one God. Muhammad declared that he was the last prophet of God. The revelation of his mission was given to him in a vision. The message which Muhammad passed down to his followers, he asserted, had been communicated to him by an angel.

Prophets are an important aspect of the Abrahamic faiths. In the Bible, prophets were individuals who were selected by God to present God's message to his people. The prophets typically came during a time when the Israelites were in danger. For example, Moses was sent to rescue the Israelites from slavery in Egypt. Other times, prophets were sent to warn the Israelites that their conduct was not pleasing to God.

The story of Jonah in the Bible is an interesting one for the fact that it presents the story of a reluctant prophet who was called to give a message to Nineveh. Jonah attempted to escape from this task, to which God sent a fish to swallow Jonah in order to bring him to Nineveh to preach about God's wrath to the Assyrians. The Assyrians repent upon receiving this message and are spared. Jonah demonstrates that not all of the prophets of God were willing prophets.

Muhammad, whom Muslims consider to be the last prophet of God, followed in the tradition of the other prophets mentioned in the Bible. Like those prophets, Muhammad came preaching a message from God and was rejected for doing so. Muhammad's new religion was not well-received and he was forced to resettle in a city known as Medina. In Medina, Muhammad continued his preaching. The move to Medina was so significant in Islamic history that the Muslim calendar marks the beginning of the Islamic era in 622, when Muhammad moved to Medina. Muhammad eventually managed to seize power in Mecca as well.

The duties of Muslims form the five pillars of the Islamic faith. The pillars include the shahada, which is a declaration that there is no god but Allah and that Muhammad is his prophet; daily prayer; almsgiving; fasting; and undertaking the pilgrimage to Mecca. The religion of Islam incorporates the prophets of the Bible including Abraham, Moses, and Jesus. The Qur'an itself recounts many of the events told in the Bible, although with some slight differences. For example, Genesis 11 in the Bible explained that humanity tested God's patience by trying to build a tower to reach the heavens, so God created separate languages among humanity to prevent humans from completing the tower. Chapter 40, verses 36-37 of the Qur'an contains a similar story of the pharaoh of Egypt attempting to build a tower to reach the heavens to look for God. These two stories about building towers to heaven, although different, are meant to display the arrogance of humanity in the eyes of God.

The Qur'an affirms that those who worship and pray to Allah are to be rewarded, whereas those who disbelieve or rebel against Allah are to endure a painful punishment. Chapter 5, verse 33, explained that the punishments for those who wage war against Allah and Muhammad are death, crucifixion, cutting off their hands and feet, or exile. This is to be followed by a tremendous punishment in the hereafter.

The absolute monotheism of Islam also influenced the relationship between Muslims and the polytheists. Chapter 9 of the Qur'an affirms that polytheists who do not believe in Allah will face a painful punishment. This chapter does encourage Muslims to honor their treaties with polytheists who have not violated those treaties and to provide protection for polytheists who ask for it, but it also instructs Muslims to kill the polytheists who have violated the treaties. Here we see Muhammad's pragmatic approach to spreading his religion. He maintained that polytheists were unbelievers who will be punished, yet he only called for violence against those polytheists who had not honored their obligations to Muslims.

In the Abrahamic faiths, the hostility towards other creeds is due to the concern that these creeds will cause people to stray away from the true understanding of God. This concern was such that Ezra 9 in the Bible denounced the fact that the Israelites had married foreign women because in doing so the Israelites also took on the practices of those people, which then led them further away from God. As was noted before, the function of the prophets was to ensure that the people remained faithful to God. Prophets served as those who upheld the creed which believers are called to follow.

45

FÉLIX HOUPHOUËT-BOIGNY, THE NEO-COLONIALIST

The impendence movements in Africa led to decolonization. This brought a formal end to colonialism in Africa, but Africa still retained a colonial relationship with its former colonial masters. This relationship has been termed "neo-colonialism." Whereas colonialism operated with the direct colonial control of the colonial power, neo-colonialism offered the former colonies a degree of political control, but real power remained within the grasp of the colonial powers. The neo-colonial system remained entrenched in Africa not only because Western nations worked to uphold such systems, but also because the African elite worked to maintain the neo-colonial system. This can be demonstrated by Félix Houphouët-Boigny who was the first president of Ivory Coast.

Under Houphouët-Boigny's leadership, independence did not result in any meaningful break with France. One observer noted of Ivory Coast that nearly "twenty years after independence, the French bureaucracy and commercial presence was still pervasive in Ivory Coast." The French population in Ivory Coast had also increased within the same time span. This proved helpful for Houphouët-Boigny as the French technical support and investment assisted with Ivory Coast's economic growth. Despite these successes, the economic recession in the 1980s also exposed the limits of Ivory Coast's reliance on cocoa and coffee exports. By 1988, nearly half of the French who were living in Ivory Coast left the country due to the economic conditions.

Houphouët-Boigny's foreign policy also reflected his neo-colonial outlook. For example, he eschewed establishing close links with the Soviet Union and China. This clearly reflected his pro-West and pro-capitalist disposition. These views also caused tension with Ivory Coast and other West African states. For example, Houphouët-Boigny's relations with Jerry Rawlings were strained given that Ghana had denounced Ivory Coast for granting landing rights to South African aircrafts and for allowing Abidjan to host Israeli intelligence services.

Houphouët-Boigny's relationship with Thomas Sankara was hardly any better. In 1985, there were allegations that Burkinabé were being mistreated in Ivory Coast. A Burkinabé businessman was also assassinated. Sankara himself was nearly assassinated in Ivory Coast in 1985. While attending a meeting for the Council of the Entente there, a bomb exploded in a hotel room that he was to occupy. No one was arrested for this incident.

The Council of the Entente was established in 1959 by the leaders of Ivory Coast, Upper Volta, Dahomey, and Niger. Togo became a member in 1966. The council helped to advance Houphouët-Boigny's objective of expanding his influence in West Africa, but Sankara's presidency proved to be a challenge for Houphouët-Boigny. Sankara had refused to sign the summit communique. Sankara went further by denouncing Togo and Ivory Coast for victimizing Burkinabé. He also accused them of supporting critics of his government and Sankara proposed the creation of a "Revolutionary Entente Council."

Houphouët-Boigny's relationship with France remained close to the point that Houphouët-Boigny took the position of refusing to condemn France's actions during the Algerian revolution. He also refused to provide support for Algeria and he remained a defender of French military intervention in Africa. Whereas Sankara sought to challenge the French colonial system, Houphouët-Boigny worked to uphold it.

46

PAUL ROBESON'S DEFENSE OF THE SOVIET UNION

Paul Robeson was a political activist and a brilliant intellectual who was a tireless opponent of the racial oppression which African Americans endured. Robeson was a Pan-Africanist who was also committed to the global liberation of African people. While in London, Robeson developed a relationship with figures such as Kwame Nkrumah and Jomo Kenyatta. He also developed an interest in studying African language, history, and culture. Robeson was also a leader of the Council of African Affairs, along with W.E.B. Du Bois.

Robeson's Pan-Africanism and commitment to fighting racism against African Americans were important aspects of his political vision and worldview. Robeson was also someone who supported the labor movement as well. This included walking on union picket lines and traveling to Detroit to support the United Auto Workers members in their conflict with Henry Ford. Given Robeson's views on labor, it is perhaps little surprise that Robeson came to support the Soviet Union.

Robeson's support for the Soviet Union was not only due to his support for working people and his embrace of socialism, but it was also a reaction to the positive reception he received while in the Soviet Union and his reaction to the brutal nature of Nazi fascism in Germany. Robeson was so concerned about the rise of fascism in Europe that he supported the Loyalists in the Spanish Civil War.

The Spanish Civil War began in 1936 when General Francisco Franco led a rebellion against the government of Spain. The rebels opposed the liberal changes which were being implemented, such as land reforms, women's education, and divorce. Franco received support from the fascist regimes in Germany and Italy for his rebellion. Other nations in Europe opted for a policy of non-intervention so as to avoid risking another World War—this second World War would happen anyway. The Spanish Republic was forced to turn to the Soviet Union for support against the rebels.

An international brigade to combat fascism was formed by volunteers who journeyed to Spain to support the Spanish Republic. Nearly 3,000 volunteers from the United States served in the war. This included about 90 African Americans. Robeson was among those volunteers. He sang to front-line troops in the fight against Franco's insurrection. Robeson described his visit to Spain as a major turning point in his life.

Robeson's embrace of the Soviet Union is an aspect of his politics which does seem troubling to his admirers given the abuses which were carried out under Joseph Stalin. Paul Von Blum wrote: "Paul Robeson's compelling and durable moral vision, far more than his problematic support for Stalinist policies, constitutes the core of his identity as one of the quintessential public intellectuals of the 20th century. Still, his pro-Soviet stance remains part of his intellectual legacy and deserves retrospective commentary and analysis. Few today would deny the appalling record of terror, corruption, anti-Semitism, and ethnic cleansing in the former Soviet Union. Only the most intractable apologists still believe that the Soviet system was compatible with the humane vision of Karl Marx and other socialist theorists. Like thousands of other intellectuals throughout the world, Robeson saw the Soviet dream as a practical fulfillment of the moral mandate to make life better for the overwhelming majority of the planet's inhabitants."

Blum suggested that perhaps Robeson had a difficult time criticizing the Soviet Union given how he was treated with "dignity and acclaim" in the Soviet Union, in contrast to the racism he experienced in America. Blum also noted that it may have been "difficult to abandon the vision of the Soviet beacon, even in the face of powerful evidence of the growing gap between socialist ideals and Soviet practices." It could have also possibly been the case that Robeson felt that the achievements of Stalin and the Soviet Union were too great to be undermined by engaging in public criticisms.

Given the politics of the Cold War at the time, any public criticism of the Soviet Union would have likely been utilized by the United States to further its anti-Soviet propaganda. Even if

Robeson had private disagreements about what was happening under Stalin's leadership, he likely would have understood how voicing such disagreements in public would have been used against the Soviet Union. The reality is that Robeson held the Soviet Union in very high regard, as demonstrated by a speech he delivered titled "The Negro People and the Soviet Union."

In the speech, Robeson quoted Mao who had stated that had the Soviet Union not existed, there would have been no victory over fascism during World War II. In this statement, Mao included China's liberation from Japanese fascism as an example of this victory over fascism during the war. Robeson began by quoting Mao to demonstrate his view that the Soviet Union had helped to shift the balance of power "in favor of the forces of peace and democracy." Robeson explained that his travels to Western Europe and Scandinavia reinforced his view that the new balance of power allowed the people in those countries to struggle "against the total colonization of their countries" by Wall Street. Robeson went further to state that the independence of India was also due to the shift in the balance of power caused by the Soviet Union.

In Robeson's view, the Soviet Union were the "real friends" of the people of Africa and the West Indies. To demonstrated this, he noted that Creech-Jones of the British Empire had told Nigerians that their demands for self-rule could not be granted because they were not ready. He also noted that it was Litvinov who supported Haile Selassie in Geneva after Mussolini had invaded the nation and dropped bombs on the Ethiopian people. The contrast was clear. The Soviet Union stood in support of Africa, whereas the British Empire stood opposed to Africa's progress.

Robeson declared: "The Soviet Union is the friend of the African and West Indian peoples. And no imperialist wolf disguised as a benevolent watchdog, and not Tito disguised as a revolutionary, can convince them that Moscow oppresses the small nations. Africa knows the Soviet Union is the defender and champion of the rights of all nations—large and small—to control their own destinies." He contrasted this with the programs of racial superiority in South Africa and the United States.

Robeson gave the specific example of Maceo Snipes who was a World War II veteran. Snipes went to vote in Alabama and an hour later he was killed on the doorstep of his home, in front of his wife and children. He was killed for daring to vote. Robeson also added that even though President Truman promised civil rights, ninety Negroes had been lynched since he was elected. The injustice was so blatant that the men who were on trial for the murder of Willie Earl were freed by the jury. This was despite the fact that several of the men admitted to being involved in killing Earl. Robeson noted that the federal government refused to intervene in the situation because Tom Clark, the Attorney General at the time, was more interested in prosecuting members of the Communist Party.

It was not only that the Soviet Union stood in contrast to the racism which the United States openly promoted, but also that socialism offered an alternative for the struggles which black people endured under capitalism. Robeson declared that there was no democracy for his people in America, as "millions of Negroes who are denied the right to vote are mountainous testimony." He also pointed out that 75 percent of black people in America earned less than one-third of what was necessary to support a family of four. This was in addition to being the last hired and the first fired.

Robeson's views were no doubt reinforced by the fact that the American government had withdrawn his passport, which prevented him from traveling. This further demonstrated that the American government was not truly committed to democracy and liberty. If Robeson did indeed have disagreements with the Soviet Union, such disagreements were very likely secondary to the real oppression which he battled in the United States. During Robeson's lifetime, the Soviet Union seemed to have offered a real alternative to the racism and the fascism which he fought against in the United States and in Europe. This is why Blum noted: "Robeson genuinely believed and fully articulated the view that capitalism promoted the most predatory features of human existence. He thought that capitalism fostered and exacerbated inequality, poverty, racism, and economic and social misery for millions of human beings. His moral vision about the superiority of a socialist transformation of society reflected the deepest humanistic features of Marxism—the Marxism that has a continuing vitality for life in the early 21st century in a global economy where transnational corporate domination continues to keep most human beings in seemingly irreversible bondage."

Robeson was not alone in his view. Du Bois was also drawn to support the Soviet Union. Du Bois went further by publishing a eulogy for Joseph Stalin in the *National Guardian*. In the eulogy, Du Bois described Stalin as a "great man" whom few in the 20th century managed to match. He wrote: "He was simple, calm and courageous. He seldom lost his poise; pondered his problems slowly, made his decisions clearly and firmly; never yielded to ostentation nor coyly refrained from holding his rightful place with dignity. He was the son of a serf but stood calmly before the great without hesitation or nerves. But also—and this was the highest proof of his greatness—he knew the common man, felt his problems, followed his fate."

Given Du Bois' view of Stalin, it is no surprise that he maintained a less favorable view of Leon Trotsky, writing: "His judgment of men was profound. He early saw through the flamboyance and exhibitionism of Trotsky, who fooled the world, and especially America. The whole ill-bred and insulting attitude of Liberals in the U.S. today began with our naive acceptance of Trotsky's magnificent lying propaganda, which he carried around the world. Against it, Stalin stood like a rock and moved neither right nor left, as he continued to advance toward a real socialism instead of the sham Trotsky offered."

In denouncing Trotsky, Du Bois not only demonstrated his support for Stalin, but his opposition to the man who emerged as Stalin's most prominent socialist critic. It is curious to note the contrast between Du Bois and C.L.R. James given that James was a Trotskyist who broke with Trotskyism because he felt that Trotsky not critical enough of the Soviet Union. Du Bois held the opposite view. In his view, Trotsky's criticisms were baseless because he only offered a sham in contrast to Stalin's advance towards "real socialism".

Much of Du Bois' reverence for Stalin was due to the manner in which Stalin stood up against fascism in Europe. Not only did the defeat of Nazism in Germany come at a great cost for Russia, but Du Bois noted that initially the Soviet Union was left alone to fend off fascism. He noted: "Western Europe and the U.S. were willing to betray her to fascism, and then had to beg her aid in the Second World War. A lesser man than Stalin would have demanded vengeance for Munich, but he had the wisdom to ask only justice for his fatherland. This Roosevelt granted but Churchill held back. The British Empire proposed first to save itself in Africa and southern Europe, while Hitler smashed the Soviets."

One could perhaps fault Du Bois for being too exuberant in his praise for Stalin, but it is also important to contextualize Du Bois' view. In Du Bois' view, Stalin not only represented the hope of socialism, but he was also a leader who boldly fought against fascism in Europe—of course, prior to the war with Germany, Stalin had demonstrated that he was willing to make deals with the fascists, but this is perhaps secondary to the fact that Stalin ultimately did play a leading role in defeating Hitler. Du Bois clearly viewed racism, capitalism, and imperialism as greater threats to the world than Stalin's socialism. Racism, capitalism, and imperialism were certainly more immediate threats to African people.

Robeson's willingness to remain silent on Stalin's abuses is understandably concerning to those who view such silence as being contrary to Robeson's general outspokenness about injustices and oppression, but such silence should be understood within the context of Robeson's struggle against American racism, European colonialism in Africa, and fascism in Europe. As flawed as Stalin may have been, the Soviet Union was a nation which stood in support of those who struggled against racism, colonialism, and fascism. For this reason, Robeson would have never aligned himself with the capitalists in America by denouncing the Soviet Union publicly, even if Robeson may have had private disagreements.

References:

Paul Robeson, "The Negro People and the Soviet Union," November 10, 1949.

"Paul Robeson in Spain," *The Volunteer*, Vol. XXVI, No. 2

Paul Von Blum, J.D. "Paul Robeson: The Quintessential Public

Intellectual," *The Journal of Pan African Studies*, vol.2, no.7, December 2008.

W.E.B. Du Bois, "On Stalin," *National Guardian*, March 16, 1953.

47

FREDERICK FORBES' NOTES ON DAHOMEY

Frederick Forbes' book *Dahomey and Dahomeans* was a recollection of two of his missions to Dahomey which took place in 1849 and 1850. Forbes' book offered some notable insights into the structure of Dahomey's society at the time. During this period Dahomey was under the rule of Gezo. Gezo is a somewhat notorious ruler in the history of Dahomey for his position as a defender of Dahomey's role in the slave trade.

Dahomey at the time was also one of the more highly militarized states in Africa. This militarization developed out of necessity given the existing political situation in Africa. Forbes wrote that for "nearly a century Dahomey could barely repel the attacks of her nieghbours." This statement demonstrated the immense pressure which states in West Africa endured due to the conflicts caused by the slave trade.

As part of the military tradition of Dahomey, the troops would march as they were reviewed by the king. Forbes observed that during the review, the troops were armed and dressed in blue and white tunics. Each army marched with their own war drums and with shields which were ornamented with human skulls. Forbes noted that the whole nation seemed to have participated in the march, including hunchbacks and dwarfs. As the soldiers marched, the king remained seated under a canopy of umbrellas. When the royal amazons advanced, they saluted the king and he joined them in performing a war dance.

The amazons were the most unique aspect of Dahomey's military. The "amazons" of Dahomey were all all-female regiment which served the king of Dahomey. The amazons were fierce warriors who were acculturated to fight to the death, if necessary, as demonstrated by a remark which Forbes recorded from an amazon who stated: "War is our great friend; without it there is no cloth, no armlets; let us to war, and conquer or die." Another stated: "I am a wolf, the enemy of all I meet who are the king's enemies, and if I do not conquer, let me die."

The review of the military which Forbes recorded demonstrated the extent to which the military became institutionalized in Dahomey. Dahomey was among the few pre-colonial African states which maintained a standing army. Forbes noted that the military in Dahomey was very well ordered. He wrote: "Order and discipline were observable throughout, uniform and good accoutrements general, and except in the most civilized countries in the world, and even there as regarded the order of the multitude, no review could have gone off better. There was no delay, no awkwardness, no accident: aides-de-camp were rushing about with orders; it was noble and extremely interesting."

Concerning justice in Dahomey, Forbes observed that the king of Dahomey oversaw trials in an open court in which any individual was free to comment. Forbes also explained that in these public and open speeches, the king was made aware of the state of the country. Anyone was free to provide a complaint to the king which would compel the king to act, though Forbes did add that the one bringing the complaint "must be careful to prove it, or woe betide him." Forbes explained that during the session he witnessed, the king's eldest brothers stated that the roads were not kept in order. Forbes observed that the next day the roads were in the process of being cleaned, which demonstrated the importance of the open court which the king held not only to oversee trials, but to also address some of the problems in the country.

Concerning the religious beliefs of the people of Dahomey, Forbes recorded that the Dahomans believe that the souls of those who die enter the land of spirits, though they may return to earth to watch over members of their family. There was also a custom in which the rich would take their slaves and wives with them, with some being voluntary sacrifices. The people of Dahomey also believed in the power of charms. Forbes noted a charm was planted under the entrances of the king's palace to protect against adultery. The understanding was that any woman who engaged in adultery would suffer from a bowl disease due to the charm. Forbes observed that this belief was so strong that some women imagined themselves ill and confessed their action, whereupon the woman and the man she engaged in the act with were both beheaded as punishment for their actions.

Forbes' interactions with Gezo are also noteworthy. Forbes

presented Gezo as a ruler who was bound by tradition. For example, Forbes noted that Gezo "has no delight in human sacrifices and continues these awful scenes solely out of deference to ancient national customs." Gezo did not abolish the sacrifices, but he did reduce them. Likewise, Gezo defended Dahomey's continued involvement in the slave trade by noting that his people were soldiers and that his revenue came from the slave trade. Gezo also stated that the slave trading of other states needed to stop before Gezo could end the trade. Gezo's response demonstrated a view that the slave trade was not only an important source of revenue for him, but that other states which were engaged in the slave trade needed to end the trade before he did.

Forbes was not able to convince Gezo to end Dahomey's role in the slave trade. Forbes did manage to rescue a young girl, however. The girl was captured during an attack on a town known as Okeadon. The girl was taken as a captive and was kept for the purpose of being sacrificed. Her parents were both killed and she was unaware of what happened to her siblings. She was held for two years. That same girl was given to Forbes as a gift. Forbes received her and she was baptized under the day of Sarah Forbes Bonetta. That this girl was to be sacrificed demonstrated the brutal reality of life in Dahomey. Indeed, this was the brutal reality of life in West Africa during the time of the slave trade.

48

A STRANGE KIND OF SOCIALISM: THE CASE OF MALI

Modibo Keita came to power as Mali's first president in 1960 when Mali gained its independence from France. Keita was notable for being one of the more visionary and ambitious of the first generation of post-colonial leaders in Africa. Keita sought to establish in Mali "a system where there will be no beggars, and where each will eat if hungry." This was a lofty vision, but one which Keita fell short of due to a number of factors.

Mali became independence in 1960 following the dissolution of the Mali Federation, which occurred when Senegal opted unliterally dissolve the federation between Lai and Senegal. Keita, who was in Dakara, was arrested and expelled from Senegal. Keita later expressed the view that the federation ended due to "fundamental political contradictions." Keita had also accused France of having a role in the breakup of the federation, though Charles de Gaulle did invite Keita to Paris for talks concerning the situation with Senegal. The federation could not be salvaged, however. In the end, Mali and Senegal moved to independence as separate countries rather than as a united federation.

As was the case with some of the leaders in Africa at the time, Keita was drawn to socialism, particularly Marxism-Leninism. Keita's Marxist vision was unique in some respects. In the first place, Keita's ideology remained rooted in Mali's history, to the point that Keita embraced the motto "Death rather than dishonour," which was attributed to Sundiata Keita who was the first ruler of the Mali Empire. Mamby Sidibe stated that Mali's socialist system was influenced "by the political doctrines of the rulers of the former great empire which disappeared at the end of the 17th century: unity of the people, thanks to the existence of a single party, happiness of each through the work of all, and vice versa…"

Keita's Marxist vision was also unique in that he rejected the atheism of Marxism. Keita stated: "Mali and her leaders draw their inspiration for socialist construction from the theory of Marxism-Leninism. But we do not adopt its materialist philosophy, and we do not adopt its atheism, because we are believers." Keita, who was a Muslim, believed that "to believe is to aspire in the beyond to a life better than one may reach on earth, in so far as one behaves as a brother and as a human being with the moral and intellectual qualities which are necessary to make of man a being fit to represent that divinity Whom we all cherish." Keita also held the view that scientific socialism must be adapted to Mali's particular situation. He explained: "We try to draw from it values which enable us to make fruitful the positive realities of Mali, with our temperament, our culture, and our heritage of mysticism."

Keita saw no contradiction in his socialist vision and his Islamic beliefs. He explained: "There is no religion more socialist than Islam, because it teaches among its principles that the rich should give, should share, should relieve the suffering of others." He also explained that, "we consider that there can be no contradictions between the practice of a religion and adherence to a socialist definition of the social relations of the various strata of population."

Mali embraced socialism for much of the same reason other African states at the time did. Capitalism was the economic system which was utilized by the colonial powers of Europe who exploited Africa. As such it was viewed as an alien system, whereas socialism seemed to be more aligned with the communal values of traditional African societies. Keita expressed the view that African society was historically and fundamentally communal. The strides which the Soviet Union and China made towards modernizing their economies also made socialism an attractive prospect to African states which hoped to also achieve such rapid development and industrialization.

The Union Soudanaise-Rassemblement Démocratique Africain (USRDA) was formed in 1946. The party initially had limited support and resources. Its members were also subjected to repression from both the colonial administration, as well as the main rival party, the Parti Progressiste Soudanais (PSP). The USRDA's alliance with the merchants in Mali helped to strengthen the party, which allowed it to gradually take control of power in Mali. This alliance was a beneficial one for both parties as the

USRDA needed the resources which the merchants supplied. The alliance benefitted the merchants as well since under the colonial administration, local merchants were unable to compete with European businesses. The merchants believed that they would benefit from the success of the USRDA.

Keita's vision for Mali was not simply a political decolonization, but a cultural one as well. Keita stated: "we must get rid of some of those inherited needs and habits which previously could be satisfied with French support, but which cannot be satisfied by the real resources of the country." To accomplish this vision, Keita needed to develop a strong national identity in Mali. The national identity which Keita sought to forge was a fragile one, however. Communities across Mali expressed a desire to secede. The Tuareg wanted their own nation, whereas locals in the region of Koulikoro wished to be annexed by Guinea.

The greatest challenge which Keita faced was the challenge of developing Mali economically. Indeed, this was the challenge which was posed to all African nations. Colonialism not only exploited African colonies, but left them in a state of underdevelopment. For Keita, as was the case for some other African leaders at the time, socialism seemed to offer a solution to Mali's underdevelopment. Not only did socialism envision a society which was free of the type of exploitation of the masses which accorded during colonialism, but the rapid modernization of the Soviet Union and China also made socialis appealing. This is why the USRDA sought to emulate the Soviet Union and China.

The economic policies which Keita's government implemented were marked by the deeply anti-democratic nature of Keita's government. In 1959, the USRDA began outlawing opposition parties. Others were coerced into merging with the USRDA. Those who refused to join were arrested in 1960 and villages that were strongholds for the opposition were razed. Amadou Ba was sanctioned for publicly stating that closing the Dakara-Niger Railway had a disastrous impact on Mali's economy. These examples demonstrated that in its early years, the USRDA was already displaying a tendency towards repression which would only become worse over time.

In 1962, the Malian franc was introduced. The introduction of this new currency further demonstrated the undemocratic nature of

Mali's policies as the government began seizing CFA francs throughout the country. Among those who were arrested was a merchant named El Hadj Kassoum Touré. Touré was an activist who had financially supported Keita for many years. His arrest resulted in hundreds of protesters gathering to demand his release. The security forces responded to this by firing on the crowd, killing one and wounding three others. The protesters gathered again later in the day and these protests were similarly put down with violence. Keita dismissed the protests as being "nothing but a phase in a grand subversive movement organized at length to topple the regime." The USRDA also took the position that the protesters were involved in a plot to assassinate some of Mali's political leaders.

The incident with Kassoum Touré demonstrated the conflict which emerged between the merchants in Mali and the government. It was noted before that the USRDA benefitted from the support of the merchants. The USRDA promised to improve the conditions of the merchants, but the USRDA did the opposite once in power. The policies pursued by the USRDA restricted the abilities of the merchants in Mali. When the merchants openly opposed these policies, they were met with repression by the government.

Robert Donald Francis Nathan noted that Sékou Touré went from leading trade unions in Guinea in the 1950s to repressing them in the 1960s. A similar situation occurred in Mali. Keita oversaw a government which was deeply authoritarian in nature. Such measures were justified as being necessary to guard the national interests of Mali and to ensure unity within the USRDA. The problem was that such repression also silenced legitimate concerns over Mali's economic policies, which were not working.

Keita's government was spending itself into deeper debt. This in turn undermined Mali's independence. In 1967, Mali decided to sign a monetary accord with France which allowed Mali to rejoin the West African Franc Zone. This effectively reestablished French influence over Mali. This was also a major blow for socialism in Mali. As one commentator noted: "The economy of a socialist country dominated by capitalists. Oh, what a strange kind of socialism." Indeed, Mali's socialism did in fact become a strange kind of socialism not only because of the fact that capitalists came to dominate Mali, but also because of the rampant clientelism within the government.

Clientelism within the USRDA developed due to the fact that the party often won support by providing favors and compensation. This was not an approach which Keita himself had endorsed. He urged party members to rise above "politics of the belly" but clientelism would remain a problem because the USRDA failed to effectively stop it. This was because the USRDA continued to utilize clientelism to its benefit by rewarding those who were loyal to the party and by punishing dissent. Those who supported the party and remained loyal to the party were rewarded with administrative and political positions. This created a culture in which positions within the party were dictated not by aptitude, but by a willingness to conform to the party.

Sustaining clientelism only worsened Mali's financial woes. Between 1959 and 1962, there was a significant increase in public sector salary, which placed Mali in debt. The expansion of the number of employees in public administration meant that Mali was spending more, but the effect of this spending resulted in marginal economic growth. Samir Amin noted that investments in administration and state enterprises were unproductive or barely productive. Amin also pointed out that the increase in administrative spending financed the inflation of staff rosters of cabinet ministers.

The creation of large state bureaucracy undermined Keita's socialist vision. Keita believed that the task of the USRDA was to root out individualism, but clientelism resulted in certain individuals accumulating resources at the expense of the masses. The problem was such that Keita had to state in 1967: "Certain comrade officials have settled into conditions of material comfort, have become 'delicate ones' hardly inclined to exert themselves... The very same ones who, yesterday, criss-crossed the bush at the time of the political struggle, village by village, living the life of the peasants, sharing their roof, their meals, and their worries, content themselves now... with making the leaders from the bush come to them in the city in order to pass on party directives!"

The remark above demonstrated that Keita was aware of the

problem. Others were aware of the problem as well. The French ambassador noted: "Currently, the true danger to Modibo Keita comes from his own political friends... Many consider themselves to have been deprived of benefits they believed they would derive from the newly acquired independence and, their hopes dashed, they complain to the members of government."

The limitations of Mali's socialist policies were also demonstrated by the USRDA's relationship with the peasant population in Mali. The USRDA came to power promising to improve conditions for peasants, but once in power peasants were confronted with policies such as increased taxation, forced labor, and forced collectivization. It was sometimes the case that police would round up peasants in the cities to move them to rural places. These policies were viewed as necessary sacrifices to improve Mali, but as the peasants were being forced to make sacrifices for the betterment of the country, officials in the government sought to improve their own comfort.

It was often the case that peasants resisted many of the government's initiatives. For example, many peasants left public work projects which they were forced to work on. The abandonment of such projects meant that projects were started, but never finished. This included a highway which was meant to connect Mali to Guinea. Others sold grain on the black market rather than selling it to the state. There even occasions in which peasants would attack and kill state representatives. The type of socialism which was developing in Mali was one which benefited the bureaucracy at the expense of the peasants. Nathan noted that "resource redistribution to clients only reduced the party's capacity to improve life's material conditions for ordinary citizens. By the time soldiers ousted President Keita in 1968, living standards had dropped."

Even as peasants resisted imposed policies such as forced labor, the government of Mali did not perceive itself as exploiters of the peasants. In his 1966 New Year Message, Keita stated that the peasants in Mali must be mobilized for economic development and that a major obstacle in this goal was those who maintained a vested interest in exploiting the peasants. Keita maintained the view that the government of Mali was one which represented the interests of the peasants. He stated that the rural population in Mali should "draw the greatest possible benefit from our administration, for our economic development." This was not the case, however.

It would have perhaps been different if the harsh measures which were imposed on peasants led to an improvement in Mali's economic conditions, but this was not the case. The poor economic conditions in Mali were such that Keita was booed in 1961 at a conference in which he discussed his government's economic policies.

The government was harshly imposing economic measures which simply were not working for the people of Mali, but there was little that the people of Mali could do about this as any public dissent or criticism was met with repression. Nathan noted that these responses to dissents "ranged from instituting laws to punish those who criticized the regime's policies, all the way to razing villages to the ground and sending troops to engage in gun battles with rural communities." Such heavy-handed responses were done to ensure the survival of the regime, but it also had the consequence of suppressing constructive criticisms of the government's failing economic policies.

The repression worsened in 1967 when Mali launched the "Active Revolution" which was inspired by Mao Tse-tung's Cultural Revolution in China. The Active Revolution, much like China's Cultural Revolution, resulted in citizens being terrorized by the militia. The aim was to repress the moderates within the party who were not totally committed to a socialist vision.

That Mao's vision in China was an influence for Mali was demonstrated by the fact that Keita had quoted Mao's remark that "the State and political power will necessarily be identical there in principle..." Mamadou Gologo also displayed this Chinese influence with his book, *China: A Giant People With a Great Destiny*. In Mali, the distinction between the party and the state was erased to justify the USRDA's control over state institutions.

The Soviet Union also served as a model for Mali as well. Maderia Keita, who served as Minister of the Interior, was noted for having a pro-Soviet view. Salah Niaré, who served as Minister of Agriculture, noted that some within the USRDA wished to impose Russia's kolkhoz system of collective farms in Mali's rural communities. The obvious problems associated with adopting such policies were dismissed by some USRDA members who believed that the negative outcomes of the Soviet policies which they sought to emulate were merely part of the capitalist effort to discredit socialism.

The repression which the government of Mali engaged in must be understood within the context of the politics of the time. The assassination of Patrice Lumumba in the Congo was an event which concerned the leaders in Mali. The concern was that French agents would also try to destabilize Mali or topple Mali's government. A circular from the government noted: "French agents will try to use all discontented elements: ex-Canton chiefs, political adversaries... waiting for an occasion to get revenge, earlier political comrades disappointed that responsibilities they believe they merited have not been given to them." Years after Lumumba's assassination, the coup which overthrew Kwame Nkrumah in Ghana further entrenched the concern about a coup in Mali. In 1966, Keita suggested that the party be restructured to prevent the type of upheaval which was experience in Ghana.

The need to guard against French destabilization efforts were not the only reason for the repressive measures which Keita undertook. It was noted before that the autocratic tendencies of the USRDA began to formulate prior to independence in 1960. In 1959, the USRDA passed decrees which made smaller parties illegal. In 1960, Keita justified implementing a single party state by stating that a country "that has only just been born to Western-style democracy" could not afford "the dispersion of efforts and good will."

In addition to outlawing opposition parties, the USRDA also eliminated canton chiefs in 1958. The USRDA took the position that canton chiefs were a vestige of the colonial era which did not fit with the party's vision. It likely did not help matters that the canton chiefs had sided with the colonial administration in opposing the USRDA. Yet another factor in the USRDA's decision to abolish canton chiefs is that the chiefs had often abused their authority.

There were elements within the USRDA which simply did not

believe in democracy. Seydou Badian Kouyaté, who was among the party members who shaped the USRDA's policies during the Active Revolution, rejected in idea of democracy in Mali. He later became an advisor to Denis Sassou Nguesso and described Nguesso as a socialist hero. Mamadou Gologo expressed the view that all outside journalists should be removed from Mali.

Nathan pointed out that Keita had been known as a mediator between the factions within the USRDA. His own political views remained enigmatic because of his tendency to avoid taking sides in the party. This is demonstrated by the fact that whereas Guinea voted against the French referendum in 1958, Keita persuaded the people of Mali to vote for it. His position at the time was that autonomy was as good as independence. At the time, Keita was also viewed as a moderate figure by the French ambassador. Given his enigmatic views, Nathan noted that Keita had been described as "a moderate, a radical, a vacillator between factions, an opportunist, and a mentally unstable autocrat." What was most clear is that by 1967, Keita had firmly sided with the radical faction within the party. This shift seemed to have been due to the fact that Keita had been a proponent of socialism in Mali and was unwilling to renounce the wing of the party which remained committed to socialism. This move matched Keita's own ideological disposition, but it may have been a mistake in that Keita was throwing his support behind the faction of the party which was quickly becoming unpopular in the country due to the failures of Mali's socialist policies.

Keita was in no easy position to be sure. The USRDA had always been an uneasy coalition of groups with different ideologies and different visions. The previously noted conflict between merchants and the USRDA demonstrated this reality. The USRDA relied on the resources supplied by the merchants to take power, but once in power some of the same merchants who supported Keita and the USRDA came to oppose government policies. There was also the fact that within the USRDA itself there were two main factions. One faction was committed to socialism in Mali, whereas the other faction was more moderate, anti-communist, and inclined to compromise. The latter was the faction which had pushed for negotiations with France in 1967.

Keita's position was also made difficult by the fact that Mali was extremely underdeveloped. Even by the standards of West African nations, Mali's economy was regarded as backward. This was a testament to how neglected Mali had been during the period of French colonial rule. This also meant that Mali was heavily dependent on French aid. This was demonstrated by the fact that the USRDA admitted that after independence it was unable to balance its budget without French subsidies. The loss of French subsidies was a significant blow to Mali's economy and Keita's economic policies only made matters worse.

Keita was confronted with the challenge of maintaining unity within the differing factions in the USRDA, maintaining popular support for the party, and developing Mali economically. Then there was also the problem of clientelism within the party, which persisted despite Keita's efforts to denounce such clientelism. Keita did not have an easy task in front of him, but he did himself no favors by siding with the radical faction of the USRDA at a time when the party was losing support from all segments of Mali's societies. The merchants and peasants felt betrayed by the USRDA's policies, but the party was also losing support from members of the government who were not pleased about cuts in their pay and the government's failure to deliver salaries on time.

The government of Mali certainly had legitimate concerns about the potential subversion, but its policies only exacerbated the problem. It deepened the divisions within the party and it deepened the tensions within Mali's society. This is why Aristide Zoldberg noted that "Mali thus reveals most acutely the fundamental paradox of the African one-party States: namely that, while observers have been busy deploring authoritarian trends, the real problem is the weakness of their political structures."

That Mali drew influence from Mao's Cultural Revolution also demonstrated the problem of ideological confusion which seemed to have plagued Mali's government as well. Keita drew from a number of ideological sources including Marxism-Leninism, Maoism, Islam, and Mali's own history. In doing so, a clear ideological direction did not seem to emerge within the USRDA, which further contributed to the problem of division within the party.

In Keita's view, the party was the main instrument which was to be used to carry out the socialist transformation of Mali. He stated, "we must have confidence in the party." Francis Synder noted that in Keita's view: "History, party, and nation are equated and combined into a single entity. Accordingly, a person who disregards one in effect betrays the others." Mali's history was an important aspect of Keita's ideological worldview. This is why William J. Foltz noted that one of the leaders of the USRDA declared: "The essential thing is to study the past to draw practical conclusions from it." This was not done by the USRDA, however.

In the first place, Mali's history would indicate that rulers who were successful were those who were effective at managing the empire. This did not simply mean having the power to conquer territories or to put down revolts. It also meant being able to effectively manage the nation's finances. Mansa Mari Jata II was remembered in Mali's history as a poor ruler in part because of his wasteful management of the country's treasury. This is why David Conrad noted that Malians "were probably relieved" when Mari Jatta died.

Yet another lesson to be drawn from Mali's history is the relationship between social classes. Historically, Mali was a society which was broadly divided into three social classes: nobles, the "nyamakalas," and slaves. The Kouroukan Fouga of Mali stated that Mali's society was "divided into sixteen clans of quiver carriers, five clans of marabouts, four groups of 'nyamakalas' and one group of slaves. Each one has a specific activity and role." The nyamakalas, who engaged in skilled labor such as making leather products, were tasked with devoting "themselves to tell the truth to the chiefs, to be their counsellors and to defend by the speech the established rulers and the order upon the whole territory."

It is notable that although Mali was divided by different social classes there was also a sense that each class had a specific role or function in society. Slaves occupied the lowest class within Mali's society, yet the Kouroukan Fouga offered legal recognition and even certain protections for slaves. As such, no social class in Mali's society was without some form of recognition.

Keita's government did make some efforts to address caste divisions within Mali. In 1968, Madeira Keita noted that the village of Mandajkuy was ruled by a feudal family which would not allow someone outside of the family—especially those from a lower caste such as a blacksmith, griot, or slave descendant—to hold a chieftaincy in the village. Given this reality, it is notable that Kouyaté came from griot origins and managed to attain a high position within the ruling party. There were others who were not of noble birth, but who were able to obtain prominent political positions. Nathan noted that this was merely a pragmatic move on the part of the USRDA, as it had also barred politicians from lower castes from running for office out of concern that such individuals could not win due to their origins. Modibo Keita himself came from a noble background.

In its effort to create a new, more egalitarian social hierarchy in Mali, the USRDA merely created new social distinctions which divided the society between those who supported the bureaucracy of the ruling party and those who opposed it. In the Mali Empire, the existence of clearly divided class structures maintained a degree of internal stability in that each class had a defined role and function in society. Under Keita's leadership, there were no such clearly defined roles and the increasingly authoritarian nature of the government meant that those who did not support the government were viewed as enemies of the state.

The lessons which could have be drawn from Mali's own history should have been the importance of maintaining political stability through effective management of the nation's finances and through clearly defining roles within the process of nation building for each social class. Keita himself stated, "we have in Mali sufficient cultural values, both past and present, to define clearly the wishes of the people and to realise them." Instead of drawing on Mali's cultural values, the radical wing of the USRD looked to Maoist China for its model of consolidating and maintaining power in Mali.

Keita's failed economic policies resulted in him being overthrow in a military coup which was led by Moussa Traoré. Traoré, who retained a single-party system in Mali, did little to significantly improve Mali's economic condition. By the 1980s, more than half of Mali's workforce was employed by government agencies and businesses which were taken over by the government.

Mali was essentially under the control of a bureaucracy which was both corrupt and inefficient, which was not much different than the situation which existed under Keita's leadership. Traoré was himself removed by a military coup following massive protests in Mali.

Keita stated: "The ex-colonial powers and others are convinced that Africans are incapable of governing themselves, that they always need a tutelary power, whether visible or not, in order to govern their countries. We must prove the contrary." Unfortunately, Keita was not able to do this. Keita was a leader with a grand vision for Mali, but the economic mismanagement under his leadership proved to be his downfall.

References:

David Conrad, *Empires of Medieval West Africa*, (Chelsea House, 2010).

Francis Synder, "The Political Thought of Modibo Keita," *The Journal of Modern African Studies*, Vol. 5, No. 1 (May, 1967), pp. 79-106

Robert Donald Francis Nathan, "Socialism and the Nation: Mali, 1957-1968," 2015.

49

T.A. MARRYSHOW'S COLONIAL VISION

T. Albert Marryshow was an important figure in Caribbean history for his role as an advocate for Caribbean unity, particularly the formation of a federation. His vision of unity was not one which promoted a radical break with the colonial structure. This was demonstrated in his article titled "The Queen Is Pasing By", which was written to celebrate Queen Elizabeth II's visit to the Caribbean. Marryshow wrote: "As one who wished and worked for years for a reigning Sovereign to visit Caribbean waters, and who conceived the idea of an all-British Caribbean welcome to Her Majesty in Jamaica, I do feel glad that my dreams have come true."

Marryshow may have dreamed about the Queen visiting the Caribbean, but by the 1970s, during the Black Power movement in the Caribbean, the Queen was viewed much more critically by those who came to reject British colonialism and all of that it represented. It was for this reason that Eric Gairy accepting knighthood from the Queen had undermined his previous perception as a leader who defended the black masses.

The Black Power movement in the Caribbean helped to shape the perceptive that black people in the Caribbean should look not to colonialism for hope and inspiration, but to their own history and culture. Maurice Bishop seemed to have recognized this, which is why one of the aspects of the revolution in Grenada during the 1970s was the promotion of culture.

In 1982, Grenada hosted a conference of intellectual and cultural workers. Among those who attended the event included George Lamming, Earl Lovelace, Merle Collins, Harry Belafonte, and Paul Keens-Douglas. Keens-Douglas' inclusion was especially notable given that he had produced a piece titled "Fedon's Flute" which framed the revolution in Grenada as a continuation of Fedon's rebellion.

Fedon was certainly a rebel leader who had no sense of loyalty to the British colonial administration which had enslaved his people. In fact, during the rebellion Fedon declared his support for

France. This reflected Fedon's support for the revolutionary ideals which were being promoted by France at the time. This included decrees which granted full citizenship to free coloreds and emancipated slaves in France's Caribbean territories. This would suggest that Fedon's loyalties were to the freedom of his people, rather than to any particular colonial power.

Grenada was involved in the process of culturally decolonizing the Caribbean by promoting local arts. The artists themselves contributed to this process by promoting the history of the anti-colonial struggle in their art as well. The movement went beyond envisioning unity in the Caribbean to promoting a type of unity which was rooted in the local culture and which rejected the colonial legacy. The Black Power movement conceptualized a unity which went beyond Marryshow's limited colonial vision.

50

MARY MCLEOD BETHUNE'S LEGACY

Mary McLeod Bethune emerged as one of the most outstanding educators and leaders of her time. Elaine Smith placed her among the "Four Greats," along with Frederick Douglass, W.E.B. Du Bois, and Martin Luther King. Bethune's greatness was not only due to the monumental feat which she accomplished in founding what was to become Bethune-Cookman University, but also her accomplishments through the National Council of Negro Women (NCNW) and her role as an advisor to President Franklin Roosvelet. That Bethune's time was split between working with the NCNW, working for her college, and her time in Washington demonstrated the nature of the type of activities which she found herself involved in.

Bethune was particularly close with First Lady Eleanor Roosevelt. President Franklin Roosevelt enlisted Bethune's service as one of two black advisers to his National Youth Administration. This administration was set up to assist young people with the struggles of the Depression. Eleanor Roosvelet recalled that Bethune "had a great deal of influence with the President, who had complete trust in whatever she told him as it affected the young people of her race while she was working with the NYA."

There were limitations to how much influence Bethune had over President Roosvelet, however. Bethune had requested that President Roosevelt consider addressing issues such as lynching and federally funded discrimination, but the president would not act on these issues. Roosevelt's unwillingness to confront racism in America was especially at issue during World War II. First Lady Roosevelt was asked how she could expect black people to remain loyal given that the armed forces still were not integrated. Her response was to argue that the "danger or disorders" of immediate integration would be worse than segregation itself.

The loyalty of black people to the American cause was partly rooted in concern over the manner in which Jews in Germany were being treated. Charlotte Hawkins Brown commented that "Hitler is endeavoring to reduce the status of Jews in Germany to that of the Negro in New York." Bethune sought to rally support for the war cause when she stated: "Armed with a faith in what we as a united group may do, we go forth to the job before us, with an undying faith in God, and in the cause to which we are committed. We must be aware of our special problems and the nature of their ultimate solution. But we must also recognize that our problems are akin to the problems of the weak and oppressed everywhere, and that our rights, like the rights of all people, are rooted in the common humanity of all men. United — We build a free world."

Bethune's vision was not shared by President Roosevelt, however. As noted previously, Roosevelt would not even see to it that the American forces were integrated during the war against Germany. The racism which persisted during the war was apparent in other areas. Millions of workers were employed to assist with the war effort, yet too few of the new employees were black. This was an issue raised by the NCNW when Bethune wrote to President Roosevelt to explain: "At a time like this, when the basic principles of democracy are being challenged at home and abroad, when racial and religious hatreds are being engendered, it is vitally important that the Negro, as a minority group in this nation, express anew his faith in your leadership and his unswerving adherence to a program of national defense adequate to insure the perpetuation of the principles of democracy."

Bethune also explained: "In the ranks of Negro womanhood in America are to be found ability and capacity for leadership, for administrative as well as routine tasks, for the types of service so necessary in a program of national defense. These are citizens whose past records at home and in war service abroad, whose unquestioned loyalty to their country and its ideals, and whose sincere and enthusiastic desire to serve you and the nation indicate how deeply they are concerned that a more realistic American democracy, as visioned by those not blinded by racial prejudices, shall be maintained and perpetuated."

Bethune's appeal was a passionate one, but President Roosvelt was not moved by this appeal. A year later A. Phillip Randolph and Walter White threatened to organize 100,000 black people to protest against employment discrimination. Bethune was prepared to mobilize NCNW members for a march on Washington. The threat of a potential mass protest forced Roosevelt to issue an executive order which barred discrimination in defense industries.

The reality was that there was little difference between the discriminatory ideology of Adolf Hitler and that of the United States. Hitler himself recognized the similarities. In *Mein Kampf*, Hitler wrote about how the eugenics laws in a number of American states were attempting to create a "master race." This served as a model which Hitler studied from. In a conversation, Hitler was quoted as stating: "I have studied with great interest the laws of several American states concerning prevention of reproduction by people whose progeny would, in all possibility, be of no value or be injurious to the racial stock."

Hitler not only studied American laws concerning eugenics, but American eugenicists also supported what was taking place in Nazi Germany at the time. Charles Goethe, who was an American eugenicist, took a number of trips to Germany. Following a trip to Germany in 1934, Goethe wrote a letter to another eugenicist named Ezra Gosney, explaining: "You will be interested to know... that your work has played a powerful part in shaping the opinions of the group of intellectuals who are behind Hitler... Everywhere I sensed that their opinions have been tremendously stimulated by American thought."

Despite the similarities between Hitler's views and the racism in America, the United States saw itself as representing liberty and democracy. This was a view which President Woodrow Wilson had expressed when he suggested that America should make the world safe for democracy. President Wilson also declared: "An extraordinary and very perilous state of affairs had been created in the South by the sudden and absolute emancipation of the Negroes, and it was not strange that the Southern legislatures should deem it necessary to take extraordinary steps to guard against the manifest and pressing dangers which it entailed. Here was a vast 'laboring, landless, homeless class,' once slaves; now free; unpracticed in liberty, unschooled in self-control; never sobered by the discipline of self-support; never established in any habit of prudence; excited by a freedom they did not understand, exalted by false hopes, bewildered and without leaders, and yet insolent and aggressive;

sick of work, covetous of pleasure—a host of dusky children untimely put out of school."

That World War I had little to do with extending democracy to black people is demonstrated by the fact that some black soldiers who fought in the war were lynched—some of them were still in their uniform as they were lunched. The situation had not changed during the Second World War. When the United States was fighting Nazism, black people were again confronted with racism from the very nation which they served. For example, the President of the North American Aviation Company noted that it was against company policy to employ black people as aircraft workers of mechanics, but that black people could work as janitors.

Bethune advocated for better conditions for black women during the war. This earned her the title of being "the surrogate mother" of black women in service. Bethune regularly sent congratulations and praise to black women in order to boost morale. In seeking to support the efforts of black service members, Bethune also seemed to have recognized the need to compromise on certain demands. Following the attack on Pearl Harbor, Bethune declared: "The National Council of Negro Women submerges any obstacles that would come between us and an all-out effort of America toward final victory."

One obstacle which Bethune was forced to submerge was the issue of segregation. Bethune refused to demand an anti-segregation clause in the Women's Army Auxiliary Corps bill before it became law. In doing so, she ignored the request of Walter White who suggested that such a clause should be made an issue.

Bethune recognized that the problem of discrimination persisted, but she also seemed to have believed that supporting the war effort was more important than protesting discrimination. Noel Campbell Mitchell remembered that Bethune had remarked to recruits for the Women's Army Auxiliary Corps (WAAC) that the War Department "did not want us in the first place, so we had to set an example." Bethune went on record to tell officer candidates: "We are asking for equal participation. We are not going to be agitators. We are real Americans, and as Americans we must give our all to protect America."

This is not to suggest that Bethune completely acquiesced to discrimination within the WAAC. Bethune organized an inquiry into discrimination at the WAAC training facility. Bethune also acted on complaints about racism. A journalist named Charles Howard was able to uncover the discriminatory practices which were taking place in the facility, which included forcing black women to eat at separate tables.

America was ultimately successful in defeating Germany in the war, but racial discrimination in America persisted, as well as the terror and violence which accompanied the discrimination. The terror which confronted African Americans was one which had personally impacted Bethune. In Florida, Harry T. Moore and his wife Henrietta were killed in a bombing. The Moores were graduates of Bethune-Cookman College. The bombing was one which troubled Bethune because the Moores were not only graduates of her school, but she personally knew Harry Moore.

The murder of the Moores was not the first time that Bethune was forced to confront racial violence in America. In 1943, before the war ended, race riots erupted throughout the nation. The NCNW responded to the uprising by urging action from the White House. Bethune sent a letter to President Roosevelt in which she wrote: "A straight forward determined statement and program of action from you that will reach the core of this problem is imperative. We urge you as President of the United States and as Commander-in-Chief of the American Armed Forces to take some firm steps immediately in suppressing this violence. We know you as the courageous leader who will not hesitate to act when the need for action is apparent."

Elaine Smith noted that Bethune wasted her time writing to President Roosevelt. President Roosevelt was content to focus on the war effort, while ignoring racial issues. This was not an issue which Bethune could ignore, however. She argued that the greatest grievance for an African American was "the failure of the Army and his government to protect him in the uniform of his country from actual assault by civilians."

Bethune acknowledged that the government would not protect its black citizens, yet she also did what she could to affirm the patriotism of the very black people who were unprotected by their government. It was for this purpose that the NCNW celebrated "We Serve America Week". Bethune stated that this was "to demonstrate to all America the contributions made by Negro women to our war effort and to the support of our democratic ideals." As part of the effort to affirm the patriotism of black people, the NCNW sponsored the launch of the S.S. *Harriet Tubman*. The NCNW assumed the responsibility of paying for the construction of the ship through the sale of war bonds.

During the 1950s, Bethune continued to advocate for integration. She praised the Supreme Court's *Brown* decision for being a step towards ending segregation. Bethune expressed the view that the integration "of the races in public education is the only democratic way." Even as Bethune advocated for integration, she also recognized the importance of building black institutions. Her view was that "as long as Negroes are hemmed into racial blocs by prejudice and pressure, it will be necessary for them to band together for economic betterment."

In the later years of her life, Bethune's efforts also took on an international significance. Bethune was appointed by President Harry Truman as America's representative to the inauguration of President William Tubman of Liberia. The time Bethune spent in Liberia was productive. She not only received the Order of the Star of Africa, but Bethune managed to organize a chapter of the National Council of Negro Women in Liberia's capital.

In 1954, Bethune visited Switzerland. She remarked that she found no segregation and discrimination, which was a marked contrast from the realities of racial segregation in America. Bethune was in Switzerland to discuss the Moral Re-Armament (MRA). The MRA was a movement founded by a clergyman named Frank Buchman in 1938. The MRA was a worldwide, anti-communist movement which sought to prevent wars and promoted morality. This was an effort which Bethune embraced.

MRA had a profound influence on Bethune, who began to examine her own life. She explained: "I realize how much of what I did was for my own glorification. ... I want to do all I can now to make right all of the wrongs." One of the wrongs which she sought to right was acknowledging that she had neglected her son in favor of public service.

In her last will, Bethune declared: "Personally and racially, our enemies must be forgiven. Our aim must be to create a world of fellowship and justice where no man's skin, color or religion, is held against him. . . . Loving your neighbor means being interracial, interreligious and international." This remark summed up a woman whose life was spent challenging racial discrimination against black people. In this regard, Bethune had truly established herself as one of the great black leaders in American history.

What is perhaps most remarkable about Bethune's legacy was her ability to pursue her vision for inclusion while also being confronted with the racism of the very institutions of power that she worked within. Not only did she serve as an advisor to a president who would not dare to act on matters of racial justice such as segregation and lynching, but during World War II, Bethune was forced to balance her commitment to the war effort with her commitment to combatting the discrimination which black people were confronted with.

Bethune was an integrationist. The challenge which integrationist leaders in American history have historically been confronted with has been the challenge of trying to assert an American identity within a nation which has never treated its black citizens as equal American citizens. In the case of Bethune, she resolved to address this issue by developing black institutions, the most notable being her school. Beyond this, however, there were clear limitations imposed on her efforts. For example, President Roosevelt had disregarded her efforts to get him to take stronger positions against racial discrimination against black people. President Roosevelt was not willing to challenge discrimination against black people, but he also relied on the black vote. Leaders like Bethune were utilized to retain his support from black voters. This was a tactic which First Lady Roosevelt encouraged. During the 1936 campaign, she wrote a memorandum to her husband in which she noted that "it would be well to ask some Negro speakers, like Mrs. Bethune to speak at church meetings and that type of Negro organization."

Bethune was not the only one who had been used to rally support for President Roosevelt. The Colored Committee of the Good Neighbor League staged a massive rally in support of

Roosevelt for the 1936 election. At the rally a large painting of Roosevelt was unveiled. The Committee was credited with winning 70 percent of the black vote for Roosevelt, but the Committee never received an audience with the president.

During the 1936 campaign, President Roosevelt had not expressed any commitment to addressing racial issues. There was no need for him to do so, as making such a commitment would have risked alienating Southern Democrats who favored segregation. President Roosevelt also recognized that his support among black voters was such that he could continue to receive their support without making firm commitments. He could rely on the endorsements of prominent black leaders like Bethune, while also making non-committal remarks about the progress which black people made since 1863.

Bethune could perhaps be faulted for being too optimistic about President Roosevelt's willingness to take action to address racial discrimination, but one cannot fault her for her genuine desire to see an end to racism in America. Bethune attempted to use her connection to President Roosevelt to advocate for racial justice in America however they could. An example of this was a situation in which a black sharecropper named Odell Waller had killed his white landlord. Bethune called the White House to get a stay of execution. She was informed that the federal government lacked jurisdiction on the matter and Walter was executed. Bethune was not successful in getting the White House to save Waller, but she could not be faulted for trying, just as she could not be faulted for trying to get President Roosevelt to commit to racial justice. Following Bethune's death in 1955, Adam Clayton Powell summed up Bethune's legacy when he declared: "We have truly lost one whose great and gentle influence has shaped our lives over many years. The people of America have lost the keen mind, the rich wisdom, and the infinite courage of a woman who has contributed so much to her country".

References:

Blake T. Hilton, "Frantz Fanon and Colonialism: A Psychology of Oppression," *Journal of Scientific Psychology*, December 2011.

Charles Hamliton and Kwame Ture, *Black Power*

Earlene Kelly Parr, "Franklin D. Roosevelt and the Negro in the 1930's," 1965.

Elaine M. Smith, "Mary McLeod Bethune and the National Council of Negro Women"

51

ON ASSATA SHAKUR AND THE BLACK LIBERATION ARMY

Nelson Mandela explained: "A freedom fighter learns the hard way that it is the oppressor who defines the nature of the struggle, and the oppressed is often left no recourse but to use methods that mirror those of the oppressor. At a certain point, one can only fight fire with fire." In this remark, he was referring to the fact that the African National Congress' struggle in South Africa initially began as a nonviolent struggle, but the circumstances in South Africa eventually forced the ANC to abandon nonviolent struggle in favor of violent resistance.

Mandela's statement can be applied to conditions of African people in the United States where groups such as the Black Liberation Army took up arms to defend themselves against the violent oppression which they confronted. One of the most prominent figures within the Black Liberation Army was Assata Shakur. Shakur, who was also a member of the Black Panther Party, came to national prominence due to her involvement in a shootout on a New Jersey turnpike which resulted in an officer named Werner Foerster being shot and killed. For her involvement in this incident, Shakur was tried and convicted of murder. Sundiata Acoli, who was in the car with Shakur, was also convicted for the shooting. Acoli was later implicated in organizing a prison riot which resulted in a corrections officer named Robert Glen Simmons being shot.

Shakur not only professed her innocence, but she claimed that she was tortured in the hospital after she was shot and that she was wrongfully convicted by a white jury. What Shakur did apologize for is that she should not have been a New Jersey turnpike considering that it was often used as a checkpoint to stop and harass black people.

Assata Shakur was accused of killing Werner Foerster with his own gun. Prior to the trial, Stanely Cohen, the lawyer who was working on her case, was found dead. Shakur recalled that the last time she saw him, he was excited because of the progress he was making on her case. Days later he was found dead in his house with evidence of trauma, although it was reported in the newspapers that he died of natural causes. After his death, the legal papers on Shakur's case went missing. The legal papers were eventually found in the possession of the New York City police. The police had taken the legal papers from Stanley's house as evidence. Some of the papers were never recovered, including all the notes on trial strategy.

There were other problems leading up to the trial. After Cohen's death, William Kunstler joined the defense team. Once he joined, the judge rescinded the order for state-paid experts. Without the state paying for expert witnesses, Shakur could not afford to hire expert witnesses for her trial. The lawyers also discovered that the offices which they and the defense team were using had been bugged.

Shakur's defense attorney, Lennox Hinds, noted that the evidence which emerged demonstrated that Shakur was shot in her back with her hands in the air, which meant that she could not raise her hand to shoot a gun. Moreover, no evidence was found that Shakur had fired a gun. There was no evidence to support the claim that she took Foerster's gun and shot him either.

Though there was no evidence that Shakur herself killed Foerster, the fact is that a shootout did take place which resulted in Foerster being killed. Even if Shakur herself had not fired the shot, the political repression which black activists at the time endured and her involvement in armed struggle practically ensured that Shakur could not beat the case. She was a revolutionary leader who was captured at the scene of an officer being slayed. Moreover, the public perception of Shakur was already that of a cop murdering, criminal. A book titled *Target Blue* claimed that Assata Shakur had been responsible for the deaths of several policemen and that she had even blown up a police car with a grenade during a police chase.

Assata Shakur was targeted because of her work as a political activist with the Black Panther Party and the Black Liberation Army. The Black Liberation Army emerged as a formation which waged an armed struggle against the state. The aim of the Black

Liberation Army was certainly ambitious, but the group proved to be ill-prepared to undertake the task which it did. Assata Shakur noted that she read about armed struggle in other places, but she had no concrete idea of how to apply those lessons to the struggle of black people in the United States. This is because the struggle of black people in the United States was unlike some of the other anti-colonial revolutionary struggles being waged around the world. In Vietnam, for example, the objective of the Viet Cong was to force an American withdrawal. In African colonies such as Mozambique and Angola, the objective was similarly to force a Portuguese withdrawal. Black Americans, however, found themselves living in the same nation as the colonial power which they waged war against. The nationalist struggle waged by the Black Liberation Army was not a struggle to drive an occupying colonial power out of the black nation, but a struggle to build a black nation by forcing the occupying colonial power to secede territory to new Afrikans.

The struggle which the Black Liberation Army waged was also unlike the struggles waged by black people during the period of enslavement. The struggle to abolish slavery in the United States was one which resulted in violent uprisings on the part of the enslaved, but such uprisings were not aimed at transforming the territorial integrity of the United States. The purpose was to liberate enslaved Africans and to bring an end to the system of slavery. In this regard, the struggle waged by Nat Turner and Harriet Tubman was more singular and focused. The anti-slavery struggle also benefitted from the fact that Abraham Lincoln was among those who favored the abolition of slavery. The Republic of New Afrika certainly could have never hoped for the support of President Richard Nixon or President Gerald Ford.

Of course, as Shakur herself pointed out, Lincoln's support for the abolition of slavery was a strategic move designed to weaken the South during the Civil War. As Shakur noted, in 1861, Lincoln affirmed that slavery was legal and that he had no right to abolish it. Lincoln also promised to enforce the Fugitive Slave Act. Shakur further pointed out that Lincoln was not in favor of having black people fight in the war. She quoted Lincoln, who stated: "I am not so sure we could do much with the Blacks. If we were to arm them, I fear in a few weeks the arms would be in the hands of the

Rebels." In the end, however, Lincoln did abolish slavery.

Yet another challenge was that the Black Liberation Army had no defined structure. Shakur explained that the Black Liberation Army "was not a centralized, organized group with a common leadership and chain of command. Instead, there were various organizations and collectives working together and simultaneously independent of each other." The decentralized nature of the Black Liberation Army was partly due to the fact that it was formed at a time when repression against revolutionary organizations was severe. Shakur noted that many revolutionaries were locked away in prison or forced into hiding. The scattered nature of the movement at the time made coordinating among the different groups very challenging. Shakur also admitted that those involved "were weak, inexperienced, disorganized, and seriously lacking in training."

The Black Liberation Army was poorly prepared to engage in the type of struggle which they engaged in, but they dared to show that black people were ready to fight back against the repression. I certainly admire the bravery which they demonstrated, though I will admit that I found their methods to be misguided. It is not that I am against armed self-defense or acts of aggression aimed at combatting oppression. My critique is that given the strength and resources of the American government, the Black Liberation Army perhaps should have been more strategic in how it conducted its activities. For example, robbing banks to fund the revolutionary struggle of the New Afrikan movement was never going to be a reliable way to fund the movement, but doing so certainly ensured further state repression against the movement.

Kwame Ture was another activist who embraced armed struggle as an aspect of the liberation struggle of African people, but his approach was somewhat different. Ture served as the chairman of the Student Nonviolent Coordinating Committee (SNCC). As the name suggested, SNCC was committed to nonviolence. Ture himself embraced nonviolence, but only as a tactic, not as a principle. Ture explained that he used nonviolence as a cover to organize revolts. He did so in such a way that the government could not prove he was responsible for organizing revolts. This would be an example of a more strategic approach towards engaging in violent rebellion.

I do not mention Ture in this context to diminish the efforts of the Black Liberation Army or Assata Shakur. Ture himself would not have tolerated any effort to diminish Shakur's significance in the struggle. Ture noted that Shakur was so respected that men in the Black Liberation Army were proud to receive orders from her. The point here is that the manner in which the Black Liberation Army conducted their efforts not only made them an easier target for state repression, but it also provided evidence which could potentially be used against them in court. For example, during her trial Shakur was informed that discussing the circumstances of how she became a fugitive could potentially "open the door" for the prosecutor to introduce evidence such as the manuals of guerilla warfare and other material which was found in the car. Shakur had acknowledged that being on the turnpike was a mistake, but being caught in a car with incriminating evidence only amplified the nature of that mistake.

Though I may not have agreed with the methods used by the Black Liberation Army, I honor Assata Shakur as a revolutionary leader who served the community and fought for the community. Her detractors may accuse her of being a violent extremist. To this I would merely point out that George Washington was also a violent extremist who took up arms to wage a war of liberation against the British colonial empire. If America can honor George Washington for his actions, then African people should be free to honor Assata Shakur for fighting against a level of repression which was worse than anything George Washington had ever experienced. Shakur herself stated it best when she explained, "always decide who your enemies are for yourself, and never let your enemies choose your enemies for you."

52

THE SLEEPING BEAUTY OF THE WORLD

In a short article titled "M is for Marxism," Kehinde Andrews wrote: "Marxism's central problem is that [it] imagines the White worker to be the hero of history, a vitally necessary part of the coming revolution. These ideas bleed into the work of revolutionary thinkers such as Franz Fanon who calls for the 'sleeping beauty' of history, the White worker, to awake and join with the global oppressed. This is a dangerous fantasy. The reality is that those in the West live in relative prosperity to the rest of the world because of *racism*."

Andrews is referring to a passage from *The Wretched of the Earth* in which Fanon wrote: "This huge task which consists of reintroducing mankind into the world, the whole of mankind, will be carried out with the indispensable help of the European peoples, who themselves must realize that in the past they have often joined the ranks of our common masters where colonial questions were concerned. To achieve this, the European peoples must first decide to wake up and shake themselves, use their brains, and stop playing the stupid game of Sleeping Beauty."

In an article published in *Catalyst: A Journal of Theory and Strategy* titled "Who Owns Frantz Fanon's Legacy?," Bashir Abu-Manneh noted that *"Wretched* is thus committedly internationalist and refuses to essentialize the West as irredeemably racist or incapable of anti-systemic mobilization." Abu-Manneh contrasted Fanon's views with those of certain critical theorists who discounted the possibility of socialist mobilization in the West. Abu-Manneh also explained that Fanon "is far from being anti-European, nor does he tar Europe as permanently disabled by its old colonial practices." That Fanon was far from being anti-European is demonstrated not only in his writings, but also in his personal life as well. Fanon was married to a French woman.

The issue is not that Europe is irredeemably racist, but that the European masses have not yet displayed a willingness to mobilize against racism. This is because, as Andrews noted, they enjoy a relatively better standard of living than colonized Africans because they benefit from racism. Andrews explained: "Black radicalism is built on an analysis that sees racism as the basis of society with class oppression produced out of that fundamental relationship. For Marxism the opposite is true, so whilst there may be Black sections and a commitment to ending racial oppression the so called 'Negro Question' is on the side lines of the struggle. It is assumed that communism will magically end racism, something we have seen is definitely not true in places like Cuba."

I do not quote Andrews to make the argument that Marxism is of no relevance to the African liberation struggle. Andrews himself noted that Black people throughout Africa and the Diaspora were attracted to Marxism because of its call to overturn the existing economy. Andrews noted that Africa and the Caribbean witnessed more Marxist revolutions than Europe did, which demonstrated the extent to which Marxism influenced the radical Black liberation struggle.

It is also true that Black Marxists have had to contend with the racism and the indifference of their white comrades. This is a reality which Abu-Manneh acknowledged, noting that "Fanon's theory of revolutionary process is based on some key historical facts. First, the communist parties in both France and Algeria had rejected Algerian political independence for the longest time, under different pretexts ranging from fighting traditionalism in Arab society to advocating gradualist political reforms in the colony. This tarred communism with political ambivalence at best, or colonial contempt at worst."

Abu-Manneh noted that the second problem was that the majority class in Algeria was the peasantry. Marx and Engels described the proletariat as the leading "gravediggers" of capitalism. In their view, the revolution to overthrow capitalism was to be led by the white working class of the industrialized Western nations, but this was the same class of individuals whom Fanon described as behaving like "Sleeping Beauty." Abu-Manneh noted that "all successful socialist revolutions took place outside of advanced capitalist countries: in Russia, not Germany, and in Cuba, not the United States."

I reference Andrews again who noted that he has been called a Marxist for criticizing racism, which he found ironic given his view "that the major problem with Marxism is its inability to truly account for the racist nature of society." In Andrews' view, the major problem with Marxism is not merely that the proletariat of developed capitalist nations have failed to mobilize a successful socialist revolution, but that racism prevented them from doing so and that Marxists have not fully accepted this reality.

It is rather curious that Fanon would have held a position which Andrews described as a "dangerous fantasy" because Fanon was not unaware of how pervasive racism against African people was. In *Black Skin, White Masks*, Fanon noted that such racism was global in nature. He wrote: "In America, Negroes are segregated. In South America, Negroes are whipped in the streets, and Negro strikers are cut down by machine-guns. In West Africa, the Negro is an animal." Fanon also wrote: "In Martinique there are two hundred whites who consider themselves superior to 300,000 people of color. In South Africa there are two million whites against almost thirteen million native people, and it has never occurred to a single black to consider himself superior to a member of the white minority." Despite being confronted with the reality of global white racism against African people, Fanon still held the view that Europeans had to play a role in the revolutionary struggle.

Fanon's view on the possibility of the European working class waking up to join the revolutionary struggle was consistent with Fanon's unwillingness to engage in racial essentialism. This was part of Fanon's critique of Leopold Senghor's ideology of négritude. Senghor celebrated African culture as being the opposite of what he perceived as Western culture. Whereas the West represented science and reason, Senghor believed that Africans represented emotion and subjectivism. Fanon rejected this premise.

The problem with Senghor's position was that Senghor was effectively embracing a Western, colonial perspective on African people. Science and reason existed as elements of African culture prior to colonialism. It is certainly true that Europe began to outpace Africa in scientific development due in large part to the Industrial Revolution, though, as Walter Rodney noted, even before the Industrial Revolution and the development of capitalism in Europe, the merchant and manufacturing class in Europe was more aggressive in developing technological innovations which led to the development of a fledgling capitalist society. Even so, it would be inaccurate to suggest that there was no interest in scientific inquiry among pre-colonial African societies. Just as Fanon rejected the essentialist view which presented Africans as beings of emotion, rather than reason, he also rejected the notion that racism was so essential to European society that the European masses were incapable of overcoming their own racism.

Fanon's critique of Senghor's ideology was valid, especially considering Senghor's status as a neo-colonialist who aligned himself with France's colonial interests in Africa to the point that Senghor opposed Algerian independence. Abu-Manneh explained: "Fanon's damning judgment was clearly expressed in *Wretched*. If négritude was a symptom of the illusory cultural politics of race, *Wretched* is where Fanon would develop his alternative political worldview, in which class politics is primary."

Within the African liberation struggle there was a debate about whether class politics or racial politics should be primary. This was connected to the issue of whether the oppression of African people was primarily racial or primarily class based. Fanon was clearly in the camp which saw the struggle as being primarily a class struggle. In taking this position, Fanon was forced to wrestle with the limitations of this analysis due to the fact that Marxism did not develop as an ideology which addressed itself to the struggles of African people. This is why Fanon explained: "In the colonies the economic substructure is also a superstructure. The cause is the consequence; you are rich because you are white, you are white because you are rich. This is why Marxist analysis should always be slightly stretched every time we have to do with the colonial problem."

A Marxist analysis has to be stretched to address the colonial problem because Marx himself was not very much interested in the colonial problem and spent little time analyzing it. Marx's interest was in the problem of the proletariat in capitalist societies. Marx's limited understanding of the role of racism and colonialism within the capitalist system perhaps led him to overestimate the revolutionary potential of the working class in Europe. As Andrews noted, the racist colonial system allowed white workers to enjoy a standard of living which is generally better than the state of colonized Africans, so that it is not even in the material interest of the white working class to fight against the very racism which they benefit from.

53

MUSIC AND THE PAN-AFRICAN MOVEMENT

Music has played an important role in fostering Pan-African unity. Artists such as Fela Kuti, Bob Marley, Calypso Rose, Ti Manno, Ras Ly, and Sonny Okosun are among the artists whom I have mentioned in my writings who have used their music to promote unity among African people. Music has also demonstrated the cultural connections among African people. This was demonstrated when Koo Nimo met with Lord Pretender and Lord Kitchener. Koo Nimo spoke about the similarities between the music of Ghana and Trinidad. To demonstrate this point, Koo Nimo played a "dagomba tune" for the two artists.

Apart from its role in fostering unity, music has also been used by African people as a tool of resistance as well. Here I would give the specific example of calypso music. I grew up with calypso music as a young child in Guyana, but I rediscovered the music in college through the music of Brother Valentino, followed by Black Stalin and Chalkdust. This was in 2011. Those who have read my writings would know that I draw on the works of calypsonians often. This is because I view calypsonians as important political and social commentators who often use wit and satire as elements of their commentary. I have also argued that in some cases the political critiques of the calypsonians have been more stinging than even that of the political opposition. Brother Valentino expressed the view that calypso is the true opposition. In any given Caribbean country, an opposition party may come into power and behave just as poorly as the previous party that was in power, but the voice of the calypsonian has remained a constant source of critique of those in power. This is not to suggest that calypsonians themselves have not been drawn into party politics in the Caribbean, but generally calypso had been the most constant source of critique of those in power.

One notable example of the political role of calypso which I have written about was De Professor's song "God Don't Sleep." In the song, De Professor called on Guyanese to hold their leaders accountable. He was also very critical of the corruption and misrule under the P.P.P. government. In the song he condemned the extrajudicial killings which took place under the government; financial mismanagement such as Clement Rohee (referred to as "Clem" in the song) spending $38 million of the country's money for a water trunk which ended up breaking down; faulty road projects; and promoting racial division. As the title of the song suggests, De Professor maintains that God does not sleep and that in the end God will punish the corrupt politicians in Guyana. Apparently, the same corrupt politicians were concerned about the punishment which De Professor was inflicting through his lyrics because the song was banned.

Calypsonians also served an important role during the Black Power movement in the Caribbean. They became voices of racial pride, cultural expression, Pan-African unity, and anti-colonialism. One example of this is Brother Valentino's song "Stay Up Zimbabwe," which was a call for support for the liberation struggles in Zimbabwe and South Africa. The roots of calypso music in the Caribbean can be traced to enslaved Africans on the plantations who used music as a form of resistance against the conditions of slavery. Gros Jean, who was a slave, is known to be the first known calypsonian. Gros Jean was the first "Maitre Casio" or "Casio Master." In the twentieth-century, calypso emerged as a music genre, with the earliest recordings of calypsos being done between 1912 and 1914.

Mighty Spoiler was one particular calypsonian whom I wrote about in *One Caribbean and Other Essays*. I am not one to use the phrase "lyrical genius" very lightly, but I think Spoiler safely fits in that category given his wit, creativity, and humour as an artist. For example, in his song "Picking Nonsense," Spoiler sang about observing various nonsensical situations in Trinidad such as an incident with a stubborn patron at the Perseverance Club or about the discussion about cricket at Arouca involving a Carriacounian who did not understand the concept of time zones.

Spoiler's accomplishment as an artist is even more impressive to me when one considers the poverty that he lived in and his struggle with alcoholism, which led to his premature death. Spoiler, in my opinion, represented the brilliance of African people, as well as the way that this brilliance is often cut short by the poverty and hardships which African people have endured.

Spoiler's fate also brings to mind the Brazilian samba artist, Geraldo Pereira. Just like Spoiler, Pereira was a heavy drinker. Pereira became bitter over the fact that his music was being played on the radio, but he was not making a lot of money from music. By the 1950s, his health declined due to his heavy drinking. Pereira was also known for becoming violent when drunk. In 1955, not long after Pereira's thirty-seventh birthday, he died following a fight with a crossdresser known as Madame Satã.

The calypso artists that I listened to were largely influenced by the Black Power movement of the 1960s and the 1970s. As such, their music often reflected themes such as anti-colonialism, Pan-Africanism, nationalism, and cultural pride. Shadow, whom I have written about, reflected the anti-colonial nature of the Black Power movement. His music celebrated Caribbean culture, while also expressing his belief in the unity of African people and his support for the liberation of South Africa. Singing Sandra's music also reflected this embrace of African culture and African roots. Chalkdust was someone who used calypso to promote African identity and Caribbean unity based on a shared cultural identity. What is especially unique about Chalkdust is that he was originally uncomfortable with the Black Power movement's emphasis on Africa, but he came to fully embrace the cultural aspect of the Black Power movement to the point that he was critical of those who tried to run away from their African identity.

Apart from the role of calypsonians as critics of the neo-colonial governments in the Caribbean, calypsonians often became important voices for promoting Caribbean unity and Pan-Africanism. Their music in turn greatly shaped my own Pan-African consciousness and my appreciation for Caribbean culture.

Chalkdust also stands out as an example of how calypso has been used as a means to engage in a scathing critique of those in power. His song "Ah Miss De Bards" (Creole for "I Miss the Bards") is a great example of Chalkdust's ability to combine history with political commentary. In the song, Chalkdust laments that the calypsonians of the modern era lack the skills to attack modern politicians. Chalkdust honored a number of great kaisonians from the past such as Lord Kitchener (Kitch),

Lord Pretender (Preddie), Mighty Spoiler, Mighty Duke, Zandolie, Maestro, Lord Melody, Growler, Lord Blakie, Ras Shorty I, Penguin, Merchant, Atilla, Caruso, Cristo, the Mighty Cypher, King Radio, Roaring Lion, Power, Houdini, Nap Hepburn, and Destroyer.

Throughout the song Chalkdust mentions various scandals involving members of the People's Partnership government which was led by Prime Minister Kamla Persad-Bissessar. Chalkdust presents Prime Minister Persad-Bissessar as an incompetent leader with a drinking problem. In the song, he mentions that Maestro would have stated that the prime minister was in "high spirits," whereas Mighty Spoiler would have stated that "she want to fall"—this is a reference to Spoiler's famous line "I want to fall," which was a reference to his own alcoholism.

Other members of the government which Chalkdust lambasts include Jack Warner, who was a former Minister of Works and Transport who was involved in a scandal in which it was alleged that he used his position as the vice president of FIFA to acquire millions of dollars; Errol MacLeod, a former Minister of Labour; Herbert Volney, the former Minister of Justice who was dismissed after being involved in a controversy relating to Clause 34 and someone who Chalkdust claims "Kitch" would have invoked the vengeance of Moko upon; Anand Ramlogan, a former Attorney General who was involved in a controversy over spending millions of dollars to purchase vehicles and also faced accusations that he was a wife beater; Roodal Moonilal, a former Minister of Housing and the Environment; Surujrattan Rambachan, a former Minister of Foreign Affairs; Wade Mark, a Speaker of the House of Representatives; and Gary Griffith, a former Minister of National Security, who is portrayed by Chalkdust as being so incompetent at maintaining security in the country that his plan for fighting crime is merely a waste of time.

There are two particular lines from this song which I referenced in my writings. The first is Chalkdust's line: "And when the speaker say that he pass all he exams up at UWI/Spoiler would say, himself gave himself a degree." This is a reference to the controversy over a degree which Wade Mark received from the

University of the West Indies (UWI), as well as a reference to Spoiler's song "Magistrate Try Himself." The second line which I have made reference to in my writings is the line: "And when Daaga get a national award from the PP crew, Merchant would say, 'Norman Daaga is that you.'" This is a reference to Merchant's song "Norman" in which Merchant utters the line, "Norman is that you?" Chalkdust references Merchant's song to draw a contrast between the Daaga the revolutionary leader with the Daaga who became part of the corrupt PP government. I respect and admire Daaga for his role in the Black Power uprising in 1970, but Daaga represented the unfortunate trend of revolutionary leaders taking counterrevolutionary positions at a later point in their life. The Daaga who was being awarded by the government of Trinidad was not the same Daaga who stood up to the government of Trinidad in 1970.

The unfortunate reality of Caribbean politics has been that radical voices for change have often reversed position. This was certainly the case with the 1970 Black Power uprising in Trinidad. Apart from Daaga, the trade union leader George Weekes joined with the National Alliance for Reconstruction government which promoted the same neoliberal policies which Eric Williams' government did. Chalkdust also criticized Weekes' decision to join the N.A.R.

Khafra Kambon is rather unique. Unlike Daaga and Weekes, Kambon did not join the ruling government of Trinidad. Instead, he became the chairman of the Emancipation Support Committee and utilized Emancipation Day as a day to promote African culture in Trinidad. The restoration of the culture of African people was one aspect of the Black Power movement, but Kambon's work with the Emancipation Support Committee represented a retreat from the demands for radical change which were expressed by the 1970 Black Power movement of which he was involved in. The fact that the Emancipation Support Committee relies on government support to fund its activities may explain Kambon's shift from radical political activism to promoting culture.

Calypso developed among the poorer class within Caribbean society. As Chalkdust himself noted, even the church in Caribbean society looked at calypso very negatively at one point. The church also had a generally negative view of carnival. This was something which the Mighty Gabby of Barbados addressed in his song "Wuk Up." "Wuk Up" was an angry response to the Catholic Church's denouncement of Crop Over in Barbados. In the song, Gabby notes the hypocrisy of the Catholic Church's condemnation of carnival given that the church has an "alcoholic sacrament" in which church goers drink wine. Gabby also notes how musical praise worship of God in the church looks very similar to Kadooment. In this regard, calypso was used to affirm the cultural identity of the African masses in the face of institutions which have sought to shame Africans for engaging in their cultural practices.

Calypso has also played an important role in discussions regarding cultural and racial identity in the Caribbean as well. This is a topic which I have explored in my writings as well. In the 1970s, during the Black Power movement, calypsonians were among those who challenged the prevailing colonial order by promoting African cultural identity in Eurocentric societies where individuals were taught to despise their African roots. Calypsonians engaged in a reappraisal of Caribbean culture and identity which shifted the focus away from the Caribbean's connection with its colonizers and shifted the focus to a connection with Africa.

The reappraisal of the Caribbean's African roots also took place within the context of debates over racial cohesion in the Caribbean, especially for Guyana and Trinidad where there are tensions between the African and Indian population. Some calypsonians have addressed this topic as well. I wrote an essay on Brother Marvin's song "Jahaji Bhai," in which he used his own mixed heritage to promote racial unity in Trinidad. As I noted in my essay, despite purporting to reflect the mixed identity of Trinidadian society, Brother Marvin expressed a clear bias towards his Indian roots. One of the ways this was demonstrated in his song is the fact that there are several Hindi phrases that are used throughout Brother Marvin's song in addition to the title. This included: Bahut Ajah (grandfather), Achcha dosti (good friend), Janmabhumi (homeland), Zindagee (life), Do chuttee, (two holidays), Anth bhala to sab bhala (all's well that ends well), Bahut achcha (very good), Haat melawo (let's join hands), Bete baat ko garro (child pay heed to what I'm saying), and Ekta me bal hai (unity is strength). In other words, Brother Marvin's attempt to foster unity in Trinidad was through displaying his connection to his Indian roots and culture, while displaying much less of a cultural connection to his African roots. In the song, he also chastised Africans in Trinidad for having strong connections to their African roots.

Brother Marvin's song was criticized by Sugar Aloes. In the view of Sugar Aloes, it was not Africans who needed a lesson on racial unity in Trinidad, but rather Indians. The perception of Sugar Aloes was that it was Indians who not only refused to support African cultural events, but Indian leaders such as Sat Maharaj expressed racist views. In the song, Sugar Aloes affirms the view that we all belong to the human race and shunned the racial ideals of Sat Maharaj, so Sugar Aloes' song was not an argument against racial unity. It was an argument against Brother Marvin's approach of placing the onus of racial unity in Trinidad on Africans.

The controversy created by Brother Marvin's song demonstrated that building a cohesive multiracial society must not be done at the expense of diminishing the history of one group. This is an issue that goes beyond Brother Marvin's song, however. Too often diversity has meant ignoring the particular needs and concerns of black people. Mutabaruka, another musician, raised this point when he noted that Jamaica's slogan about "one people" was accurate because in Jamaica it was only "one people" who struggled, black people. This is also the same problem with Brazil's national myth about "racial democracy." It is a myth which was used to mask the racism against black people in Brazil.

Music genres such as reggae and calypso have contributed to sustaining the spirit of the Pan-African movement even in the face of efforts by the colonial powers to destroy the Pan-African movement through targeting certain individual Pan-African leaders and Pan-African organizations. As important as music has been to the revolutionary Pan-African struggle, I do think it is important to note that music by itself cannot make or sustain a revolutionary movement. This is a point I have certainly explored in my writings. This is not to diminish the important role of music, but to point out that music itself cannot create the type of structural changes which are necessary.

In an article titled "How to Emancipate Yourself From Mental Slavery" which was published in the *Jamaica Gleaner*, an author and motivational speaker named Glenford Smith made the important point that many of those who know of Bob Marley's music do not take the time and effort to read Marcus Garvey. He explained: "True emancipation from mental slavery can be achieved only by gaining new knowledge, insights, ideas and paradigms. Although learning through entertainment is important, it is also very limited. Not every important idea you can make into song, chant, or drama." Indeed, we must go beyond music if we are to build real revolutionary movements.

Bob Marley is a figure whom I cite to make the point about why revolutionary movements need to go beyond music. Marley used his music to promote revolutionary ideas, but Marley was not a revolutionary himself. I believe that Marley was someone who genuinely cared about the suffering of the masses of people in the Caribbean and in Africa, but there were contradictions between the message of Marley's music and the realities of his life as an internationally famed musician. I state this not to diminish the importance of the message of Marley's music, but it is difficult to be an internationally famous musician and a revolutionary. This is exemplified by the fact that Marley's music was popular among white people in the United States, but he struggled to attract black audiences in part because they could not afford ticket prices. Marley himself admitted that he didn't understand politics or "big words like 'democratic socialism.'"

Another example is the Mighty Gabby. In *One Caribbean and Other Essays* I wrote about his song, "Gabby is a Bee." The song was an angry response to those who criticized Gabby for changing his political alliances. I understand Gabby's point that he had a democratic right to choose which party he wanted to support, but it did seem hypocritical that the man who proclaimed there was no difference between the D.L.P. and the B.L.P. would switch between the two parties. It seemed to be especially opportunistic because Gabby ran as a candidate for the D.L.P. in 1994. In the song, Gabby expressed that his anger was that people who were once his friends were criticizing his decision to change political parties.

The problem with "Gabby is a Bee" was that Gabby responded to criticisms of his political positions with very personal attacks. In the song, Gabby dismissed Romeo as an alcoholic whose drinking problem caused him to neglect personal hygiene, singing: "That boy should go min' he teeth/no time of the day the man smelling sweet." Gabby suggested that Classic engaged in bestiality, singing: "Classic should go and take married vows, and stop having sex with the people cows." Gabby also boasted that unlike Classic, he never faced judgment for stealing cement. The most troubling part of the song was Gabby's treatment of Kid Site. Gabby mentioned that Kid Site's mother was killed by his father, singing, "how come he ain't tell none a wunna, he father kill he mother."

Gabby's response was in very poor taste. He resorted to very personal attacks to respond to political criticisms and, in the case of Kid Site, Gabby even resorted to digging up very painful family history. I saw this as an effort on Gabby's part to publicly humiliate his critics into silence. This is an example of what I refer to as Gabby's tendency to abuse and intimidate others. This may not be physical abuse, but I would consider bringing up a person's traumatic family history to shame them into silence as a form of emotional or psychological abuse.

I admired what Gabby represented as someone who used his music to promote positive values such as anti-colonialism and Caribbean unity, but I saw this response as troubling not only because of what I saw as hypocritical opportunism on his part where politics were concerned, but also because of the manner in which he addressed those who criticized this opportunism. Gabby demonstrated that even political artists in the Caribbean are not immune from the type of opportunism which plagues Caribbean politics.

54

THE EARLY ROOTS OF PAN-AFRICANISM

In 1900, Henry Sylvester Williams organized a Pan-African Conference. It was from Williams' Pan-African Conference in 1900 that the term "Pan-African" came into common usage to describe this vision of a united African people. As I explained in *The Life, Goals, and Achievements of Marcus Garvey*, Williams' vision for Pan-Africanism was not a particularly revolutionary one. He did not advocate for the independence of Africa or the end of colonial rule. Despite this, Williams did make an important contribution to the global African struggle by organizing the first Pan-African conference. It was out of this conference that a genuine revolutionary Pan-African struggle eventually emerged.

Williams gave us the phrase "Pan-African," but the vision of an international unity of African people certainly did not begin with him. A very early example of this was Haiti's 1816 constitution which declared that anyone with African blood who came to live in Haiti would be recognized as a Haitian citizen. In *Black in Latin America*, Henry Louis Gates explained that Haiti's constitution from 1816 "can be thought of as one of the earliest, and perhaps the earliest, signal acts in the history of Pan-Africanism, the first time certainly that a government thought of all persons of African descent positively as 'citizens' or members of a unified or related group [...]". Ngũgĩ wa Thiong'o declared: "The journey of the African idea, beginning in Haiti and championed by Pan-African congresses, reached its climax in the independence of Angola, Guinea Bissau, and Mozambique and the liberation of South Africa in the 1980s and 1990s."

It was precisely because of what Haiti represented to Africans globally that the Western powers felt that it was necessary to conspire to ruin Haiti. Haiti was made to pay very dearly for the success of its revolution. The situation in Haiti demonstrated why Anténor Firmin's vision for Haiti and for the African race remained very relevant. Firmin was an individual who understood that Haitians needed to take control of their own destiny by

285

defending their nation from foreign exploitation. Doing so also meant stabilizing Haiti politically. Firmin was a very visionary leader. He attended the Pan-African Conference in 1900 and was one among the early pioneers of the Pan-African movement. He was also an early advocate for Caribbean unity, which is a point that I noted in *One Caribbean and Other Essays*. Firmin was also a man who was firmly committed to combatting racial prejudice. His most well-known book was *On the Equality of Human Races*, in which he argued that there are no superior and inferior races. His premise was that all races are capable of noble aspirations and of degradation.

I did take issue with some of Firmin's views, however. For example, Firmin relied on sexism to counter Clémence Royer's racist arguments by suggesting that women do not have the temperament and education to understand complex topics. To be clear, I am in full support of Firmin's criticism of Royer's racism—I certainly will not be the one to defend a racist white woman. Even so, Firmin's comment about Royer not understanding a complex topic because she was a woman was a comment with troubling implications. As I noted in my essay, Firmin did not elaborate on this point, so one is not sure if Firmin believed that women were biologically incapable of understanding complex thoughts or whether he felt that this was due to society's socialization of women. Whatever the case may have been, this is certainly one aspect of Firmin's views which did trouble me.

Apart from his views on women, Firmin also expressed Eurocentric standards of beauty, which is a point I made in *Essays Towards Restoring the African Mind*. Even though Firmin expressed views which I am strongly opposed to, I still view him as a great statesman, a great scholar, and one of the great men of history. Firmin was arguably the most important political leader in Haiti's history since the leaders who fought in the Haitian Revolution and he was one of the most prominent Pan-African thinkers to emerge from the Caribbean. This is something which I attempted to convey in my essay on him.

W.E.B. Du Bois does deserve credit for his role for promoting anti-colonialism as an aspect of the Pan-African movement. Du Bois was also an attendee at the 1900 conference. Unlike Williams, Du Bois' vision for Pan-Africanism was decidedly anti-colonial.

Du Bois' greatest contribution to the Pan-African movement was his scholarship. Du Bois was a great researcher and a prolific writer. He was not a leader or organizer, however. Reflecting on his role in the Niagara Movement, Du Bois explained: "I was no natural leader of men. I could not slap people on the back and make friends of strangers. I could not easily break down an inherited reserve; or at all times curb a biting, critical tongue." He also admitted that his inexperience with organizations caused the movement to suffer.

Unlike Du Bois, Garvey was a natural leader of men. This is why Garvey's organization managed to organize millions of Africans across the world. Garvey stands out as not only one of the most remarkable leaders within the history of the Pan-African movement, but one of the most remarkable leaders in world history. Garvey was a controversial figure, but I view him as a man who sincerely dedicated his life to the cause of justice. Garvey was a proud African who centered his work on the liberation of African people. This racial pride caused Garvey to take a strong position against race mixing. Even so, Garvey was no racist. He stood against the oppression of all people, regardless of their race.

55

ON THE POLITICS OF CHANGE

In my view, activism work is important because this is where change truly comes from. Activism is often necessary within political systems which are undemocratic in nature. Such systems ensure that change must come from those who exert pressure on the system to demand the change because the system would otherwise be unresponsive to more passive demands for change.

Democratic representation is an important aspect of politics and governance. Democracy is a term which comes out of the political system which developed in Athens. In Athens, citizens were selected to actively participate in the government. Although the term "democracy" is Greek, the concept of democracy is not solely Greek in nature. Democracy essentially refers to a political system in which citizens are given an active role in the government of the country. Forms of democratic systems existed in African societies as well.

The United States and other nations which have a representative democracy often suffer from the problem of what Marxists would refer to as "bourgeois democracy" or a form of democracy in which the masses are free to participate by electing political representatives, but have limited ability to control politics beyond this. This is a type of democracy in which the interests of the ruling class are secured because the bourgeoisie remains in power, regardless of the outcome of the election. I understand this is a very Marxian way of looking at elections, but I think it is also an accurate understanding of how electoral politics tends to work in capitalist societies.

Capitalism also creates a disparity between the political elite and ordinary citizens which insulates politicians from the issues which ordinary citizens endure. Political leaders who do not have to struggle and suffer like the citizens who elect them often do not have much of an urgency to produce sweeping societal changes because they do not feel the pain that their citizens feel. These political leaders may even impose austerity measures on citizens which impose a heavy burden on citizens in the form of taxation and reducing subsidies. In the Caribbean, we refer to this sort of thing as politicians wanting people to "ban they belly." This essentially means that people are expected to go without food due to the poverty they must endure, but our political leaders are never asked to ban their own bellies.

Change rarely comes from electoral politics because citizens elect leaders who have no incentive to produce change. It is often the case that these elected officials join the same corrupt system and become part of the problem. In his song "Oppression," Alston Cyrus Becket lamented: "You vote brother to help fight oppression/Brother get in there and join the bandwagon." And whereas Judas in the Bible hanged himself after betraying Jesus because of the guilt that he felt, the elected betrayers of the people have no guilt about taking their pieces of silver.

Another problem with electoral politics is demonstrated in yet another story from the Bible. The story in question is when a Jewish crowd is given the option to select either Jesus or Barabbas. The crowd opted to release Barabbas and let Jesus be executed. The lesson is that an ill-informed population will select the wrong individual, so effective democratic representation does require an informed voting population.

In the book, *Politics Among Nations*, Hans Morgenthau defined political power as the "psychological control over the minds of men". I find this to be an apt description for what political power is. Political power is indeed the power to control the minds of others. This is why politicians invest so much effort in propaganda. This is true across all forms of political systems, be it monarchy, dictatorship, or electoral democracy. The political party or leader in power strives to get the population to believe in the propaganda of those in power. For this reason, it can be difficult for ordinary citizens to decipher for themselves whether or not the information they are being given is accurate.

It is important to note that propaganda is not always dishonest. Propaganda is spread simply to promote a particular position or viewpoint. The type of propaganda which dedicated political activists seek to spread is the type which will both educate and empower citizens to improve their own conditions. The propaganda of the political elite may or may not be rooted in falsehoods, but the objective is typically to win election or reelection. The party in power must convince voters to allow that party to remain in power, whereas opposition parties seek to convince voters to remove the party in power.

I make none of these points to discourage black people from voting as a means to create change, although I do recognize certain limitations which come with voting. Within the context of the African American struggle, there are certainly instances in which significant gains came out of electoral politics. An example which I have written about is Booker T. Washington's program at Tuskegee which was made possible through electoral politics. Adam Clayton Powell's political career is also an example of the power of electing true representatives, although very few black political leaders in American history have been as committed to their constituencies as Powell was. Voting can create change, but voting alone does not create change. It is also important to note that Powell's work as a politician was a continuation of the work which he was engaged in as a community activist, so he would also stand out as an example of an individual who worked to produce real meaningful change outside of public office before he was elected to public office.

Most who have come to occupy political office have not been as productive nor as uncompromising as Powell was. An example of this was John Lewis. Lewis opted to join the system, whereas Kwame Ture (who was also a member of SNCC) worked outside of the system, struggling for change. Admittedly, I tend to agree more with Ture than with Lewis. Like Kwame Ture, I am a Pan-Africanist who believes that African people around the world share a common struggle. I am also not a staunch adherent to non-violence like John Lewis was. I certainly would never thank a police officer for brutalizing me as Lewis did.

Lewis decided to join the system by becoming a politician. In the years that he served as a representative, Lewis never produced the type of change that was produced by the civil rights movement which he was involved in. I mention this to show that the most significant political change which Lewis was involved in came from his work as an activist, not from his work as a politician. Of course, Lewis was no Powell. By this I mean that Lewis was more of a moderate figure than Powell was. This was true even when Lewis was a political activist. Unlike Powell, Lewis could be controlled and tamed. I state this with the utmost respect for Lewis. I respected his courage and willingness to suffer for what he believed in, but Lewis also represented a wing of black leadership which was not as forceful or uncompromising as needed.

Within the liberation struggle, there has always been a segment of the leadership which adopted a more moderate approach. An example of this would be Kenya's liberation struggle in which the Mau Mau played a most important role. It was undoubtedly true that the Mau Mau rebels were very violent in their methods, but the British administration left little alternative. British colonialism in Kenya was extremely brutal. Harry Thuku attempted to nonviolently confront British colonialism, only to be imprisoned and for his supporters to be massacred. One certainly has to admire Thuku for his commitment to Kenya's freedom, but he was limited by his moderate approach. Thuku's views were not unlike the more moderate approach to black freedom in America taken by leaders like Lewis and Martin Luther King. Much as Thuku opposed the Mau Mau, King and others could not fully endorse the more revolutionary approach of those like Malcolm X and Kwame Ture.

Within the ranks of the leaders of the Mau Mau, I rank Musa Mwariama higher than Dedan Kimathi because Kimathi's leadership was marked by his jealousy and tendency towards dictatorial control. This was not merely a character flaw, but also something which ended up weakening Kimathi as a resistance leader. His desire for power eventually isolated him. I mention this to make the point that the violence within any liberation movement must be directed at the enemy. Kimathi began to direct violence against those within the Mau Mau movement in an attempt to assert his control. This was a mistake which ultimately led to him being captured and executed.

Even with his flaws, Kimathi remained a leader who was respected as a man who struggled for Kenya's freedom. The love Kenyans maintained for Kimathi explained why Ndirangu, the man who shot and captured Kimathi, faced the scorn of the Kenyan people. Ndirangu bought a truck with the reward he received for capturing Kimathi. He tried to use the truck as a van, but the villagers refused to ride it. When he attempted to run a hotel, the people refused to patronize it, which resulted in the business going bankrupt.

The colonial administration attempted to portray the Mau Mau rebels as savage terrorists, but the reality was that the Mau Mau were dedicated nationalists who wanted to free Kenya from colonial domination. Malcolm X was a staunch supporter of the Mau Mau. He had even met some of them when he was in Kenya. He remarked: "Don't you ever be ashamed of the Mau Mau. They're not to be ashamed of. They are to be proud of. Those brothers were freedom fighters. Not only brothers, there were sisters over there. I met a lot of them. They're brave. They hug you and kiss you—glad to see you."

Whereas Lewis remained committed to moderation, Powell embraced the radicalism of the Black Power movement. This embrace may have been for political purposes. I make this suggestion because Powell saw King as someone who challenged his position as a black leader in America. Powell was willing to go so far as to spread a lie about King to damage King's reputation to ensure that King's activism would not pose too much of a problem for Powell's Democratic Party. Embracing Black Power became way for Powell to distinguish himself from King and the other leaders within the civil rights movement who were losing popularity among the frustrated youth who embraced more radical alternatives for change.

Powell was a rare figure in American politics who could exercise significant political influence without seemingly compromising his previous work as activist by doing so. The great problem with Powell was his conduct. As I explained in my essay "The Emperor of Harlem," Powell was known to flaunt the lavish lifestyle that he lived because of his status as a politician. He was also known for his womanizing which led to a couple of divorces, heavy drinking, and he faced numerous allegations of misappropriation of funds—behavior which was unbecoming for a public official who was also a religious leader. He was no saint, but Powell's constituents were willing to continue their support for him because he got the job done. Not only did his committee get legislation passed, but he consistently opposed racism.

In the end, what caused Powell's downfall was that his colleagues in the House of Representatives were not as forgiving of Powell's conduct as voters in Harlem were. Powell was barred from taking his seat in Congress. The decision to bar Powell was eventually overturned by the Supreme Court, but the damage had been done. Powell returned to Congress, but he did not have the influence that he once had. Powell's frequent absences from Congress also made some of the residents of Harlem feel as though they were left without representation. This contributed to Powell being defeated in his final election.

Flawed as he may have been, there have not been many black political leaders in America's history who were like Powell. Barack Obama certainly was not, although it is unlikely that Obama would have ever been elected president if he was willing to take the type of stances which Powell took. Powell was a rarity in American politics, but his political career demonstrated that electing the right people into power can produce necessary results. The challenge is finding or producing leadership like Powell.

Producing proper leaders requires a certain type of culture to be in place. Great leaders do not produce themselves. They must be cultivated. One challenge for African people is that colonialism essentially destroyed the existing structures that we had. The external pressure has also made it difficult to develop and sustain effective leadership because that leadership is always subject to undue influence from outside of the community.

I also have a very strong belief that proper leadership must be democratic in nature. By this I mean that the leadership must govern in the interest of the masses and with the consent of the masses. I use Sékou Touré as an example to illustrate this point. Touré was admired as a Pan-Africanist who challenged colonialism, but the other reality is that he was a leader who did carry out repression against his own people. In *Black Power and Post-Colonial Society*, I specifically made reference to my own experience with political repression in Guinea. Before Farida Nabourema left Africans Rising, the last effort that we worked on together was the situation in Guinea. There were protests against Alpha Condé who was ready to serve a third term, which was a violation of the constitution. Not only were the protests crushed with violent force, but activists were being kidnapped and detained as well. Africans Rising launched a campaign for the release of Ibrahima Diallo and Sékou Koundouno, who were both detained by the regime. Farida had made plans to organize an activity with them in the Gambia, but they were arrested and Farida was unable to attend an activity to support Guinea due to being in poor health.

I mention this to demonstrate that Touré's policies of political repression in Guinea had a lingering impact on the politics of Guinea. This was something that activists were wrestling with many generations later. This is important to understand because these critiques are coming from those who have had to wrestle with the consequences of how policies of the past impact the present. I have tremendous respect for Kwame Ture, but I think he may have been too closely attached to Sékou Touré to understand just how completely the revolution in Guinea had been betrayed by Touré himself and the lingering impact that Touré's policies would have in Guinea.

I saw Ture as someone who went in the opposite extreme of his fellow SNCC colleague John Lewis. Whereas Lewis found himself becoming part of the establishment which he struggled against, Ture became a revolutionary ideologue who remained so dogmatically attached to a particular vision of revolutionary struggle that he was unable to adapt when circumstances had changed. In my view, political activists should be cautious to avoid compromising too much, but should also avoid the mistake of becoming too inflexible. Compromising too much or not compromising enough can prove to be detrimental in the long-term. One of the critiques I have of Nelson Mandela is that I believe that he too made the mistake of compromising too much.

The problems relating to Sékou Touré's government is why I stress that the Pan-African movement must be democratic in nature. By democratic I am not referring merely to having free and fair multi-party elections, but a political system in which the masses have true representation within the government as opposed to a system in which an individual leader claims to represent the masses and then uses this vested authority to justify repressive measures in the name of defending the revolution.

There may be some who believe that any measure is acceptable so long as it is done in service of achieving the desired outcome. I am not someone who believes that the ends justify the means. I find such an approach immoral and impractical. It is immoral because it suggests that any action, no matter how harmful or egregious it is, can be justified by the outcome. This approach can also become impractical given that the means may produce the desired outcome in the short-term, but it may also result in long-term problems which undermine the main objective. A state which is oppressive and dictatorial may very well have a logical reason for adopting such measures. Such policies may be seen as a means to an end. The problem is that people generally do not like to feel oppressed and too much oppression can breed rebellion. A good example is Henri Christophe of Haiti. Under his leadership there was an improvement of the national economy, although he also implemented a very strict regime which he quickly lost control of when his health diminished. In the short term his oppressive measures did produce results, but he could not sustain it.

I can also point to Jerry Rawlings who ultimately implemented neo-liberal policies in Ghana. The problem with leaders who implement such harsh measures in the name of revolution is that these harsh measures are never applied to the leaders themselves when they decide to compromise the principles of the revolution which they claim to be fighting for. This was true of Touré and it was true of Rawlings. This again is why I stress the importance of the democratic nature of the Pan-African movement. It cannot be a movement led by an authoritarian leader who implements repressive measures to sustain the revolution, especially given that there is nothing to prevent said leader from reversing position.

I understand that some degree of force or coercion is necessary to manage and protect a state structure, so I am not suggesting that states never undertake forceful measures. What I am suggesting is that there must be a balance which restricts the degree to which governments or political leaders are able to impose forceful measures. Too often we have seen examples of governments which implement forceful measures which have a determinantal impact in the long-term. True meaningful political change cannot come at the expense of suppressing the masses.

56

A RESPONSE TO APOLOGISTS FOR COLONIALISM

I know that apologists for Western colonialism would argue that African people also engaged in conquest and colonization of other Africans prior to European colonialism. To show the difference between Western imperialism in Africa and African imperialism one can look at the number of powerful African kingdoms which had once been subjugated by other powerful states. This included Kush, Mali, and Songhai. When one African state subjugated another state, the people were not dehumanized in the same manner that European colonialism did to African people. They also were not typically dispossessed of their land and resources, which is why certain subjugated states could rise to become powerful in their own right. Under European colonialism, no African state could have hoped to develop to reach the standard of the colonial powers of Europe. The structure of colonialism ensured that the colonized African states were to remain in a perpetual state of underdevelopment, even after the formal end of colonization.

All empires are built and sustained through some level of force and coercion. I do not believe that the use of state force is always a negative thing as coercion may be needed to maintain law and order within a political structure. We have certainly seen examples where a weakened state results in chaos and widespread violence, so there are certain benefits to having a strong and stable state in power which is able to enforce the rule of law, although the use of state force to maintain the stability of the state is always a balancing act in which there must be a check against excessive abuses on the part of the state as well.

Maintaining powerful empires was certainly to the advantage of African states which were confronted with the threat of colonialism. Within the context of the anti-colonial struggle against French imperialism, Samory Toure is certainly regarded as a heroic figure for the resistance he put up against the French, yet it is also important to note that among African people Samory Toure was not universally regarded as a hero. By this, I am pointing to

296

the fact that Samory Toure did establish an empire which was built and sustained through conquest. Those who were conquered by Toure obviously would have resented living under his imposed rule, yet it was also these very conquests which allowed Toure to expand his empire and to build up an army which was strong enough to put up the fierce resistance which he managed to engage in against the French. That stable and unified empires were viewed as a threat to the colonial powers in Europe can be further demonstrated by the manner in which the British colonial administration moved to overthrow Prempeh when they realized that Prempeh was finding success at rebuilding the strength of the Asante Empire through some of the conquests which he engaged in. Prempeh managed to reorganize the Asante Empire after a period of political instability which weakened the empire.

The use of force to retain power or to suppress others was an aspect of Africa's social development. At times this did have the positive effect of bringing stability and peace, but the use of force among the ruling class also included raids, the forced seizure of certain possessions, and enslavement. In general, however, there were observed limits to the violence. By contrast, colonialism in Africa led to a significant increase in violence and instability in Africa.

Rwanda and Burundi are examples of this given that both nations experienced a brutal genocide which was the result of divide and conquer policies which were implemented during colonialism. This is not to suggest that the relations between the Tutsis and Hutus were free of any antagonisms. The Tutsis were the ruling elite and the Hutus were the workers. This was a class distinction, not a tribal one, however. The two groups not only shared a common culture, but intermarriage further blurred distinctions between the two groups. There were Tutsis who worked as farmers and Hutus who owned cattle. Moreover, there was no Tutsi or Hutu state. Rather there were the kingdoms of Rwanda and Burundi. The ethnic violence in Rwanda and Burundi was not the product of pre-colonial social relations in both societies, but rather the result of the deliberate policy of the colonial powers to impose division among the Tutsis and the

Hutus.

To further illustrate this point, I turn to Anténor Firmin who suggested that the oppression which Africans endured at the hands of white people was an echo of the past when at one time black people in Egypt oppressed white people. He was pointing out that there was a time in history when a black empire oppressed white people. I understand the point, but where I disagree is that Egyptian civilization was not one which oppressed people on the basis of race. Moreover, Egypt itself had been subjected to numerous invasions. The Egyptian empire of the 18th dynasty emerged following a period when invaders from West Asia ruled over Egypt. Egypt expelled the Hyksos and then expanded its power into West Asia which ensured Egypt's protection from further invasions. In essence, Egypt's decision to build an empire was done as a defensive action. I address these differences not to make apologies for the harms that come with imperialism, but simply to make the point that African empires cannot be compared to the destructive force which was Western colonization in Africa and the rest of the world.

This is not an attempt to romanticize African history to present an idyllic African past. African history certainly has had its share of violent rulers. There are several examples of this in my writings. Shaka certainly stands out in this regard. Shaka built a powerful Zulu state through his innovative military strategies. The problem with Shaka was that he was noted to be excessively violent and he was himself eventually killed by his half-brothers who took control of the throne. I have demonstrated in the chapter I wrote on the Zulus that the European accounts of Shaka's brutalities were often exaggerated as there were examples in which Shaka spared his foes. Moreover, those who were brought under Zulu rule were assimilated into Zulu society and became Zulus. This was much different than European colonialism in South Africa which created an apartheid system to discriminate against the African population.

Another example would be the kingdom of Buganda. The ruling class of Buganda developed a reputation for harshly oppressing commoners. Mutesa of Buganda was especially noted for his cruel and warlike manner. Mutesa's cruelty was not without its setbacks, however. Mutesa broke Buganda's policy of peace with the Bayuma people which resulted in him being defeated in battle. It was left to Mutesa's son and successor, Mwanga to restore Buganda's peaceful relationship with the Bayuma people.

Any state in which a hierarchy of classes emerges will inevitably be confronted with the issue of abuse as the dominant class seeks to exploit those who lack power. There will also be the problem of militarism as the state seeks to expand its power, influence, and resources at the expense of conquering and dominating others. This is a reality which has confronted all human societies and Africa has been no different in this regard. My point is to note that the level of imperialistic violence which European societies engaged in was generally not matched by African societies. Moreover, imperialism in Africa never developed into the type of racial superiority which European societies came to promote. As such, it would be incorrect to point to Africa's history to make an apology for what Europeans did in Africa.

It was also the case that the European intervention in Africa gave rise to greater violence and repression. Dahomey developed a very infamous reputation for being a warlike, slave-raiding state which practiced ritualistic human sacrifices. This development should be seen in the context of the slave trade, however. The slave trade disrupted West African societies. Dahomey's militarized nature developed out of the need for Dahomey to protect itself against raids from rival kingdoms, while also being able to carry out its own raids for access to European goods. Gezo was noted as the ruler of Dahomey who resisted attempts to end the slave trade. The same Gezo was also noted for being a monarch who was concerned with the well-being of his people to such an extent that he reformed the laws of Dahomey to provide for more humane treatment of his people.

The complexity of Gezo is that he was a ruler who truly cared for the well-being of his own people, but displayed little regard for Africans from other states to the point that he continued Dahomey's tradition of human sacrifice. So long as Dahomey could benefit from the capture and sale of others, Gezo was not only willing to participate, but reluctant to end the slave trade. The slave trade actually had a determinantal impact on Dahomey's development, but there was little Dahomey alone could have done to stop it. Agaja had tried, but was forced to make a compromise with the European slave traders. Gezo also seemed to have recognized this problem as well, which is why he argued that he could only end Dahomey's role in the slave trade if other nations ended their involvement as well. The rulers of Dahomey embraced the slave trade and restructured the society of Dahomey to help sustain Dahomey's participation in the trade. These developments were a response to external pressures imposed on Dahomey by outside influences.

Ethiopia presents a most interesting example of this point. For centuries, Ethiopia had dealt with violent disruptions. This included the Oromo migration, which became very bloody and destructive as the Oromo warred on others. The Oromo people engaged in raids for cattle and captives. Apart from this, there was also a period known as the *Zemene Mesafint* (Era of Princes) in which Ethiopia no longer had a centralized kingdom.

The *Zemene Mesafint* was the result of the nobles exercising too much power in Ethiopia. This was demonstrated by the influence of Ras Mikael Sehul, who managed to control a powerful army of his own. His power was such that he ordered the number of two kings and placed a weak ruler on the throne whom he could control. This began a period in which the monarchy in Ethiopia was reduced in power. The kingdom eventually devolved into bloody conflicts for control. By 1800, there were as many as six rival emperors.

The Ethiopian monarchy was consolidated under these chaotic conditions under the leadership of Tewodros. Yohannes and Menelik II would continue this process of consolidating power in Ethiopia under a centralized monarchy. I have explained before that Menelik was the most challenging African personality to write about because of his complexity. Menelik was noted for being a very caring and patient ruler who enjoyed feeding his people. He was also a very involved leader who oversaw the modernization of his country. He became a heroic figure internationally for defeating Italy.

Despite the great things that could be stated of Menelik, it was equally true that his wars of conquest were extremely bloody and destructive. Menelik managed to establish centralized authority in

Ethiopia. The establishment of a central authority is something which can bring peace and stability among a disunited and warring people. To a degree Menelik was able to achieve this. The problem was that even though Menelik ordered an end to the aggression, the aggression continued and the victims were left with no means of redress. This was because the state which Menelik built was somewhat decentralized in that certain regions of Ethiopia were left under the rule of Rases who were left to exploit the conquered populations.

The wars between the Amhara and the Oromo in the past were very bloody and destructive, but neither side was able to prevail over the other, which resulted in a degree of assimilation on both sides. Oromo conquerors did assimilate those who were conquered and the Amhara ruling class also embraced Oromo culture to such an extent that Oromo was the primary language spoken in the court of the Ethiopian monarchy.

What changed this relationship was the introduction of European weapons, which allowed the Ahmara ruling class to establish a feudal state which engaged in a level of repression which was previously impossible. This created a system of total political and cultural domination. It also created hardened distinctions between Amhara and Oromo which previously did not exist in Ethiopia. The Oromo were always decentralized to the point that they often engaged in brutal wars with each other, but the state which Menelik II established and which Haile Selassie inherited was one in which the Oromo were forced to develop a collective ethnic identity to resist the imposition of an Amhara identity which was imposed by the ruling class.

To be clear, Menelik's conquests were aided by Oromo such as Ras Gobana. Oromo Nationalists tend to view Ras Gobana and others who fought against other Oromos as collaborators working against the interest of the Oromo people, but the reality is that there was not a collective Oromo identity until after Menelik II consolidated his state.

The Ethiopian state which Menelik II established was fragmented precisely due to the imbalance of power between the ruling elite which was culturally Ahmara and the others who were not Ahmara. The conquered Oromo were not assimilated in any meaningful way and they were also dispossessed of their land. As I noted in my essay on this topic, the development of this oppressive feudal state was made possible because of the European intervention in Ethiopia's political development. This was not something which developed wholly as a result of Ethiopia's own internal political evolution.

Apart from the racism of Western colonialism and the manner in which it adversely impacted Africa's own development, there is also the fact that the scope of Western colonialism became so large that the colonies found themselves drawn into the wars of the colonial powers. No empire in Africa, for example, was responsible for conflicts as bloody and destructive as the World Wars were. In short, not all empires are the same and not all forms of exploitation are the same.

In making the argument which I made, I am aware that I am contradicting Frantz Fanon who wrote: "All forms of exploitation are identical because all of them are applied against the same 'object': man." It is precisely because apologists for colonialism attempt to draw comparisons between different forms of exploitation to defend Western colonialism that it becomes necessary to make distinctions between different forms of exploitation. The exploitation of Western colonialism was something which was unique in its destructive impact when compared to the empires in Africa.

57

SEND THEM BACK

In *Black Skin, White Masks*, Frantz Fanon noted the divisions which existed among colonized Africans. Fanon explained that those born in Dahomey or Congo would pretend to be from the Antilles, while those from the Antilles would be annoyed if they were suspected of being Senegalese. This was because within the colonial system, those from the Antilles were regarded as being more "civilized" and closer to the white man than those from Africa. Fanon also noted that among black people from the Antilles there were also divisions as well. Fanon recalled a conversation with someone from Martinque who told him that black people from Guadeloupe were more savage than those from Martinique.

The colonial system is one which relies on promoting divide and rule tactics among African people. This is something which Ti Manno noted in his song "Black Against Black." This song by Ti Manno was about how black people allowed colonialism to create divisions among them. Among the divisions he noted in the song is that black people from Queens do not view themselves as comrades with those from Brooklyn, or black people from Pétion-Ville believe themselves to be superior to those from Carrefour. Assata Shakur also noted the divide and conquer methods in her autobiography. She wrote about being told not to trust West Indians because they'll stab you in the back or not trusting Africans because they think that they are better. She explained that these were lies which were told to create confusion and division.

Given the legacy of division among African people which was promoted by colonialism, it was particularly disappointing to see an artist like Chalkdust contribute to this division with a song that he composed regarding the differences between West Indians and African Americans. Chalkdust himself noted that the song was controversial, although he personally did not seem to understand the controversy around the song.

The song was based on an exchange Chalkdust had with a white man who wanted to send all of the West Indian immigrants back to the Caribbean because, in his view, they were bringing crime to New York. Chalkdust's response was to argue that it was really African Americans who were abusing drugs and mugging white people. Chalkdust sings: "Culture makes us different if you please. Caribbean and black American come like chalk and cheese."

It was disappointing coming from Chalkdust considering that he at times has been an advocate for Pan-African unity. For example, his song "Immigration Problems" suggested that nationality does not count among descendants of the slave trade whose ancestors were forcibly scattered throughout the Americas. In "It Ain't We," Chalkdust discarded the Pan-Africanism expressed in "Immigration Problems" to blame African Americans for crime in New York as a way to defend the West Indian community against the comments from a bigoted white man. Chalkdust sought to highlight the differences between African Americans and West Indians in such a way as to present West Indians in a more favorable manner. Chalkdust did something similar in "We Is We" when he suggested that black people from Trinidad are not like those in Africa because Trinidad does not have tribal war.

The proper response from Chalkdust would have been to denounce the racism of the white man who wanted to send back all Caribbean immigrants over crime being committed by some black people in Brooklyn. Instead, Chalkdust decided to respond by presenting African Americans as being the true criminals. In doing so, Chalkdust was upholding racist stereotypes about African Americans in his attempt to defend West Indian immigrants. Chalkdust may not have understood why the song was controversial, but the critics of the song rightfully understood that it was yet another example of divide and conquer being promoted among African people.

58

THE WOLF AND THE FOX

Malcolm X spoke about the wolf and the fox. The point he was making is that whereas the wolf is openly hostile, the fox is cunning and friendly. He explained that both are canines who humiliate and mutilate their victims, but they have different methods of doing so. In making this remark, Malcolm was referring to two different forms of racism. One form of racism is more vicious, while the other one appears to be more friendly, but both forms of racism are harmful towards black humanity.

Malcolm's point can be demonstrated by an individual such as Robert De Niro. De Niro emerged as a prominent critique of Donald Trump, yet as one concerned Barbudan named Rosanna Harris noted, De Niro professed that he wanted to punch Trump, but De Niro was really no different than Trump. She was referring to De Niro's involvement in the struggle over Barbuda's communal land ownership. The issue stemmed from De Niro's effort to gain control of land in Barbuda to build a resort. The plan to build this resort became entangled in the struggle over Barbuda's tradition of communal land ownership, which Prime Minister Gaston Browne sought to undermine.

After the destruction caused to Barbuda by Hurricane Irma, the recovery effort was slow. De Niro appealed to the United Nation for help in rebuilding Barbuda. This was a noble deed, except for the fact that De Niro had a financial interest in rebuilding Barbuda due to his plans to establish a resort on the island. It was really an appeal for the United Nations to help him secure his financial interests.

In the Caribbean, the tourism industry has been connected to the legacy of foreign control of the Caribbean which enriches foreigners while leaving the locals not only impoverished, but also unable to access their own land. One doubts that De Niro was aware of this legacy or that he even cared to understand it. He was certainly willing to benefit from it. De Niro was even appointed as the economic envoy to Antigua and Barbuda. He was appointed to this position by Gaston Browne. An aspect of this legacy of foreign control over the Caribbean is that the Caribbean leadership is often all too willing to give control to foreigners.

De Niro represents the wealthy white liberal who views himself as being humanitarian, but is actually someone who benefits from the system of colonialism and white supremacy. I state this in spite of the fact that De Niro was, for twenty years, married to a black woman with whom he had two children with. That De Niro was married to a black woman does not negate the reality that in his plans to build a resort in Barbuda, De Niro was primarily concerned with his own enrichment and expressed little regard for the concerns expressed by the people of Barbuda over the control of their land. Barbuda's unique legacy of communal land ownership or the legacy of foreign exploitation which comes with tourism in the Caribbean were of no concern to De Niro.

De Niro is an example of the fox which Malcolm warned about. The wolf and the fox are both part of the same system, though they operate within the system differently. De Niro would find Trump offensive because Trump is a fox who does not attempt to disguise his nature in the manner that De Niro does, but Harris was correct to claim that De Niro was no different than Trump. Both are wealthy capitalists who have no interest in combating the colonial system because they benefit from it. They are also unconcerned with the humanity of those who are made to suffer due to the same system. This is why Malcolm stated that "all these white liberals have definitely failed the Negro."

White supremacy persists not only because of white people who are outwardly racist, but also because of those who remain complacent in upholding the system which they benefit from. Such individuals are the foxes that Malcolm warned about. These individuals may denounce the more overt forms of racism from leaders like Trump. They may even marry black people, but at the end of the day they continue to uphold the colonial system of white supremacy because they benefit from it. Where African people are concerned, there is little distinction between Trump and De Niro. They are simply the wolf and the fox.

59

CHIEF ADOGBEJI SALUBI OF THE URHOBO PROGRESS UNION

Thompson Adogbeji Salubi did not know the date and year of his birth since there was no system to register births and deaths in the district where he was born. Salubi decided on 1906 as his birth year, although he strongly believed that he was born after 1906. Salubi's given name at birth was Odebo. His name was later changed to Adogbeji by one of his family members who had a vision which indicated to him that Salubi was given the wrong name.

Salubi recalled that he was a very active child. He was fond of fishing and working. He often went to farm with his father and prepared food for him as well. The relationship which Salubi had with his father was a very close one. Salubi noted that his father was very caring and loving towards him. Salubi described himself as a troublesome child who would cause quarrels with others, and then run to his elder brother to fight for him. Salubi also recalled that he had trouble walking due to an injury he sustained as a child after a dog bit his leg. The wound became infected and developed into an ulcer. It eventually healed, although that injury continued to give Salubi problems.

Salubi's village was one which encouraged hard work. Peter Ekeh noted that *ovwiere*, which means lazy person, was a term which was viewed as an insult. Salubi grew up in this culture which promoted and honored hard work. Salubi also admired the fact that his father was a hard-working man with several professions. His father was a palm-cutter, farmer, trader, fisherman, and hunter. The principles of hard work and discipline which Salubi learned in his childhood were principles which he carried with him throughout his life.

Salubi began his schooling in 1917. His father was initially reluctant to send him to school, but when his mother agreed to send him to school, his father allowed it. The first teacher at the school that Salubi attended was Mr. Robert. Mr. Robert was the only teacher in the school. In 1919, Salubi went to Lagos to continue his studies. It was also in 1919 that he was baptized. Prior to going to Lagos for his studies, Salubi's father sought the consent of his mother before letting him go. Once she granted this consent, Salubi was allowed to attend school in Lagos.

Salubi's father had seven wives. Of the seven, Salubi described his mother, Ovire, as being his father's favorite wife. Salubi's father was surprised to find that she was a virgin when they married, so he paid a sum of money to her and her parents as a reward for this. This began the tradition in Ovu of men rewarding a bride who was a virgin before marriage. Salubi described his mother as thus: "She was and is still faithful. Very honest and hard-working; always contented with her lot, unlike most women, she is never covetous. She is a woman with a clean great heart." Salubi was the second of Ovire's five children.

Interestingly, despite coming from a polygamous family, Salubi himself expressed a preference for monogamous marriages, as demonstrated by the fact that he had only one wife. He explained: "I had a natural inclination of keeping only one wife in my house. I never believe in keeping two, three or so many at a time as my [Urhobo] people used to do and are still doing. This might be due to the fact that I was not trained in such an environment at home [in Urhoboland]. But I feel that I am not naturally inclined that way. I had always liked to lead a respectable and peaceful life." Salubi did note that prior to his marriage, he had a connection with three women which he described as his "concubines." He regarded these relationships as giving him experience with women, which helped him to remain faithful to the one wife which he had.

Salubi first met Angela as he was going to Faji Market. It was raining and she took shelter by the side of a house. He saluted her and give her a shilling. Upon meeting her, Salubi took interest in her and wrote a love letter to her. The two began to exchange love letters. A distance between them eventually grew when Angela became interested in a man named James Okito. Salubi recorded that he withdrew his feelings for her and began to insult her whenever he saw her. Salubi went so far as to attend a Corpus Christi procession just to hurl insults at Anegla simply to satisfy himself.

Salubi's abuse of Angela demonstrated the extent to which her rejection hurt him. Rather than handling the rejection with maturity and grace, Salubi decided to engage in harassment and verbal abuse. When Salubi's friend Oboraje asked Angela if she knew Salubi, she described him as a bad boy who was abusing her constantly. She also complained to a man named Vincent Oniwo. Vincent confronted Salubi about this and Salubi admitted that what Angela had complained about was true.

Vincent liked Salubi, so he decided to improve the relationship between the two so that they could continue their love. Despite the hurtful things he said to Angela, Salubi's position was that he did not want Vincent to bring undue pressure on Angela to force her to love someone that she did not want to love. This demonstrated that he still maintained a degree of care and respect for her. Perhaps in that moment, Salubi recognized that he cared for Angela enough that he would have preferred her to pursue whoever made her happy. He certainly still had strong feelings for her and it would turn out that she still had strong feelings for him as well.

Vincent was able to get Angela and Salubi to mee at his house. At the meeting, the two agreed to forget their troubled past and vowed to be one together in the future. Prior to getting married, Angela made Salubi change from being an Anglican to a Catholic. The two were married on July 12, 1932. In addition to the children which the two had together, they also adopted an orphan named Stephen. Stephen was abandoned at birth because his mother died. Salubi was unable to find Stephen's relatives and expressed frustration that the relatives would abandon the boy. He and Angela decided to adopt Stephen.

That Salubi decided to maintain only one wife may very well have been due to the Western influence. He did embrace Christianity, after all. Salubi's views on marriage may have also been shaped by his father's experiences. For example, he noted that a wife named Overare brought ruin and misery to his father when she absconded with his father's properties. She was eventually traced and returned home, but the beads and trinkets which she took were lost. Overare then ran away a second time with a slave girl named Emuoborowho. Emuoborowho was sold to

Salubi's grandmother when she was young. Emuoborowho was also one of the seven wives of Salubi's father. The problems caused by these dissatisfied wives were indicative of some of the problems which emerged in polygamous marriages in Africa. That Salubi stated he preferred to maintain a peaceful life would suggest that he believed having multiple wives would have led to the type of problems his father dealt with. Salubi does not state this outright in his writings, but one would imagine that this contributed to his decision to have a single wife.

What does seem apparent from Salubi's writings is that his views on gender relations were very much influenced by Urhobo cultural norms. For example, he regarded unrestrained relations between members of both sexes as one of the peculiarities of the British. Salubi explained that he found this as strange to him as witchcraft beliefs and fetish worship were to Europeans. Of this he noted that each racial group has their different peculiarities.

The peculiarities were not the only observations which Salubi made while he was in the United Kingdom for his studies. Salubi was also impressed by the ingenuity of the British. He described those who created the steamer, the railway, the motor, and the aeroplane as having "wonderful brains." Salubi also noted that the brilliance of the British meant that there was no justification for the poverty which he witnessed as well. He explained: "There are enough brains, enough ingenuity, skill and wisdom in that country to make everybody happier, contented and prosperous. And it seems to me that those slums, squalor and abject poverty which I saw, had no justification to be, except through human failings, greed and avarice."

Salubi described both the wonders of civilization, as well as its flaws. He noted: "Behold Civilisation! She is beautiful, she's attractive and beckons to me for a kiss but as I went near, I saw that she had a foul mouth, and at a closer examination, I observed she possessed an arm of clay and a wooden foot! Not all of it is made of gold! I observed she was not all wholesome. She was diseased in part." Salubi was certainly impressed by the scientific advances of Britain, but he also recognized that these advances were not being properly utilized to serve humanity. In his observations of Europeans, Salubi was also careful to avoid the very prejudices which Europeans engaged in. He explained: "It's no use saying glibly that white men are like this, or like that. If we are not careful, we are going to be the same as the white men."

Salubi was also a very deeply religious man. It was noted before that Salubi was a Christian. Salubi described his religious philosophy as follows: "I believe in doing good always to a fellow man and I refrain from doing unto others what I would not like them to do unto me. I have the fear of God in my heart. I believe in retributions. Whatever thou sowest, that wilt thou reap. I believe that there is no good without associating evil and no evil without any good accompanying it."

Much like in many other African traditions, Urhobo people believed that ancestors upheld the moral order of Urhobo society by rewarding good deeds and punishing bad deeds. The punishments for the bad deeds could be alleviated through a proper sacrifice and atonement. In addition to ancestors, the Urhobo also believed that each person had a personal spirit which helped to guide them as well. There were also witches who were blamed for the misfortunes in the community. Salubi recounted that his grandmother was accused of witchcraft and was forced to raise large sums of money in order to clear her name. Salubi also noted that his mother was never accused of witchcraft, which was rare for a woman of her age.

Some of the Urhobo who converted to Christianity still practiced their traditional religious practices. This included communing with personal spirits for assistance. Salubi dismissed certain aspects of Urhobo religious practices as superstitions, though Salubi generally respected the traditional practices of the Urhobo people. This can be demonstrated by the fact that he kept the name Adogbeji, which he was given as the result of divination.

The Urhobo people formed the Urhobo Brotherly Society to protect their interests and to portray a positive image of the Urhobo people to the rest of Nigeria. From this organization came the Urhobo Progress Union. The first president general of the organization was Chief Mukoro Mowoe. Mowoe was a very respected figure among the Urhobo people. His death in 1948 was a great loss as the leaders who followed him could not match his charisma and organizational abilities. From 1949 until 1961, the organization continued its initiatives, but it declined in significance. Salubi took over leadership in 1962. He proved to be just as capable a leader as Mowoe was.

Among the aims of the Urhobo Progress Union was the maintenance of Urhobo traditions and culture, and the development of agriculture. Salubi noted that the growth of scientific agriculture was a challenge due to the conservative nature of Urhobo society. In Salubi's view, the Urhobo people needed to modernize and move away from certain superstitious practices. He declared: "We must be determined to wage war vigorously against poverty, disease, illiteracy, ignorance and superstition. These ills are a dead weight on us. Wherever they exist, enlightened progress does not thrive. There is real poverty in Urhobo at the moment." He also encouraged embracing modern medical methods to treat the sick.

Salubi understood the importance of modernization, yet he still remained grounded in the culture of the Urhobo people. This is important because the colonial mission in Africa was one which was framed in terms of civilizing African people by making them more European. Salubi embraced certain aspects of European culture and technological knowledge, but only to the extent that he believed it would benefit the Urhobo people. Salubi's view was that Africans could draw ideas from Europe, but must remain rooted in their own cultural identity. Salubi noted that most of the attributes of the British "are very good and worthy of emulation; but some are abominable and repugnant to African concepts."

The motto of the Urhobo Progress Union was that unity is strength. This was why the first objective of the organization was to foster unity among the Urhobo people. The second objective was to promote education. The organization also sought to promote Urhobo traditions and culture. This included organizing traditional dances for national occasions such as the coronation of King George VI in 1937, the visit of Queen in 1959, and for Nigeria's independence.

That the Urhobo Progress Union would celebrate occasions involving British monarchs is noteworthy here given that the Union came into existence to challenge British colonial polices in Nigeria. Even so, the Urhobo Progress Union also sought to engage in national celebrations in Nigeria which would showcase the culture of the Urhobo people. The anti-colonialism of the Urhobo Progress Union was pragmatic in this regard.

It is important to note that the Urhobo Progress Union also developed in response to British colonial policies which disadvantaged the Urhobo people in favor of the Itsekiri. This was a reversal from the prior approach of favoring the Urhobo people against the Itsekiri ruler, Nana Olomu. Nana attempted to intimidate Urhobo communities to assert his domination over the Urhobo when he felt that the British were establishing control of Urhobo territories. Kemi Rotimi noted that the British utilized Nana's attempt to establish control over the Urhobo territories to wrongfully accuse him of terrorizing the Urhobo. There were other wrongful claims made against him to support the invasion.

The British presented Nana as a threat who needed to be removed for the protection of the Urhobo people, but there was some hypocrisy involved in this intervention. Salubi noted that the Europeans who met Nana "had nothing but great admiration for his outstanding personality, intelligence, wealth and hospitality." When Nana challenged Britain's economic interests in the region, they decided that he was a destabilizing force who needed to be removed.

The other aspect of the hypocrisy involved is that the British acted on the claim that they were attempting to protect the Urhobo people from Nana, yet in deposing Nana, the British also brought the Urhobo under a more direct form of domination under an Itsekiri ruler. Nana exercised economic influence over the Urhobo via controlling trade in the region, but his relationship with the Urhobo people was not totally hostile. Nana's mother was a Urhobo woman. This connection to the Urhobo people was something which Nana was apparently proud of. Nana was able to speak the Urhobo language, which won him the favor of the Urhobo traders. To further secure his connection with the Urhobo people, he also took wives from the leading Urhobo clans. Nana had enough force to bring to submission those who interfered with his trade, but it would appear that his interest was mainly in controlling trade. Salubi explained: "Chief Nana did not establish any form of native government in Urhobo land. All his interest was in trade, and only when his trade was interrupted was there any friction between his canoe-boys and the people. In many cases, settlement of such frictions was peaceful."

With Nana Olomu removed, another Itsekiri ruler named Dore Numa came to power. He attempted to assert control over Itsekiri and Urhobo affairs. Peter Ekeh described Nana's attempt to assert control over the Urhobo as an act of "marauding violence" but, as Salubi noted, Nana was interested in controlling trade, not in controlling the politics of the Urhobo people. Dore Numa was more ambitious as he sought to assert direct control over the affairs of the Urhobo people. Moreover, unlike Nana, the British supported Dore's efforts. This was due to the fact that Dore Numa had supported the British expedition against Nana.

It would appear that Dore Numa opportunistically sided with the British against Nana to accomplish his goal of obtaining absolute political power over both the Itsekiri and the Urhobo. Whereas Nana waged war against the British to defend the independence of his state, Dore Numa was content with submitting to British rule to advance his own position. This came at the expense of the Urhobo people, however. Salubi's son described Dora Numa's rule as "an absolute tragedy and a disaster for the Urhobo people." It was a disaster because Dora Numa weakened the power of the Urhobo people and he was able to accomplish this with the support of the same British colonial administration which removed Nan Olomu. After Dore Numa's death in 1932, the Urhobo began to organize against British colonial policies by demanding that Urhobo and Itsekiri affairs be treated separately. From this demand eventually came the Urhobo Progress Union.

Salubi was also involved in Nigeria's politics. He was initially a supporter of Nnamdi Azikiwe and his political party, the National Council of Nigeria and Cameroons (NCNC). This support came from the fact that Azikiwe provided support for the Urhobo Progress Union in the 1940s. There was another political party known as the Action Group which was led by Chief Obafemi Awolowo. The Action Group aligned itself with the Itsekiri. Given the Urhobo support for the NCNC, they faced persecution from the Action Group.

The NCNC eventually proved to be unsympathetic to the concerns of the Urhobo people. Among the leaders within the

NCNC was Festus Okotie-Eboh. Okotie-Eboh desired to continue the pattern established by Dora Numa of establishing Itsekiri domination over Urhobo affairs. It was determined that Okotie-Eboh would be tasked with producing the list of candidates from the Urhobo regions. Salubi objected to the idea that anybody should select candidates for the Urhobo people. He also pointed out that since 1952, all Urhobo candidates for the NCNC were selected by the Urhobo Progress Union.

Azikiwe decided not to intervene in the dispute. He referred the issue to Michael Okpara. Okpara attempted to placate both sides, but he did not make a definitive decision. The dispute caused Salubi to leave the NCNC for a regional party known as the Midwest Democratic Front (MDF). It is important to note that some leaders and members of the Urhobo Progress Union remained in the NCNC. Apart from the issue regarding selections for Urhobo candidates, Salubi also had other misgivings about the NCNC. He felt that the NCNC was using the police to oppress political opponents. This was demonstrated by a situation where the Urhobo Progress Union was granted a police permit for a general meeting. Two days before the meeting was to be geld, Salubi was informed by the Divisional Police Officer of Warri that the event would have to be canceled.

Salubi decided to go ahead with the meeting, but he called upon the assistance of the Igbu to protect the attendees. The Igbu were Urhobo warriors who were noted for wearing spiked feathers on their caps. The number of feathers represented the number of men that the warrior had killed in war. The Igbu came to the meeting prepared for battle, but no confrontation took place. When the police arrived and saw that the meeting was orderly, they decided to leave to avoid bloodshed. It was at this meeting that Salubi announced that he had left the NCNC and he urged other Urhobo to do the same. The fact that the NCNC attempted to use the police to intimidate Salubi as a means of forcing him to cancel the scheduled event demonstrated why he felt it was necessary to leave.

After Okotie-Eboh declared that Salubi would never be elected, Salubi decided to run as a member of the MDF. The MDF managed to win a number of seats in the region. Salubi was the only MDF candidate in Urhoboland to win a seat, however. The other MDF candidates in Urhoboland lost due to irregularities in the election. The rigging of elections and the use of the police to harass political opposition marked the early stages of what was to become a pattern of abusive and undemocratic practices which has been a stain on Nigeria's politics. The first republic of Nigeria came to an end due to a military coup. Okotie-Eboh was among those killed in the coup.

Salubi managed to receive a position in the military regime which was established following the coup. Colonel David Ejoor was appointed to the Midwest Region where he established his own government. He appointed Salubi as the Commissioner of Agriculture and Natural Resources. Despite the fact that Salubi found himself working in the government of the military regime, he cautioned that the Urhobo Progress Union should maintain a low profile and suspend its usual activities to avoid drawing the ire of the military administration.

Salubi served in a number of governmental positions from 1967 until 1972. He finally decided to retire to allow others the opportunity to serve. Salubi's decision to retire was also due to the direction of the military administration. He explained, "out of share disgust as the administration was tailing to what I could not, from my sense of administration and long experiences, understand, decided whether or not I should continue in the way the Government was being run. I found myself unable to continue." Salubi was not content with remaining in a government which was not being run efficiently.

Salubi's decision to retire from politics to let others serve and because of his disgust with the manner in which the government was run demonstrated the type of politician that he was. Unlike so many other political leaders who cling to power and are even willing to support inefficient government for the sake of having a high position, Salubi was different. He entered into politics to serve others, not to advance his own interests. He also retained his principles. Despite the wealth which Salubi amassed from his career, he was not someone who was engaged in corruption. Salubi was among the few former ministers who were completely exonerated from any corruption during a mass probe which was conducted. In 1967, Salubi was brought to a tribunal. The justice who discharged Salubi stated: "Chief Salubi is a most honest Minister who should not have been invited before the Tribunal for trial."

In addition to being an advocate for the Urhobo people and a commitment servant to the people of Nigeria, Salubi was also someone who expressed concern for the plight of African people elsewhere. In 1961, Salubi led Nigeria's delegation to the International Labor Organization in Switzerland. On this occasion he was able to succeed in passing a motion to expel South Africa from the organization due to the nation's apartheid policies. Salubi was very critical of racial prejudice and the impact that it had on African people. He explained that racial prejudice "creates an unhappy situation; it makes the African a psychological case. If he moves too fast, or too slow, it is because he is an African, and not an individual with his characteristics; thus the poor man moves about always conscious, sensitive, and hypersensitive of himself." Salubi described America and South Africa as "the two blackest spots for Africans and people of African descent in the world today."

Salubi died in 1982. His legacy was not only that of someone who was a tireless defender of the rights of the Urhobo people, but someone who displayed the type of integrity and morality in public service which is desperately needed in Nigeria and many other African nations. As corruption and abuse of power began to emerge in Nigerian society, Salubi remained incorruptible.

References:

Kemi Rotimi, "Jaja and Nana in the Niger Delta Region of Nigeria: Proto-Nationalists or Emergent Capitalists," *The Journal of Pan African Studies*, vol.2, no.7, December 2008.

Peter P. Ekeh (editor), *T.E.A. Salubi: Witness to British Colonial Rule in Urhoboland and Nigeria*, 2008.

60

AMILCAR CABRAL'S ANTI-COLONIAL VISION

An important aspect of Amilcar Cabral's approach to military struggle was to convert enemy forces. He suggested that members of his party should do "everything possible to help enemy soldiers to desert, ensuring them safety through all the means necessary, in such a way as to encourage them to take the decision to desert." He also advocated that political work be done among Africans who serve the enemy, whether they be civilians or soldiers. The aim was to convince such individuals to change course. This magnanimous approach did not extend to those who "knowingly betray" the people. Cabral urged that the knowing betrayers of the people and those who take up arms on the side of the enemy be eliminated.

Cabral understood that the struggle against Portuguese colonialism was not merely an armed struggle, but a struggle against colonial propaganda as well. This meant countering the propaganda of the colonial powers with propaganda designed to win over the African population to the anti-colonial struggle. It also meant weaponizing disinformation against the enemy. Cabral explained: "Trick the enemy with false news, make them fall into traps so that we can destroy them in large numbers." The effort to confuse the enemy was combined with a careful study of the enemy. Cabral urged the members of his party to develop intelligence networks to gather information about the enemy. The goal was to be better informed and better prepared than the enemy.

There was also an economic aspect to the war as well. Cabral urged that members of the party must destroy the economy of the enemy and build their own economy. Building this economic meant developing agricultural production in the liberated areas. Cabral urged members of the party to pay special attention to the development of food crops and the care of livestock. Cabral encouraged that the spare time of the armed forces should be spent assisting farmers. In the zones occupied by the enemy, Cabral encouraged sabotage as a means of destroying the colonial economy. This included destroying the shops and warehouses of the enemy.

Concerning discipline, Cabral understood that it was important that each combatant be aware that they are "serving the people." He explained that no combatant or worker had the right to use weapons to terrorize the people, or to obtain person advantages against the interests of the people. Cabral was aware of the danger that soldiers could become exploiters and abusers of the very people whom they took up arms to defend. Discipline within the party was upheld by a people's court. Cabral explained that these courts must practice justice and judge each case with care.

Cabral was not merely waging a struggle to liberate his own nation from colonial domination. He recognized that Guinea-Bissau's struggle was related to the African liberation struggle. In a speech delivered at the Conference of the Nationalist Organizations of the Portuguese Colonies, Amilcar Cabral affirmed his support for Pan-Africanism. He explained: "We are, in Africa, for African unity in favour of African people." He also added that he viewed unity as a means, not an end. As such, he was in no rush to claim African unity, for he believed that it must be a step by step process. In this regard, Cabral differed from Nkrumah who differed with the gradualist approach to unity.

Cabral was also concerned with African nations respecting each other's territories. He stated that his only condition for unity is that the gains of the revolutionary struggle in Guinea-Bissau should not be compromised by unities with other peoples. Respect for neighboring African countries was also something which Cabral advocated within his own party. Cabral stated: "Do not allow any member of the Party to meddle in the internal affairs of those countries: be watchful in respect of elements of those countries who seek to meddle in our life or make use of our struggle."

Cabral not only benefitted from Pan-African solidarity in his struggle, but he recognized that Portugal benefitted from the solidarity of the West. Not only did NATO provide support for Portugal, but Portugal was backed by South Africa, Ian Smith in Rhodesia, and Franco's government in Spain.

Cabral's solidarity extended beyond African unity to include support for the people of Palestine. He explained, "we support with all our hearts' strength all that the children of Palestine are doing to free their country and we support with all our might the Arab countries and the African countries in general helping the Palestinian people recover their dignity, their independence, their right to live."

Following his assassination, *New York Times* published an article on Cabral which noted that Cabral expressed the view that he wanted his nation to be like Brazil, "a former Portuguese colony that has close ties with Lisbon." The fact that Cabral still wished to retain such close ties demonstrated that Cabral still retained some degree of psychological connection to the colonial power, though Cabral separated Portuguese colonialism from the people of Portugal. Cabral had consistently expressed the view that the war which he was engaged in was not a war against the Portuguese people or Portugal, but against Portuguese colonialism which was overseen by a fascist regime. Cabral declared: "The people of Portugal are our ally; the people of Portugal are aware of the fact that colonial war is a crime, not only against our people but also against themselves, and we are doing all we can, through this struggle, to strengthen our solidarity with that people, who have lately decided to use even violent methods against the Portuguese colonial war machine."

Cabral's anti-colonial vision was one which promoted a radical break with Portuguese colonialism. He declared that "whatever God is with the Portuguese colonialists, whatever civilization the Portuguese colonialists represent, we are going to destroy them because we *shall destroy* any kind of foreign domination over us." Cabral was willing to take up arms to destroy this domination, but he also still remained hopeful of a future where Guinea-Bissau remained close to Portugal.

61

MY VIEWS ON MARXISM-LENINISM

The character of Tony Baker from my books *The Black African Crisis in the Age of a Black President* and *From Colin Kaepernick to Donald Trump: A New Age of Crisis* was intended to provide a critique of a dogmatic Marxist-Leninist position. Baker is a Marxist-Leninist who supports Pan-Africanism to the extent that Pan-Africanism works to unite the African working class as part of the larger effort to unite the global working class. Baker is opposed to Garveyism because views Garvey as a petty-bourgeois ideologue who preached a reactionary version of Pan-Africanism. By contrast, Baker is an admirer of W.E.B. Du Bois because, in his view, Du Bois was a Pan-African intellectual who embraced Marxism and class struggle.

Baker is also an apologist for the Soviet Union. I understand the defense of the Soviet Union from the perspective that the Soviet Union did not maintain colonies in Africa and that the Soviet Union had even supported anti-colonial struggles in Africa. This is why Paul Robeson defended the Soviet Union as being a friend to the Negro people around the world. I also understand that the Soviet Union was engaged in an ideological contest with the United States. Soviet policies in Africa were designed to oppose American policies. This was beneficials for Africa when opposing the United States meant supporting anti-colonial struggles, but it was a problem when Soviet policy resulted in taking positions such as supporting the Derg government in Ethiopia or continuing to supply oil to Italy after the Italian invasion of Ethiopia.

The revolution in Russia initially inspired the hope of a genuinely socialist revolution which would create a workers' society. What followed was the creation of a totalitarian state under the leadership of Joseph Stalin. This is not to suggest that the Soviet Union ceased serving a progressive role in the world. After all, the Soviet Union did help to support liberation movements in Africa. The problem was that the nature of the Soviet regime undermined the goal of establishing workers' control. Leon

Trotsky emerged as a leading Marxist theoretician who denounced the abuses which were taking place under Stalin, but, as C.L.R. James noted, Trotsky underestimated the extent to which the revolution in the Soviet Union had been betrayed. In James' view the Soviet Union was not a degenerated workers' state as Trotsky had argued; it simply was not a workers' state at all. Trotskyists did not appreciate the extent to which the revolution in Russia had been betrayed and continued to defend the Soviet Union as a degenerated workers' state. This is why the Spartacist League supported the Soviet invasion of Afghanistan out of the misguided view that the social gains of the Russian Revolution could be exported to Afghanistan through military force.

The other reality is that Trotskyists were historically never in a position to produce a viable alternative to what they denounced as degenerated and deformed workers' states because they never managed to seize power anywhere. Trotsky was assassinated by Stalin. His followers faced similar persecution. For example, in Cuba, Fidel Castro's government engaged in the suppression of the Trotskyist movement. There was an even more severe repression in Vietnam where Trotskyists were murdered by Ho Chi Minh's party.

Baker reflects the worldview of the individuals such as Henry Winston. I wrote a response to Winston's criticism of Pan-Africanism in *Abraham's God and African People*. I am not in complete variance with Winston's positions. For example, I myself share some of the criticisms which he raised of George Padmore's politics. Where I take issue with Winston is that I found his treatment of Pan-Africanism to be misleading because of the way that he selectively presented information to support his arguments. I also found Winston's attitude towards nationalism to be overly dismissive. He wrote: "In colonially-subjugated countries, the people's movement emerges in the struggle for independence from foreign domination of the country and its economy. When independence is won, the economy of the country, depending on circumstances, comes either under the control of the people or of the national bourgeoisie allied with and accommodating itself to neo-colonialism." Winston doubted that the black bourgeoisie or black masses could truly take power in America, but this is precisely what took place in South Africa in which a white minority seized power and ruled the black majority.

Given that racial segregation in America had resulted in African Americans being alienated from the capitalist system, it became rather natural for nationalists to advocate for a position of self-determination in the form of controlling the wealth and resources within black communities. Kwame Ture explained: "The struggle for Black Power in the United States, and certainly around the world, is the struggle to free these colonies from external domination, but we do not seek merely to create communities where black rulers replace white rulers, controlling the lives of black masses and where black money goes into a few black pockets. We want to see it go into the communal pocket . . ."

Winston dismissed this view, but what Ture was expressing was a desire to create black communities which are not only controlled by black people, but which have an economic system which is independent of the dominant American capitalist system. Winston acknowledged that the Communist Party in America "recognized that Blacks were oppressed as a people and that labor with a white skin and labor with a Black skin could not be free unless the special demands of the triply oppressed Black people were put at the center of the struggle for progress and socialism." Winston noted that the Communist Party later discarded its position on self-determination for black people when the Communist Party believed that the conditions in the South had changed.

Tony Baker's debates with Eddie Wilson center around the larger debate around the relevance of Marxism-Leninism in the Pan-African struggle. Eddie Wilson's position is more aligned with my own personal view on the topic. I am not a Marxist-Leninist. I am not necessarily opposed to Marxism-Leninism either. I think Karl Marx and Vladimir Lenin raised valid criticisms of capitalism. As I noted, I am also willing to recognize that the Soviet Union did make some important contributions to the African struggle against colonialism. I state that I am not opposed to Marxism-Leninism in theory, but I also recognize that in practice there have been certain challenges when it comes to implementing Marxism-Leninism. I do acknowledge that this may be due to problems with improper implementation of Marxist-

Leninist ideals rather than a deficiency in the ideology itself. Yet, I am not a Marxist-Leninist, so I do not see it as my duty to correct the flaws made by Marxist-Leninists of the past. That is a task reserved for those who still advocate for Marxism-Leninism as a solution for the oppression of African people. I maintain that I am ideologically flexible, so I do not oppose Marxism-Leninism in theory, but I also do not adhere to it myself.

The anarchist critique of Marxism-Leninism argues that Marxism-Leninism is conceptually flawed because it is based on the notion that a vanguard which seizes power can produce anything other than an oppressive hierarchy. Mikhail Bakunin, who was one of the most influential figures in developing anarchism, was a critic of Karl Marx's view on revolution. Bakunin accused Marxists of wanting to concentrate power into their hands. In *Statism and Anarchy*, Bakunin argued: "Ultimately, from whatever point of view we look at this question, we come always to the same sad conclusion, the rule of the great masses of the people by a privileged minority. The Marxists say that this minority will consist of workers. Yes, possibly of former workers, who, as soon as they become the rulers or the representatives of the people, will cease to be workers and will look down on the plain working masses from the governing heights of the State; they will no longer represent the people, but only themselves and their claims to rulership over the people. Those who doubt this know very little about human nature." Bakunin also argued that the state which Marxists sought to establish would be "nothing but a despotic control of the populace by a new and not at all numerous aristocracy of real and pseudoscientists."

Whereas Bakunin dismissed Marx's theories as an attempt to establish control, Marx dismissed Bakunin as someone who did not understand revolution. Marx wrote: "He [Bakunin] understands absolutely nothing of social revolution, only its political rhetoric; its economic conditions simply do not exist for him. Now since all previous economic formations, whether developed or undeveloped, have entailed the enslavement of the worker (whether as wage labourer, peasant, etc.), he imagines that radical revolution is equally possible in all these formations. What is more, he wants the European social revolution, whose economic basis is capitalist production, to be carried out on the level of the Russian or Slav agricultural and pastoral peoples..."

Engels countered anarchist criticisms by arguing that with the introduction of the socialist order, the state will dissolve itself and disappear. Engels also dismissed the notion of a free people's state, explaining that the proletariat would make use of the state "not for the purpose of freedom, but of keeping down its enemies and, as soon as there can be any question of freedom, the state as such ceases to exist." Engels argued that the Paris Commune represented an example of a situation in which the state was dissolved. Lenin later elaborated on this when he argued in *The State and Revolution* that the Commune not only ceased to be a state, but that it had to suppress not the majority of the population, but rather the minority of exploiters.

Anarchists following the line of Bakunin would argue that the establishment of a state capitalist bureaucracy in the Soviet Union was inevitable because it is human nature to use the power of the state to oppress others. The failure of the Soviet Union certainly demonstrated the challenges with implementing Marxism-Leninism in practice, but these were challenges which Lenin himself was aware of. In Marx's view, capitalism would have to be overthrown at its core. Lenin understood this as well. A socialist revolution did not sweep across Europe as Lenin had anticipated. Lenin found himself in a position of having to implement capitalist reforms in Russia. Moreover, to maintain the control of the Communist Party, Lenin opposed expanding the power of trade unions because doing so would pose a potential challenge to the party's power. Thus, Lenin found himself in a position of trying to protect the revolution from external and internal challenges. Its is important to understand this point because the establishment of Stalinism was not merely due to human nature, but also certain material conditions in the Soviet Union as well. Much like Trotskyists, anarchists never managed to mobilize a successful revolution to develop a workable alternative to Marxism-Leninism.

I agree with Kwame Ture, who argued that a people's ideology must be rooted in their culture. Marxism-Leninism is not rooted in African culture. Marxism-Leninism arose from the Soviet Union's attempt to implement Marx's theories to the material conditions of

Russia. Marxism-Leninism did not emerge out of Africa's struggle against imperialism. Moreover, the ideals which Marx and Lenin advocated for were ideals which may have been radical in European society, but these ideals were not new to Africans. African societies developed models of what Amilcar Cabral referred to as "horizontal" societies in which there were no class hierarchies. Africa also did produce many societies which did have class hierarchies and the type of exploitation of labor which comes with that, but even in some of those societies there were still elements of communalism which were generally lacking in more individualistic European societies.

What the character of Baker is meant to convey is the hardline approach to Marxism-Leninism, which I am opposed to. For African people, racial oppression has been a much greater burden than class oppression has been. This has been reinforced by the fact that the white working class has displayed racist behaviors as well. The character of Baker is not intended to be a critique of Marxism-Leninism as an ideology, but rather a critique of a particular type of approach to Marxism-Leninism which I am opposed to.

62

ON LOVE AND MARRIAGE

Love is a complex concept because it is subjective. It means different things to different individuals. It also means different things to different cultures. Love is a concept that refers to a very strong feeling of desire or affection. In the English language, this feeling is measured in degrees. For example, "love" represents a stronger feeling of affection or desire than "like" does. This is not true of other languages. In French, for example, the word "aimer" means both like and love. The same is true in Lingala, where the word "kolinga" means to love, to like, and to want. This is what to love someone really means. It means to want a person; to want to be with that person and to make a commitment to being with that person.

I have written about the fact that in many traditional African societies, marriages were arranged. This meant that individuals did not marry purely due to love. There were advantages to this. Both parties typically went into the marriage with clear expectations about the marriage. Rather than subjective feelings of love, marriages were based on a shared understanding of societal norms and expectations. There was also the element of communal support for the arrangement which is often lacking in the modern Western romantic approach to marriage which views marriage as an arrangement between two individuals, rather than an arrangement between families or clans. The communal aspect is important because marriages were viewed as a union of families. There were disadvantages as well. Arranged marriages mean that the individuals do not get to select their partner. Marriages under such circumstances can work, but there are also instances in which a person is forced into a bad marriage.

Polygamy is also a common marital practice in Africa. Polygamous marriages served the purpose of creating larger family units and securing political alliances among the ruling class. Having multiple wives also provided the advantage of increasing the labor capacity of a single household. This was obviously an advantage for a man with multiple wives, but there were some cases where African men who preferred to have one wife were driven to polygamy by wives who desired to have cowives to assist with the housework. This was an observation which Mary Kingsley made when she wrote: "The more wives the less work, says the African lady; and I have known men who would rather have had one wife and spent the rest of the money on themselves, in a civilised way, driven into polygamy by the women; and of course this state of affairs is most common in nonslave-holding tribes like the Fan."

Polygamy did pose certain challenges as well. This included conflicts among co-wives and among the children of these wives. The downfall of the Songhai Empire is an example of how polygamous marriages in Africa caused political strife. The greatest emperor of this empire was Askia Muhammad or Askia the Great. Askia was a great warrior, but he was also known as a great ruler who maintained peace and stability throughout his empire. His great downfall was his sons. Askia fathered many children with different women. As his sons grew older, Askia had a difficult time controlling them. Askia was deposed by a son named Musa. This same son began killing his brothers. Musa was himself killed by some of the surviving brothers. Over the next several years, the Songhai Empire weakened due to the conflicts over power among Askia's many sons. The rivalry between the half-brothers Maqoma and Sandile presents another example of how polygamous marriages among the ruling class could lead to the problem of disunity among half-brothers who are in competition for their father's position.

I also want to add here that polygamy was more than just having multiple partners to have sex with. Polygamous arrangements were legally recognized arrangements and in some societies each woman was meant to have their own house. As I have noted in my essay "Civilized and Savages: The Myth of the European Civilizing Mission," adultery was not uncommon in polygamous African societies and in African societies such transgressions were often punished very harshly. Olaudah Equiano noted that in the society which he came from, men were allowed to have numerous wives, but the punishment for adultery was slavery or death.

Polygamy in African cultures was not the same thing as the type womanizing which some men engage in. One difference is that given that polygamous marriages were legitimately recognized, the children of such marriages were legitimacy recognized and raised as such. Adogbeji Salubi, for example, was one of his father's twenty-two children by his several wives. Salubi recalled that his father was very caring towards him. The Xhosa ruler Sandile was also noted to be very affectionate towards the children of the many wives that he had. This is obviously different than a situation in which a man has several children with different women without being present in the lives of these children. I recall the case of the football player Adrian Peterson who had several different children by several different women. One of his children was a two-year-old named Tyrese who was killed after being beaten by his mother's boyfriend. The first time that Peterson ever saw his son was when his son was in a coma shortly before the child died. Peterson paid child support to take care of his children, but one of the mothers complained that he did not spend much time with his children.

I also noted in my essay "Civilized and Savages: The Myth of the European Civilizing Mission" that the polygamous nature of African marriages clashed with European missionary efforts since the missionaries denounced the tradition of polygamy. The New Testament itself urged that church leaders should have one wife—see Titus 1:6 and 1 Timothy 3:12. Polygamy is never explicitly forbidden in the Bible, however. In the Old Testament, polygamy was practiced among the Hebrew people, which was famously demonstrated by Solomon's 700 wives and 300 concubines. It seems that as Paul worked to spread the doctrine of Christianity, he held the view that it was better for church leaders to have only one wife. This was not an unreasonable view given that Solomon's many wives caused the downfall of the united Israelite kingdom. Paul's instruction for monogamy was explicitly directed at church leaders, though monogamy was eventually adopted as general practice among Christians.

Apart from the Christian missionary influence, there have been other sources of opposition to polygamy in Africa. Shamba

Bolongongo outlawed polygamous marriages among his people to end the fighting among cowives. Thomas Sankara outlawed polygamy in Burkina Faso as part of his effort to uphold the rights of women. Most interesting was the opposition to polygamy from Mahmoud Muhammad Taha's Islamic religious movement, which also sought to uphold women's rights. This is interesting because Islam expressly allows polygamous marriages. Chapter 4, verse 3 allows a man to take as many as four wives, but Taha believed that polygamy was not an original precept in Islam, so he outlawed it among his followers. I have expressed in the past that my personal view on the matter is that I am not wholly opposed to polygamy, although I recognize the potential problems involved. I certainly have no interest in perusing polygamous relationships as I have always preferred to give all my attention to a single person.

I am not suggesting that the traditional African system of marriages was perfect, but there was a certain logic to how those marriages were structured which I understand and respect. Western cultures are more individualistic and out of this individualism emerged the concept of romantic love. This is a concept in which marriage is based on meeting someone who makes you feel happy. The entire arrangement is based on the happiness and fulfillment of the individuals involved, but a person can never receive all of this from another individual. Our happiness and fulfillment come from within, not from the people whom we date and marry. I am not suggesting that individuals should be miserable in their marriages, but at the same time there must also be more to a marriage than seeking some sort of personal fulfillment through one's partner. In communal African societies, the view was that marriage was not simply about the individuals involved. It was about the best interests of the community at large.

There is a political aspect of marriage as well. Marriage is typically thought of as a private affair, but it does have public implications for political figures. I refer again to African history. Nana Olomu, for example, married women from the leading Urhobo clans to secure his alliance with the Urhobo people. Amenhotep III of Egypt maintained a harem of foreign princesses which he had married. This helped to secure Egypt's diplomatic connection with the nations which that Egypt ruled over at the time. The marriages of ruling kings in African societies were not only a public concern insomuch as these marriages represented political connections, but the fertility of the king represented the well-being of the nation. Louis Regis noted that there was a practice in "some West African communities in which the sexuality of the king is connected organically to the fertility of the land—and thence the well-being of the people." Ruling kings were often expected to take many wives and produce many children, though a king who failed to exercise discipline did risk placing himself in danger. In the history of Oyo, Amuniwaye is remembered as a weak leader whose affair with another man's wife resulted in that man killing Amuniwaye.

Among black public figures, marriage is also used to judge commitment to the community and the cause of black freedom. Interracial marriages create suspicion because one's loyalty to the black community is questioned. There is also the sense that by selecting a partner outside of the African race, one may also be affirming Eurocentric standards of beauty, thereby displaying a sense of psychological colonization. These judgments may not always be accurate or fair, but these are some of the reasons why black people who date and marry non-black partners are viewed with suspicion. It is sometimes the case that one's partner does reflect one's political disposition. For example, Harry Belafonte's marriage to a white woman was consistent with his integrationist outlook. The same is true of Frederick Douglass' marriage. Olaudah Equiano came to view the white people who enslaved him as being superior and he sought to imitate them to the point of marrying a white woman.

One must also be careful when it comes to selecting the proper partner. Malcolm X explained in his autobiography that he distrusted women because he had seen many men ruined by women. He even gave the example of Samson who was a biblical warrior who became involved with a woman named Delilah. She managed to get Samson to expose the secret of his strength and when she discovered this, she cut his hair. He was then captured and blinded. Samson was so strong that he killed 1,000 men with a jawbone, but his weakness was that he trusted the wrong woman. As distrusting as Malcolm was of women, he eventually married

Betty Shabazz. The two not only went on to have several children together, but Betty became a very important source of support for Malcolm. In his biography of Malcolm, Manning Marable attempted to depict Malcolm's marriage to Betty as one in which Malcolm displayed very little affection for Betty, but this was not the case.

Ideally, the proper partner should be someone who is caring, understanding, and supportive. It is also important that the partners share the same values or perhaps even the same objectives. To give a historical example, we can look at Marcus Garvey and Amy Jacques Garvey. Marcus Garvey himself admitted that he sacrificed his wife and his home for his work. Amy, in turn, noted that Marcus was very demanding of her. They became estranged near the end of his life because he was building the organization while she was concerned with raising the children. What caused their relationship to withstand the strain was that the two shared a commitment to African unity and liberation. This is why Amy Jacques Garvey continued to represent her husband's legacy after he died. They both shared a vision which was stronger than the tensions in their relationship. Amy Jacques Garvey was Garvey's second wife. The first marriage was short-lived and not as productive for Garvey as the second marriage was, which further demonstrates the importance of selecting the right partner.

63

RACE AND THE AFRICAN STRUGGLE

I have described race as being a social construct which is rooted in certain biological realities. This is to state that there are physical and phenotypical differences among humans which exist as a biological reality. This biological reality alone is not the sole basis for race, however. Apart from being physical, race is political and cultural as well. As such, when I speak of the African race, I am speaking not only of people who look a particular way, but also of a people with a shared experience and culture. Out of this experience and culture comes a certain general worldview which is found across the African world. The same could be stated for other groups which are classified as "races." East Asians for example do share certain physical features, but there are also certain shared cultural traits as well.

These physical and cultural differences are not immutable. We know that throughout history, as different racial groups interacted with each other they also exchanged cultures. These interactions have also resulted in miscegenation, which further reinforces the fact that racial divisions are more social than they are biological. As W.E.B. Du Bois pointed out: "Differences, and striking differences, there are between men and groups of men, but they fade into each other so insensibly that we can only indicate the main divisions of men in broad outlines." Miscegenation is also political as well. Miscegenation was encouraged by some white supremacists as a means of biologically eliminating the African population. This was the position supported by George Rawlinson of the Church of England, who advocated intermarriage as a means of eliminating the black race. Other white supremacists opposed miscegenation out of a desire to keep the white race pure. Black Nationalist groups such as the Universal Negro Improvement Association and the Nation of Islam opposed miscegenation to uphold racial purity as well, although both organizations were also willing to accept mixed race members.

In *Hackers, Politicians, and Monarchs*, there is a chapter titled

333

"Biracial and Racially Neutral" which addresses those biracial individuals who try to take a neutral position on racial matters. In the essay, I specifically refer to Meghan Markle as an example of this. In a number of my essays, I have written about mixed race individuals who either take a neutral position on matters of racial discrimination or who side with the oppressor. Take for example Elizabeth Key's white descendants. Key was a biracial woman who escaped from slavery and married a white man. Her descendants later became slave owners themselves.

As I stated previously, miscegenation is not merely biological, but it is political as well. There are some black people whose descendants not only become biologically assimilated into white society through intermixing, but they become culturally and politically assimilated to the point where they become part of the white supremacist system which exploits the masses of black people. These are individuals who adopt the values of the dominant society. They become white not only physically, but politically as well. Such individuals represent not only a biological erasure of the African identity, but a cultural and political erasure as well.

Miscegenation certainly does raise questions around racial identity as well. After all, would it be practical to label people as European, African, or Asian given that so many of us are not purely of one racial group? This is where race as a social concept becomes important. I can state that from the African context, there have been mixed individuals—including myself—who have firmly identified as African or black. Therefore, African identity has never been rooted in the understanding that to identify as African or black one must be purely African or black from a biological perspective. The same has been true for white people. It has certainly been the case that individuals who have identified as white have African ancestry. I have even written of examples where white people have paid to cover up any record of their African ancestry.

The concept of race as it would come to be known became relevant during the age of colonization. The roots of Western racial supremacy can be found in the history of Greco-Roman society. Ancient Greece and Rome were not racial societies in the way that Western societies would later become, but Western imperialism was an outgrowth of the imperialism of Alexander the Great and the imperialism of the Roman Empire.

Following the discovery of the New World, the nations of Western Europe began to expand themselves globally. This expansion involved seizing territory from Native Americans and enslaving the people of Africa. It was in these New World colonies that a racial hierarchy developed which placed certain racial groups above others. It was during this period where the white identity came into existence.

What is generally known as Western civilization was the product of a historical process which began with the rise of Greece and Rome. Greek city-states provided a foundational basis for the development of Western civilization. The Romans built on those cultural foundations by developing a massive empire which unified Europe under Roman rule. Roman rule also provided a Latin cultural basis which would form an important basis for Western cultural identity. Western European languages such as Italian, French, Spanish, Portuguese, and English all reflect this Latin influence.

I offer some examples of this Latin influence in European languages. The English word "construct" and the French word "construire" come from the Latin word "constructum." The French word "contre," the Spanish word "contra," and the English word "counter" come from the Latin "contra" which means to oppose or to be against. The French word "amour" and the Spanish word "amor" come from the Latin word "amor" which means love. The English "idea" and French "idée" come from the Latin word "idea." The English words "save" and "salvage," and the French words "sauver" and "sauvegarder" come from the Latin "salvare." The English word "render" and the French word "rendre" come from the Latin word "reddere." The English word "corpse" and the French word "corps" come from the Latin word for body, which is "corpus". From the Latin phrase "ad libitum" (which means at one's desire) comes the English phrase "ad lib" which refers to something which is done without prior preparation or planning. The connection is that when a person decides to ab lib, they are speaking or singing as they desire rather than as was originally planned. Coitus is an English word for sexual intercourse which comes from the Latin word "coition, which means "a coming together."

Success comes from the Latin word "succedere." The English word annual which refers to something which happens yearly, and the French word for year, "année" comes from the Latin "annus." The English word "via" comes from the Latin "via," which means a path or way. The phrase "mea culpa" comes from a Latin phrase which means "through my fault." The word private comes from the Latin word "privare," which means "to deprive of" because one who owns private property has the ability to deprive others of the use of such property. The word vex comes from the Latin "vexare".

There are some words in English which are of Greek origin as well. One example of this is didactic, which comes from the Greek word, "didaktikos." Dialogue comes from the Greek word, "dialogos" which means to have a discourse or conversation. The word phobia is a Greek word for fear. Democracy is a word which is of Greek origin and it's a system of a governance which developed out of Athens. All of this demonstrates the extent to which Greece and Roman influenced the development of Western civilization.

I am not suggesting that racism is so deeply rooted in Western society that no white person can support the African struggle. I would cite John Brown as the standard for white people who fight against white racism. This is because Brown was willing to take up arms and risk his own life in the fight to end slavery. There were also other white abolitionists who also put themselves at risk to help liberate black people. There is the example Sherman Booth who broke the law to help free enslaved Africans. Though I have been critical of the hypocrisy surrounding the abolitionist movement, I do recognize that there were white abolitionists who did risk their own freedom and well-being to end slavery. Marilyn Buck was a revolutionary white woman who was involved in the effort to help Assata Shakur escape from prison. Much like John Brown, she faced a harsh penalty for supporting the African struggle in America. I found Che Guevara's intervention in the Democratic Republic of Congo to be indicative of Guevara's misguided revolutionary adventurism, but one must grant that

Guevara was willing to take up arms to fight against the Western backed regime in Congo. There is also Peter Garlake, who was forced into exile for challenging the racist historical narrative being promoted by the government of Rhodesia.

There have been some white people who have stood against racism and supported the cause of African freedom, but reality is that within the system of white supremacy, a large number, if not the majority, of white people are comfortable with the status quo. They see nothing fundamentally wrong with the system as it is, so they are not willing to radically alter it. There are the conservative whites whose mission is to leave the system as is; to conserve it rather than to change it. Then there are the moderates who believe in incremental change. The problem with the moderates is that their vision of change is not change at all and they frequently become obstacles in the path of those who do believe in change.

The problem which confronts African people is not merely white racism alone. Racism against Africans in Arab societies predated Western colonialism in Africa. The Arab slave trade also predated the European slave trade. During the anti-colonial struggles of the 1950s and 1960s there was some sense of solidarity between Africans and Arabs given that both groups were waging an anti-colonial struggle against a common European colonizer. Apart from having a common enemy, there was also geographic location. Due to the Arab presence in North Africa, the Pan-African movement in Africa developed as one which included Arabs as part of Africa's unity. There were even certain Arabs who professed a Pan-African vision as well such as Ben Bella of Algeria, Nasser of Egypt, and Gaddafi of Libya.

The problem was that even though Africans and Arabs faced a common colonial enemy, Arab racism towards African people, which predated European racism, persisted. This racism also included attempts to impose Arab culture on Africans through a process of Arabization. This forced Arabization led to civil wars in Sudan. Nasser, who professed support for Pan-African unity, was also a Pan-Arabist who officially declared Egypt as an Arab republic. This continued the process of Arabizing Egyptian society. One problem with the Arab inclusion within Pan-Africanism has been this dual commitment to African unity and Arab unity which has ultimately resulted in the imposition of Arab cultural identity over an African one. Of Nasser, Kwame Nkrumah remarked: "He would have done so much better for Egypt if he had looked towards Africa instead of towards the Middle East."

In the case of Gaddafi, he began as an advocate for Arab unity. He advocated for a federation of Arab states. In 1969, Gaddafi signed a federation between Libya, Egypt, and Sudan. This federation and other federation attempts failed. In the end, Gaddafi fell out of favor with the Arab world and the Arab League had even supported the NATO led coalition which toppled him. Gaddafi eventually turned to Pan-Africanism where he found more success than he had with his efforts at Pan-Arabism.

It is certainly true that Gaddafi supported various anti-colonial struggles in Africa such as the struggle against Portuguese colonialism in Angola. He also provided support for the liberation struggle in South Africa. It is also true that Gaddafi played a very divisive role in Africa as well given his tendency to intervene in internal conflicts to support one side over the other, or his decision to wage war with Chad over territory. For this reason, I viewed Gaddafi as a typical opportunist whose policies shifted based on whichever position was most favorable for him. This is why Gaddafi, who denounced the United States for its imperialism and capitalism in the 1980s, became so close with the United States in the 2000s that the C.I.A. was assisting him torturing critics. Of course, Gaddafi would learn—much as Saddam Hussein had learned—that the United States' political leaders are also opportunistic. This is why President Barack Obama could shake Gaddafi's hand and then later celebrate Gaddafi being overthrown.

The same point can be made of the relationship of African people to Asians. Mahatma Gandhi was a man who was admired by prominent African leaders such as Marcus Garvey and Martin Luther King, but the reality is that Gandhi was an Indian nationalist who was primarily concerned with Indian people. Cheddi Jagan was an anti-colonial leader in Guyana. Even though Jagan was a Marxist, he was also an Indian who placed the interests of Indians in Guyana first and foremost. Jagan was an Indian first and a Marxist second. The Chinese revolutionary leader, Mao Zedong, was also respected by prominent African leaders and intellectuals, even though he eventually led the Chinese government down the path of siding with American imperialism in Africa. Mao was a Marxist, but he was also a nationalist leader as well and he put China's nationalist interests over Marxism where his foreign policy in Africa was concerned.

The historical connection between Asia and Africa is obviously one which is of particular interest for me given that I am of both African and Asian ancestry. Both Africans and Asians have had to confront the struggle against global European domination. This shared struggle against European colonialism did help to foster a sense of Afro-Asian solidarity in the 1900s, but there were also limits to this solidarity. Jagan's position on the West Indies Federation and Mao's policies in Africa demonstrated the limits of that solidarity.

I do not intend to give the impression that the history of Afro-Asian unity has always been a history of betrayal. In South Africa, for example, there were Indians who did align with African people in the struggle against apartheid. In 1947, Monty Naicker of the Natal Indian Congress and Yusuf Dadoo of the Transvaal Indian Congress signed the "Doctor's Pact" with Dr. Xuma of the ANC. This was an important step towards the unity of the African and Indian movements. This first step eventually led to the Defiance Campaign which was organized by the ANC and the South African Indian Congress (SAIC). It was not the case that there was no genuine support for the African liberation struggle on the part of Asians, but tensions persisted because of conflicting interests.

64

ON RELIGION

Religion is an abstract concept. This means that religion ultimately exists within the thoughts and beliefs of the believer. For instance, going to a mosque and reading the Qur'an does not make one a Muslim. What makes one a Muslim is what one believes about the Qur'an. A Muslim is one who chooses to believe that the Qur'an was divinely revealed and that Muhammad was the last of God's prophets. Reading the Bible does not make one a Christian, but accepting Jesus Christ as lord and savior does. Even those who practice a particular religion may have differences, which is why different sects can emerge within the same religion because beliefs vary among individuals and groups. The pope is the leader of the Catholic Church. A Christian who does not belong to the Catholic Church obviously would not share such a view because their faith is different from the faith of a Catholic, though they are both Christians who accept that Jesus is lord and savior.

The same is true of Islam. The split between Sunnis and Shia began following the assassination of Ali ibn Abu Talib. Shia Muslims held the view that the leader of the Islamic faith should be a descendant of Muhammad. Sunnis, however, held the position that the caliph must be elected. Given that the Sunnis were the larger faction, they came to be viewed as the orthodox branch of Islam. Sufism developed as a practice of Islam which emphasizes mystical knowledge of God. Sufism was criticized by some orthodox Muslims for being in contrast to the intellectual and legalistic emphasis of Sunni theology. There is also the Nation of Islam, which developed its own interpretation of the Islamic faith. The Five Percent Nation developed as breakaway sect from the Nation of Islam.

In stating that religion is an abstract concept which exists in the beliefs of the practitioner, I do not want to give the impression that I am dismissing the importance of religious beliefs. I think that we must also look at the functions of religious belief. How does believing in a religion impact the lives and the behaviors of the believer? The answer to this varies. Religious faith may be abstract in the sense that the religion exists in the minds of the believer, but the actions which are motivated by religious beliefs are very much real and tangible. It is for this reason that I view religion as a tool. Some have used it as a source of motivation to work towards the advancement of humanity. Others have used it to justify horrible deeds. These are both realities of religious faith. Religion is only as wicked or as righteous as the deeds of the believer. This duality is even found in the Bible. God in the Bible is both a vengeful and jealous creator who frequently punishes those who disobey his commands. Yet, God in the Bible is also presented as a loving and forgiving God who was willing to sacrifice his own son for the redemption of humanity.

One criticism which atheists raise of religion is that all religions cannot be true. It is certainly the case that all religions cannot be true, but I do not think that necessarily makes them totally false either. By this, I mean that even if a religion is not literally true, there still may be some moral or philosophical value found in the religion. For example, if Jesus never existed at all—a position which some have argued—it would not invalidate the positive values of the teachings which are attributed to Jesus in the gospels of Matthew, Mark, Luke, and John. It is the case that religious tales and characters do not have to be real for the values or morals of the religion to be real. There is a philosophy of religion which, I would argue, still maintains its validity even if one dismisses the stories as being purely mythological.

Obviously, the premise that Jesus never existed would be unacceptable to a Christian who believes that Jesus was not only a historical figure, but the Messiah as well. For Christians, the doctrine of Christ is not merely a philosophy, but it is the sole path to salvation (John 14:6). What matters for such believers is not what can be proven about the existence of Jesus, but what is to be believed about Jesus. What matters is faith in Jesus. Rex Nettleford explained: "An immaculate conception, a resurrection, and an ascension may be challenges to historical investigation, but not to faith. Faith has a unique approach to facts."

The debate around the historicity of Jesus is due to the way that his life was documented. Matthew, Mark, Luke and John are the four gospels which tell the story of Jesus' birth, his preaching, death, and resurrection. These gospels were written after Jesus' death, so they do not provide actual contemporary accounts of Jesus while he was alive. Moreover, the gospels were written as religious texts which were meant to portray Jesus as the Messiah who was sent as a fulfillment of God's prophecy to the Israelites.

One of the texts in the Bible where this prophecy is to be found is in Isaiah 9, where God proclaims that a child will be born who will be called the prince of peace. This child was also prophesized to reign over David's throne with justice. In 2 Samuel 7:8-16, God promised David that when David's days are over, God will raise up a successor to David. This successor will establish a house in God's name and will be God's son. Through this new king, David's kingdom will be established forever.

Not only is Jesus' birth framed as a fulfillment of the prophecies of the Old Testament, but many aspects of Jesus' life and works continue themes mentioned in the Old Testament. For example, Jesus being forced to hide in Egypt to escape the wrath of Herod invokes the story of how Moses was hidden in a basket to escape the wrath of the Pharaoh who ordered that every Hebrew boy should be killed. Many of Jesus' miracles are also continuations of the type of miracles which prophets of God performed in the Old Testament. In 2 Kings 5, Elisah heals a man named Naaman who was suffering from leprosy. In Luke 17, Jesus heals ten men with leprosy. Elijah raises the son of a widow from the dead (1 King 17:17-24) and Jesus raises Lazarus from the dead (John 11). And much like how Elijah is taken up to heaven in a chariot, Jesus ascends to heaven as well.

Jesus' narrative also continues the theme of the Jewish rejection of the prophets of God. Elijah was threatened by the queen Jezebel for his preachings (1 Kings 19:1–4). The people of Judah reacted to Jeremiah's prophecies by threatening to kill him because he prophesied against the city of Judah (Jeremiah 26). Jeremiah's life was saved because of some leaders who recounted that when Micah prophesied about the destruction of Jerusalem, King Hezekiah did not put him to death. Jeremiah had previously been beaten and put in stocks for his prophecies (Jeremiah 20). Nehemiah 9:30 explains that God had patiently sent prophets to warn the Israelites, but the prophets were ignored. Psalm 118:22-

23 explained that the stone which is rejected by the builder has become the cornerstone due to the Lord's work. Jesus, like the prophets before him, was a rejected stone.

Paul not only had a major role in the spread of Christianity, but he also authored many of the books found in the New Testament. Paul, who was originally known as Saul, was not one of the Twelve Apostles. According to the Book of Acts, Saul was someone who persecuted Christians due to his zealous commitment to Judaism (Galatians 1:13-14). This changed when Paul was encountered by a vision of Jesus. Saul became baptized and began to preach that Jesus was the Messiah. Acts 9: 22-25 explained that there was even a conspiracy to kill Paul on the part of Jews who were baffled by Paul's growing influence, demonstrating that Paul too became another rejected prophet.

I mention all of this to demonstrate that Jesus' life as depicted in the gospels served as a continuation of certain themes found in the Old Testament. If Jesus was indeed a literary creation, then these similarities could be seen as an attempt by the writers of the gospel to draw a connection between Jesus and the prophets of the Old Testament in order to present Jesus as the fulfillment of the prophecies mentioned in the Old Testament. Like the prophets of old, Jesus was a miracle worker who was rejected and persecuted by God's chosen people.

The point here is that everything that is known about Jesus' life comes from books which were written as religious propaganda to spread the doctrine of Christianity. This does not necessarily mean that everything about Jesus written in those books was fabricated or that Jesus himself never existed, but it is also important to understand that the gospels were not written during Jesus' lifetime. They were written by individuals who never met Jesus, but were convinced of his divinity. Again, I state that even if there was no historical Jesus, it would not negate the validity of Jesus' teachings as conveyed in the gospels.

Religions generally concern themselves with morality; with how humans ought to treat each other. This imposed not only a duty to avoid mistreating others, but also a duty to act in service of those who are in need or of those who are being mistreated.

Religions also uphold a certain moral standard. This includes sexual morality which is an important aspect of Abrahamic religions. The Bible and the Qur'an both express the view that fornication and adultery are sins. Chapter 24 of the Qur'an instructs that men and women who engage in fornication and adultery be given one hundred lashes. This is actually a less harsh punishment than the Book of Leviticus which offers death as the punishment for adultery. Both the Bible and the Qur'an mandate that sexual relations between a man and a woman be done only through the bond of marriage.

The reason for the harsh punishments on those who failed to uphold sexual morality seems to have been out of a desire to protect the family institution by ensuring that children are not born out of wedlock. The strict laws against adultery are to protect the institution of marriage by ensuring that married couples remain faithful to each other. It also protects the feelings of the parties involved, as the feeling of betrayal that adultery can invoke in a relationship is a very painful one.

The particular concern with sexual morality in Abrahamic religions is interesting given that many of the prominent figures in these religions fall short of such moral standards. David very infamously committed adultery and then had the husband of the woman he committed adultery with killed to cover his actions. Genesis 38 conveys the story of Tamar who married Judah's son Er. Er was later killed by God for being wicked and Er's brother Onan was instructed by Judah to impregnate Tamar. Onan refused and he was put to death by God for refusing to impregnate his brother's wife. Later in the story, Tamar disguises herself and Judah mistakes her for a prostitute. When Judah finds out that Tamar engaged in prostitution and became pregnant, he was ready to burn her to death until he realized that he was the one who impregnated her. Tamar later gave birth to Judah's twins. The only thing which saved Tamar's life was that she had sex with Judah. Otherwise, Judah, who engaged with prostitutes, would have had no problem with putting his daughter-in-law to death for prostitution.

The sexual morality imposed within Abrahamic religions also included a prohibition against homosexuality. The Book of Leviticus in the Old Testament of the Bible commanded the

Israelites to kill men who had sex with other men. The tale of Sodom and Gomorrah also exemplifies the opposition towards homosexuality which is found in Abrahamic religions. Genesis 19 noted that the men in Sodom wanted to have sex some of the men who were staying with Lot. Jude 7 indicates that Sodom and Gomorrah were destroyed for sexual immorality. The Qur'an, chapter 7:80-84, explained that Lot scolded the men of Sodom because they lusted after other men rather than women.

Religions are a product of the cultures which produce them. Likewise, the conceptions of God in each religion are also culturally relative. Whereas many African religions viewed God as a distant creator being who is not actively involved in human affairs, the Abrahamic creator is depicted as being involved in human affairs. This is why God in the Old Testament is frequently punishing humanity for its rebellion. Genesis 6 tells the story of God wiping out most of humanity with a flood. Humanity became so wicked that God regretted creating humanity, but God spared Noah because Noah found favor in God's eyes. Humans repopulated after the flood, but Genesis 11 explains that humanity tested God's patience again by trying to build a tower to reach the heavens, so God created separate languages among humanity to prevent humans from completing the tower—this is a myth designed to explain the different languages among humans.

The values and ethics of a religion comes from the culture from which the religion emerges. God in this context is a philosophical concept which represents the highest aspirations of a culture. I am not referring here to the concept of God as a literal divine being or divine source, although I am not arguing against such a belief either. What I am suggesting is that God as a philosophical concept represents the greatest aspirations of a particular culture or society. Thus, to be godlike is to represent the highest expression of human consciousness or what Abraham Maslow referred as self-actualization. Religion at its best leads individuals to this elevated consciousness. I am also aware that religion at its worst leads to dogmatism, dangerous superstation, and violence. This is the duality of religious faith.

Central to the philosophy of most religions is the idea of an eternal human soul. The concept of the soul is one which suggests that there is a spiritual essence of a human being which transcends our physical self. In many religions, it is believed that the soul lives on after the human being dies. One obviously cannot know what happens to a person after death because no one has ever returned from the dead, yet there are those who came close to dying and have reported being able to see or communicate with deceased loved ones. Those who have near death experiences also reported seeing a being of light.

Dr. Pim Van Lommel began studying near death experiences after reading a book on the topic. He began to ask some of his patients about their near death experiences. Their responses led him to become curious because what his patients were telling him contradicted the generally held view in the scientific community that individuals could not experience consciousness during cardiac arrest.

In 1988, Dr. Lommel engaged in a prospective study of patients who experienced near death experiences. He noted such experiences were generally viewed as being the result of hallucinations, the effect of drugs, or lack of oxygen. Prior to this, no scientific study had been conducted. From these studies, Dr. Lommel concluded that there was no physiological explanation for such experiences.

One interesting feature of near death experiences which Dr. Lommel noted was that those who have experienced them reported feeling connected to the consciousness of others. What Dr. Lommel described here was that those who had such experiences came to understand the interconnected nature of human existence; the understanding that we do not exist as individuals, but that our lives are connected to others.

In Christianity, Islam, and many traditional African religions, the understanding of human existence is that we are born into the world, we die, and our soul returns to the realm from which our souls came. Upon this return, our souls are then judged based on the actions which we undertook during our lives. Interestingly, some who have experienced a near death experience have recalled undergoing a life review. The understanding is that what we do during our lifetime will determine what happens to us in eternity. Not all religions believe in an afterlife, however. The Bafia people did not believe in an afterlife. The Nation of Islam also taught that there was no afterlife. The Nation of Islam's view on the matter was that the resurrection of the dead mentioned in the Bible described not a physical resurrection of the dead, but rather a mental resurrection.

65

THE CASE AGAINST COLONIALISM

In an article published in *Third World Quarterly* titled "The Case for Colonialism," Bruce Gilley attempted to not only defend colonialism as something which was a benefit for the nations which were colonized by the Western powers, but he also advocated for a return of colonialism. Gilley opened his piece by writing: "For the last 100 years, Western colonialism has had a bad name. Colonialism has virtually disappeared from international affairs, and there is no easier way to discredit a political idea or opponent than to raise the cry of 'colonialism'." He continued to note that Helen Zille was vilified for attributing Singapore's success to its ability to build on the "valuable aspects of colonial heritage".

I will state here that the problem with Zille's remark is that Singapore was given the ability to build on the positive aspect of its colonial heritage. Africa was not afforded the same opportunity. This is a point which Gilley consistently ignored throughout his defense of colonialism. For example, Gilley wrote: "Patrice Lumumba, who became an anti-colonial agitator only very late, praised Belgian colonial rule in his autobiography of 1962 for 'restoring our human dignity and turning us into free, happy, vigorous, and civilized men.'" Lumumba was anti-colonial in that he wanted his nation to be independent from colonial rule, but Lumumba was not seeking to completely sever ties with Belgium. Lumumba was willing to work with the West. It was Belgium and the United States which conspired to have Lumumba eliminated.

Amilcar Cabral is another example. Gilley wrote: "In launching a guerrilla war against Portuguese rule in 1963 Cabral insisted that it was 'necessary to totally destroy, to break, to reduce to ash all aspects of the colonial state in our country in order to make everything possible for our people'." What Gilley leaves out is that Cabral launched a guerilla war out of necessity. Cabral would have preferred a peaceful transition to independence. Even as he engaged in a war with Portugal, Cabral continued to insist that he was combating Portuguese colonialism, not Portugal or the

Portuguese people.

Independence for Guinea-Bissau was a necessity. Gilley claimed that colonialism "quadrupled rice production" and "initiated sustained gains in life expectancy" but this must be viewed within the context of the exploitation and abuses which were inflicted upon the people of Guinea-Bissau. Colonialism restricted Guinea-Bissau's true developmental potential because the economy was structured to benefit the colonial powers at the expense of the people of Guinea-Bissau. Thus, Barbara Harrell-Bond and Sarah Forer explained that "instead of being able to concentrate on growing their own subsistence foods, African farmers were forced in a variety of ways to concentrate on cash crops, rendering them victims of the commercial companies which were expanding their exploitation of the economies of the colonies." They continued to note: "Cash-cropping soon reduced the variety of foodstuffs grown and adversely affected the nutritional standards of the peasants." Gilley mentioned the increase of rice production as if it was a positive metric, but Harrell-Bond and Forer pointed out that growing only rice resulted in the food needs of the peasants of Guinea-Bissau being inadequately met.

This was not only an issue in Guinea-Bissau, but in other colonies as well. In the Gambia, for example, Gambians were made to abandon the cultivation of rice to produce groundnuts. Rice had to imported. In Guinea, Africans in the Futa Jallon area produced rubber, which led to a rice shortage in 1911. Rice in Guinea had to be imported as well. Gilley praised rice production in Guinea-Bissau, but neglected to mention the determinantal impact which the colonial mode of production had on food production in African colonies.

Gilley mentioned that the "war killed 15,000 combatants (out of a population of 600,000) and at least as many civilians, and displaced another 150,000 (a quarter of the population)." This was a war which was waged by Portugal to maintain its control of Guinea-Bissau. The human cost of the war demonstrated the fact that the colonial powers were largely unconcerned with the number of Africans who were killed. As was already noted, Cabral himself hoped to maintain good relations with Portugal. It was Portugal which made this reality an impossible one.

What is astonishing is that Gilley mentioned Cabral's war against the Portuguese, but in the same article he also suggested that colonialism cost Europe more than Europe gained from colonialism, which is why Europeans "gave up their colonies so easily, as Wu also showed with regard to the Dutch surrender of Taiwan." The Dutch may have surrendered Taiwan, but that was not universally the case for other colonial powers. Portugal would not give up its colonies without a war. Likewise, France went to war to maintain Algeria. Britain developed the practice of imprisoning anti-colonial advocates in an effort to stifle the anti-colonial movement. This is an example of how Gilley was extremely selective in his handling of colonialism.

In the course of the war Cabral was assassinated. Gilley rightfully noted that once Guinea-Bissau became independent, rice production fell and that this was accompanied by the violent repression of dissidents. Gilley suggested that confused Marxist scholars blamed the legacy of colonialism for Guinea-Bissau's struggles following independence, but the legacy of colonialism certainly did not help. Portuguese rule in Guinea-Bissau was brutal, which is hardly surprising given that Portugal itself was under the authoritarian rule of Antonio Salazar.

Gilley ignored the reality that many former colonies inherited violent and repressive colonial institutions. Take for example Haiti, where leaders such as Toussaint Louverture and Jean Jacques-Dessalines developed a state which resembled France under the rule of Napoleon Bonaparte. Toussaint and Dessalines made an important contribution to the liberation struggle by combating slavery in Haiti, but the success of their military struggle was limited by their inability to develop a model outside of the colonial system which they inherited from France. The same problem existed in Africa, where colonialism eroded existing political institutions and replaced those institutions which were much more repressive.

Gilley perplexingly described Haiti as a nation without a significant colonial history. This is rather odd considering that Haiti waged a war for its independence and then spent several generations after independence struggling with the legacy of

French colonialism. He also included Libya among the list of nations which had no significant colonial history. This is also perplexing. Italy gained control over Libya in 1912 after signing a treaty with the Ottoman Empire which effectively granted control of Libya to Italy. What followed was the Italo-Sanusi War which lasted from 1914 until 1917. The second Italo-Sanusi War began in 1923. The second war lasted until Umar al Mukhtar was captured and executed in 1931. Italian rule did not end until 1947 when Italy was made to renounce its claims to its African colonies as a condition for losing World War II. Libya finally became independent in 1951. One supposes Gilley made this suggestion on the basis that Haiti became independent before most other Caribbean nations did and that Libya became independent before many other African nations did, but it is strange to suggest that nations with a history of combatting colonialism could be described as nations with no significant colonial history.

Gilley described the post-colonial struggles of Guinea-Bissau as "the half-century anti-colonial nightmare of Amilcar Cabral." This is dishonest because Amilcar Cabral never had a chance to govern an independent Guinea-Bissau. It is difficult to determine if Guinea-Bissau could have avoided its post-colonial struggles had Amilcar Cabral not been assassinated. We will never know because he was killed by the very colonial forces he was fighting against. Colonialism developed the habit of eliminating the more visionary leaders in Africa. Gilley argued: "For 60 years, Third World despots have raised the spectre of recolonization to discredit democratic oppositions and ruin their economies." Gilley neglected to mention that many of these despots have been able to remain in power and suppress democratic opposition with the assistance of Western nations. For example, when Lumumba was assassinated, Western governments gave full support to Joseph Mobutu, in spite of the human rights abuses which took place under his leadership. Gilley neglected to mention this history.

Gilley stated: "Scholars in full Eurocentric mode prefer to churn out books on colonial atrocities or to suggest that 'colonial legacies' have something to do with the follies and body blows inflicted on these countries by their anti-colonial leaders." Such scholars would be correct, but Gilley preferred not to address the nature of the colonial legacies in the colonies. Gilley argued that the problem in post-colonial nations is that too many of them are stuck in anti-colonial protest identities. Gilley did not provide specific examples to illustrate this point, however.

It is not clear how Gilley defined "anti-colonial" because he argued that "otherwise liberal and democratic states such as India, Brazil and South Africa continue to style themselves as enemies of Western colonialism." It is not apparent how Brazil can truly be regarded as an enemy of Western colonialism considering that Brazil has kept the racist system of Western colonialism in place, resulting in continued racism against the black population in Brazil. A stronger case could be made for South Africa styling itself as an enemy of colonialism, but given the Western support for apartheid in South Africa, could one fault South Africa for taking a critical position of the West?

Gilley cited Chatterjee Miller who argued that "the foreign policies of these former colonies continue to be driven by a sense of victimhood and entitlement rather than rational self-interest or global responsibility." Gilley failed to provide a specific example of what a foreign policy driven by "victimhood" looks like. Is a "victimhood" foreign policy one which sustains a close bond to the former colonial powers or is it one which seeks to break the connection to the former colonial power? Gilley did not elaborate. Gilley mentioned Zimbabwe as being an example of a nation which is a voice of anti-colonialism, but for much of Robert Mugabe's leadership he retained such a close connection to Britain that he was even knighted by Queen Elizabeth. Mugabe, who received a mission education, also retained the Christian faith of the missionaries.

Mugabe's relationship with Britain eventually deteriorated following Mugabe's controversial fast track land reform program. When Zimbabwe found itself in economic turmoil, Mugabe blamed the turmoil on Britain and the World Bank. Britain again became a target for blame by Mugabe when his party, ZANU-PF, narrowly won a majority of seats in 2000. Mugabe charged that Britain and other forces were attempting to overthrow him by supporting the political opposition. Mugabe also charged that the opposition leader Morgan Tsvangirai was a puppet who served the interests of the British and the white settlers.

Mugabe used anti-colonialism to deflect away criticisms of his policies which had a detrimental impact on Zimbabwe's economy, but he was a leader who actually embraced the colonial system rather than breaking away from it. Mugabe mobilized the security forces in Zimbabwe to intimidate and attack his political opposition just as the colonial state of Rhodesia did. Mugabe was himself detained along with hundreds of others by Ian Smith's government after Smith banned Mugabe's party. Mugabe was detained for ten years along with Joshua Nkomo before both men were released. After being released in 1974, Nkomo was willing to enter negotiations, but Mugabe committed himself to a revolutionary struggle against white rule.

In 2007, as part of the "Save Zimbabwe Campaign," Mugabe sent riot police to arrest demonstrators. The demonstrators were taken to a police station where they were beaten. Tsvangirai arrived at the police station to investigate and he too was seized. He was held down and beaten. Mugabe admitted to telling the police to beat Tsvangirai. The election which was held in 2008 witnessed a campaign of terror in which villagers were beaten to intimidate them into voting for Mugabe. A number of MDC organizers were abducted and killed. The violence worked as Tsvangirai pulled out of the election for avoid more bloodshed. Mugabe did not inherit a democratic political system. Rather, he inherited a system which was decidedly repressive and undemocratic. It is for this reason that the violence which Mugabe unleased upon his citizens could rightfully be viewed as part of the legacy of colonialism.

Gilley argued that it was the responsibility of the West to help former colonies "kick the habit" of victimhood. Gilley explained: "After all, Britain's rise is surely inseparable from the ways that it embraced and celebrated its colonisers from the Romans through to the Normans. If anti-colonial sentiments had gone unchallenged in Britain, the country today would be a backwater of druid worshippers." By comparing Western colonialism in Africa to the Roman colonization of Britain, Gilley exposed his superficial understanding of colonialism in Africa.

Colonialism by its very nature involves a degree of force and exploitation. Western colonialism in Africa was not unique in this respect. What made Western colonialism in Africa unique was its racism. The doctrine of racism meant that Africans were not only viewed as subhumans, but that Africans could never be fully accepted as citizens within the colonial empire. When Roman rule expanded into Britain, the British underwent a process of Romanization in which the British adopted aspect of Roman society such as Roman clothing, baths, and Roman temples. The British were able to become fully recognized Roman citizens. This was never the case for Africans in the European colonies.

Another important difference is that after the fall of the Roman Empire, Britain was effectively free to develop its own system. In Africa, a number of powerful states were once colonies or tributaries, but upon freeing themselves they were able to develop into powerful states themselves. For example, Kush was once under the domination of Egypt. The powerful Songhai Empire was once ruled by Mali. It is true that it was sometimes the case that nations which were formerly subjugated could become powerful states themselves, but this did not happen following the end of European colonialism in Africa for a particular reason. Following independence in Africa, the colonial powers of Europe continued to interfere in Africa's politics. Very often, this interference meant toppling leaders who were viewed unfavorably and supporting those who were viewed favorably by the West.

Gilley quoted Chinua Achebe who stated that it "is important to face the fact that British colonies were, more or less, expertly run." Achebe had more to say on this matter, however. In an interview with Barbara Ellington, Achebe stated: "We all are disappointed that things are not going well in Africa now. But we understand why, and one of the reasons is the nature of independence that was granted to the various colonies." He continued to explain: "The weaknesses specifically built into the newly created independent states are now showing." Achebe also added: "Part of the hoax called independence, is to give us leaders who do not understand what happened to us. As long as they are running things, they run Africa to the ground. We have to understand leadership more broadly than just one person in one country."

The remarks which Achebe made to Ellington are important for understanding the lingering impact of colonialism. The struggles which many former colonies in Africa experienced are the result of the fact that British colonialism was expertly run. It was designed to allow the colonial power to effectively exploit the resources of the colonies. This system continued even after African nations became independent. What changed was that the system of exploitation was directly overseen by African leaders who continued to use colonial institutions to repress their own citizens. In some parts of Africa, independence was followed by instability and civil war. This is hardly surprising given that most African nations were arbitrability created by the colonial powers, as well as the fact that the colonial powers often exploited ethnic differences to sustain its rule.

Gilley stated: "Colonialism is credited with near-magical powers to sweep away everything good in its path (like tribal chiefs or ethnic identity) and with equally magical powers to make permanent everything bad in its path (like tribal chiefs or ethnic identity)." What Gilley described as magical powers was actually the expert management which Achebe mentioned. It is not so much that colonialism swept away the good and made the bad permanent. Colonialism swept away that which threatened to undermine colonialism, while entrenching that which upheld colonialism. Not everything which colonialism swept away was good, but what was bad was the loss of African sovereignty.

Gilley overlooked the real impact that colonialism had on the lives of African people. For example, he argued that the abolition of slave-trading was an undoubtable benefit of colonialism. The problem here is that the colonial powers of Europe were the ones who not only developed the Transatlantic slave trade, but they sustained it for several centuries, often violently suppressing acts of resistance by African leaders who tried to oppose the slave trade. Thus, Gilley wanted to give colonialism credit for an injustice which colonialism itself developed and benefitted from.

The "bad" of colonialism would also include those killed in the Congo under the rule of King Leopold II and the Belgian state or those killed by the Germans in Namibia. This violence is not offset by some supposed benefits such as expanded education or improved public health, especially considering that by the time of independence, many Africans nations were still underdeveloped. In Tanzania, for example, Julius Nyerere noted that most adults were illiterate and the nation only had a few graduates.

Gilley was largely unconcerned with the "bad" aspects of colonialism. Despite the fact that Belgian rule in the Congo resulted in millions of Congolese being killed, Gilley suggested that "the Belgians should come back." Gilley also quoted Van Reybrouck who concluded that since Congo became independent, Congo "never had an army comparable in efficiency and discipline to the former [Belgian colonial] *Force Publique*". The Force Publique was responsible for the atrocities which were inflicted on the Congolese. If anything, the instability in Congo due to violent rebels would indicate that the Congolese learned very well from the Belgians.

Gilley very deliberately avoided mentioning the true violent nature of colonialism because to do so would weaken his argument that colonialism was a benefit for the colonized and that it should return. Using Gilley's logic, one could also call for a return of Nazism considering that under Adolf Hitler's leadership, Germany had a very efficient and disciplined military which rivaled the military power of Britain. Such a call would obviously require ignoring the millions killed by the Nazi regime and the disastrous results of World War II. Likewise, calling for the return of Belgium rule in Congo similarly requires ignoring the millions killed and the instability which colonialism in the Congo caused.

Gilley does not completely avoid the topic of colonial violence. Gilley attempts to justify colonial violence as being necessary to secure order. In the case of Kenya, for example, Gilley quoted Daniels who suggested that "[h]ad the British left Kenya to the Mau, there would have been anarchy and further civil war, perhaps even genocide". There is no basis for this claim whatsoever. The fact is that the Mau Mau was a rebel movement which was formed specifically to combat the British. After Kenya gained independence, the Mau Mau did not cause any anarchy or civil war. Most of the Mau Mau rebels returned to civilian life.

In Gilley's view, the violence utilized by the British to put down the Mau Mau was justified. Gilley does not mention that the Mau Mau resorted to violence after the nonviolent methods of those such as Harry Thuku were suppressed with violent force by the British. The violence of the Mau Mau was a response to the violence of the British colonial state. Gilley stated that "the independent Kenyan government long applauded the historic contribution of the British in suppressing the movement." The same independent Kenyan government which praised in the British for suppressing the Mau Mau betrayed the very struggle which the Mau Mau waged.

Those who defend the supposed modernizing aspect of colonialism are arguing that colonialism was the only means by which Africa could have modernized, but the reality is that colonialism actually hindered modernization in Africa. In *How Europe Underdeveloped Africa*, Walter Rodney pointed out that African rulers were often very willing and eager to adopt the technological advances of the West, but this process was hindered by the fact that West was more interested in exploiting African labor and resources than developing Africa. In the previously mentioned book, and in *A History of the Upper Guinea Coast*, Rodney demonstrated that the slave trade had a determinantal impact on Africa, but African rulers engaged in the slave trade because they wanted European goods and slave trading was the form of trade which Europeans were most interested in engaging in.

The example of Ethiopia under Menelik II's leadership demonstrated that African leaders were eager to embrace European technology and adapt it to their own societies. Colonialism slowed this process by restricting the ability of Africans to adopt European technology. Gilley also mentioned "female rights" as a gain under colonialism, but this ignores the reality that in some parts of Africa colonialism actually resulted in women losing certain rights. These examples indicate that far from progressing Africa, colonialism actually hindered African development in a number of ways.

A. Abu Boahen noted that existing pre-colonial industries in Africa produced items such as building materials, soaps, beads, iron tools, and cloth. These industries were not promoted or modernized during the colonial period. Boahen explained that "these crafts and industries were all virtually killed as a result of the importation of cheap commodities produced on a mass basis into Africa. African technological development was thereby halted and was never resumed until after independence."

Boahen also noted that whatever economic growth was achieved during the colonial period was done at an unjustifiable cost to Africans who endured "compulsory cultivation of certain crops, compulsory seizure of land, forced movements of populations with the consequential dislocation of family life, the pass system, the high mortality rate in the mines and on the plantations, the brutality with which African resistance and protest movements generated by these measures were suppressed, etc." Yet another issue is that monetary policies tied the currencies of the African colonies to that of the colonial powers, which further entrenched the colonial domination of African economies.

Gilley stated that "rule has often been legitimate in world history because it has provided better governance than the indigenous alternative." The problem is that Gilley spent very little time addressing indigenous governance. He appeared to be working from the assumption that "European colonialism appears to have been highly legitimate and for good reasons." If this was the case, why then did Africans put up such fierce resistance against colonialism? Moreover, if colonialism was legitimate, why then did the colonial powers have to resort to such brutal methods to sustain colonial rule?

Gilley argued that certain areas should be recolonized. The reality is that if colonialism failed the first time, there is no reason to believe that it would work again. Gilley acknowledged that recolonization would require making colonialism acceptable to the colonized. Gilley held the view that "colonialism usually spread with a significant degree of consent from politically salient actors." Such a remark obviously ignores the numerous wars which were fought in Africa by those who were opposed to colonialism. The violence and racism of colonialism was what made colonialism unacceptable to the colonized, and Gilley's obvious disregard for the harmful legacy of colonialism only further reinforces the fact that Western colonialism in Africa is rooted in a lack of recognition of the humanity of African people.

What needs to be done is not a return to colonialism because colonialism never truly ended. Kwame Nkrumah coined the term "neo-colonialism" to describe the post-colonial relationship between Africa and the West. This is a relationship which has been marked by the continued exploitation of Africa by Western powers. Gilley argued: "The notion that colonialism is always and everywhere a bad thing needs to be rethought in light of the grave human toll of a century of anti-colonial regimes and policies." I would argue that the human toll has come from regimes which have not been anti-colonial enough. What Africa needs is not recolonization, but a complete decolonization.

66

KWAME NKRUMAH: THE PAN-AFRICANIST AND THE STATESMAN

Ali Mazrui argued that Kwame Nkrumah was a great Gold Coaster for leading the country to independence, he was a great African for working hard to keep Pan-Africanism warm as a political ideal, but that Nkrumah fell short of being a great Ghanaian. Nkrumah himself dismissed Mazrui, describing Mazrui as one of the "black neocolonialist intellectuals". In a separate letter, Nkrumah dismissed Mazrui's writings as "thrash".

Nkrumah had good reason for feeling this way considering that Nkrumah had been overthrown in an American backed coup and Mazrui's article on Nkrumah in *Transition* was part of a number of publications which the magazine made which were critical of Nkrumah. This included publishing an interview with K.A. Busia, who would later become the prime minister of Ghana. Busia was questioned about Mazrui's essay which described Nkrumah as a Leninist czar. Busia responded that Mazrui had made Nkrumah a better Leninist than he actually was. Busia also argued that socialism was "not compatible with the megalomaniac search for eminence of one individual."

Another essay titled "Did Nkrumah favour Pan-Africanism?" was written by a white journalist with ties to the Central Intelligence Agency named Russell Warren Howe. Howe charged that Ghana under Nkrumah's leadership was a "typical fascist state." Howe went further to charge that Nkrumah was not a Pan-Africanist at all because Nkrumah actually wrecked African unity. Howe also depicted Nkrumah as being mentally unbalanced.,

In "Kwame Nkrumah and Ali Mazrui: An Analysis of the 1967 *Transition* Debate," Michael O. West explained: "Howe's article ranked high on the list of the absurd. It truly qualified as trash, the language Nkrumah used to describe Mazrui's essay. Not just by comparison, but also on its own terms, Mazrui's essay was a model of credible (if debatable) analysis and balance, rendering unwarranted Nkrumah's characterization of it. Even Nkrumah's most rabid critics, like the Ghanaian military men who staged the

360

coup against him, refrained from treading where Howe did."

In her response to Howe's essay, Ama Ata Aidoo criticized Mazrui and "all other objective and non-partisan African intellectuals and journalists who make the writing and publication of papers like Mr. Howe's possible." Munhamu Utete was even more direct by arguing that Mazrui had reproduced "all the innuendo, baseless insinuations, and propaganda slanders of world imperialist and reactionary circles that Nkrumah oppressed the people of Ghana." The view among some was that by writing an essay which was critical of Nkrumah, Mazrui had aligned himself with the imperialist and reactionary forces which opposed Nkrumah.

The negative responses to Mazrui's essay were valid, especially considering that his essay became the basis for Howe's piece on Nkrumah. Even so, I would argue that Mazrui did raise an interesting point by separating Nkrumah's anti-colonialism and Pan-Africanism from Nkrumah's role as the political leader of Ghana. This distinction demonstrated the complexity of Nkrumah's legacy in Africa's politics. Nkrumah was indeed a committed anti-colonial revolutionary and Pan-Africanist, but his tenure as a statesman who led Ghana's government could rightfully be criticized for certain missteps on Nkrumah's part.

In the first place, Nkrumah pursued economic policies which were misguided. In *Personal Rule in Black Africa*, Robert Jackson and Carl Rosberg argued that realistic economic principles "were never understood by Nkrumah". They noted that under Nkrumah's leadership, Ghana developed into a dirigiste state in which there was an increase in the government budget, but a decrease in capital expenditures. Yoichi Mine summed up Nkrumah's time in office as follows: "Nkrumah's personal cult, intolerance, and economic mismanagement had accumulated strong discontent among civil servants and army officials."

Apart from the poor management of Ghana's economy, there was also the question of how to effectively implement socialism in Ghana. Selwyn Ryan argued that Nkrumah struggled with this because "cadres were scarce" and that Nkrumah lacked a secure base of power "outside of those who benefitted directly from his regime." Walter Rodney noted yet another mistake which Nkrumah made while he was in power in Ghana was that he failed to fully accept the idea of class struggle in Africa. Rodney argued that it was only after Nkrumah was overthrown by a reactionary petty bourgeois coup d'etat that Nkrumah became convinced that there was a class struggle in Africa, and that this class struggle required leadership which was loyal to workers and peasants.

Indeed, it was after the coup that Nkrumah published books which explored his vision for a Pan-African revolution rooted in a class analysis of African society. One such book was *Class Struggle in Africa*. In the book, Nkrumah explained: "Class divisions in modern African society became blurred to some extent during the pre-independence period, when it seemed there was national unity and all classes joined forces to eject the colonial power. This led some to proclaim that there were no class divisions in Africa, and that the communalism and egalitarianism of traditional African society made any notion of a class struggle out of the question." Nkrumah continued to add that this fallacy was exposed after independence.

In tracing the origins of class in Africa, Nkrumah applied a Marxist understanding of history to argue that at the opening of the colonial period, Africa was passing through the stage of communalism and that feudal relations were emerging. This was true of certain parts of Africa where large kingdoms and empires had emerged, but there were other societies which remained more decentralized. Nkrumah is correct to note that colonialism resulted in the collapse of communalist socio-economic patterns as export crops were introduced. The economies of the colonies also became interconnected with world capitalist markets.

Nkrumah expressed the view that in all non-socialist societies there are two main classes; the ruling class and the subject class. The difference between the two is that the ruling class possess the major instruments of economic production and distribution, whereas the subject class serves the interests of the ruling class. Nkrumah argued that in pre-colonial Africa where capitalism had not emerged, there were only "embryonic class cleavages." These class differences fully developed due to the era of colonialism, creating an identifiable class of proletariat and bourgeoisie.

One aspect of how colonialism altered social relations in Africa is that it eroded certain democratic features of African societies. Nkrumah noted that before the colonial period, the power of ruling chiefs was limited. This was due to the fact that the "stool" and not the chief was sacred. Moreover, there was a council of elders which exercised control. Nkrumah noted that colonialism developed a system of indirect rule which reinforced the power of the chiefs. These chiefs became known as "warrant chiefs."

This system in which the power of the ruling class was limited by a political body such as a council existed to check the power of ruling monarchs was replaced with what Nkrumah described as "a veneer of Parliamentary democracy concealing a coercive state run by an elite of bureaucrats with practically unlimited power." Nkrumah argued that this ruling class also slavishly accepted the ideologies of the capitalist world, while developing ideologies of its own which reinforced the capitalist structure in Africa. One such ideology was that of "negritude" which Nkrumah dismissed as a "bogus" pseud-intellectual theory which served as a bridge between the African middle class and the French cultural establishment. Nkrumah also dismissed "African socialism" as being meaningless and irrelevant because it was used to deny class struggle in Africa.

Nkrumah also criticized the armed forces and police, which he explained came into existence as part of the colonial coercive apparatus. Considering that Nkrumah was overthrown in a military coup, the chapter in *Class Struggle in Africa* which addressed the problem of the role of the armed forces in carrying out coups was of personal significance for Nkrumah. Nkrumah noted that in instances where the armed forces do engage in coups, in most cases "there has been no mass participation." This is because the armed forces generally do not overthrow existing states on behalf of the masses. Nkrumah pointed out that armed forces in Africa are deliberately alienated from the masses because a large number of them are illiterate and are taught to obey orders without question.

Concerning imperialist backed coups such as the one which overthrew Nkrumah, Nkrumah explained: "Reactionary, pro-imperialist coups signify that imperialism and its internal allies, being unable to thwart the advance of the masses and to defeat the socialist revolution by traditional methods, have resorted to the use of arms." Nkrumah viewed this as a last ditch stand by the indigenous exploiting class and the neocolonialists to preserve the reactionary status quo. Nkrumah noted that from January 1963 to December 1969, Africa had experienced twenty-five coups, as well as a number of coup attempts and assassination attempts. In Nkrumah's view, such coups would continue until the political unification of Africa is achieved.

Nkrumah concluded that socialist revolution was needed to empower the masses and to bring an end to the capitalist exploitation of Africa. In Nkrumah's view, the socialist revolution in Africa "must be based on the peasantry and the rural proletariat." Nkrumah noted that this was the class which formed the overwhelming majority of Ghana's population. This is where we see a break between Nkrumah's policies as the political leader of Ghana and Nkrumah's vision as a revolutionary Pan-African theorist because Nkrumah's policies in Ghana were criticized for neglecting the rural areas of the country to concentrate on developing the urban areas of the country.

As the president of Ghana, Nkrumah was not focused on developing the rural areas, but in *Class Struggle in Africa*, Nkrumah identified the rural workers in Ghana as forming the class which served as the basis for the socialist revolution in Africa.

It was in *Handbook of Revolutionary Warfare* that Nkrumah promoted his vision for what the socialist revolution in Africa is to look like. Nkrumah was developing a manual of guerilla warfare prior to being overthrown in 1966. The handbook which he published represented a new approach to the topic of revolutionary armed struggle.

Nkrumah affirmed the Pan-African nature of the revolution he promoted when he declared: "The Black Power movement in the U.S.A., and the struggles of peoples of African descent in the Caribbean, South America and elsewhere, form an integral part of the African politico-military revolutionary struggle. Our victory will be their victory also, and the victory of all the revolutionary, oppressed and exploited masses of the world who are challenging the capitalist, imperialist and neo-colonialist power structure of reaction and counter-revolution." Nkrumah called for the development of the All-African People's Revolutionary Army (AAPRA) to carry out establishing the objectives of the liberation movement, which Nkrumah defined as nationalism, Pan-Africanism, and socialism. Nkrumah noted that socialism implied common ownership of the means of production and planned methods of production by the state.

In *Class Struggle in Africa*, Nkrumah explained that the army is part of the class struggle because it represents one class or another. The AAPRA was intended to represent the African masses in their struggle against the ruling class. Nkrumah explained that the aim of the AAPRA was to unify the liberation forces to carry the armed struggle through to final victory. He also advocated for the creation of the All-African People's Revolutionary Party (AAPRP) to "co-ordinate policies and to direct action." In addition to training fighters in combat, Nkrumah also wrote about the need to provide political education as well so that every fighter understood against whom they are fighting and why they are fighting.

Nkrumah died in exile in 1972. He was never able to reclaim state power in Ghana. His vision for the development of the AAPRP persisted, however. Kwame Ture, who was formerly known as Stokely Carmichael, became an organizer for the AAPRP. Ture himself made the distinction between Nkrumah as a statesman and a revolutionary Pan-Africanist when he argued that Nkrumah sacrificed Ghana for Africa.

Ture was attempting to frame Nkrumah being overthrown in Ghana as an act of sacrifice in which Nkrumah gave up his power in Ghana for Africa. This was a somewhat misleading analysis, however. Nkrumah being toppled in Ghana was not an act of sacrifice on Nkrumah's part. Nkrumah did not intend to surrender power in Ghana. This was demonstrated by the fact that his objective while he was in exile was to be restored to power in Ghana. Even if one takes the position that Nkrumah's overthrow was somehow a sacrificial act done for the sake of Africa, one struggles to see how Nkrumah being overthrown was beneficial for Africa in the long-term. If anything, losing Nkrumah's government in Africa was a blow to the revolutionary Pan-African movement.

Ture's line of defense for Nkrumah being overthrown may not

have been convincing, but the implication of his manner of defending Nkrumah demonstrated that in Ture's view, Nkrumah's most significant contribution to Africa was his revolutionary Pan-African vision and not the work that he did as president of Ghana. This line of defense seemed to reinforce the distinction Mazrui made between Nkrumah as an African and a Ghanian. Their intentions were clearly different, however. Whereas Mazrui offered a critique of Nkrumah's time in power in Ghana, Ture was defending Nkrumah by suggesting that Nkrumah being overthrown was an act of sacrifice on Nkrumah's part rather than being the product of the mistakes which Nkrumah made.

Nkrumah certainly made a number of missteps in Ghana—some of which have been recounted here. Yet, for all that could be said of Nkrumah's mistakes as a political leader, few leaders in Africa matched Nkrumah's genuine commitment to the complete liberation and unification of Africa. In short, it could accurately be stated that Nkrumah was a better Pan-Africanist than he was a president of Ghana.

67

THE POLITICS OF INDIFFERENCE

Wilt Chamberlain was one of the most successful players in the history of the National Basketball Association. He enjoyed success off the basketball court as well. Chamberlain became a successful businessman after his retirement. This included buying a nightclub called Big Wilt's Smalls Paradise. Chamberlain also owned race horses, real estate and invested in stocks. Chamberlain did well for himself financially, which is why it was so easy for him to remain silent on racial issues. At a time when the civil rights movement was taking place, Chamberlain preferred to remain silent.

Bud Furillo stated that he enjoyed that Chamberlain never brought up racism. That a white man would make such a remark would indicate that Chamberlain allowed himself to symbolize the "safe" athlete. Whereas Muhammad Ali was someone who did denounce racism and took a stand against the Vietnam War, Chamberlain would not upset white people or make them feel uncomfortable by denouncing the abuse of black people. Yet, even Furillo seem to have found it odd that Chamberlain became a supporter of Richard Nixon. Chamberlain, who was silent on racism, received criticism from the black community for publicly endorsing Nixon as president. John Lewis explained that it was disappointing that someone like Chamberlain would support the opposition.

Chamberlain defended his support for Nixon by claiming that black people should try to infiltrate the Republican Party to get the most out of their votes. He was not wrong in theory. The problem was that Chamberlain demanded nothing from the Republican Party for the black vote. At the time, the majority of black voters supported the Democratic Party because that was the party which not only expressed more support concerning civil rights, but had also passed civil rights legislation. There is a great deal the Democratic Party at the time could be criticized for in relation to its policies towards black people, but the point here is that the black vote shifted towards the Democratic Party largely because of what Democrats were doing for black people.

Chamberlain defended his support of Nixon as an action undertaken to empower black people, but in reality, it was Chamberlain supporting his own self-interests. Chamberlain was successful enough as a basketball player and a businessman that he saw no need to pursue radical change, so he avoided supporting the civil rights movement and opted to vote for Nixon.

Harry Edwards stated that Chamberlain was a phenomenal athlete who became less relevant off the court. Edwards argued that perhaps being a great athlete was enough, but I would disagree. One of the reasons why slavery was so dehumanizing is that it reduced black people to being labor. We were viewed as little more than beasts of burden. To suggest that being a great basketball player is enough, in my view, only continues this historical legacy of dehumanizing black people by reducing us to our physical labor and nothing else. Too many athletes are conditioned to believe that their only contribution to society is to provide entertainment to spectators through their athletic skill.

I would argue that an athlete must not only strive to be a great athlete, but to be a great human being as well and to make a contribution to the advancement of humanity. This cannot be done by remaining indifferent to the suffering of others. As Farida Nabourema put it, "I genuinely believe that every human being is supposed to be an activist because an activist is just somebody who believes in justice." She continued to explain that "when you are a human being you have to leave a legacy and that legacy is to leave the world better than you found it." We must transcend the politics of indifference to make a real impact in the world.

68

ON PAN-SLAVISM

Pan-Slavism developed as a movement which sought to unite the Slavic peoples of Europe. The movement came to prominence at a time when most Slavs found themselves under the subjugation of others. The South Slavs were under Turkish Ottoman rule. The western Slavs were part of the German dominated Hapsburg Empire. Poland was divided between the Hapsburg Empire and Russia. Russians were the only Slavic group at the time which was not under foreign rule. Russia posed an important challenge among those who advocated Pan-Slavism. Russia was the only Slavic nation which was not under foreign control, yet Russia was not actively pursuing a program to unite and liberate the Slavs. Russia's domination over Poland further complicated the Pan-Slavic project.

At a Slav Congress in Prague in 1848, Mikhail Bakunin expressed his vision for Slavic unity. He later elaborated on this vision in a pamphlet titled *Appeal to the Slavs*. In this appeal, Bakunin explained: "[W]e made a strong appeal to that great Russian people which, alone of all the Slavs, has been able to preserve, its national existence. We entreated the Russians to give serious thought to what they know only too well-that their nationality and their greatness mean nothing so long as they themselves are not free, so long as they permit their power to be used as a scourge against unhappy Poland and as a perpetual threat to European civilization."

Bakunin's vision found little support among the leaders who organized the Slav Congress in Prague. Bakunin's vision was also criticized by Frederich Engels in an article titled "Democratic Pan-Slavism." Engles explained: "There is not a word about the actually existing obstacles to such a universal liberation, or about the very diverse degrees of civilisation and the consequent equally diverse political needs of the individual peoples. The word 'freedom' replaces all that. There is not a word about the actual state of things, or, insofar as it does receive attention, it is described as absolutely reprehensible, arbitrarily established by 'congresses of despots' and 'diplomat': To this bad reality is counterposed the alleged will of the people with its categorical imperative, with the absolute demand simply for 'freedom' ...."

The Marxist critique of Bakunin's program was that he called for the unity of all Slavs without regard for class. In reality, most Pan movements seek to unify a group on the basis of a shared identity. Such a unity can at times obscure real class divisions within the group. Even so, the advocates of Pan-Slavism saw themselves as representatives of all Slavs, including the oppressed opposed. Walter Rodney explained that the "Slav intelligentsia who advocated Pan-Slavism were spokesmen of emergent bourgeois forces in the clash against feudalism, and their position also reflected some sympathy for the oppressed peasantry since it was in the interests of capitalism that serfdom be removed."

Pan-Slavism struggled to gain support outside of the intelligentsia which Rodney mentioned. The Austo-Hungarian Slavs felt that it was more realistic to remain loyal to the Austro-Hungarian monarchy. In Russia, the Pan-Slavic movement was limited and received no official support. Bakunin envisioned not only Russian support for Pan-Slavism, but also the establishment of a democratic republic in Russia. Such a viewpoint was obviously unpopular with the Russian Tsar. Bakunin was later arrested and imprisoned. It was under these conditions that Bakunin produced a confession to the Tsar in which he admitted his guilt.

Pan-Slavism also developed as a movement which positioned itself against Germans, who were presented as the enemies of the Slavic people. Danilevsky argued that Slavic unity was necessary to defend Slavic culture. He argued that whereas Romano-Germanic culture was individualistic and egocentric, Slavic culture was marked by a spirit of national unity and Orthodox Christianity. Bakunin similarly framed Pan-Slavism in opposition to German culture when he stated: "Hatred for the Germans is the primary basis of Slav unity and mutual understanding among the Slavs." Jan Kollar's *Slavy Dcrea* depicted Germans as the traditional enemy of the Slavs. George Guins noted that hatred "towards the Germans had been the most effective unifying stimulus among Slavs." Hatred for Germans was not enough to establish a political base for Pan-Slavism, however. The Russian Revolution exposed this.

The success of Lenin's revolution in Russia was an ideological blow to the doctrine of Pan-Slavism. Rodney noted that the advocates of Pan-Slavism had failed to unseat the indigenous and external feudal oppressors, including the Slavic ruling class in Tsarist Russia. The failure of the Balkan bourgeoise to carry out the task of national liberation and unification created a situation in which it "was left to the Balkan masses under working class leadership albeit under conditions of war to tackle effectively the problem of nationalism and of broader eastern European unity in the period after the Second World War."

The federation of Slavic countries finally came with the emergence of the Soviet Union. This was not a federation based on Slavic unity or identity, however. Guins explained that the Soviet Union was more interested in "unification through the understanding of class interests and class solidarity, not through national kinship." Under Soviet policy, Pan-Slavism was utilized merely to advance the Soviet Union's communist vision. This was a vision which concerned itself not with the regional unification of Slavs, but with the struggle of the proletarian International. This vision not only included Slavic nations, but also non-Slavic nations as well.

For a Pan movement to be successful, it must have a clear basis for unification and establish a base of support. Pan-Slavism developed as a movement supported by the intelligentsia, but it never developed a real support base among the Slavic masses or the Russian ruling class. As Guins noted, Russia never "evidenced, at least officially, any desire to swallow all Slav nationalities or even unite them into one Slav union." Bakunin himself abandoned Pan-Slavism following the Polish uprising against the Tsarist autocracy in 1863. His vision for a Pan-Slavic unity led by a democratic Russia never came.

Bakunin later advocated for anarchy and became an ideological rival to Karl Marx. It is rather ironic that the success of Russian Revolution was not only a blow to the Pan-Slavic vision which Bakunin once advocated, but it was also a blow to anarchism in

Russia given that the Bolsheviks were able to garner a larger mass following than the Russian anarchists did.

References:

George Guins, "The Politics of 'Pan-Slavism'," 1949.

Spartacist League, "Marxism vs. Anarchism," 2001.

Walter Rodney, "Aspects of the International Class Struggle in Africa, the Caribbean and America," 1974.

69

THE COMPLEX LEGACY OF JOHN MAGUFULI

Since the 1960s, Africa has produced many flawed leaders who had great visions, but whose policies and approaches to leadership often fell short of fulfilling the visions which they articulated. One such leader was Kwame Nkrumah. Nkrumah had a grand vision for Africa. He argued that Africa must unify in order to truly liberate itself from colonialism. Nkrumah's setback was that his economic policies resulted in Ghana becoming both bankrupted and deeply in debt to the very imperialist entities which Nkrumah decried. This is why I have argued that Nkrumah was a better revolutionary Pan-African theorist and visionary than a statesman.

Sekou Toure similarly advocated for a revolutionary and anti-colonial Pan-African vision. This vision made him a target. He experienced attempts to sabotage Guinea's economy, as well as several assassination and coup attempts. The result of all of this was that Toure established a dictatorship in which dissent was brutally repressed in the name of protecting Guinea's revolution, although Toure would himself betray the revolution when he began to move away from socialism in favor of a pro-Western, capitalist approach to development.

Julius Nyerere of Tanzania promoted a socialist vision for Tanzania which encouraged national unity and self-reliance. Nyerere oversaw an improvement in healthcare and education, but these gains were financed through foreign aid which placed Tanzania in further debt. Nyerere also had the tendency to be autocratic. This resulted in stifling criticisms while continuing to stubbornly pursue economic policies which were not particularly effective. To his credit, Nyerere did eventually peaceful relinquish power rather than dying in office or being removed by force as is often the case for African leaders.

Haile Selassie inherited a feudal monarchy. He developed the reputation of being a reformer who sought to modernize Ethiopia. He was also respected—and deified among some—for his commitment to Pan-African unity and his support for anti-colonial causes. Selassie's setbacks were that his reforms were too gradual, he was too much of an autocratic, and he displayed a callous indifference to the suffering of the Ethiopian masses. His autocratic approach also resulted in him sometimes using unnecessary force to suppress dissent, and his desire to consolidate power over Eritrea resulted in a costly war for both nations. He remained a popular Pan-African figure outside of Ethiopia, but in Ethiopia he was a divisive ruler who was overthrown in a military coup.

Patrice Lumumba was a genuine nationalist who wanted his nation to be both united and free from foreign domination, but Lumumba proved to be too mercurial and too inexperienced to confront the many obstacles which he found himself facing in Congo. Samora Machel of Mozambique was a revolutionary leader who came to power after waging a struggle against the Portuguese. Machael remained committed to anti-imperialism, but under his leadership Mozambique struggled economically. Of course, in fairness to Machel, he did have to contend with destabilization efforts from South Africa and a costly civil war, but some of his misguided policies certainly contributed to Mozambique's struggles.

Nelson Mandela was a courageous and committed revolutionary who spent more than two decades in prison for the struggle against apartheid. Mandela emerged victorious and became the president of South Africa. He served one term and then relinquished power, rather than clinging to power as so many other African leaders have done. During his short time in power, Mandela did implement some important policies, but Mandela, who was ideologically moderate, did not pursue a sweeping change of South Africa's system. Mandela also failed to crack down on corruption within his party. The issue of corruption would only worsen in the years following Mandela's departure from power. Mandela occupied a rather interesting position of being too moderate for some of his critics who denounced him as a sellout, while being too radical for others.

Robert Mugabe rose to power as a revolutionary soldier who fought against white rule in Rhodesia. Once in power, Mugabe developed a repressive dictatorship and oversaw the economic collapse of Zimbabwe due to some of his policies. Mugabe's most controversial measure was the Fast Track Land program which was designed to take land away from white settlers and return the lands to African people. The problem with the policy is that it descended into a violent land grab which largely benefited the political elite and those who were loyal to Mugabe. And unlike Mandela who resigned from power after one term, Mugabe was forced out of power in a coup after clinging to power for decades.

I have argued that Thomas Sankara was the most outstanding political leader which Africa has seen in the post-colonial period largely because he was an anti-imperialist leader who avoided many of the mistakes made by the leaders whom I previously listed. He avoided Nkrumah and Nyerere's economic failures, while also avoiding descending into the type of repressive despotism that some others engaged in. If anything, one might argue that Sankara was not forceful enough as he was aware of the conspiracy against him, but he refused to act on it. Sankara preferred to be a martyr than to compromise the revolutionary ideals which he believed in.

There are also the leaders who are less overtly anti-colonial. These were leaders who maintained a more favorable disposition towards the West. Rather than seeking to break the Western domination of Africa, such leaders have utilized their connections with the West to fund their development programs. A typical example of this type of leader was Félix Houphouët-Boigny. In Côte d'Ivoire, Houphouët-Boigny produced what was known as the "Ivorian Miracle" because he managed to build a nation which was economically successful relative to his African neighbors. The problem was that his model was not sustainable and collapsed after he died.

Sir Seretse Khama led Botswana to independence. Khama, who was married to a white woman, oversaw the development of a nation which has been more stable and peaceful than many other African nations. Botswana has also struggled with poverty, wealth inequality, and its dependency on exports has resulted in a situation where the San people were dispossessed of their land.

Paul Kagame in Rwanda came to power following the horrific massacre in 1994. Under his leadership, Rwanda has not only seen a return to peace, but he has also managed to lift a significant number of Rwandans out of poverty. Kagame managed this with the assistance of Western foreign aid. Western governments, leaders, and institutions have praised Kagame while also largely ignoring some of Kagame's repressive measures, including imprisoning political opponents and instances where critics of Kagame's have died under mysterious circumstances. Some of these critics charge that Kagame's policies have impressed Westerners, but have not done enough to improve the lives of ordinary Rwandans.

Tanzania's John Magufuli is an interesting case. He is a leader who is regarded as having left a mixed legacy and it is not difficult to understand why. When Magufuli came to power in Tanzania, he immediately addressed corruption, laziness, and wasteful spending within the government. His commitment to avoiding wasteful spending was demonstrated when he canceled independence day celebrations because he felt that the revenue would be better spent improving the lives of Tanzania citizens. The money was instead spent on expanding a road in Tanzania to reduce traffic congestion. In lieu of an independence day celebration, Magufuli urged that citizens come out to clean up their country. Magufuli led by example by taking to the streets to join his citizens in the cleaning effort. Magufuli's reduction of wasteful spending also included forcing government officials to fly economy and reducing the size of his own presidential convoy.

There was also an incident in which Magufuli made a surprise visit to a hospital. When he saw the horrible conditions of the hospital, including patients on the floor, he fired the director of the hospital. He also demanded equipment which was not working be repaired otherwise the new director of the hospital would be fired as well. This was very encouraging to Africans who are not accustomed to seeing leaders in Africa take such an approach to leadership. Magufuli seemed to be a man who was committed to improving the conditions of his people. This approach to leadership drew some comparisons to Sankara.

Another aspect of Magufuli's presidency which was comparable to Sankara was his desire to break the foreign control over African economies. The Economic Partnership Agreement (EPA) was developed to establish an economic partnership between East

Africa and the European Union. The deal was signed by Rwanda and Uganda, but Magufuli denounced the deal by comparing it to colonialism. He was concerned that giving European countries access to African markets would undermine Tanzania's development.

Magufuli, who was known as the "Bulldozer", led in a manner which was befitting of his title. Magufuli imposed his vision through force. This was praised when Magufuli forcefully tackled waste and corruption, but this forceful impulse also led him to crack down on free speech. This included closing down some newspapers and implementing internet regulations to restrict free speech. Opposition lawmakers were arrested. Some politicians, journalists, and critics went missing. Others were reportedly shot.

Whereas Sankara sought to change Burkina Faso's institutions, Magufuli's campaign for change was driven solely by his personal dictates. An example of Magufuli's approach to change was demonstrated during the inauguration of a new bridge. During the ceremony, Magufuli publicly mentioned to the crowd before him that the bridge was built through fraud. He then used the occasion to publicly fire the official on the spot. There was no investigation.

P.L.O. Lumumba compared Magufuli to Julius Nyerere. Nyerere could be autocratic himself, although Nyerere was not as forceful in suppressing criticism as Magufuli was. Magufuli created a political environment of fear and paranoia that Tanzanians were not familiar with. One could perhaps argue that Magufuli's intolerance to criticism was a product of his impatient desire to produce meaningful change for Tanzania. The problem was that, as opposition parliamentarian Zitto Kabwe argued, such an undemocratic approach is not sustainable. The effort to crack down on corruption on Magufuli's part was not an effort conducted through institutional changes, but was done through decrees and arbitrary terminations without an official investigation or due process.

What makes Magufuli's legacy so complex is that his crackdown on corruption and inefficacy made him popular because this approach was so unlike the trend of corruption and waste that has unfortunately become typical in Africa, yet his autocratic tendencies were disappointingly very typical of the manner in which many African leaders governed. Both tendencies were driven by Magufuli's philosophy regarding leadership, which is that leadership is purely the product of individual decision making rather than the actions undertaken by an individual leader within the confides of existing norms and institutions.

The complexity of Magufuli's legacy is also related to the fact that his forceful approach to power was not backed by any discernible ideological vision. He was not an anti-imperialist like Nkrumah, Toure, or Sankara. At the same time, Magufuli seemed more willing to challenge what he perceived as colonialism in Africa than Kagame was, as demonstrated by his criticism of the EPA which Kagame signed. This nebulous ideological approach makes it difficult to place Magufuli within a particular framework of post-colonial leadership. He was not as radical as the anti-colonial radicals, yet he also was not as moderate as those who have gained favorable reputations within the West.

70

ON THE MORALITY OF LEADERSHIP

How much does personal morality influence leadership? The answer to this varies. Immoral leaders can sometimes be otherwise effective at their work. Take for example Adam Clayton Powell whose legislative success made him a popular leader among his constituents who were willing to continue to support him in spite of certain unbecoming aspects of his personal conduct. There are other instances where immorality on the part of a leader can become too much of a distraction or even disrupt the work which the leader is trying to undertake.

Elijah Muhammad offers an interesting example given that he was a religious leader who imposed a strict moral code within his organization. This became a problem when Malcolm X was forced out of the Nation of Islam. After facing threats against his life, Malcolm publicly disclosed that he felt the attacks on him were due to the fear that Malcolm might expose that Elijah Muhammad had fathered several children with women in the Nation of Islam.

For some time, there were problems within the Nation of Islam concerning women being impregnated by the same man. Malcolm became aware of these rumors, but he never imagined that the man who was impregnating these women was Elijah Muhammad himself. Malcolm explained that Wallace Muhammad was the one who first informed Malcolm that Elijah Muhammad was the father of the women. In a documentary titled *Make It Plain*, Wallace Muhamamd confirmed that he gave Malcolm information about his father's domestic life, but he noted that he only did so after Malcolm had witnessed the situation himself.

Malcolm recalled that when he confronted Elijah Muhammad about this, Elijah Muhammd compared himself to Prophet Muhammad who had several wives. He also compared himself to David and Solomon. The problem with this comparison was that women proved to be the downfall of David and Solomon. The actions of David and Solomon created disunity and chaos among their people. Elijah Muhammad's actions also created disunity and disruption within the Nation of Islam.

Another example of how immorality can hinder leadership is Benjamin Chavis, Jr. He served as the youth assistant to Martin Luther King and was a director of the National Association for the Advancement of Colored People. He was forced to resign from the NAACP in 1994 after it was disclosed that he had used organizational money to pay a settlement to a woman who accused him of sexual harassment. Not only was this action immoral, but it was also harmful to the interests of the organization as he was taking funds away from the organization to spend it on his personal interests. He later joined the Nation of Islam, but left following another sexual misconduct allegation. Leaders cannot be and will never be morally perfect, but the expectation of leaders is that they be effective enough at their work so that their moral failures do not adversely impact their work or their organizations.

71

MARCUS GARVEY'S APPEAL

Despite the lynchings and other brutalities which African people endured in America, Marcus Garvey still continued to believe that he could appeal to the soul of philanthropic, liberty-loving white America when he declared: "I appeal to the considerate and thoughtful conscience of white America not to condemn the cry of the Universal Negro Improvement Association for a nation in Africa for Negroes, but to give us a chance to explain ourselves to the world." Garvey also stated in his appeal: "I do not desire to offend the finer feelings and sensibilities of those white friends of the race who really believe that they are kind and considerate to us as a people; but I feel it my duty to make a real appeal to conscience and not to belief."

Garvey also understood that this appeal needed to be accompanied by a forceful demand for independence. He declared: "They said we were heathens; we were pagans; we were savages and did not know how to take care of ourselves; that we did not have any religion; we did not have any culture; we did not have any civilization for all those centuries, and that is why they had to be our guardians. Well, we are satisfied that they were our guardians for all this while, because we did not have the civilization; we did not have the culture; we did not have the Christianity. But thank God we have them all now, as we are asking that you hand back to us our own civilization—hand back to us that which you have robbed and exploited us of in the name of God and Christianity for the last 500 years. We are asking England to hand it back; we are asking France to hand it back; we are asking Italy to hand it back; we are asking Belgium to hand it back; we are asking Portugal to hand it back; we are asking Spain to hand it back, and by God, the Moroccans made them hand it back."

Garvey's gratitude to our "guardians" may have been made in a wry manner considering that Garvey had also complained that the white world tried to discredit black history. Garvey declared:

"Every student of history, of impartial mind, knows that the Negro once ruled the world, when white men were savages and barbarians living in caves; that thousands of Negro professors at that time taught in the universities in Alexandria, then the seat of learning; that ancient Egypt gave to the world civilization and that Greece and Rome have robbed Egypt of her arts and letters, and taken all the credit to themselves."

The point about guardians aside, I bring attention to the fact that Garvey praised the rebellion in Morocco against Spanish rule. Garvey appealed to white America in hopes that white America would support Garvey's endeavors, but he also understood that force would be required if white people were not willing to support the demands for an independent Africa.

In a speech delivered at Liberty Hall in 1922, Garvey explained: "The U.N.I.A. is preparing to go the way of all other peoples who have fought for liberty. We are preparing to go the way of George Washington and the noble patriots of this great country. It is the way of the sword and of blood." Here again, Garvey was expressing the view that African people should be willing to take up arms to fight for their liberation. Garvey's appeal to white people was done out of the desire to win over the support of those white people whom he believed would sincerely support efforts to advance the African race, but Garvey was not naïve about the realities which confronted African people. Our history demonstrates that progress could only be made through forceful struggle, not merely appeals to the conscience of white people alone.

72

PROPERLY UTILIZING HISTORY

In his book *The Falsification of Afrikan Consciousness*, Amos Wilson stated: "Mere knowledge, morality, values, though of great importance are not going to be enough to extricate us from the situation that we are in." He was referring to nationalists who concern themselves merely with educating black people on the greatness of our history without also engaging in a program which seeks to improve the actual material conditions of the people. He also asked: "Is our study of Egyptology a persona and collective defense mechanism, a means of dealing with our hurt pride? [...] Is our hang-up with history and the exaggeration of certain of our achievements means by which we try to salvage a damaged ego?" Amos Wilson was making the argument that the glorification of our history was done as a way to salvage a damaged ego by some individuals who promoted history in a manner which was disconnected from the material conditions which confront us today.

This is not to suggest that history cannot serve the role of instilling a sense of pride in African people. To some degree, utilizing history as a means to restore the pride of African people is a necessary exercise to combat the legacy of colonialism which instilled in the minds of African people the notion that we are lacking a history. We have to go beyond this, however, to view history not only as a celebration of past achievements, but also as a blueprint for development.

73

RACISTS AND SEX

In *The Psychopathic Racial Personality*, Bobby E. Wright argued that white racists display certain psychopathic traits in their treatment of black people. One example which Wright provided is the history of sexual abuse inflicted against black women. Wright noted that psychopaths are usually "sexually inadequate with a very limited capacity to form close interpersonal relationships." Wright viewed practices such as streaking, swapping mates, and orgies as "a desperate attempt to achieve meaningful relationships" on the part of the white people who engage in such actions. Wright argued that the rape of black women was also part of this attempt by racist psychopaths to achieve sexual gratification.

Even as racists engaged in such abuses of black women, they also justified the castration of black men as an attempt to contain the "animal passions" of black men. This concern with containing the sexuality of black men was also rooted in a fear of sexual relations between black men and white women. In *Black Skin, White Masks*, Frantz Fanon explained: "We know historically that the Negro guilty of lying with a white woman is castrated. The Negro who has had a white woman makes himself taboo to his fellows." Fanon also argued that this act of castration was an act of annihilating the very manhood of black men. René Etiemble explained: "Racial jealousy produces the crimes of racism: To many white men, the black is simply that marvelous sword which, once it has transfixed their wives, leaves them forever transfigured."

The system of white supremacy was one which brutalized black women, while also holding the view that the sexuality of black men must be kept in check through violent force. Fanon noted that white women developed their own perspectives on the sexuality of black men. Fanon noted: "The women among the whites, by a genuine process of induction, invariably view the Negro as the keeper of the impalpable gate that opens into the realm of orgies, of bacchanals, of delirious sexual sensations." In his autobiography, Malcolm X recalled a white woman who was known as "Alabama Peach." Of her, Malcolm stated that "she started hearing older girls in grade school whispering the hush-hush that 'niggers' were such sexual giants and athletes, and she started growing up secretly wanting to try one." Malcolm explained that her first experience with a black man was one who worked for her father. She threatened that if she refused to have sex with him, she would accuse him of attempted rape.

74

FROM BLACK POWER TO NKRUMAHISM

Kwame Ture's embrace of Pan-Africanism represented a logical development in his political ideology. As the chairman of the Student Non-Violent Coordinating Committee, Ture, who was then known as Stokely Carmichael, popularized "Black Power." Black Power represented a radical demand for change in America. It also represented a demand for change which was more forceful than the nonviolent approach which Martin Luther King and others represented.

Ture's role in the civil rights movement of the 1960s was unique in the sense that he represented a bridge between the nationalists and the integrationists. This ideological conflict was perhaps best represented by the ideological differences which existed between Malcolm X and Martin Luther King. SNCC was founded with the assistance of Ella Baker. Baker had served as a member of King's Southern Christian Leadership Conference. In 1960, a group of college students protested against segregation at a lunch counter. Baker decided to leave SCLC to help the students organize.

Ture eventually became a member of SNCC. As was noted before, his leadership helped to shift SNCC in a more radical direction. He worked with King and other civil rights leaders, but Ture never fully embraced King's nonviolent tactics nor King's vision for integration. Instead, Ture promoted armed self-defense and rebellion. Rather than integration, Ture preached black empowerment and control.

Ture's vision was expressed in *Black Power*, which was co-written with Charles Hamilton. In the book, they argued that black people "must begin to think of the black community as a base of organization to control institutions in that community." After moving to Guinea and working with Kwame Nkrumah, Ture's vision expanded. He embraced Pan-Africanism and Nkrumahism.

Ture's new direction was expressed in a speech he delivered in 1971 during Black Culture Week. In the speech, Ture argued that the capitalist system must be destroyed in order for African people to be liberated. In *Black Power*, Ture explained: "Our basic premise is that money and jobs are not the final answer to the black man's problems." In the book, Ture and Hamilton are critical of what they refer to as "welfare colonialism" which exist for the purpose of pacification rather than as a genuine solution. Ture and Hamilton note that Gandhi refused food shipments in England because he saw them as tools of pacification.

By 1971, Ture was not only criticizing federal programs which were designed to give funds to pacify the black community, but he was also criticizing the structure of the capitalist system itself. He described it as a system in which the white capitalist owns the means of production. Ture gave the example of Muhammad Ali and Joe Fraizer, explaining that the white capitalists made more money from their fight than the two boxers did, despite the fact that the white capitalist never had to train or step into the ring.

Ture was describing a system in which the capitalist owner makes most of the wealth while doing little or none of the manual labor which is done by black people who generate the wealth for capitalists. Ture made sure to distinguish his criticisms of capitalism from the Marxist-Leninist criticism of capitalism. In his 1971 speech, Ture argued that Marx and Lenin observed the relationship between capital and labor, but that they did not invent the science known as Marxism-Leninism.

Ture held the view that Africans needed to go beyond Marxism and Leninism. He stated: "Thus, if you are an African, it makes little sense for you to stop at Marxism and Leninism. You should come home to the roots. You must come to Africa. Marxism and Leninism is a science. It is an instrument, a tool, a weapon, for dissecting one's history, that's all it is." In Ture's view, coming home meant embracing not only Pan-Africanism, but the ideology of Nkrumahism. Ture envisioned Nkrumahism as an ideology which promoted socialism, but also incorporated a Pan-African vision rooted in African culture. For Ture, this meant embracing the communalistic aspects of African culture. Ture explained: "Our ancestors, being very intelligent people, knew that there could never be such a thing as private property. Nobody came with land, nobody was going to take any when they left, so how could they own the land. It was there for everybody. Thus, the land belonged to the community. The land belonged to the community. The community worked the land and the profits from the land was divided equally amongst the community. A communalistic society." Ture argued that African people must take the guidelines of communalism and bring them into modern day society.

One of the apparent weaknesses in Ture's presentation was the question of how to modernize communalism within the context of an industrialized society. Marxists dealt with this problem by holding the position that overthrowing capitalism to produce a society which would increase productivity. As one commentator explained: "What we're ultimately about is providing all members of society, here and elsewhere, with the capacity, to do creative work, what Marx called free or unalienated labor."

Marxism-Leninism did not advocate modernizing a previous mode of production within the context of industrialization, but the development of an entirely new system which would improve worker productivity in comparison to capitalism. Ture, who was not a Marxist-Leninist, believed that African communalism served as the foundation for how to build a socialist society in which the means of production are owned and controlled by the masses.

It was not clear on precisely how Ture believed that African communalism could be adopted to an industrialized society in such a way that the masses would control the means of production. Moreover, Ture's call for the "masses" to control the means of production was also somewhat vague in comparison to Marxism-Leninism's call for the proletariat to seize the means of production.

It is worth noting that Kwame Nkrumah himself argued in *Class Struggle in Africa*: "A modern proletariat already exists in Africa, though it is relatively small in size. This is the class base for the building of socialism, and must be in the context of the international working-class movement from which it derives much of its strength." Nkrumah also argued that it is the proletariat in Africa which must be tasked with winning over the peasantry to the revolution. Whereas Nkrumah's vision for precisely which class was to lead the revolution and seize the means of production was clearer, Ture's vision was somewhat vague in that he framed his vision in terms of the masses seizing control of the means of production. Within the Marxist-Leninist understanding of class divisions, the "masses" do not represent a single class. Rather, the "masses" could comprise of several classes. After all, the anti-colonial struggles in Africa were mass struggles. Nkrumah noted that the mass nature of these struggles blurred the class distinctions which existed.

In the speech, Ture did state: "The interests of the bourgeoisie are diametrically opposed to the interests of the proletariat. Diametrically opposed. Thus, it's impossible for them to make an alliance." Ture certainly recognized the type of class divisions and conflicting class interests which Marxist-Leninists typically recognized, but Ture also viewed socialism not in terms of a seizure of the means of production by a particular class. He described a socialist society as one in which "the means of production is owned and controlled by the masses of people and the profits are divided equally among the masses." In Ture's view, this socialist society in Africa would operate as a modernized version of African communalism.

Ture's vision for how a scientific socialist society in Africa would function and what it would look like was not so clear, but his analysis of race was much clearer in his speech. Ture explained: "The African is not racist. The African is not racist because the African has never propagated a theory of pure race. The theory of pure race has always been propagated by the European, not the African." In making this statement, Ture was clarifying that the problem of racism was one which emerged from white people.

Ture argued that to effectively confront white racism, Africans in America must unite with other Africans just as Jews around the world united with "world Jewry". Ture noted that when Israel waged war with Egypt, Jews from America came to support Israel. Ture argued that Africans in America must do the same by siding with Africa.

For Ture, this was not merely a sentimental connection, but one rooted in history. He explained: "Many people when they try to analyze the problems of the African in America calls it a problem peculiar to America. They take the history back to the Africans when they came to America. That's absurd. The problem didn't start in America. The problem started in Africa when the first white man came to rape us of our continent and of our people. That's where the problem started." Ture reasoned that since the problem began in Africa, there can be no solution which did not involve Africa.

Ture also invoked the history of the slave trade to demonstrate the connection between Africans in the Caribbean and those in America. He explained: "There is no difference between us. I was born in Trinidad in the Caribbean. There is no difference between me and you. The only difference is when the slave ship got to Trinidad, they kicked me off in Trinidad and brought you here. That's the only difference. We are the same people."

Of the connection between Black Power and Pan-Africanism, Ture explained: "If you accept Black Power, you must accept Pan-Africanism because it is the logical and consistent development. The highest political expression of Black Power is Pan-Africanism. It is the logical and consistent development." Indeed, embracing Pan-Africanism did represent a logical development for Ture considering that he recognized that the struggles of African Americans was related to the collective powerlessness of African people everywhere.

75

W.E.B. DU BOIS AND RACE

In *Dusk of Dawn*, W.E.B. Du Bois explained that his paternal great-grandfather Dr. James Du Bois was a white man. James Du Bois was a slave owner in the Bahama Islands and he kept one of his slaves as a common-law wife. Together they had two sons, Alexander and John. Alexander was Du Bois' grandfather. The two boys were brought to America and were white enough to pass for white.

Du Bois explained: "If Alexander Du Bois, following the footsteps of Alexander Hamilton, had come from the West Indies to the United States, stayed with the white group and married and begotten children among them, anyone in after years who had suggested his Negro descent would have been unable to prove it and quite possibly would have been laughed to scorn, or sued for libel." Alexander did not stay with the white group, however. Du Bois noted that his grandfather married into "the colored group" and that his son did the same. Du Bois' father was born in Haiti in 1825. Of the meeting between his parents, Du Bois explained: "My father, by some queer chance, came into western Massachusetts and into the Housatonic Valley at the age of forty-two and there met and quickly married my brown mother who was then thirty-six and belonged to the Burghardt clan."

Du Bois came from a multiracial background, yet throughout his life he consciously identified with his African identity and with the African struggle. Du Bois could not recall how he came to develop his own views on race. He explained: "I do not know how I came first to form my theories of race. The process was probably largely unconscious. The differences of personal appearance between me and my fellows, I must have been conscious of when quite young." Du Bois suspected that his views on race developed due to his observation of different appearances. Du Bois' experiences at Fisk further entrenched his racial identity such that when he went to Harvard, he did not seek any contract with white students.

Du Bois' views on race were also shaped by the international nature of the racist suppression of African people. The international nature of this racist system was apparent when the United States seized control over Haiti. Du Bois explained: "The United States seized Haiti in 1915. It was not alone the intrinsic importance of the country, but Haiti stood with Liberia as a continuing symbol of Negro revolt against slavery and oppression, and capacity for self-rule; and the sudden extinction of its independence by a President whom we had helped to elect, followed by exploitation at the hands of New York City banks and plundering speculators, and the killing of at least three thousand Haitians by American soldiers, was a bitter pre-war pill."

In the same year that Haiti's independence had been snatched away by the United States, the new invention of the moving picture would help to reinforce racism in America with the release of *Birth of a Nation*. The film led to the rebirth of the Ku Klux Klan and an increase in lynchings of African Americans. The movie itself was based on the writings of Thomas Dixon. Dixon was a man who was regarded as "the most bitter and greatest arch enemy of the Negro race." *Birth of a Nation* created outrage throughout the nation, though the film was screened at the White House and received the praise of Woodrow Wilson.

That America took control of Haiti during the same year that the KKK would be reborn indicated the global connection between the struggles of African people. Du Bois, whose father was born in Haiti, was keenly aware of this connection. In 1919, following the end of World War I, Du Bois decided to call a Pan-African Congress in Paris. Du Bois recalled that the experience in Paris convinced him of the need for unity. Du Bois explained: "I was convinced, however, by my experience in Paris in 1919 that here was a real vision and an actual need. Contacts of Negroes of different origins and nationality, which I had then and before at other congresses and the Races Congress were most inspiring." Du Bois organized a second congress in 1921, which was better organized and better attended than the first congress.

As Du Bois was formulating his vision for Pan-African unity, the global European order was fragmenting. Europe had already experienced World War I prior to Du Bois' 1919 Congress. Yet a second one would follow. Du Bois understood that the unraveling of Europe during these wars was the product of its own racism. Of Hitler, Du Bois explained: "Hitler is the late crude but logical exponent of white world race philosophy since the Conference of Berlin in 1884. Europe had followed the high, ethical dream of a young Jew but twisted that ethic beyond recognition to any end that Europe wanted."

Nazism represented the tendency of racism to destroy not only black people, but white people as well. Yet despite inflicting centuries of violence against the non-white populations of the world and plunging the world into two World Wars, white people still viewed themselves as more civilized than the other races of the world. Du Bois explained this when he wrote that "Negroes in Africa, Indians in Asia, mulattoes and mestizoes in the West Indies, Central and South America, all explain the attitude of the white world as sheer malevolence; while the white people of the leading European countries honestly regard themselves as among the great benefactors of mankind and especially of colored mankind."

76

HUGO CHAVEZ'S REVOLUTION

When Hugo Chavez was elected as the president of Venezuela in 1998, he undertook a very ambitious project of transforming Venezuelan society. Chavez was a soldier who rose through the ranks of the military. In 1992, Chavez led a failed coup attempt. The attempt failed and Chavez spent two years in prison before being released. He subsequently campaigned and was elected president of Venezuela. Once in power, Chavez was free to pursue the vision for change which led him to attempt a coup in the first place.

Chavez came to power following a very difficult period in Venezuela. The economy was struggling. This forced Venezuela to seek loans from the International Monetary Fund, which resulted in the devaluation of Venezuela's currency and the elimination of subsidies for essential items. Chavez's government represented a break with these neoliberal policies.

Chavez launched a number of programs to improve conditions for the poor. This included state-subsidized food markets. The 2001 Land Law was passed to distribute underutilized rural land property to peasants. Chavez also established missions to serve poor areas in Venezuela. These missions established literacy programs, provided access to free community health care, and low-income housing construction.

Apart from addressing wealth inequality in Venezuela, Chavez also confronted the issue of race. This has been a personal issue for Chavez, who dealt with racism in Venezuela to his own mixed ancestry. Cynthia McKinney argued that Chavez did not fully embrace being "Black" until after the 2002 coup attempt which was followed by racist vitriol against him. That Chavez decided to embrace his African ancestry in response to the racist backlash he endured is interesting given that Chavez had used his marriage to a white woman to advance his political career.

It was suggested by some commentators that Chavez's marriage to his second wife, Marisabel Rodriguez, served Chavez politically. She has been described as a "trophy wife" who was utilized by Chavez's advisors during his 1998 presidential campaign. Rodriguez herself stated that she was used to lower her husband's rejection rate and to win over segments of the population that were unwilling to support him. The fact that she is a blue-eyed white woman seemed to have helped Chavez in a society where men are encouraged to marry white women to improve the race.

The marriage was one which initially served Chavez during his campaign, but Rodriguez eventually became one of his most bitter rivals. Following their divorce, the two engaged in a very public legal battle over visitation rights regarding their daughter. Rodriguez expressed concern for her safety and declared that she was a victim of harassment on the part of her ex-husband. The dispute was not merely personal, but political in nature as well as Rodriguez emerged as a vocal critic of Chavez's policies and urged voters to reject his constitutional reform.

It seemed to have become apparent to Chavez that using his marriage to a white woman did little to win over the segment of racist white Venezuelans who denounced Chavez by using terms such as "monkey". The dissolution of his marriage and his ex-wife's subsequent role as a member of the political opposition against Chavez further demonstrated the futility of his attempt to integrate himself into white society in Venezuela. It would seem that Chavez had no choice but to embrace that side of his ancestry which had been denounced by racists. As Askia Muhammad argued in *The Final Call*, Chavez used his African heritage as a bludgeon against his critics.

Chavez's embrace of his African ancestry was followed by an embrace of Africa itself. He declared: "We love Africa." This was a profound remark coming from the president of a nation which has historically sought to deny its African roots in favor of a *mestizaje* identity which privileged European roots over African roots. In 2005, Chavez established a post to handle Afro-Descendant affairs within the Ministry of Culture. In 2011, Venezuela included Afro-descendants on the census. This demonstrated that Chavez's embrace of his African roots was accompanied by policy changes which gave increased visibility to black people in Venezuela. The 2011 Law Against Racial Discrimination also demonstrated the concern with ending racism as well.

Chavez's presidency was also marked by his public criticisms of the United States. In 2006, at a speech at the United Nations General Assembly, Chavez famously called George W. Bush the devil and accused the American empire of placing humanity at risk. Chavez certainly did not hesitate to denounce American policies, yet his own position was somewhat weakened by the fact that he continued to rely on trade with America to bolster Venezuela's economy. An article in *New Yorker* explained: "If this is socialism, it's the most business-friendly socialism ever devised …. The U.S. continues to be Venezuela's most important trading partner. Much of this business is oil: Venezuela is America's fourth-largest supplier, and the U.S. is Venezuela's largest customer. But the flow of trade goes both ways and across many sectors. The U.S. is the world's biggest exporter to Venezuela, responsible for a full third of its imports. The Caracas skyline is decorated with Hewlett-Packard and Citigroup signs, and Ford and G.M. are market leaders there. And, even as Chávez's rhetoric has become more extreme, the two countries have become more entwined: trade between the U.S. and Venezuela has risen thirty-six per cent in the past year." This reality led the League for the Revolutionary Party to criticize Chavez's approach to socialism as being one which has "not reduced the level of imperialist investment and operation in Venezuela."

Chavez relied on trade with America to sustain his socialist programs in Venezuela. The rise in oil prices allowed Chavez to increase government spending. The oil revenue allowed Chavez to implement programs to address inequality and poverty, but the inability to diversify the economy proved to be a problem. The problem with Venezuela's reliance on oil was demonstrated in 2002 when workers at Venezuela's state-owned oil company rallied to force a new presidential election to remove Chavez. The workers' strike stopped oil production, which caused nearly $14 billion in lost revenue. This in turn reduced the government's capacity to push social programs. It also resulted in a scarcity of goods because the lack of petroleum meant that goods could not be transported to shops and markets.

Venezuela was also hindered by American sanctions. These sanctions were levied by President Trump in 2017. The sanctions limited Venezuela's access to American markets. This was done in an effort to pressure Chavez's successor, Nicolás Maduro, out of power. In addition to sanctions, Trump also called for an embargo against Venezuela. This policy further weakened Venezuela's economy and exacerbated Venezuela's food crisis.

There have been other factors which contributed to the food crisis which developed in Venezuela. Chavez's land distribution program resulted in violent clashes between landowners and peasant farmers. The program also faced problems with depopulating urban areas to replace the farmers in rural areas because the majority of Venezuelans moved to the urban areas to obtain easier access to subsidized goods and to find employment. The higher wages in oil producing regions in Venezuela resulted in reduced capacity and a shortage of agricultural goods. Bea Sophia Pielago concluded that "the fall of the agricultural sector could be attributed to the government's weak oversight and their mere offers of generous credit to poorly trained and inexperienced farmers."

It should seem obvious that denouncing the American president as the devil while also relying on the United States to help sustain Venezuela's economy would pose problems for Venezuela at some point, but this was the nature of Chavez's government. His socialist populism made him a target of the United States, which began plotting for ways to create regime change, including supporting the 2002 coup attempt. On the other end, Chavez's policies were also not radical enough for Marxist critics who noted that even as Chavez denounced American imperialism, he still relied on American imperialism to sustain his country's economy.

Indeed, Chavez himself saw his revolution as more of an attempt at some socialist reforms rather than a revolution in the Marxist sense. Chavez had dismissed Marxism as "a dogmatic thesis that has already passed out of style" and argued that "the working class as the motor of socialism and the revolution are obsolete." The end result was a government which implemented policies which improved the conditions of the poor through welfare programs which did not necessarily address the structural basis for the wealth inequality in Venezuela in the first place.

Chavez perhaps viewed Marxism as being dogmatic and outdated because of the fall of the Soviet Union and the general decline of Marxism-Leninism as an ideology among world leaders following the Soviet Union's fall. The question does arise, however, if Chavez rejected Marxism as an ideology, then what was the objective of the type of socialist society which he intended to build? It would seem that his vision for socialism in Venezuela was not allowing workers to take control of the means of production. Rather, his brand of socialism amounted to utilizing Venezuela's oil wealth to develop welfare programs to improve conditions for the poor. The success of the welfare programs helped to ensure that Chavez's party remained in power. The fact that these programs served a political objective is important to note as well given that Pielago also pointed out that welfare became politicized in Venezuela. Maduro introduced the CLAP program to strengthen subsidized food, but CLAP boxes were only given to those who voted for the government through their ID cards.

The League for the Revolutionary Party criticized Chavez for attempting to create socialism "within the framework of a bourgeois nationalist developmental scheme". They further criticized the fact that the United Socialist Party of Venezuela included workers and peasants, as well as sectors of the capitalist class who supported Chavez. They argued that Chavez's true allies were the capitalists. Chavez's aim was to dissolve unions into his party to put an end to union autonomy, which led the League for the Revolutionary Party to conclude that "Chavismo only has room for union and left leaders and organizations that are willing to function as tools of the bourgeois state apparatus."

In fairness to Chavez, geopolitical circumstances would have rendered more radical attempts at socialist transformation difficult. When Fidel Castro led his revolution in the 1950s, he was faced with an American embargo. The Soviet Union did provide some support for Cuba until it fell. By the time that Chavez was elected in 1998, there was no Soviet Union to provide support in the event that pursuing Marxist policies resulted in sanctions against Chavez's government. Given how damaging the sanctions which were imposed on Venezuela after Chavez's death have been, one can certainly appreciate the threat which sanctions would have posed to Chavez's government. Thus, even if Chavez truly desired to pursue a revolutionary Marxist policy of completely overturning capitalism in Venezuela, his options were severely limited by the lack of international support and the threat of American sanctions.

Chavez's revolutionary vision was one which was able to improve conditions for poor Venezuelans, but his revolutionary government was not without its contradictions and problems. Ultimately, the Bolivarian Revolution suffered from the fact that it was as contradictory as the man who initiated it.

References:

Bea Sophia Pielago, "Uncovering the 5 Major Causes of the Food Crisis in Venezuela," *Glocality*, 3(1): 4, 1–8.

Cynthia McKinney, *"El No Murio, El Se Multiplico!" Hugo Chávez: The Leadership and the Legacy on Race.* 2015. Antioch University, Doctoral dissertation

Simon Romero, "Venezuela's President Scorned by Bitter Political Foe: His Ex-Wife," *New York Times*, May 12, 2008.

"Venezuela: Chávez vs. Working Class", *Proletarian Revolution* No. 80, Fall 2007.

77

CONTESTING BOOKER T. WASHINGTON

Booker T. Washington rose to prominence as a leader of black America following his 1895 speech which was known as the "Atlanta Compromise". In that speech, Washington suggested that black people focus on acquiring wealth and education rather than agitate for political rights. This speech demonstrated Washington's own approach to addressing the race problem. Washington focused primarily on industrial training while avoiding direct agitation for political rights.

The flaw in his approach was not necessarily that Washington encouraged industrial efficiency and labor, but that his views often matched white stereotypes about black people being lazy and lacking ambition. Washington explained: "I consider labor one of the greatest boons which our Creator has conferred upon human beings." The problem for black people was not an unwillingness to engage in labor. After all, during slavery black people were made to labor without pay.

Washington understood that individuals who lacked a formal education were not stupid. Some of these individuals possessed practical skills and knowledge. He explained: "Many of these seemingly ignorant people, while not educated in the way that we consider education, have in reality a very high form of education— that which they have gotten out of contact with nature." He gave the example of an old farmer named James Hill who gave a presentation before a Farmers' Institute in which he explained that although he never studied science, he was able to make some science for himself. He went on to explain how he was able to improve the soil so that the stalk of cotton he cultivated went from only two bolls to four, and then six. He continued to process until he was able to make a single stalk of cotton produce as much as fourteen bolls.

In Washington's view it was not merely enough for a person to be educated in industry. He argued that one must become ambitious as well. In Washington's view, black people lacked ambition and that it was only through emulating the conduct of white people that black people could achieve their full potential. This is why he stated that the "trained American Negro has learned to want the highest and best in our civilization, and as we go on giving him more education, increasing his industrial efficiency and his love of labor, he will soon get to the point where he will work six days out of each week." Washington extended this view to the conditions of black people in South Africa, explaining: "They have never been educated in the day school nor in the Sunday-school nor in the church, nor in the industrial school or college; hence their ambitions have never been awakened, their wants have not been increased, and they work perhaps two days out of the week and are in idleness during the remaining portion of the time."

Ida B. Wells-Barnett was a prominent critic of Washington. She explained in her autobiography that she and her husband were involved in a discussion of W.E.B. Du Bois' book *The Souls of Black Folk*. Most of those who were present took issue with Du Bois' chapter arraigning Washington's methods, but Wells-Barnett and her husband defended Du Bois. Their view was that Washington's focus on industrial education "would mean to rob the race of leaders which it so badly needed; and that all the industrial education in the world could not take the place of manhood."

Wells-Barnett also took issue with Washington's willingness to publicly denounce black people for the benefit of white audiences. There was an instance in which Washington wrote an article in the *Christian Register* in which he claimed that two- thirds of the Negro preachers of the south were morally and intellectually unfit to teach or lead the people." Wells-Barnett held the view that it "was a wrong thing for him to have made that criticism in a white paper so far away from home." She viewed this as Washington telling "our enemies abroad."

Wells-Barnett recalled an exchange with one Mr. Sachs who attended a speech by Booker T. Washington in which Washington joked about a man whose wife left him, and that she left the chicken coop door open so that all the chickens left too. He laughed as he told the story, but Wells-Barnett was not amused. When Sachs noticed that she did not laugh at his joke, he asked her if black people accepted Washington as their leader. Wells-Barnett responded by explaining, "a great many of us cannot approve Mr. Washington's plan of telling chicken- stealing stories on his own people in order to amuse his audiences and get money for Tuskegee."

Washington's methods were effective in getting money for Tuskegee by attracting white support. Washington's views also attracted white audiences outside of the United States. Lord Grey of the British South Africa Company which controlled Rhodesiasuggested that Washington could be employed to report on the best methods "to raise, educate, and civilize the black man." Grey was even willing to pay Washington's expenses. Washington declined the offer on the ground that his main responsibility was black people in America, but he did agree to reconsider the offer.

Washington was consulted on developing a plan for education in South Africa. His advice was that black people in South Africa be taught to love and revere the English government. For Washington, doing so meant replacing the "tribal system of government". Washington also encouraged training to "fit them to go out into this rich country and be skilled laborers in agriculture, mining and the trades." South Africa had little interest in training Africans to be skilled laborers, whoever. Africans were excluded from skilled trade.

Unlike Washington, Wells-Barnett was not interested in appeasing white people. When William Monroe Trotter was being denounced by black newspapers over a disagreement between him and President Woodrow Wilson over the latter's inaction concerning racism, Wells-Barnett's organization invited him to deliver a speech. She explained: "We thought that the race should back up the man who had had the bravery to contend for the rights of his race, instead of condemning him."

Washington's views on progress for black people won him the support of white people in America and elsewhere because he did not demand radical changes, nor was he someone who advocated for direct political agitation for change. The weakness of Washington's approach was demonstrated by President McKniley's failure to respond to the Wilmington riots in which black people were killed by white mobs. Washington's accommodationist approach did not protect black people from racist violence. As Wells-Barnett pointed out, success sometimes made black people the targets of lynching. Washington was cautious about denouncing lynchings. Following the brutal murder of Samuel Hose, who was wrongfully accused of raping a white man's wife, Washington commented after T. Thomas Fortune appealed to him to do so. Washington explained that lynching injured the "moral and material growth" of the region, but he also added that black people should repudiate "the beast in human form guilty of assaulting a woman."

Wells-Barnett noted that she was not against industrial education. She explained black people objected to "being deprived of fundamental rights of American citizenship to the end that one school of industrial training shall flourish." Of Washington, he stated he should "refrain from assuming to solve a problem which is too big to be settled within the narrow confines of a single system of education."

Wells-Barnett's criticism of Washington should also be viewed within the context of the leadership void which was created by Frederick Douglass' death. Wells-Barnett's close relationship with Douglass led to some viewing her as his successor. A paper titled the *Nashville Citizen* went so far as to endorse Wells-Barnett as "the proper person to succeed Frederick Douglass as leader of the Afro-American race." Wells-Barnett seemed to have viewed herself as Douglass' successor. Following his death, she wrote: "For the first time since the burden of race defense was laid upon me, I cannot have the help and support of Frederick Douglass." Blanche Bruce was a Senator who became a critic of Wells-Barnett. He accused her of delegating "to herself the care and keeping of the entire colored population of the United States." Following Washington's famed Atlanta speech, Bruce mocked Wells-Barnett by writing, "Can it be that this new Mrs. Moses has been shelved so quickly?"

Part of the issue with Wells-Barnett's position as a leader in the black community was due to her gender. E.E. Cooper openly expressed disagreement with Wells-Barnett's election as secretary of the Afro-American Council was a mistake since, in his view, it was a man's job. Wells-Barnett's temperament also did her no favors. She developed the reputation as a leader who was not shy about criticizing those whom she disagreed with. This may have worked against her in that it alienated Wells-Barnett, but her boldness in daring to contest Washington's approach did accurately expose the weakness of his position. As Wells-Barnett so adequately understood, industrial training alone could not protect black people from racist violence.

78

THE TIME OF JUDGES

Joshua is identified in Numbers 13:1 as one of the twelve spies of Israel who were sent by Moses to explore Canaan. Joshua rose to become the leader of the Israelites following Moses' death. It was Joshua who led the Israelites in their conquest of Canaan. These conquests establish a homeland for the Israelites. This is an important moment in the Bible because it marks the fulfillment of God's promise to give a nation to the Hebrews whom God saved from captivity in Egypt. It is also important because it represents a period of turmoil among the children of Israel which results in the eventual establishment of a monarchy. The Book of Judges is set during a time when Israel had no king and instead relied on the leadership of judges who were sent by God to save the Israelites.

The first judge was Othniel. The Bible explains that by this time, the Israelites began to worship foreign gods, so God allowed them to be dominated by Cushan-Rishathaim. Othniel liberated the Israelites. This began the cycle throughout the Book of Judges in which the Israelites turn away from God only to be oppressed by their enemies until they are rescued by a judge. The next judge was Ehud who rescued the Israelites from Eglon of Moab. The Bible explained that Ehud was left-handed due to an apparent limitation in his right hand. The Bible is not clear on precisely what the problem with Ehud's right hand was. Ehud was left alone with Eglon who killed Eglon after claiming that he had a secret message.

Once again, the Israelites turned away from God. Shamgar was the next judge. Shamgar is stated to have struck down six hundred Philistines with an ox goad. A prominent theme in the Book of Judges is that some of the judges are portrayed as having supernatural abilities which allows them to overcome their enemies in combat. After Shamgar, the next judge mentioned in the Bible is Deborah. Deborah was the only female judge. Deborah is mentioned to be a prophet who held court and settled disputes. Deborah was called by God to raise an army. This army overcame the enemies of Israel only for Israel to commit more evil in the eyes of God.

The next judge sent by God is Gideon. Gideon is presented not as a brave warrior, but as a reluctant judge. When Gideon is informed by an angel that he had been selected by God, Gideon agreed to confront Israel's foes, but he asked for signs from God. He placed a wool fleece on the floor and requested for dew to be on the fleece only, while the ground remained dry. This is precisely what happened. Gideon then asked for the opposite miracle to be done, so that the fleece would be dry and the ground covered with due, which God did.

When Gideon was finally ready to confront his foes, he began with an army of 32,000 warriors which God reduced to 300 men. The 300 men were selected by how they drank water. With these 300 men, Gideon overcame Israel's foes. After his victory, the Israelites request that Gideon rule over them as a reward for saving them from Midian. Gideon refused and told the Israelites that God will rule over them. In doing so, Gideon demonstrated his loyalty to God, but he made the mistake of requesting that the Israelites each give him an earring from their share of the plunder. The rings were used to create a gold ephod which was then worshiped by Israel, demonstrating once again Israel's disloyalty to God. After Gideon's death, the Israelites begin to worship Baal-Berith as their god. The Bible also mentions that Gideon's son Abimelech attempted to seize power for himself by murdering seventy of his brothers. Jotham, who was Gideon's youngest son, escaped the slaughter. Abimelech ruled for three years before God turned the people of Shechem against him to punish Abimelech for his actions.

After Gideon, the next judge is Tola. Tola is stated to have led Israel for twenty-three years. Not much else is stated about Tola, but it appears that his rule witnessed a prolonged period of peace for Israel. This was followed by twenty-two more years of peace under Jair. This peace is broken when the Israelites again do evil in the eyes of God, which resulted in them being conquered by the Philistines and the Ammonites. When the Israelites cry out to God for help, in his anger God tells the Israelites to turn to the other gods to save them. Out of desperation, the Israelites removed the foreign gods among them to serve God. When they did this, God sent Jephthah to save the Israelites.

Jephthah was a rather unusual judge. The Bible noted that he was born to a prostitute and a man named Gilead. Jephthah was driven away by the sons which Gilead had with his wife. Jephthah was called out of exile by the very people who had driven him away so that he could fight the Ammonites for them. Jephthah overcame the Ammonites. The problem was that prior to the war, Jephthah promised to sacrifice whatever came out of his door when he returned home. When he returned home, his daughter came out to greet him. Jephthah was true to his vow and sacrificed her. The tragedy of this moment is not only that Jephthah sacrificed his daughter, but that he felt that he had to do so for God. This moment indicated that the Israelites had strayed so far from God that they were now sacrificing their children to God, despite God commanding them not to.

Ibzan was the next judge. Ibzan had thirty sons and thirty daughters. He married his children off to those outside of his clan. This would indicate that Ibzan was a judge who utilized marriage as a form of diplomacy to strengthen the bonds between his clan and other clans in Israel. Not much else is stated of Ibzan, other than he led Israel for seven years. One would assume that Ibzan secured peace in Israel through alliances forged through marriage.

The next judge is Elon who ruled for ten years. After Elon is Abdon. By this point, one gets the impression that Israel was enjoying a period of relative peace under the rule of successive judges. The final judge in the people is Samson. Samson was born to deliver the Israelites from their enemies. Samson is a powerful warrior, but his weakness proved to be his love of women. This alluded to when the Bible mentions that Samson had sex with a prostitute he saw in Gaza. He later falls in love with Delilah who learns that Samson's powers come from his hair. Samson is captured and taken into a temple where he causes the temple to collapse, killing himself and his enemies.

The Book of Judges ends with a civil war in Israel which is started by a very brutal action. Chapter 19 recounts that a Levite man was traveling with his concubine. The concubine is raped by a group of Benjaminite men. The abuse was so vicious that the concubine subsequently died. The Levite man cut the concubine up into twelve pieces and sent each piece to a different area of Israel so that the Israelites could see what had happened. The Levite informed the people of Israel of what happened.

In response to the murder of the concubine, the rest of Israel goes to war against the people of Benjamin. The war is a bloody one, which ends with Israel attacking all of the towns of Benjamin and killing everyone save for 600 men who were allowed to escape. The brutality does not end here. The men of Israel took an oath not to marry any of their daughters to a Benjamite. The people of Israel grieved for the fact that Benjamin had been isolated from the rest of Israel and the remaining Benjamite men were without wives. To resolve this problem, the Israelites attack Jabesh Gilead, killing all the men and every woman who was not a virgin. The 400 virgin women which they found were then taken and given to the remaining Benjamite men. The problem was that there were not enough women for the 600 men, so the remaining Benjamite men were instructed to seize the women of Shiloh to become their wives.

The Book of Judges concludes by stating that at the time Israel had no king and that everyone did what they saw fit. The impression given was that the lawlessness in Israel was the result of this lack of a political authority figure, when the problem was that the children of Israel had turned away from God. This is further reinforced by later stories which demonstrate that the people of Israel continued to stray away from God even after God allowed them to have a king.

As a religious text, the Book of Judges is a warning against disloyalty and ungratefulness towards God, but, as is the case with many of the books of the Old Testament, the Book of Judges is also a political text as well given that the judges are not only military leaders, but some of them serve as political leaders as well. Throughout the book, there are moments in which Israel seems to enjoy a prolonged period of stability and peace under the rule of certain judges. As was stated, Ibzan had even used his sizable family to secure alliances in Israel to sustain the peace. The problem was that the judges were not established as a permanent authority in Israel, so periods of time where Israel was without any judges often resulted in Israel falling under subjugation or falling victim to internal strife. The Bible's narrative suggests that Israel never truly needed a king, but so long as the Israelites continued to stray away from God, having a central authority under the rule of a king offered more stability than the infrequent rule of judges did.

79

RELIGION AND THE AFRICAN PERSONALITY

Na'im Akbar explained that it would be "impossible to speak accurately of Black personality without speaking of Black religion." Akbar also quoted Sterling Plump who defined Black religion as "those ways in which Black people in Africa and later in America, conceptualized to explain the universe and man's relationship to it and to subsequently govern man's relationship to man." Religion in any given society encompasses not simply belief in the divine, but also a philosophical and cultural framework for understanding the world. This is particularly true for African people given the deeply religious nature of African cultures.

John Mbiti noted that traditional religions in Africa recognized no formal distinction between the sacred and the secular. Anton Lembede explained: "Africans are a deeply religious people. To them the doctrines of Christ, Mahomed, Buddha, Confucius, do not sound strange, queer or foreign. This explains our eager and ready acceptance and adoption of Christianity." Of religion, Akbar explained: "Certainly, the most consistent characteristic of Black people throughout the world is their fervent belief and practice in some form of religion. Though the practice comes in many forms, it consistently seeks to reaffirm the notion of oneness within and between people as well as with the source of divine force that flows through all human beings."

Akbar contrasts the deeply religious nature of Black culture with that of the material definitions which predominate Western psychological approaches such as behaviorism and Freudianism. Whereas African culture did not seek to separate the religious from the secular, there arose among certain Western psychologists the view that the two were separate matters. Sigmund Freud, in particular, became a critique of religion. He wrote that "religion, consumed in moderation, stimulates the digestion, but that taken in excess it harms it." As Freud grew, so did his intolerance for religion grow to the point that he argued that religious believers should be denied the ability to attend universities.

Freud's earliest encounters with religion came from his Catholic nanny who brought him to church. Freud's parents were also Jewish, so religion was a topic which Freud was confronted with for most of his life. Despite being raised in a Jewish family, Freud violated rules for kosher meals and forbade his wife to light Sabbath candles. In 1910, Freud wrote to Carl Jung to explain: "It has occurred to me that the ultimate basis of man's need for religion is *infantile helplessness*, which is so much greater in man than in animals. After infancy he cannot conceive a world without parents, and makes for himself a just God and a kindly nature, the two worst anthropomorphic falsifications he could have imagined." In Freud's view, religion was a thing invented by the imagination of man to provide comfort. Freud ultimately believed that reason would overcome religion.

Much like Freud, Karl Marx argued that religion offered comfort. Marx went further to argue that there was a class component to religion as well, which allowed religion to be utilized as an instrument for the ruling class to subjugate the working class. Vladimir Lenin, who was influenced by Marx's theories on religion, declared: "No amount of reading matter, however enlightened, will eradicate religion from those masses who are crushed by the grinding toil of capitalism and subjected to the blind, destructive forces of capitalism until the masses themselves learn to fight against the social facts from which religion arises in a united disciplined, planned and conscious manner".

In Lembede's view, Marxism argues that "God is merely a complex of ideas engendered by the ignorance of mankind and by its subjection firstly beneath the forces of nature, and secondly, by class oppression. By spreading and disseminating scientific knowledge among the masses and by abolishing social classes, religion and belief in the gods will automatically disappear." Spreading scientific knowledge was not the only means by which communists attempted to cause the disappearance of religion. In Albania, Enver Hoxha sought to dismantle religion through brutal force.

In 1967, Hoxha declared Albania to be the first atheist state.

This was a continuation of the process of implementing atheism which became when Hoxha seized power in 1945. This hostility towards religion was informed by his admiration for Joseph Stalin. When Hoxha met Stalin in 1949, Stalin informed Hoxha to take a strong stand against religion. He also told Hoxha that the Vatican was a center of reaction. Hoxha became so hostile towards religion that he declared: "We hated religion with all the power of our reason because the revolutionary practice of our people had brought to light the profoundly reactionary and anti-popular role of religious doctrines, which supported the feudal-bourgeoisie of the country and the foreigners who oppressed us."

Hoxha's criticism of religion was not only rooted in a critique of religion for being a tool of the ruling class, but he also accused religion of providing support for the foreigners who oppressed Albanians. This was a reference to the fact that Albania had been under Ottoman rule. When Albania became independent from the Ottoman Empire, most of the population were Muslims. Hoxha also identified Roman Catholicism and the Orthodox church as foreign influences. He saw the Vatican as an extension of the Catholic Church and associated Catholicism with Italy, which was a nation that Albania fought during World War II.

The effort to abolish religion was framed in terms of being sympathetic towards believers. In a letter he explained: "Religion is the opium of the people. We must do our best so that everyone can understand it, even those who are poisoned (which are not few). We need to heal them. This is not an easy task, but not impossible." Hoxha's remark about needing to heal those who had been "poisoned" by religion masked the reality that what Hoxha truly intended was to brutally crush religion in Albania by force.

Religion was made illegal in Albania. Those who violated this law were punished harshly. Religious leaders were sent to concentration camps. It was reported that a Catholic priest had been executed for baptizing a child in a concentration camp in 1973. The *Catholic Bulletin* reported that 164 priests and bishops had been killed by the regime by 1985. The bulletin also listed 28 Muslims. Churches and mosques were also destroyed. Muslims were barred from using religious words such as "inshallah" and "mashallah." Muslims were also deliberately served food during Ramadan. The punishment for being caught with a Bible was 10 years in prison.

Hoxha opposed religion, yet his opposition to religion was rooted in his own dogmatic and zealous understanding of Marxism-Leninism. He denounced Josip Broz-Tito for revisionism and later cut ties with the Soviet Union. Hoxha also distanced himself from China in 1978. Hoxha insisted on a hardline approach to Marxism-Leninism and proved to be unforgiving of those who did not share his views. The violence of his regime also targeted those within Hoxha's own government. All of Hoxha's ministers of the interior were killed. Five of the six co-founders of the Albanian Party of Labor were killed or imprisoned, and half of the members of the Central Committee who were appointed in 1948 were executed.

Hoxha offered an extreme example of atheistic intolerance for religion, but the larger point here is that European atheists developed a critique of religion which dismissed religion as a backwards ideology which needed to be overcome by reason and science. This is not to suggest that African people have not developed their own critiques of religion, but such critiques have generally been more tolerant of religion due not only to the deeply religious nature of African culture, but also due to the fact that African people have historically been more tolerant of religious differences than Europe has been. As such, Africans often sought to resolve the conflict between religion and science in ways which acknowledged the role and function of both. This is why Lembede argued: "Religion and Science are not irreconcilably opposed to each other. Religion should remember that as the human mind progresses and explores uncharted regions of knowledge, human ideas are born, mature and 'senesce.'"

References:

Anton Lembede (author), Robert R. Edgar and Luyanda ka Msumza (editors) *Freedom in Our Lifetime*, 1996.

Christfried Tögel, "Freud and Religion," *Balkan Journal of Philosophy*, Vol. 2, 2010.

İbrahim Karataş, "State-Sponsored Atheism: The Case of Albania during the Enver Hoxha Era," *Occasional Papers on Religion in Eastern Europe*: Vol. 40, Issue 6, Article 8.

Na'im Akbar, *Akbar Papers in African Psychology*, (Mind Productions & Associates, Inc.)

80

IN DEFENSE OF KWAME TURE

David Garrow's "The Tragedy of Stokely Carmichael" was written in response to Peniel Joseph's book, *Stokely: A Life*. In his article, Garrow dismissed Stokely Carmichael as someone who became irrelevant within the black struggle. For example, Garrow quoted *The Economist* which described Carmichael as "a rather ridiculous" figure who was little more than "a nonentity" in Guinea. This was a rather odd remark to make about a man who served as the political advisor for the Democratic Party of Guinea. Garrow also quoted John D'Emilio who remarked that Carmichael "took a long, tragic detour away from political effectiveness and social influence."

Such remarks about Carmichael—who later became Kwame Ture—are misleading and unfair. It is true that by the 1990s Carmichael seemed less relevant than he had been in the 1960s as an organizer with the Student Non-Violent Coordinating Committee, but it is not because Carmichael himself took a detour. It was because he remained on the path struggling for change when so many others in the movement had changed their direction. Whereas some of the other members of SNCC such as John Lewis and John Wilson decided to join the Democratic Party, Carmichael continued to wage a struggle against the system rather than from inside of the system. Carmichael expressed the view that he was continuing the work that his colleagues in SNCC had ceased doing.

Garrow argued that by the time that Carmichael was thirty "his political obituary was all but complete." In the very next sentence, he explained that Carmichael would continue to make speaking forays to "scores" of college campuses. Garrow mentioned the outrage from Carmichael's 1986 statement that "the only Good Zionist is a dead Zionist". Garrow offers no real insight into Carmichael's specific criticisms of Zionism. The implication was obviously to present Carmichael as a man who was given to sensationalized remarks rather than an activist who was engaged in a well-reasoned political analysis of the history of Zionism and the manner in which it oppressed the people of Palestine.

Garrow also quoted the *Washington Post* which described Carmichael as giving a "rambling" talk. The speeches which Carmichael gave would indicate that his speeches were far from ramblings, but Garrow is more concerned with presenting the image of Carmichael as someone who became politically irrelevant rather than actually engaging in the substance of Carmichael's ideology and vision.

Carmichael was faced with the impossible task of being the successor to Malcolm X. This is not a task which he assigned for himself, but this is how the media saw him. In 1966, *New York Times* described Carmichael as a "new Malcolm X". Julius Lester, who worked with Carmichael in SNCC, held the view that Malcolm was "the most important black political figure of the 1960s". Lester compared Carmichael to Malcolm in a manner which was unfavorable to Carmichael by stating: "Though dead, Malcolm is terrifyingly alive in his speeches; Carmichael is alive, but his speeches are depressingly dead." Lester concluded: "Malcolm X was one of the makers of history. Carmichael was a reflector of it."

Lester's remarks were somewhat unfair to Carmichael because the circumstances around his rise to national prominence were different from Malcolm's. Malcolm came to national prominence as the representative of Elijah Muhammad and the Nation of Islam. This was a position which carried different responsibilities than the role which Carmichael occupied as the chairman of SNCC. Carmichael was also much younger than Malcolm was when Malcolm rose to prominent national attention. For this reason, Carmichael should be assessed on his own terms rather than compared to Malcolm. Such a comparison was especially unfair because Malcolm's assassination ensured that his legacy would be that of a martyr for black freedom.

Garrow's view was that Carmichael's descent into "political irrelevance" culminated when he relocated to Guinea. He also argued that Carmichael's appeals for black power and black unity offered no concrete solutions. Garrow quoted Christopher Lasch's remark that Black Power as a slogan contained "very few political ideas at all." What Garrow does not seem to realize is that Carmichael's move to Guinea may have made Carmichael politically irrelevant where the civil rights movement was concerned, but this move to Guinea was followed by an ideological shift. Black Power was a slogan which embodied a radical approach which broke with the nonviolent, integrationist strategy of many of the civil rights leaders, but the critics were correct to point out that Black Power offered no concrete programs or solutions. In Guinea, Carmichael believed that he found the proper solution, which was Pan-Africanism and socialist revolution.

It is important to note that the importance of Black Power was that it clearly articulated that the fundamental problem for black people was a lack of power. Garrow himself noted that on the evening that Carmichael famously delivered the speech in which he called for black power, he had stated that he had been arrested 27 times and was "going to jail no more." Black Power was a rejection of a type of approach to struggle in which black people were expected to suffer in the hope of producing change. Black Power was a call for resistance, a call for self-determination, and a call for unity.

Carmichael recalled that in addition to Black Power, the Meredith March Against Fear was also utilized to promote SNCC's opposition to the Vietnam War—Garrow failed to mention Carmichael's role in opposing the war. The night that Carmichael gave the speech, Martin Luther King was away. This was a fortunate development for Carmichael and others who understood that King would attempt to water down the call for Black Power. Carmichael himself did not expect such an enthusiastic response.

Garrow noted that Carmichael "had transformed from a full-time local organizer in rural Lowndes County to a full-time traveling speech-maker whose unpredictable remarks increasingly angered his SNCC colleagues." As Garrow noted, Carmichael himself felt that he was perhaps too young for the job of being SNCC's chairman. He expressed that he needed time to read, learn, and reflect. The speeches which Carmichael gave did reflect a retreat away from the political work which Carmichael had been doing, but it also reflected that Carmichael was searching for a new approach and a clear solution to the problem. He found this approach and this solution through the ideologies of Kwame Nkrumah and Sekou Toure.

As noted before, Garrow does not engage with Carmichael's ideological vision, so his article amounts to criticizing Carmichael for breaking with the organizational work which SNCC was engaged in to pursue revolution in Africa. The impression that Garrow attempted to give was that Carmichael became irrelevant. To some degree, this is true. By the 1990s the politics of the movement had changed dramatically. SNCC was gone. The Black Panther Party was gone. Sekou Toure died and his political party in Guinea had been overthrown. Those colleagues of Carmichael who were politically "relevant" were the ones who joined the Democratic Party and in doing so joined the very system which Carmichael continued to resist against.

One could argue that Carmichael's political relevance became restricted by the fact that the global black liberation struggle was hindered by the backlash which it faced, but his ideas remained very relevant. This can be demonstrated by the presidency of Barack Obama. Garrow quoted Barack Obama, who described Carmichael as having "the eyes of a madman or a saint". Garrow also dismissed Peniel Joseph's assertion that Obama displayed an "inability to comprehend the full meaning" of Carmichael's rhetoric.

Obama's presidency witnessed a number of instances of African Americans being violently killed by the police, African Americans being killed in gang violence, a record number of Americans living in poverty, and the destabilization of Libya due to an American supported intervention by NATO. What this demonstrated was that Carmichael's criticism of America's racism, capitalism, and imperialism remained relevant because these problems remained. This would have been no surprise to Carmichael who pointed out that black people in the Democratic Party had limited power. He was particularly critical of Tom Bradley's handling of the Rodney King case.

Carmichael's support for Palestine's liberation was also relevant during Obama's presidency. At a town hall meeting in Florida, Obama was asked a question about America's support for Israel given Israel's occupation of Palestine. Obama seemed uncomfortable with the question given that he stalled for a bit by addressing a member of the audience before stating, "The Middle East is obviously an issue that has plagued the region for centuries." This slip of the tongue could perhaps be explained by Obama being distracted as he searched for an answer to the question. Obama asserted that Israel is one of America's strongest allies, while also acknowledging the plight of the Palestinians. Obama expressed his support for a two-state solution which required both sides to negotiate and come to an agreement.

The point is that the very issues which Carmichael raised in his lifetime continued to be relevant after he died. Had Carmichael opted to join the Democratic Party as some the others in SNCC did, he would have been more "relevant" as a personality, but his ideas less so. Carmichael was unwavering in his commitment to meaningful change, which he believed could only be carried out through a socialist revolution.

Garrow noted that it was on the question of socialist revolution where Peniel Joseph is most critical of Carmichael. Joseph explained that moved to Guinea where he supported Sekou Toure, whose "one-party state ruthlessly dispatched enemies and imprisoned former allies" at Camp Boiro. Joseph argued that Carmichael's failure to criticize Sekou Toure was a "moral failure as well as a political one". He also criticized Carmichael's connections with Muammar Gaddafi, Idi Amin, and Louis Farrakhan.

This where Malcolm and Carmichael can be compared in a manner which is more favorable to Malcolm. Malcolm was able to recognize the contradictions in the Nation of Islam and provide a critique of Elijah Muhammad, but Carmichael remained so deeply attached to Sekou Toure that he never publicly acknowledged the extent to which the revolution in Guinea was betrayed. The problem in Guinea was not merely that Sekou Toure's government was one which harshly dealt with dissent, but that these harsh measures were justified as being necessary to protect the socialist revolution. In the end, Sekou Toure adopted a more pro-capitalist, pro-Western approach.

That Carmichael's support for Sekou Toure was misguided does not erase everything else which he fought for. Carmichael did not correctly identify all of the answers, but Carmichael did correctly identify the problems which confronted African people globally. What makes his legacy so important was that in addition to identifying the problems, he took action and tried to do something about those problems through his work with SNCC and later the All-African People's Revolutionary Party. Kwame Ture (and I deliberately refer to him as Kwame Ture here) was not a tragedy. He was a man who committed his life to the liberation and advancement of not only African people, but all of humanity.

81

MALCOLM X AND THE CIVIL RIGHTS MOVEMENT

John Henrik Clarke argued that Mahatma Gandhi's passive resistance was a strategy and that Gandhi had a violent alternative waiting in case the nonviolence did not work. Clarke disagreed with Martin Luther King utilizing nonviolence not as a strategy, but as a way of life. For King, there could be no alternative but nonviolence. His commitment to Christ's teachings on turning the other cheek meant that he could see no alternative but to utilize a nonviolent approach. Clarke described King as a "dreamer". Despite his disagreements with King, Clarke noted that one should be slow to criticize King because he was brave enough to put his life on the line for what he believed.

Clarke placed Malcolm X over Martin Luther King in terms of significance of leadership. Part of Malcolm's significance as a leader was his willingness to provide a bold criticism of the limits of the civil rights movement and the leaders of that movement, particularly Martin Luther King. Malcolm could be particularly harsh in his criticisms of King, but what Malcolm understood was that the civil rights movement was limited not only by its commitment to a nonviolent response to a violent enemy, but also its inability to break with the very power structure which was responsible for the oppression of black people in the first place.

Concerning nonviolence, Malcolm stated: "If the leaders of the nonviolent movement can go into the white community and teach nonviolence, good. I'd go along with that. But as long as I see them teaching nonviolence only in the black community, we can't go along with that. We believe in equality, and equality means that you have to put the same thing over here that you put over there. And if black people alone are going to be the ones who are nonviolent, then it's not fair." Malcolm clearly understood the hypocrisy involved in the manner in which nonviolence had been promoted as a tactic among black people. He also explained: "My experience has been that in many instances where you find Negroes talking about nonviolence, they are not nonviolent with each other, and they're not loving with each other, or forgiving with each other. Usually when they say they're nonviolent, they mean they're nonviolent with somebody else. I think you understand what I mean. They are nonviolent with the enemy."

Malcolm's more forceful approach was in some respects a benefit to the civil rights movement. Malcolm made this observation when he noted that the Nation of Islam made the civil rights movement not only become more militant but also "more acceptable to the white power structure." Gloria Richardson was among those in the civil rights movement who benefitted from Malcolm's approach.

Richardson, who led the Cambridge movement, invited Malcolm to Cambridge after listening to one of Malcolm's speeches. Richardson recalled that Malcolm was not available to speak to Cambridge. She believed that it was Louis Farrakhan who was sent instead. She described him as "just horrible" because the group which came wanted nothing to do with the demonstration which was being planned. Despite this, Richardson recalled that the connection which they established with Malcolm was very useful because it allowed Cambridge to go to meetings in which they declared that the white power structure would either deal with Cambridge or deal with Malcolm. Malcolm did not play much of a direct role in the civil rights movement, but his influence was undeniable.

82

THE EUROCENTRISM OF C.L.R. JAMES

Upon reflecting on his friendship with C.L.R. James, John Henrik Clarke described James as a brilliant man who could lecture about any topic. He recalled that on one occasion while having some drinks with James, James began to lecture about the history of stained glass windows. Clarke jokingly told James that he could probably lecture on the origin of shoelaces. James then proceeded to lecture on the origin of shoelaces. Clarke explained, "I don't know a single thing that man didn't know."

Indeed, James was a brilliant scholar, but one struggles to resist pointing out that James' brilliance may have been limited by his Eurocentric outlook. Within the Pan-African liberation struggle, there arose the view that African people must define the world from our own cultural and historical experiences. This was a necessary aspect of the struggle given that one of the means by which colonialism dehumanized African people was to present the narrative that Africans were an uncivilized people who produced no civilizations or cultures of consequence. Therefore, understanding Africa's historical accomplishments became necessary to not only restore the psyche of African people, but to restore the very humanity of African people.

James provided a strong intellectual critique of colonialism which was rooted in a Marxist understanding of capitalist oppression, but the component which was missing was the cultural component. James remained so fundamentally attached to Western civilization that of Kwame Nkrumah he would write: "He could lead the people because his genealogical tree is to be found not among Africa flora but because he is the fine flower of another garden altogether, the political experiences and theoretical strivings of Western civilisation." This is a view which Nkrumah himself likely would not have endorsed given that Nkrumah's identity was always firmly rooted in Africa. Like James, Nkrumah was influenced by Marx, but unlike James, Nkrumah's politics was grounded in his African identity and this informed Nkrumah's zeal for African unity, which he envisioned would lead to the formation of the United States of Africa.

In "Decolonizing Revolution with C.L.R. James," Matthieu Renault referred to this paradox as James' Eurocentric anti-Eurocentrism. This is the paradox of a man who denounced colonialism while also referring to himself as a "British Negro". James also explained: "It is in the history and philosophy of Western Europe that I have gained my understanding not only of Western Europe's civilization, but of the importance of the underdeveloped countries. And that is still my outlook." The notion that one could develop an understanding of the importance of underdeveloped countries through the history and philosophy of Western Europe is indeed a curious one. As Renault noted, "James believed that the destiny of the non-Western world was to be Westernized."

This Eurocentrism also informed James' Marxist vision. In *World Revolution*, James wrote: "We may well see, especially after the universal ruin and destruction of the coming war, a revolutionary movement which, beginning in one of the great European cities, in the course of a few short months, will sweep the imperialist bourgeoisie out of power, not only in every country in Europe, but in India, China, Egypt and South Africa." Whereas Black Nationalists and even some non-European Marxists did not accept the notion that the revolution to overthrow imperialism would begin in Europe, James fully accepted this view. In 1960, during a series of lectures in Trinidad, James declared that "the basic opposition must come from the proletariat of the advanced countries".

James' attachment to Western civilization—and perhaps his marriages to white women—had blinded him to the reality that socialism developed its strongest appeal among the peoples who were the furthest removed from Western civilization. Socialist revolution took place in what Lenin referred to as the "weakest link" in the European imperialist system. James' views were certainly consistent with the orthodox Marxist view that revolution must come from the "advanced countries" but the historical reality is that the proletariat in Western capitalist countries have proven to be the less revolutionary and most reactionary of the world's working classes partly because they have a vested interest in sustaining a system which allows them to live relatively better than those in the colonies and also because of their racism towards the colonized. It seemed that James' attachment to Western civilization prevented him from fully understanding the nature of Western racism and Western imperialism.

83

EDUCATION FOR POWER

In his book, *The Mis-Education of the Negro*, Dr. Carter G. Woodson wrote: "If the Negro in the ghetto must eternally be fed by the hand that pushes him into the ghetto, he will never become strong enough to get out of the ghetto." In this sentence, Woodson expressed why the mis-education of black people was a necessity to keep white supremacy intact. The purpose of mis-education is not merely to keep black people ignorant, but it is also designed to keep black people powerless and perpetually dependent on those who benefit from the powerlessness of black people

Woodson noted that this mis-education impacted all aspects of the social, economic, and political life of black people in America. Concerning religion, Woodson noted: "In schools of theology Negroes are taught the interpretation of the Bible worked out by those who have justified segregation and winked at the economic debasement of the Negro sometimes almost to the point of starvation. Deriving their sense of right from this teaching, graduates of such schools can have no message to grip the people whom they have been ill trained to serve. Most of such mis-educated ministers, therefore, preach to benches while illiterate Negro preachers do the best they can in supplying the spiritual needs of the masses." Woodson also noted: "The large majority of Negro preachers of today, then, are doing nothing more than to keep up the mediaeval hell-fire scare which the whites have long since abandoned to emphasize the humanitarian trend in religion through systematized education. The young people of the Negro race could be held in the church by some such program, but the Negro's Christianity does not conceive of social uplift as a duty of the church; and consequently Negro children have not been adequately trained in religious matters to be equal to the social demands upon them."

Woodson argued that education must empower black people to work towards their own social uplift. He quoted Frederick Douglass who said in 1852, "It is vain that we talk of being men, if we do not the work of men. We must become valuable to society in other departments of industry than those servile ones from which we are rapidly being excluded. We must show that we can do as well as they." Woodson recognized that the unfortunate reality of mis-education is that rather than viewing leadership in terms of service, too many mis-educated individuals viewed leadership in terms of competition. He explained that he "has known numerous cases of Negro lawyers, physicians and business men who, while attending local Sunday schools, churches, and lodges, have fallen out about trifles like a resolution or the chairmanship of a committee, which so embittered them as to make themselves enemies for life and stumbling blocks preventing any such thing as organization or community cooperation." Woodson lamented that everything in the community "must yield ground to this puerile contest."

The essential problem which Woodson was exposing was that a people who are mis-educated to think in terms of individual advancement at the expense of others within the race are not a people who will work in the service of the race. These are not a people who will think in terms of developing and sustaining group power. Woodson published his book decades before Kwame Ture popularized the term "Black Power," but Woodson was still dealing with the problem of powerlessness among black people. A people who think in terms of power are a people who operate differently from those who are not concerned with power.

The work of Dr. Amos Wilson is also important for understanding the nature of power. Wilson argued that the African American condition was comparable to conditions of Africans in other parts of the world as well. Much like Woodson, Wilson understood that the powerlessness and mis-education of African Americans was part of the largely global condition of African people. Much like Woodson, Wilson also argued that overcoming this powerlessness meant that African people had to change the way they thought about their condition and their history. Wilson argued that simply because an idea appeared later in history does not mean that this idea represents an advancement over an idea which had appeared earlier. His point was that the knowledge and wisdom of ancient African cultures are not irrelevant or rendered meaningless because of the point in history in which these ideas appeared. Wilson argued that there was a great deal one could learn from the wisdom of ancient cultures.

An example which Wilson provided was the story of Joseph in Egypt in the Bible. He noted that the story was essentially a story of how an ancient African society dealt with drought. What this indicated to Wilson was that drought was a problem which African societies were confronted with and learned to manage. He argued that European agrobusiness and cash crops resulted in Africans producing food to feed others in such a way that they could not take care of themselves. Colonialism created monocultures in which Africans produce resources for others while being unable to feed themselves.

In Wilson's view, the state of African nations was not unlike the condition of African American communities. He described African Americans as being a Third World nation as well. The crime in African American communities, Wilson argued, was rooted in the same thing which caused crime in Africa and in Caribbean nations such as Jamaica and Trinidad. Wilson also noted the parallel between assimilationism in America and neo-colonialism in Africa. In both instances, black faces were placed over white power such that black people in positions of political power in Africa and the United States still served the interests of the colonial powers.

Wilson found the conditions of African Americans especially shameful given the access to knowledge which African Americans possessed. He argued that in America, one had to will themselves to be dumb given the access to libraries and other forms of information which were lacking in poorer nations. Wilson argued that this mis-education was rooted in the fact that African Americans also possessed a monoculture economy in which labor was the primary resource which African Americans provided.

Wilson also argued that electoral politics itself was not real power because electing a person in office was not the same thing as getting an elected official to serve the interests of those who elected him. Woodson made a similar point when he wrote that political education was neglected so that "the few Negroes who are elected to office are often similarly uninformed and show a lack of vision. They have given little attention to the weighty problems of the nation; and in the legislative bodies to which they are elected, they restrict themselves as a rule to matters of special concern to the Negroes themselves, such as lynching, segregation and disfranchisement, which they have well learned by experience."

Both men ultimately concluded that power was something which African Americans had to seize. Woodson lamented: "We do not show the Negro how to overcome segregation, but we teach him how to accept it as final and just." Woodson argued that racism was not a thing which was to be accepted, but that it should be resisted. He noted that the education which black people received was one which glorified the actions of the conquers. He noted: "The oppressor has always indoctrinated the weak with this interpretation of the crimes of the strong." Woodson's Association for the Study of Negro Life and History put forward a program of education which was designed to educate black people on "whether these forces have come into his life to bless him or to bless his oppressor." This was relevant not only for African Americans, but those in Africa as well, as Woodson explained: "Liberia must not wait until she is offered to Germany before realizing that she has few friends in Europe. Abyssinia must not wait until she is invaded by Italy before she prepares for selfdefense." Woodson understood that African people must learn to think for themselves and develop for themselves, rather than relying on the very people who oppressed them. He stated: "At present the Negro, both in Africa and America, is being turned first here and there experimentally by so-called friends who in the final analysis assist the Negro merely in remaining in the dark."

Wilson expressed a similar view regarding power. He cited the Bible story of Jesus and the rich young man. Wilson noted that when the rich man was told that he must give up his worldly wealth to enter into heaven, he refused. For Wilson, the lesson was if a rich man can reject God, then there was no reason that African Americans should expect that one day white people will share their wealth simply out of the goodness of their heart. Wilson explained that African Americans would have to take this wealth. Power cannot be obtained by relying on those in power to share it freely.

The work of Dr. Carter G. Woodson and Dr. Amos Wilson is

instructive for understanding education for power. They both understood that education for power required not only understanding the conditions which confront African people, but also developing solutions for those problems and developing the proper temperament to become a solution-oriented servant of the people as opposed to someone seeking individual advancement at the expense of the collective.

84

SOCIETY AND RACIAL IDENTITY

In his autobiography, Jamil Abdullah Al-Amin (formerly known as H. Rap Brown) explained: "I was born into a family of dark-skinned negroes, but I'm what many consider a red nigger. My mother, my father, my brother Ed and my sister are all darker than I am. Because I was lighter, it meant that I was supposed to get ahead. So my mother gave me what I would call preferential treatment. Because of this there was a lot of rivalry between my brother Ed and myself. He and I weren't 'tight' when we were young. He thought that our mother treated me better than she did him."

What Al-Amin was explaining was that the racism which black people endured in American society impacted not only the manner in which black people related to white people, but how they related to each other as well. He also explained: "The first thing you learn is that you are different from whites. The next thing you learn is that you are different from each other. You are born into a world of double standards where color is of paramount importance. In your community a color pattern exists which is closely akin to the white man's, and likewise reinforced from both ends of the spectrum." Black people in America have been confronted with the challenge of navigating the standards set by the dominant white society and the manner in which such standards have impacted social relations within the black community.

This is not only an American challenge. It is a global one for black people. In *Black Skin, White Masks*, Frantz Fanon recounted the impact that the racism of French colonial society had in Martinique and the other French colonies. Fanon noted that black people in the French colonies were educated to think of themselves as being French, yet they are not French, and they realized this when they went to France. Fanon explained: "For the Negro in France, which is his country, will feel different from other people. One can hear the glib remark: The Negro makes himself inferior. But the truth is that he is made inferior. The young Antillean is a

Frenchman called upon constantly to live with white compatriots." Fanon continued to note that any black person from the Antilles who desired to climb into European society must reject his own family to do so. The black man or black women who wished to become successful in French society had to cease being black to become like the colonizer.

Fanon recognized that Alfred Alder's individual psychology could not be easily applied to the condition of black people in the Antilles because their behaviors were shaped by the society itself. Fanon explained: "The Antillean is characterized by his desire to dominate the other." He continued to describe the people of Martinque as being "greedy for security." Fanon noted that Alder's psychology of the individual encountered difficulties in the Antilles because, as Fanon observed, inferiority was an Antillean characteristic. Fanon explained that "Antillean society is a neurotic society, a society of 'comparison' Hence we are driven from the individual back to the social structure." For this reason, Fanon argued that the "taint" was not in the soul of the individual, but in the environment of the individual.

Isaac Prilleltensky and Lev Gonick noted in a paper titled "Polities Change, Oppression Remains: On the Psychology and Politics of Oppression" that those who experience oppression internalize negative conceptions of the self. They explain: "The feelings of guilt, shame, and worthlessness sexual abuse are painful reminders internalized of the susceptibility by victims of child of vulnerable groups to negative judgments imposed on them by perpetrators."

The problem of racism and its impact on black people is not an individual problem. It exists at the societal level and therefore must be confronted at the societal level. Similarly, it must be understood that racial identity exists not only as a product of an individual's perceptions and desires, but also as a product of the society as a whole. A racist society produces racial identities which work to sustain the racism. The only solution is direct confrontation with such a system.

85

SETTING OUR OWN STANDARD

My interest in studying African history truly began after listening to a lecture by John Henrik Clarke. In the lecture, he was speaking about Islam. What caught my attention was that he stated that in traditional African societies there was no word for jail. I could not believe this, so I did my own research and I discovered that he was correct. In traditional African societies, there were no jails. This was not because African societies were utopias. This was because African societies possessed a degree of humanity such that criminal offenses were often settled through fines or other means which did not involve jailing someone. The colonial powers which invaded Africa deliberately presented African people as being savages, but this was not the case at all.

The West possesses no superior mortality over African people. At the time when European nations held control over colonies in Africa, professing to bring civilization to the colonies, Europe managed to start two World Wars. In 1922, Marcus Garvey predicted that in "another few years we are going to come in contact with the bloodiest war mankind has ever seen. The stage is set for a bloody holocaust." Garvey was indeed correct. The 1930s would witness the start of World War II, and during this conflict the Nazis would orchestrate the holocaust of the Jewish population. This is why we must define our history on our own terms rather than using those who have colonized us as the standard.

James Henry Breasted's suggestion that Thutmose III was the Napoleon of Egypt is an example which demonstrates the need to define our history on our terms. Thutmose III came to power following the death of Hatshepsut. He proved to be an energetic conqueror who engaged in military campaigns to the east. By the end of his reign, Thutmose III not only secured Egyptian power through a number of successful military campaigns, but he also left behind a kingdom which was in good order. This can be contrasted with Napoleon whose ambitions proved to be very destructive for Europe.

Napoleon Bonaparte emerged as one of the great military personalities in Europe's history. In his biography of Napoleon, titled *The Story of Napoleon*, Harold Wheeler declared that there "is no more marvellous story in human history than that of Napoleon I., Emperor of the French." What made his story so marvelous was his rise to power. Through his military skill and determination, Napoleon became, for a brief time, the most powerful man in Europe. There was also a bit of ruthless opportunism in his rise to power as well, as demonstrated by the fact that when his army in Egypt encountered difficulties, he decided to abandon his army to make his way back to France. Baron de Frénilly noted: "A general does not flee—he retreats. But Bonaparte was ever the general of Fortune, and every time that she abandoned him he fled like a soldier, leaving the others to get out of the difficulty as best they could. This man, then, crept out of Egypt by night, glided between the English frigates and entered Paris. There he had to stoop and take what he wanted. France—after passing, during eight years, from the anarchy of revolutionaries to the anarchy of political comedians—was eager for the despotism of a single man."

Napoleon left Egypt to return to France on October 16, 1799. He eventually seized power on November 9. Napoleon, ever the conqueror, turned his attention to expanding France by conquering territories in Europe. This included waging a war against Austria which ended with Austria ceding territory to Napoleon in 1809 following the Peace of Vienna. Territory was also ceded to Bavaria, Russia, and the Grand Duchy of Warsaw.

Napoleon would also go on to marry Marie Louise, who was the daughter of the Emperor of Austria. This was Napoleon's second marriage. His first wife Josephine was unable to produce an heir for Napoleon, so he left her for Marie. Marie herself did not seem particularly fond of this arrangement, considering that she had described Napoleon as the "Anti-Christ." European missionaries tended to view polygamous marriages in Africa negatively, but one of the advantages of polygamy where the ruling class was concerned was that rulers were able to produce heirs without having to divorce a wife who did not produce an heir. Henry VIII is particularly notorious for resolving this matter by divorcing and executing two of his wives.

Napoleon's ambitions began to crumble following an ill-fated invasion of Russia. Napoleon was forced to retreat from Russia to return to France, leaving behind his forces. It was estimated that as many as 500,000 French soldiers were lost in the war. The disaster in Russia was followed by the Leipzig campaign in 1813, which also ended in defeat for Napoleon. It is estimated that as many as 120,000 men were killed or wounded in this conflict. Napoleon was eventually defeated and exiled after plunging Europe into a destructive war. In my view, he was no Thutmose III, but James Henry Breasted's claim does demonstrate the need for African people to decolonize how we think about history by defining history on our own terms rather than on terms which center European figures as the standard by which all other important historical personalities are to be judged.

I also want to note that for many years, Egyptologists had dismissed the notion that Egyptian civilization could have been produced by black people. The Egyptians did not see themselves as being black, but one could make the argument that at least some of Egypt's rulers would fall under the category of what we would describe as being "black," meaning that they were dark-skinned individuals of African ancestry. Henry Aubin's book *The Rescue of Jerusalem* focuses on the Kushite rulers of the 25th dynasty, which he notes was the only dynasty in Egypt's history which all historians agree was black as the term is used in North America. This is because the 25th dynasty was a purely Nubian dynasty, but if we take the position that the Nubians were black and the Egyptians were not, then there would have been other black dynasties such as the 12th dynasty which was founded by Amenemhat I who had a Nubian mother from Ta-Seti. We would also have to acknowledge the possibility of other Egyptian dynasties being "black" as well due to the close connection between Upper Egypt and Nubia. This would include the 18th dynasty.

When addressing this debate over the racial identity of the ancient Egyptians, it is also important to look beyond race as a biological classification to look at the culture of Egypt as well. Dynastic Egyptian culture shared some very obvious similarities with the cultures of Africa as well. Thus, we can take the conservative position that at least some of the rulers of Egypt's major dynasties were black as the term is generally understood.

The reason why I mention this is because Egyptian history is connected to the larger debate around the history of African people. Part of the effort to dehumanize African people has been to rob us of our sense of historical accomplishment. As a result of this one of the reasons why we have the problems which we have is because we have forgotten who we were. Amos Wilson argued that the true history and culture of "Afrikan peoples must be *re*discovered, *re*examined, and *re*integrated by Afrikan peoples." Bobby E. Wright advocated for the creation of a Black Social Theory. He explained: "The ultimate achievement of a Black Social Theory would be the reintegration of a worldwide Black culture." We must look at our history and draw from our history the lessons which are needed to guide us forward. This means recapturing the positive aspects of our civilizations.

One of the great achievements of Mali was its constitution which was known as the Kouroukan Fouga. This constitution was formed after the Battle of Krina in which Sundiata Keita seized power by overcoming his enemy. The constitution was very remarkable for its time. It established a political system under the rule of the Keita family, but it also allocated duties to other clans as well, demonstrating a degree of decentralized political leadership. The constitution did not abolish slavery, but it ensured that slaves were treated humanely. It also ensured the right to life and safety, established a system to fight laziness, encouraged mutual condolences, encouraged humility, barred the mistreatment of foreigners, and ensured the respect of women.

One provision of the Kouroukan Fouga that I want to bring attention to is the provision which stated: "You can kill the enemy, but not humiliate him." The understanding is that in combat one may kill an enemy, but one may not humiliate the enemy. This shows that even in the heat of combat when the objective is to kill or be killed, one can still retain respect for one's enemy and recognition of the enemy's humanity. Wars are an unfortunate reality of human history. Throughout history wars have been fought to advance a political or economic objective. Wars are by their very nature violent, although this does not mean that there are no limits to the depravities involved in war. The Kouroukan Fouga demonstrated that centuries before the Geneva Conventions, African people developed humane conceptions of warfare.

The code of laws which existed in Mali were far from perfect. For example, article 17 states that lies which have lived for 40 years should be considered to be truths. The intention behind the provision is that if a lie is able to persist unchallenged for so many years that it should be accepted as true to avoid any further conflict over the matter, but I think any lie which is exposed as such should never be regarded as truth regardless of how long it had been unchallenged. As I pointed out, the Kouroukan Fouga provided that slaves should not be ill-treated. I would argue that slaves in Mali certainly were not as poorly treated as African slaves in the Americas and slaves in Greco-Roman society were treated, but slavery existed nevertheless and the existence of slavery is incompatible with a view of human rights which suggests that a human being should not be legally held as the property of another human being, no matter how humane the system of slavery is.

The Kouroukan Fouga also allowed for women to be beaten as a form of discipline. This may seem like a contradiction of the provision regarding respect for women, but women in Mali did have recourse in situations where they were unjustly punished. Mungo Park explained that among the Mandingo people "if any one of the ladies complains to the chief of the town, that her husband has unjustly punished her, and shewn an undue partiality to some other of his wives, the affair is brought to a public trial." Therefore, women in Malian society were not completely without redress if her husband became too overbearing in his punishment of his wife. It is not as though a husband was free to mistreat his wife however he saw fit, which is why the constitution of Mali urged respect for women. This is not to justify corporal punishment of women, but simply to point out that there were protections in place for women. Even so, I would argue that the use of corporal discipline against one's partner is a practice which is archaic and should be abolished along with slavery.

Apart from the Kouroukan Fouga's provision concerning warfare, there are other examples I can point to demonstrate the humane approach to war which existed in Africa, such as Piye of Kush who was noted for conquering entire cities while avoiding bloodshed when possible. Ezana was known to sometimes provide food for his vanquished foes. Moshoeshoe did something similar by providing cattle to those whom he defeated in battle. Shamba Bolongongo encouraged his warriors to use non-lethal methods in warfare. In Southern Africa, there was a tradition of fighting wars away from civilian populations to avoid civilian casualties in combat.

It was also even the case that when African societies did wage brutal and bloody wars against each other, the resolution was some form of peaceful coexistence. Take for example the history of Egypt and Nubia, especially during the 18th dynasty of Egypt. This dynasty established the first empire in Egypt's history. This dynasty came to power following the expulsion of the Hyksos invaders. Once Ahmose I expelled the invaders, he set about consolidating Egypt's power. This included securing the Syrian border and conquering Nubia. When Ahmose I died, his son Amenhotep I took power. Amenhotep I undertook a campaign into Nubia. Amenhotep I was followed by Thutmose I. Thutmose was a military man who married into the royal family. Thutmose boasted that he expanded the boundaries of Egypt "as far as that which the sun encircles." This was the first time in Egypt's history that its territory had expanded so far into West Asia.

The 18th dynasty was one which preoccupied itself with expanding the boundaries of Egypt beyond what prior dynasties had done. This was done not only to expand Egypt's power and access to resources, but it was also a defensive action as well. Prior to the Hyksos invasion, Egypt had made efforts to secure itself against invasions from West Asia. The rulers of the 18th dynasty understood that the only way to ensure Egypt's protection against continued invasions was to expand its power eastward. Egypt came to rule over the very lands from which the Asiatic invaders came from.

This period was also marked by several military campaigns into Nubia to put down rebellions. For example, during the reign of Thutmose II, it was recorded that there was a revolt in Nubia. Thutmose was so enraged by this that he sent an army to Nubia to crush the revolt. It was recorded that all of the males had been killed with the exception of one of the sons of the prince of Kush who was returned as a prisoner. During the reign of Amenhotep III, it was recorded that a rebellion in Nubia was crushed. The recording of this event boasted that 740 Nubians were captured and 312 were slain.

Egypt's relationship with Nubia during this period was a complex one. Nubia was often referred to as "the wretched land of Kush" which demonstrated the hostile view that the rulers of Egypt had of Nubia. Yet Nubia was also an important region for Egypt because of the wealth it produced. Henry Aubin noted that Egypt developed a plantation economy in Nubia. There, farmers "worked on large estates owned by the pharaoh, by the local nobility or by the temples that were established throughout the territory." From Nubia, Egypt acquired gold, cattle, honey, and wine.

What makes the relationship between Nubia and Egypt so complex during this period is that although the connection between the two states was marked by frequent rebellions by Nubia and Egyptian campaigns to brutally suppress such rebellions, but it was also marked by collaboration which would result in Nubians not only adopting certain Egyptian customs, but also viewing Egypt as "a kindred land, not a foreign one." The relationship between Egypt and Nubia demonstrated that Egypt's relationship with its African neighbors was marked by war and confrontation, but also by building mutual alliances as well.

Hatshepsut stands out as one of the most remarkable rulers of the 18th dynasty. She initially ruled as the co-regent with Thutmose III, but she subverted his position and seized power for herself. To justify her seizure of power, Hatshepsut constructed a temple which depicted her mother being visited by Amun to emphasize that she had been conceived by Amun. Presenting herself as being selected by Amun was the means by which she justified her claim to the throne.

One of the most notable moments from Hatshepsut's reign was an expedition which she sent to Punt. There the Egyptians encountered the queen of Punt, Eti. This was yet another example which demonstrates the existence of mutually beneficial relations between African nations. The empire which Egypt established during the New Kingdom did not solely rely on military might in its dealings with its neighbors.

To be clear, dynastic Egyptian society was a society which was stratified along the basis of an entrenched class system which was often harsh in its exploitation of those who were conquered and enslaved. Egypt was an empire and like all empires, there was a degree of brutality in the expansion and maintenance of the empire. My point here is not to diminish this aspect of Egyptian society, but to point out that even in an empire such as Egypt recognized that it could not sustain itself through brutal force and violence. The rulers of Egypt's empire seemed to understand what Napoleon had not understood about power.

86

RACISM AND STATE ACTION

The protections offered by the Constitution are limited by the state action doctrine which established that the protections of the Equal Protection Clause do not extend to the conduct of private citizens. The scope of the state action doctrine is one which has been criticized for being incoherent due to the difficulties involved in defining the difference between state action and private action. Joseph William Singer explained that the state action doctrine was created by the Supreme Court shortly after the Fourteenth Amendment was enacted. This was due to the language of the Fourteenth Amendment, which stated: "No State shall make or enforce any law which shall abridge the privileges or immunities of citizens of the United States; nor shall any State deprive any person of life, liberty, or property, without due process of law; nor deny to any person within its jurisdiction the equal protection of the laws."

In 1875, the Supreme Court in *United States v. Cruikshank* interpreted the language of the Fourteenth Amendment as limiting the scope of the Fourteenth Amendment to state action. In this case, the Supreme Court overturned the convictions of white supremacists who were involved in the Colfax massacre in which over one hundred black people were killed. In 1879, the state action doctrine was applied by the Supreme Court in *Commonwealth of Virginia v. Rives* to deny an appeal from a black defendant who argued that an all-white jury had violated the Equal Protection Clause. In *Civil Rights Cases* the Supreme Court held that Congress did not have the authority to enact the Civil Rights Act of 1875 which prohibited racial discrimination in places of public accommodation. Apart from ruling that there was no authority to be found in the Thirteenth or Fourteenth Amendment, Supreme Court also reasoned that discrimination was acceptable because during the time of slavery there were freed black people who appeared to be fine with the discrimination. The Supreme Court's opinion stated: "There were thousands of free colored people in this country before the abolition of slavery, enjoying all the essential rights of life, liberty and property the same as white citizens; yet no one, at that time, thought that it was any invasion of his personal status as a freeman because he was not admitted to all the privileges enjoyed by white citizens, or because he was subjected to discriminations in the enjoyment of accommodations in inns, public conveyances and places of amusement. Mere discriminations on account of race or color were not regarded as badges of slavery."

The state action doctrine was also utilized to weaken the protections offered by the Fifteenth Amendment. After the Fifteenth Amendment was ratified, southern states responded with measures to restrict the ability of black people to vote. Congress responded to this by passing the Enforcement Act of 1870. The act was enacted pursuant to the Fifteenth Amendment which was ratified to protect voter rights. Despite this, in 1903 the Supreme Court invalidated key provisions of the Enforcement Act in *James v. Bowman*. The case involved a writ of habeas corpus filed by Henry Bowman who was indicted for bribing and intimidating black voters in violation of the Enforcement Act of 1870. The Supreme Court held that the state action doctrine prevented Congress from regulating private behavior under the Fifteenth Amendment. In 1935, in *Grovey v. Townsend*, the Supreme Court used the state action doctrine to hold that the Texas Democratic Party's exclusion of black people from primary elections was insulated from constitutional challenge.

From the examples above, it is clear that the state action doctrine frustrated efforts to address racial discrimination in America. This is precisely why Joseph William Singer explained: "The state action doctrine has substantially harmed individuals and groups since its inception in the late nineteenth century. Minority populations—particularly African Americans—have been especially vulnerable to the collateral damage of the state action doctrine." Singer also noted that the state action doctrine was used to shield private citizens from acts of discrimination even in situations where private actors relied on the law to carry out their racial discrimination. Erwin Chemerinsky explained that "in announcing the state action doctrine, the Court assumed that the common law protected against private discrimination and private violations of rights."

In time, the Supreme Court eventually relaxed the state action doctrine by including exceptions. One such exception are public function cases in which private entities perform the function that a government traditionally performs. This exception was displayed in 1944 in *Smith v. Allwright* in which the Supreme Court held that the state action doctrine did not protect voter suppressing tactics, effectively reversing the decision in *Grovey* by holding that an entity which regulates elections performs a public function and is subject to the Fifteenth Amendment. In *Marsh v. Alabama*, the Supreme Court held that a company which owned a town in Alabama was not shielded by the state action doctrine because the company-owned town functioned like a traditional municipality, and therefore could not restrict the appellant's First Amendment right by denying him the ability to distribute leaflets. Similarly, in *Evans v. Newton*, the Supreme Court held that parks serve a public function and that when a private entity manages a park, it is subject to the Equal Protection Clause.

In *Evans*, property in a charitable trust was bequeathed to the city of Macon in Georgia to be used as a park for white people only. The city was named a trustee and named a board of trustees who operated the park in a segregated manner. The city eventually acknowledged that it could not continue maintaining a public facility in a segregated manner, so the board of managers sued the city and asked for the title to be transferred to private trustees so that segregation could continue. The Supreme Court ruled that the state court's transfer of title from the city to private trustees did not shield the private trustees under the state action doctrine, holding that "when private individuals or groups are endowed by the State with powers or functions governmental in nature, they become agencies or instrumentalities of the State and subject to its constitutional limitations."

The other exception to the state action doctrine are entanglement cases. Entanglement cases involve situations in which the government authorizes, encourages, facilitates, or becomes involved with private discrimination. This is demonstrated by the 1948 ruling in *Shelley v. Kraemer* in which the Supreme Court held that the judicial enforcement of racially restrictive covenants constituted a state action violation of the Equal Protection Clause. This case involved a racially restrictive covenant which was implemented in Missouri. Neighbors sued to uphold the covenant when several landowners sold parcels of land to African Americans who moved into the homes. The covenant was upheld by the Missouri Supreme Court, but it was overturned by the Supreme Court. Curiously, in upholding the covenant, the Missouri Supreme Court held that the covenant did not violate state policy, despite the fact that it imposed a partial restraint on alienation of fee simple interests, which could have easily been found to have been a violation of the common law rule against unreasonable restraints on alienation. The Missouri Supreme Court had struck down restraints on alienation of fee simple interests as a violation of public policy in prior rulings. On appeal, the respondents argued that the racially restrictive covenant was a private contractual agreement which was beyond the strictures of the Constitution and that judicial enforcement of the agreement was not state action. The Supreme Court disagreed. The Supreme Court held that the judicial enforcement of racially restrictive covenants was state action. The Supreme Court concluded that the "action of state courts and of judicial officers in their official capacities is to be regarded as action of the State within the meaning of the Fourteenth Amendment."

In *New York Times v. Sullivan*, the Supreme Court held that a state's enforcement of its common law libel rule constituted state action which violated the First and Fourteenth Amendments. Just as in *Shelly*, the Supreme Court ruled that the involvement of the court in this matter resulted in state power being exercised. A third entanglement case was *Adickes v. S.H. Kress Co.* in which Sandra Adickes was arrested and convicted of vagrancy after she entered a restaurant with African American students. The Supreme Court held that a state enforced custom of segregation constituted state action to the same degree as a statute mandating segregation.

In *Robinson v. Florida*, a restaurant manager called the police after a group of African Americans refused to leave a racially segregated restaurant. They were arrested for trespass. At issue in this case was whether or not state action was involved. The state government contended that there was no state action because a private business had carried out the discriminatory conduct, not the state. The Supreme Court disagreed, finding that there was state action under the theory of entanglement. The Supreme Court reasoned that while "these Florida regulations do not directly and expressly forbid restaurants to serve both white and colored people together, they certainly embody a state policy putting burdens upon any restaurant which serves both races, burdens bound to discourage the serving of the two races together." The Supreme Court concluded that this was government entanglement which constituted state action and violated the Equal Protection Clause.

Granting exceptions to the state action doctrine allowed the Supreme Court to remedy acts of private discrimination. Congress itself also found a means by getting around the restrictive nature of the state action doctrine through utilizing the Commerce Clause of the Constitution. A note from the *Harvard Law Review* explained that the Commerce Clause contains no state action requirement, which makes it "a more significant and invasive power than the powers provided under the Fourteenth Amendment." This clause allowed the federal government to regulate individual behavior so long as that behavior could be characterized as economic activity which affects commerce.

That the Commerce Clause has been utilized to regulate individual behavior can be demonstrated by the use of this clause to prohibit racial discrimination. *Heart of Atlanta Motel, Inc. v. United States* involved a case in which a motel in Atlanta refused to rent rooms to African Americans. The owner of the motel filed an action to have Title II of the 1964 Civil Rights Act invalidated as being unconstitutional. The Supreme Court upheld the Act on the basis of the equal protection clause of the Fourteenth Amendment and the Commerce Clause. The Court noted the "overwhelming evidence of the disruptive effect that racial discrimination has had on commercial intercourse." The Supreme Court reasoned that though the Heart of Atlanta Motel may be a local, intrastate operation, its discriminatory practices may have "a substantial and harmful effect upon that commerce," which therefore authorized Congress to regulate it.

Katzenbach v. McClung was yet another case in which the

constitutionality of the Civil Rights Act was upheld by the Commerce Clause. This case involved Ollie's Barbecue, which was a small restaurant. The Supreme Court concluded that the discriminatory practices of Ollie's discouraged African Americans from traveling, which resulted in fewer interstate goods being sold than if discrimination did not exist. The Commerce Clause in the previously mentioned two cases ensured a different outcome from the *Civil Rights Cases* in which the Supreme Court invalidated the Civil Rights Act of 1875 because the Fourteenth Amendment did not empower Congress to regulate private actions.

The Supreme Court did restrict the Commerce Clause in *United States v. Morrison* by striking down the Violence Against Women Act of 1994 because violence against women did not constitute an economic activity. This was reinforced in *Lopez v. United States* and in *National Federation of Independent Business v. Sebelius*. The ruling in *NFIB* permitted both state regulation and federal regulation under the Taxing Clause but limited the commerce power.

The state action doctrine was designed to separate government action from the action of private citizens, but, as Singer pointed out, discriminatory laws can only exist to the extent that the state allows and enforces such laws. Singer gave the example of apartheid in South Africa where 10% of the population held 90% of the land. Singer noted that ending apartheid laws would not be sufficient to remedy the problem if white owners continued to refuse to sell their homes to black buyers. Singer explained that apartheid would have continued under the mechanism of private property law if white people were allowed to engage in discriminatory practices.

Louis Michael Seidman explained that "private action always occurs in the context of background state action that molds and enables private choice." Singer gave the specific example of property law to demonstrate the connection between state activity and private conduct, explaining: "Anyone who tries to create a fee tail today will be unsuccessful. State property law will convert those interests into a fee simple. Anyone who tries to impose a restraint on alienation of a fee simple interest is likely to be successful in only a narrow set of cases. Anyone who tries to create a homeowners' association that has the power to divest an owner of their rights without compensation will be unsuccessful. State law protects unit owners from unfair retroactive changes in their property rights." Similarly, anyone who wants to own a slave will be unsuccessful because the Thirteenth Amendment will prevent his. Singer concluded that: "Democracies do not allow for the creation and enjoyment of all types of property rights no matter their scope and content."

References:

Joseph William Singer, "Things Invisible To See: State Action & Private Property," *Texas A &M Law Review*, (2018).

"NFIB v. Sebelius and the Individualization of the State Action Doctrine," note from *Harvard Law Review*, (2014).

87

ADDRESSING CONTRADICTIONS

In an edition of *Negro Digest* in 1970, Tchaiko Kwayana (who was at the time known as Ann Cook) published an article titled "Black Pride? Some Contradictions." The article served as a critical analysis of certain expressions of black pride which were taking place at the time. Kwayana was able to recognize that much of what was being celebrated as a newfound cultural pride often reflected a Eurocentric influence. For example, she questioned if the emphasis on great kingdoms such as Songhai, Bornu, Ghana, and Mali was because "these kingdoms were similar in structure and size to European ones and serve as reassurance to us that we had the same thing they had, even when, as with Islam, these kingdoms were not the norm?"

Kwayana also noted that she heard music and read plays in which African languages were simply "mumbo jumbo" rather than authentic representations of African language. The phrase mumbo jumbo in English has come to represent something which appears to have meaning but is effectively meaningless or nonsensical, but the phrase is itself is of African origin. One is not sure if Kwayana was aware of this when she published her article, but her point that many artists did not make the effort to authentically represent African languages in their works is well taken.

Kwayana also expressed concern that some individuals were duping African people by telling them that anti-Africanism must be viewed as a secondary concern to "Karl Marx's priorities." She also questioned whether the embrace of the Third World was being done by those who unconsciously did not want to truly deal with Africa itself.

Kwayana's travels allowed her to see firsthand that the contradictions existed not only in the United States. She recounted that in Brazil she met a white man who proudly exclaimed to Kwayana that his grandmother was a Negro. When Kwayana stated that she was not surprised because it showed in his features, he panicked and insisted that he had no Negro features. What she discovered was that in Brazil "it is quite all right to have African blood if it does not show." Thus, people who appeared white had no problem boasting to a black foreigner of their "Negro blood" but became defensive at the suggestion that they had Negro features.

Kwayana concluded by explaining that there was no "substitute for hard organizing." She pointed to the work which was done by ASCRIA in Guyana as an example. ASCRIA was led by Eusi Kwayana who would become her husband. She described Eusi as "a giant of a man." What Kwayana understood was that the work to be done to create an effective cultural revival among African people not only required making an effort to truly connect with African history and culture in a manner which was removed from the influence of Eurocentrism, but that such efforts also needed to be connected to organizing activities. She explained: "We must think in terms of building and sustaining our own institutions—a herculean task for organizers." Unfortunately, she also concluded, "Our leaders are still looking for easy ways out."

Kwayana also recognized a deliberate effort to keep African people divided. She explained: "The West is aware of the vast potential we have as a people. It is for that reason that we have been kept so cleverly fragmented. The publicized enmity between American Africans and West Indian Africans and between Western Hemisphere Africans and the Africans of our motherland has certainly been a vast and successful propaganda ploy." Kwayana's Pan-African work represented an attempt to combat this ploy. It also represented an attempt to address the contradictions which existed in the movement.

88

AFRICANS IN AMERICA

Malcolm X once stated, "we discovered that deep within the subconscious of the black man in this country, he is still more African than he is American. He thinks that he's more American than African, because the man is jiving him, the man is brainwashing him every day. He's telling him, 'You're an American, you're an American.' Man, how could you think you're an American when you haven't ever had any kind of an American treat over here?" He continued to state: "I'm not a diner until you let me dine. Just being at the table with others who are dining doesn't make me a diner, and this is what you've got to get in your head here in this country."

Many of the civil rights leaders were optimistic about producing change in America, but this optimism was somewhat misguided. Malcolm understood this clearly. Malcolm understood that the race problem existed because America did not intend to allow African Americans to truly become equal citizens under the law. In Malcolm's view, African Americans were more African than American not only culturally, but politically as well.

In her autobiography titled *To Praise Our Bridges*, Fannie Lou Hamer provided a rather touching account of her trip to Guinea in 1964. It was very inspirational for her to see black men flying airplanes, driving buses, and doing other things that she was accustomed to seeing white people do in America. Shortly after arriving in Guinea, Sekou Toure visited her and invited her to the presidential palace. In America, President Lyndon B. Johnson interrupted Hamer's Congressional testimony with a press conference in an attempt to silence her. The president of Guinea gave Hamer respect which the president of America had not extended to her. Hamer herself acknowledged that she was treated better in Guinea than she was in America.

What was most touching about her account was that Hamer saw women in Africa who reminded her of her mother and her grandmother. Despite not being able to speak French, Hamer felt a closeness in Africa because of the connection between the women in Guinea and her family in America. This connection was reinforced when she heard the people in Guinea singing a song which she did not understand, but the tune sounded just like a song she heard her grandmother sing. She explained: "It was just so close to my family that I cried."

Hamer resolved that she would not relocate to live in Africa permanently because black people had contributed more to America than any other race. She was correct, but the challenge for African Americans has been that this contribution has meant very little to the ruling class in America which has never viewed black people as citizens, or even as human beings for that matter. This was a reality which Hamer herself had to confront. She acknowledged that America could have resolved the terror inflicted against black people in Mississippi if America wanted to. This was not due to ignorance of the brutalities which black people experienced. Hamer herself stated, "They know what they have done to us." White America did know, but also collectively did not care enough to fix the problem. As Hamer herself saw, she was more welcomed and respected in Guinea than she was in America.

The solution would not have been as simple as renouncing America to return to Africa. Guinea itself had its share of problems, so it would have been the case of leaving one struggle for another—this is in fact what Kwame Ture did when he relocated to Guinea and became involved in the political struggle there. The revolutionary Pan-African vision of Malcolm was one which recognized that liberation meant that the struggles being waged in America needed to be connected with the struggles being waged in Africa. Malcolm looked beyond America. After leaving the Nation of Islam, Malcolm renounced the teachings of Elijah Muhammad which said that the white man is devilish by nature and was therefore destined to be destroyed by God. Malcolm no longer saw white people as being collectively irredeemably racist, yet he also recognized there was little to be gained from trying to force brotherhood on white racists who did not understand the language of brotherhood.

Malcolm understood what so many other civil rights leaders failed to understand, which is that the American power structure simply did not view African Americans as American citizens and had no intention of treating African Americans as such. One cannot take away from the commitment and bravery of Fannie Lou Hamer and others who struggled for the advancement of African Americans, but the civil rights movement did not advance far enough. One could argue that the civil rights movement actually regressed the moment that the leaders of the civil rights movement decided to join with the very Democratic Party which tried to silence Fannie Lou Hamer.

The nationalist tradition of black ideological thought has always viewed racism as being fundamental to America's existence. Racism exists not simply as an attitude, but as an embedded aspect of America's society and cultural identity. As such, nationalists traditionally did not frame their activism around this notion that white racists will eventually change their ways and accept African Americans as equal citizens. Wyatt Tee Walker admitted that he and others in the civil rights movement of the 1960s were guilty of being too optimistic about change. President Barack Obama was guilty of the same optimism. Obama expressed the view that Donald Trump would not be elected to his first term. Not only was he wrong, but Trump managed to win a second term after being convicted for a criminal offense. Malcolm understood that the political destiny of African Americans was connected to the larger international struggles of African people globally. He was not as optimistic as the civil rights leaders were, and he was correct to be skeptical.